needed to organize a WDW visit right down to the smallest detail: When To Go; Reservations; How To Get There; Answers To The Tough Questions On Budgets and Packages; Hints On Traveling With Children; Hints For The Handicapped, For Singles, and For Older Visitors; plus lots more indispensable information.

AND ACCOMMODATIONS
Similarly, the complex transportation system within the World moves millions of visitors by monorail, bus, and various waterborne vehicles. It's organized to provide swift, efficient access to all facilities, but it is complicated. Here are all the details.

THE MAGIC KINGDOM
Here is a land-by-land guide to all that there is to see and do, where to shop, and how to avoid the crowds, plus lots of other special tips to make your visit most pleasant and most rewarding.

WORLD AND WORLD SHOWCASE
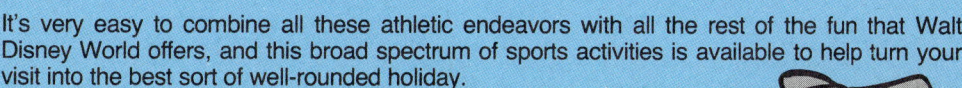
entertainment worlds that offer every visitor the opportunity to be a global and cerebral voyager without ever setting foot out of Central Florida. Here's how to make the most of this unique and fascinating attraction.

ELSE IN THE WORLD
here for a visitor to enjoy. Whether you want to ride down high watery slides, shop at elegant boutiques, wander among exotic birds, or "go to school" behind the scenes, here's all the information you need to find your way to the wonders.

It's very easy to combine all these athletic endeavors with all the rest of the fun that Walt Disney World offers, and this broad spectrum of sports activities is available to help turn your visit into the best sort of well-rounded holiday.

AND GREAT TIMES
area-by-area directories that let you know which restaurants are where and what specialties they offer. From fried ice cream to special French toast, from foie gras to sushi, we put all the dining choices right on your plate.

CONVENTIONS
Here's all the information you need to help plan a perfect conference or seminar, plus all the opportunities for nearby accommodations and the best possible after-hours activities.

complement to the World's own attractions, with all sorts of restaurants, shops, and other sights to see. Here is comprehensive data on the world surrounding Walt Disney World, with emphasis on its major urban neighbor.

For Alex, who went on all the rides.

Copyright © 1984 by Diversion Communications, Inc.

All photographs and artwork Copyright © 1984 by
Walt Disney Productions

All rights reserved. No part of this work may be reproduced or transmitted in any form by any means, electronic or mechanical, including photocopying and recording, or by any information storage or retrieval system, without permission in writing from the copyright holders.

ISBN: 0-395-36528-7

Printed in the United States of America

<u>*Other 1985 Steve Birnbaum Travel Guides*</u>
Canada
Caribbean, Bahamas, and Bermuda
Disneyland
Europe
Europe for Business Travelers
France
Great Britain and Ireland
Hawaii
Mexico
South America
United States
USA for Business Travelers

STEVE BIRNBAUM
BRINGS YOU THE BEST OF

Walt Disney World®

STEPHEN BIRNBAUM
EDITOR

PAUL POSNICK
DESIGN DIRECTOR

KAREN CURE
EXECUTIVE EDITOR

ASSOCIATE EDITORS
Janet Bennett
Sandra Miller
Tom Passavant
Wendy Spritzer
David Walker

ART DIRECTOR
Phyllis Busell

HOUGHTON MIFFLIN COMPANY & DIVERSION COMMUNICATIONS, INC.

CONTENTS

7 GETTING READY TO GO
The key to a completely successful visit to Walt Disney World is planning—careful planning that coordinates all the elements of your stay to make the most of all of WDW's vast and varied pleasures. So here is all the practical information

39 TRANSPORTATION
The most basic questions at Walt Disney World are where to stay and how to get around. There is such a wide variety of accommodations—scaled to fit any budget—that choices vary from lush hotel suites to modest campsites.

69 AN ESSENTIAL GUIDE TO
The magic of the Magic Kingdom is most apparent in the host of attractions and amusements that fill this, the most famous entertainment oasis anywhere. It's hardly surprising that it has enchanted tens of millions of visitors of all ages.

103 EPCOT CENTER: FUTURE
A gleaming silver geosphere introduces Walt Disney World's newest and perhaps greatest adventure, an exploration of the world of the present—and the future. Twice the size of the Magic Kingdom, Epcot Center features two new

129 EVERYTHING
Beyond the boundaries of the Magic Kingdom and Epcot Center are 27,000 acres full of the kinds of wonders for which WDW is famous. Sports, shopping, campgrounds, and more are all

145 SPORTS
Walt Disney World boasts more tennis courts and golf holes than most posh resorts, and there's lots of acreage devoted to boats, bikes, horseback riding, swimming, and fishing. There are also programs available to help improve your sports skills.

153 GOOD MEALS
Restaurants around the Walt Disney World property run the gamut from simple snack shops to bastions of elegant haute cuisine. The choices are nearly endless, so we've organized these eating opportunities into meal-by-meal and

177 MEETINGS AND
From the Contemporary Resort Hotel's exhibit areas to the almost infinitely flexible meeting rooms at the Conference Center, there are facilities to accommodate almost any sort of get-together.

181 ALL ABOUT ORLANDO
In the years since Walt Disney World opened, the Orlando area has grown from a rural agricultural center to the vibrant heart of Central Florida. The diversions surrounding Walt Disney World make a fine

A WORD FROM THE EDITOR

I suspect that my wife may be the most blasé traveler I know. I've actually come home and asked if she'd like to go to Paris for the weekend, only to have her answer that she was planning to wash her hair.

So you can understand why I was a little apprehensive the first time I asked her if she'd like to spend a few days at Walt Disney World. It is perhaps the ultimate tribute to the appeal of this extraordinary place that my otherwise demure and dignified spouse immediately began jumping up and down, screaming, "Can we go on all the rides?"

My wife's reaction was clearly not very unusual, since Walt Disney World occupies the unique position of being the most popular man-made attraction on this planet. On a slow day (admittedly a relative term, and usually the by-product of unseasonable cold, wind, or rain), more than 25,000 visitors still find their way into WDW, while a really busy day in the Magic Kingdom and Epcot Center can mean as many as 125,000 souls streaming onto the premises.

Because I first experienced Walt Disney World as an unescorted, raw tourist, I feel eminently qualified to edit this guide. I believe I'm able to lead readers to Walt Disney World because I personally made just about every possible error an unknowing guest could make. Like many other uninitiated visitors before me, I wasted enormous amounts of time queuing up at attractions I should have left for another time, and finally missed a lot of things I really wanted to see because time ran short. I didn't allow enough days to do even a major fraction of all that was available, and I even chose the wrong time of the year to come to the park as a first-timer. I picked one of the most crowded times, when the mass of other visitors made orientation difficult and exaggerated every problem that one encounters at any truly popular destination.

I also committed the ultimate sin where Walt Disney World is concerned: I believed that the Magic Kingdom amusement area was all that Walt Disney World included. So the pleasures of places like River Country, Discovery Island, and the trio of first-class golf courses were never encountered by me until far later in the course of the research for this guide. The presence of vast, inspiring Epcot Center only exaggerates this abundance of riches.

So what we've tried to do in designing this book is to keep you and yours from making the same mistakes that dogged my own early encounters with Walt Disney World. Even the most willing vacation planner needs adequate information in order to prepare an intelligent itinerary and daily plan, and what we hope we've done is to organize all the information necessary for a productive visit into as accessible and comprehensible a context as possible. Anyone who will take the time to read even the outlines of the pages that follow will find an emerging pattern that fits his or her special tastes; for those unwilling to exert even that much effort, we've compiled specific prospective day-by-day itineraries for several lengths of visits in order to protect you from yourself.

Travel guides of any sort are, of course, ultimately reflections of personal taste, and putting one's name on a title page obviously places one's preferences on the line. But I think I ought to amplify exactly what "personal" means with reference to this book. Literally dozens of very talented people have worked on preparing this guide, and what you will read on the pages that follow is the collected wisdom of myself and Karen Cure, amplified and expanded by comments from other knowledgeable editors, friends, and Disney World staff members whose tastes most closely approximate our own. We've tried to avoid doggedly alliterative or oppressively onomatopoetic text in favor of simple, straightforward descriptions of what we think is good and bad.

So despite the considerable numbers of contributors, what follows is as close to the gospel according to Birnbaum as you're likely to find. It represents as much of my own taste and preferences as possible, and it's likely, therefore, that if you like your steak medium rare, your ice cream served only in a sugar cone, and can't tolerate fish that's been frozen or overcooked, we'll probably have a long and meaningful relationship. Readers with dissimilar tastes may be less enchanted.

This guidebook also owes an enormous debt to one of the most extraordinary groups of executives and operations people ever assembled—the ladies and gentlemen who manage and run Walt Disney World. Despite the designation of *Official Guide,* I should say that the Walt Disney World staff has exercised no veto power whatever over the contents of this book. Quite the contrary, they have opened their files and explained operations to us in the most generous way imaginable, so that we could prepare the comprehensive appraisals, charts, and schedules that were necessary to help visitors understand the very complex workings of a very complex enterprise.

I daresay there were times when Disney folk were less than delighted at some of our opinions or conclusions, yet these analyses all stayed in. Furthermore, we've been flattered again and again by Disney staff members who've commented about how much they've learned about some unfamiliar aspects of Walt Disney World from the material in this guide.

But the fact remains that this guide could never have been created without the extremely forthcoming cooperation of Walt Disney World personnel on every level. Both in the park and behind the scenes, they've been the source of the most critical factual data. I can only hope that I'm not omitting any name in thanking Jim Bertoluzzi, Walter Meyer, Bob Ziegler, and Jim Athanas (Foods); Sara Beverly and Larry Brooks (Wardrobe); Sherri Johns (Marketing); Ralph Mitchell and Dale Walker (Casting); Bill Dennis (Disney University); Deede Sharpe (Wonders Program); Gary Hallman, Jim Beckwith, Gene Terrico, Judi Daley, Bill Burns, Mary Ann Goloversic, Tom Turley, and Bob Lamb (Operations); Jerry Szenfeld, Harold Bay, Spencer Craig, Jim Gilliam, and Wayne Busch (Merchandise); Rich Taylor, Tom Rother, and Ben Rossi (Entertainment); Bob MacKinnon and Chris Moore (Resorts); John Dreyer and Bob Mervine (Publicity); Wilbur Moore (Finance); Bill Spidle, Bill Marshall, and Chris Biondo (Photography); Pete Bloustein (Epcot Show Development); Ray Powell and Tony Schroeder (Epcot Merchandise); Ken Fuller, Mike Latoria, Bruce Laval, Eric Gatley, and Jim McNalis (WED Florida); Ed Beaver (Walt Disney Travel); Jean Besterman and Jim Rye (WDW Sales); Bob Horton, Ed Stair, Dale Stafford, and Sally Davis (WDW Village); Hideo Amemiya (WDW Village Hotel Plaza); Jim James (WDW Village Training); Danni Mikler (Guest Relations); Lee Blankenship, Sharon Wolf, and Marianne Raver (Central Reservations); Mark Russell and Eric Frederickson (Golf Resort); Steve Babb (Tennis); Charlie Cook (Discovery Island); Greg Emmer, Dwight Dorr, and Phil Holmes (Transportation); Jill Krotky (Employee Relations); Bob Obenour and Spencer Oberle (Fort Wilderness); and Pat McCarty (Horticulture).

In addition, Joice Veselka of the Florida Division of Tourism, Bonnie Manjura of the Orlando Area Chamber of Commerce, and Norman Glass of the Greater Orlando Aviation Authority deserve a tip of the editor's pen for assistance well beyond the call of duty.

To Don MacLaughlin, Norm Doerges, Marty Sklar, Betsy Richman, Charlie Ridgway, Linda Hallman, and Roni Wieners, who did so much to make our job easier (and often possible), more thanks for their extraordinary help.

Most of all, we owe a debt of gratitude larger than we can say to those Walt Disney World executives and their staffs who believed in and nurtured this project, and who allowed us to do it—often against their basic instincts and better judgments. To Vince Jefferds, Bo Boyd, and Tom Elrod there are no words to say thanks in quite the way we mean it.

Lastly, I should also point out that every worthwhile travel guide is a living enterprise; that is, this book may be our best effort at explaining how best to enjoy Walt Disney World at this moment, but its text is in no way cast in bronze. In each annual revision—you've got the fourth installment in your hand—we expect to refine and expand our material to serve our readers' needs even better. To this end, no contribution is of greater value to us than *your* personal reaction to what we have written, as well as information about *your* own experiences while you were trying our suggestions. We eagerly and enthusiastically solicit your comments about this guide, and your opinions and perceptions based on your own visit. In this way, we are able to provide the best and most current information—including the actual experiences of individual travelers—and make it more readily available to others. So please write me at 60 East 42nd Street; New York, New York 10165.

I sincerely hope to hear from you.

Steve Birnbaum

GETTING READY TO GO

- 8   When to Go
- 12   Planning Ahead
- 17   Reservations
- 19   How to Get There
- 24   Tough Questions
- 26   How to Get the Best Photos
- 28   Hints on Traveling with Children
- 30   Helpful Hints
- 33   Other Information

The key to a successful visit to Walt Disney World is advance planning. In the most simple terms, this vast attraction is just too complex and too varied to allow a spontaneous visit to be accomplished with notable success. That doesn't mean that even the most casual visitor can't have a fair amount of fun, but rather that such a visitor is likely to discover a host of opportunities that were missed because of the pressure of time or the absence of knowledge.

What follows, then, is intended to provide a sensible scheme for organizing a prospective visit to Walt Disney World, one that will allow the maximum amount of enjoyment and produce the minimum level of frustration. (Unless otherwise noted, all phone numbers are in area code 305.)

WHEN TO GO

When talk finally turns to the best time to make a trip to Walt Disney World, Christmas and Easter are often mentioned, as well as summer vacation—especially if there are children in the family. But there are good reasons to avoid these periods, chief among them that almost everybody else goes then, and when Walt Disney World is crowded, it can be very crowded indeed. On the busiest days, visitors may wait more than an hour for admission to some particularly popular attraction—at least twice as long as at less crowded times of year.

Considering both the weather and crowd patterns described in the charts below, optimal times to visit WDW are September, October, and early November, the six weeks before and after spring school vacations, and the early part of June. Room reservations in the area are easiest to obtain from September through November. Youngsters who need to be taken out of school to visit at these times can enroll in WDW's innovative Wonders of Walt Disney World, a day-long educational program that uses the World as a classroom.

WDW WEATHER

	Temperature			
	Average high	Average low	Mean	Average rainfall
January	70	50	60	2.28
February	72	51	62	2.95
March	76	56	66	3.46
April	82	61	71	2.72
May	87	66	76	2.94
June	89	71	80	7.11
July	90	73	81	8.29
August	90	74	82	6.73
September	88	72	80	7.20
October	82	66	74	4.07
November	76	57	67	1.56
December	72	52	62	1.90

SPECIAL EVENTS

INSIDE WALT DISNEY WORLD: Special festivities are often staged not only to celebrate holidays but to salute special groups by offering special admissions to the Magic Kingdom and Epcot Center.

JANUARY: Walt Disney World New Year's Eve Celebration (Dec. 31). There are parties in all the hotels and an extra-large fireworks display over the Magic Kingdom, which is open until 2 A.M. for the occasion. The celebration at the Top of the World, the stand-out, sells out a year in advance, despite its relatively hefty cost. The glass-walled room here gives a fantastic view of the pyrotechnics.
Resident Salute. Throughout the month, Florida residents pay special low admission prices to enter the parks.
WDW Village Wine Festival. Sixty wineries from the U.S. and Europe participate. For details, contact Special Events; WDW Village; Box 35; Lake Buena Vista, FL 32830.

EASTER SUNDAY: A holiday show at Cinderella Castle and a promenade-style Easter Parade help make this holiday celebration special in the Magic Kingdom, during a very busy time of year. Both the Magic Kingdom and Epcot Center stay open late during this season.

MAY: Armed Forces Days. WDW salutes members of this group with the same special admission fees offered to Florida residents in January. Held again in November.

MAY: Grad Nites. Top rock entertainment is presented, and the park is open from 11 P.M. to 5 A.M. for graduating high school students, who may buy specially priced tickets. Held on two consecutive weekends. Special attire is required. For details, contact the Grad Nite Office; Box 40; Lake Buena Vista, FL 32830.

JULY 4: Fourth of July Celebration. In the evening fireworks are set off above Cinderella Castle in the Magic Kingdom—as is usual when the park is open until midnight—and over the Seven Seas Lagoon as well. There's a spectacular show, Laserphonic Fantasy, featuring lasers and fireworks at Epcot Center, too. Very busy.

SEPTEMBER: Night of Joy. Two nights of gospel contemporary Christian music.

SEPTEMBER: Sport Goofy International Tennis Tournament. A year-long, worldwide tournament culminates at WDW.

OCTOBER 1 TO DECEMBER 15: Young at Heart Days. During this period, those Florida residents 55 and over receive special low-cost admission values.

OCTOBER: Walt Disney World Classic. Top PGA Tour players compete alongside amateurs in this big tourney.

OCTOBER 31: Halloween. At night on the holiday itself, youngsters can get dressed up and join Disney villains in the Halloween Procession at WDW Shopping Village.

NOVEMBER: Festival of Masters at WDW Shopping Village. One of the best of the area's art shows draws exhibitors from all around the country.

DECEMBER: Christmas celebrations. Nightly at Walt Disney World Shopping Village, from mid-month until the eve of the holiday, some 40 players present a nativity pageant. In the Magic Kingdom, a large, perfect Christmas tree is erected in Town Square; Main Street is decorated to the nines and patrolled by groups of carolers; a special Christmas parade and show are staged. Special tickets are available for Mickey's Very Merry Christmas Party, featuring all of the above—plus more holiday entertainment. The Magic Kingdom stays open late throughout the season, as does Epcot Center, where there is also a special show throughout the season.

OUTSIDE WALT DISNEY WORLD: Several major events in the Central Florida communities around Walt Disney World are also worth a visit.

JANUARY: Orlando; Scottish Highland Games. The sizable Scottish population of the area turns out in force for Highland dancing and bagpipe competitions, as well as such traditional field events as tossing of the caber. Scottish shops are also set up. Details: Scottish-American Society of Central Florida; Box 2149; Orlando, FL 32802; 644-0516.

FEBRUARY: Tampa; Gasparilla Pirate Invasion. Costumed as renegades of the pirate band led by the legendary José Gaspar, members of a local club sail into Tampa Harbor in a full-sized buccaneer ship (accompanied by a flotilla of local boats), claim the city as their own, and then parade through the streets. Among the activities during the subsequent two weeks are another raid, this one on Ybor City—Tampa's Latin quarter—and a Spanish bean soup day during which this thick, delectable broth is served free (along with Cuban bread and Cuban coffee). An illuminated parade winds up the event. Details: Ye Mystic Krewe of Gasparilla; Box 1514; Tampa, FL 33601; 813-228-7338.
Daytona; Speed Weeks. All the top names in stock-car racing are on hand at the Daytona International Speedway for two weeks of almost-daily competitions, culminating in the Daytona 500. Details: Daytona International Speedway; P.O. Drawer S; Daytona Beach, FL 32015; 904-255-5301.
Grant; Grant Seafood Festival. Some 75,000 visitors show up to eat fresh Indian River seafood at this huge affair staged by a small community on Florida's

east coast. Details: Seafood Festival; Box 44; Grant, FL 32949; 723-6811 or 723-0898.

Kissimmee; Silver Spurs Rodeo. This three-day event, held annually since 1944, draws professional cowboys from all over the United States to compete for thousands of dollars in prizes. Also held July 4th weekend. Details: Kissimmee–St. Cloud Convention and Visitors Bureau; Box 2007; Kissimmee, FL 32742; 847-5000.

MARCH: Orlando; Bay Hill Classic. Held annually early in March; Arnold Palmer hosts this PGA Tour event, one of eight in the state of Florida, at the Bay Hill Club. Details: Bay Hill Club; 9000 Bay Hill Blvd.; Orlando, FL 32819; 876-2888.
Sarasota; Medieval Fair. Hundreds of entertainers from all over the country and abroad join in a human chess match, jousting, processions, singing, and other medieval merriment at the Ringling Museums complex. Everything from the food and drink served (pot pies, giant turkey legs, and ale) to the crafts sold and the language spoken by participants is authentically medieval. Details: Ringling Museums; Box 1838; Sarasota, FL 33578; 813-355-5101.
Winter Park; Winter Park Sidewalk Art Festival. Held annually during the third weekend of the month, this display of etchings, pottery, paintings, sculpture, and other artwork and craft items also features concerts, strolling musicians, and a folk sing; it's one of the most prestigious events of its type in the Southeast. The backdrop is a small municipal park full of ancient trees draped with Spanish moss; the town itself is as tony as they come in Central Florida, with its array of chic boutiques and elegant French restaurants. Details: Chamber of Commerce; Box 280; Winter Park, FL 32790; 644-8281.
Orlando; Minnesota Twins Spring Training. The season at Tinker Field begins early in March and continues through the month with exhibition games daily until the first week in April. The Orlando Twins, a Minnesota farm team, play a full schedule during the summer months. Details: Tinker Field; 287 Tampa Ave. S.; Orlando, FL 32805; 849-6346.

APRIL: Titusville; Great Indian River Festival. This community near the Kennedy Space Center makes an annual tribute to the celebrated Indian River with a weekend of arts and crafts, carnival rides, food, and the Great Indian River Raft Race, in which any kind of craft that floats can participate. Details: Titusville Area Chamber of Commerce; 2000 S. Washington Ave.; Titusville, FL 32780; 267-3036.

MAY: Zellwood; Zellwood Sweet Corn Festival. The Zellwood area, about 20 miles northwest of Orlando, is famous for its production of sweet corn, and it celebrates its bounty every year at the end of May (or early June, depending on the crops) with this festival. There's a corn-eating contest and entertainment by bluegrass bands; corn is sold by the crate; and hundreds upon hundreds of ears are devoured at stands on the spot. Details: Zellwood Sweet Corn Festival; Box 628; Zellwood, FL 32798; 886-0014.

JUNE: Kissimmee; Boat-A-Cade. *Reader's Digest* called this affair "the world's greatest outdoor event," for it brings Florida boat owners out in droves for a six-day cruise that begins on Lake Tohopekaliga and winds through state waters. Barbecues, banquets, and other land activities are staged at docking points en route. Details: Kissimmee Boat-A-Cade; Box 1855; Kissimmee, FL 32742; 847-2033.

OCTOBER: Orlando; Pioneer Days. Two days of folk music, square dancing, and other old-fashioned good times. Details: Pioneer Days; 5903 Randolph St.; Orlando, FL 32809; 855-7461.

NOVEMBER: Kissimmee; Florida State Air Fair. The U.S. Navy's Blue Angels headline a two-day roster of activities that also includes aerial acrobatic demonstrations and aeronautical displays. Details: Kissimmee–St. Cloud Convention and Visitors Bureau; Box 2007; Kissimmee, FL 32741; 847-5000.

DECEMBER: St. Petersburg; Florida Tournament of Bands. Marching bands from all over the state get together to vie for top honors in a series of competitions that will send shivers up and down the spines of anybody who ever loved a parade. Details: Florida Tournament of Bands; Box 1731; St. Petersburg, FL 33731; 813-898-3654.

OPERATING HOURS

Hours of operation of the Magic Kingdom and Epcot Center—which may also figure in decisions on when to go—vary from season to season. For about a third of the year—in September, October, parts of November and December, and all of January—the Magic Kingdom is usually open from about 9 A.M. to 6 P.M. (Main Street stays open until 7 P.M.). Hours are extended to 10 P.M. during Washington's Birthday week and during spring school breaks; and to midnight for summer and certain holiday periods (Thanksgiving weekend, Christmas, and the two weeks straddling Easter). On New Year's Eve, an additional couple of hours is added to the nighttime schedule.

Epcot Center is usually open from 9 A.M. to 8 P.M.; hours are extended during Washington's Birthday week, spring school breaks, summer months, and certain holidays.

Occasionally, during busy periods, the parks may open earlier or close later. Call 824-4321 for up-to-the-minute details.

WHICH DAYS TO VISIT: Most visitors to Walt Disney World routinely assume that weekends are by far the busiest days on the property. But in Epcot Center every day is about equally busy, and in the Magic Kingdom Saturday is busiest *only in the fall, not during the summer.* In the summertime, *the biggest crowds are usually found on Tuesdays,* with Wednesdays and Mondays just about as busy. Saturdays and Thursdays rank next. So it's a wise visitor who knows that Fridays are usually the quietest days of the week, with Sunday (particularly Sunday morning) the least crowded time in the Magic Kingdom and Epcot Center.

HOW BIG ARE THE CROWDS?

The following statistics on the average number of people in the Magic Kingdom or Epcot Center on any given day amply illustrate the optimal times for a visit.

January through the first week in February	15,000 to 25,000
Second week of February to beginning of Washington's Birthday week	20,000 to 35,000
Washington's Birthday week	30,000 to 50,000
The period from the end of Washington's Birthday week until the beginning of college spring breaks	25,000 to 40,000
College spring break weeks	30,000 to 45,000
The two weeks around Easter Sunday	35,000 to 65,000
Easter to early June	25,000 to 35,000
EXCEPTION: Memorial Day Weekend	30,000 to 45,000
Mid-June through mid-August	30,000 to 60,000
Mid-August to Labor Day	30,000 to 45,000
September through November	15,000 to 30,000
EXCEPTION: Thanksgiving weekend	30,000 to 50,000
Thanksgiving to beginning of Christmas holidays (the least busy time of year)	10,000 to 20,000
Christmas holidays through New Year's Day	35,000 to 65,000

What the Statistics Mean

15,000	Exclusive		40,000	Getting busy
20,000	Semi-private		50,000	Highly active
30,000	Longer lines but still comfortable		60,000	Crowded
			70,000 and up	Body to body

PLANNING AHEAD

Mapping a trip properly takes time, but most travelers find that the increased enjoyment is well worth the effort. Such planning goes most smoothly when it's done in an organized fashion, and kids will enjoy their trip all the more if they're involved in the planning process, too. First, assemble all the options available from the various sources listed in this guide. Then study these materials and begin to make specific decisions. Just be careful not to try to see and do too much in too short a period of time.

SAMPLE SCHEDULES: It's no exaggeration to say that a visitor could stay in Central Florida for three weeks and not see everything. Walt Disney World alone requires every bit of four days—two of them in the Magic Kingdom and two in Epcot Center—and that doesn't begin to allow enough time to truly discover River Country, Discovery Island, Fort Wilderness, and the fine golf courses, beaches, and other sports facilities.

The suggested schedules described here, which are predicated on a late afternoon arrival, should put you on the right track—and keep you there. Any deviations from the programs suggested here should be based on our "Tips from WDW Veterans" (pages 102 and 128). In general, count on visiting seven or eight attractions per day in the Magic Kingdom and about five pavilions in Epcot Center. That leaves time for some shopping, the inevitable waits at some attractions, and some unhurried eating. During the less crowded seasons, it may be possible to accomplish significantly more.

It's very important to begin days in the Magic Kingdom and Epcot Center at park opening. Note that Epcot Center occasionally opens a full hour before the official posted time.

One-day visit: There is so much to see and do at WDW that we don't recommend this length of visit. But if that's all the time you've got, first decide which of its two prime areas (the Magic Kingdom or Epcot Center) you want to see, and then study all available material in advance so that you're familiar with your destination's layout and offerings. Be sure to arrive on the property very early and move quickly while you're there. For optimal results, follow our schedules to the letter. **Note:** Because one-day tickets permit visitors to enter either Epcot Center *or* the Magic Kingdom *but not both*, you must concentrate on one or the other.

• If you choose to tour the Magic Kingdom, be in the parking lot at least 45 minutes before the scheduled park opening so as to be at the Central Plaza end of Main Street at the official opening time. From then on move rapidly and purposefully from one attraction to the next—first to Space Mountain, then to the Haunted Mansion, Big Thunder Mountain Railroad, Country Bear Jamboree, Tom Sawyer Island, Pirates of the Caribbean, and the Jungle Cruise. Plan on lunching at 11 A.M. to avoid mealtime lines. If time remains after the Jungle Cruise, see the Enchanted Tiki Room and the Swiss Family Island Treehouse before eating; otherwise go to those attractions after lunch. Then begin making a second trip around the area, stopping at If You Had Wings, American Journeys, It's A Small World, the Penny Arcade, the Main Street Cinema, the shops and entertainment en route, and anything else that catches your eye. Then, having made reservations before leaving home, leave the Magic Kingdom at about 4 P.M. for Fort Wilderness and the Hoop-Dee-Doo Revue.

In busy seasons, when all WDW attractions are open late, you may be able to follow this dinner show with a couple of hours at River Country and then another short visit to the Magic Kingdom, where fireworks, the Electrical Water Pageant, and the late installment of the Main Street Electrical Parade comprise the prime diversions.

In other months (or if you could not get reservations for the Hoop-Dee-Doo Revue), head for Walt Disney World Village and spend the evening aboard the *Empress Lilly* in one of its restaurants and the Baton Rouge Lounge.

• If you choose to spend the day in Epcot Center, arrive approximately one half hour before the park's official opening and wait at the gate until the turnstiles are unlocked. Then send the fastest member of your party ahead to Earth Station to make a 5 P.M. dinner reservation at one of the special restaurants in World Showcase or Future World. Pick up an entertainment schedule while there. That done, visit The Land and then Journey Into Imagination, in Future World, then head quickly for World Showcase and see *O Canada!* in the Canada pavilion and *Impressions de France* in the France pavilion. Then backtrack to *Le Cellier,* in the Canada pavilion, for lunch around 11:15 A.M. Afterwards, enjoy the World Showcase entertainment and browse through the shops in Canada, the United Kingdom, France, Japan, Germany, Italy, and Mexico. Keep an eye on the time so you're out of Mexico at about 3:30 P.M.; then head for Future World at about 3:45 P.M. Visit Spaceship Earth or participate in the Electronic Forum Future Choice Theatre there, and spend the time before 4:45 P.M. at the various exhibits in Epcot Computer Central or the

Energy Exchange. Leave CommuniCore promptly at 4:45 P.M. for your dining spot. Plan to finish your meal by 6:30 P.M. Spend the time until 9:30 P.M. in the China pavilion (for one of the last showings of the exciting film there), World of Motion, and Universe of Energy.

Two-day visit (includes 3 evenings): The following plan is recommended *only* for the highly energetic, and with the following qualification: WDW comprises a great amalgam of striking sights and fascinating attractions, so in two days it's only possible to see the high points.

During peak seasons, nothing less than two full days and three evenings will do the trick. Note that late afternoon arrivals in both Epcot Center and the Magic Kingdom are a key to successful completion of our full program. Be sure to check (the night before) on required transportation time for early-morning hours, and allot plenty of extra time for potential delays. On each day, the idea is to make a quick tour of the premises, visiting the major attractions during the most uncrowded hours of the early morning, then repeat the circuit of the park once again later on.

• Before leaving home, make reservations for a 5 P.M. seating at the Hoop-Dee-Doo Revue for the evening of the first *full* day of your stay. Then, on your first evening at WDW, go directly to Epcot Center after arrival (try to arrive before 5 P.M.). Purchase a three-day World Passport for the best value, even though you will not have three full days. Have a quick bite at one of the restaurants in CommuniCore East or West. Then visit the Universe of Energy and the World of Motion (skipping the TransCenter for the time being). This should take about an hour. Next, walk over to Journey Into Imagination, where you should count on spending at least an hour and a half. Depending on how much time remains before closing, proceed to Spaceship Earth, which requires about half an hour, figuring a ten-minute wait to get in, or The Land, to whose trio of major attractions a full hour and a half should be allotted.

• On your first full day, have breakfast as early as possible so as to arrive at the Magic Kingdom turnstiles half an hour before scheduled opening and to be able to be at the Central Plaza end of Main Street at the official opening time. Once the gates open, make a beeline for Space Mountain, and then head for the Haunted Mansion, Big Thunder Mountain Railroad, Country Bear Jamboree, Tom Sawyer Island, Pirates of the Caribbean, and the Jungle Cruise in quick succession. If you're hungry, have lunch at the Adventureland Veranda or the Crystal Palace. Otherwise, go next to the Enchanted Tiki Room and the Swiss Family Island Treehouse—but be sure to arrange your meal schedule to have lunch shortly after 11 A.M. After lunch, begin making the day's second circuit of the park, visiting If You Had Wings, American Journeys, It's A Small World, the Penny Arcade, the Main Street Cinema, and anything else that seems appealing. Then, having been careful to reserve in advance, leave the Magic Kingdom at about 4 P.M. to head for Fort Wilderness and the Hoop-Dee-Doo Revue. During busy seasons it's possible to follow dinner with a couple of hours at River Country—and then return to the Magic Kingdom for the fireworks, the Electrical Water Pageant, and the late installment of the Main Street Electrical Parade.

In other months (or in the event that reservations were unavailable for the Hoop-Dee-Doo Revue), either return to Epcot Center and see some of the Future World attractions you missed the night before and then visit World Showcase, or head for Walt Disney World Village and spend the evening aboard the *Empress Lilly*—don't miss the Baton Rouge Lounge.

• On your second day, arrive at Epcot Center about half an hour before the park's official opening, and wait at the gate until the turnstiles are unlocked. Then make the hundred-yard (or so) sprint to Earth Station to make an 8:45 P.M. dinner reservation either at Germany's Biergarten, Les Chefs de France, or at Alfredo's. That done, take in any major attractions in Future World that you haven't already seen. Then decide on a specific World Showcase restaurant for lunch, and head straight for that pavilion to book a midday mealtime. Next begin visiting the nearby attractions, working your way around World Showcase Lagoon but skipping the shops and the entertainment until lines have begun to build up. When that happens, bypass the attractions, do some shopping in World Showcase, and stop in Future World at CommuniCore East and West and the TransCenter in the World of Motion. The hours between 6 P.M. and your scheduled dinner reservation should be devoted to seeing any major attractions that might have been missed earlier in the day. After dinner, skip dessert and instead treat yourself to pastry and espresso at the Boulangerie Pâtisserie, in the France pavilion.

Three-day visit: A stay of this length, while not exactly leisurely, is still the shortest time that can be conscientiously recommended for families with young children, older visitors, or anyone else who wants to visit WDW at less than breakneck speed.

• Before visiting, read as much as possible about the WDW attractions and their locations. This is a must—because although the pace on this three-day program is significantly slower than that required during a two-day visit, it is still necessary not to waste time in order to cover all of the high points. Remember, too, that the first order of business (before leaving home) is to make a 7:30 P.M. reservation for the Hoop-Dee-Doo Revue for the first full day you'll be at WDW.

• On the evening of the day of your arrival, visit Epcot Center. Purchase a four-day World Passport for the best value in admission media. Have a quick bite at one of the restaurants in CommuniCore East or West. Then proceed as for the first evening of the two-day visit described above.

• On the first full day of your visit, arrive at the Magic Kingdom 45 minutes before the official park opening. The Town Square Café and the Crystal Palace buffeteria, on Main Street, begin serving early, so have breakfast at one of them, and be at the Central Plaza end of Main Street at the park's official opening time. Then begin circumnavigating the park, taking in just the major attractions en route—as described for the first morning of a two-day visit.

During busy seasons, when the park is open late, first go to the Jungle Cruise and Pirates of the Caribbean in Adventureland, Country Bear Jamboree in Frontierland, and to the Hall of Presidents in Liberty Square. Afterwards, leave the park at about 11 A.M. for Discovery Island, River Country, or the Polynesian Village Resort Hotel. Have lunch at your destination, and pursue the available activities there. The Polynesian is a good spot for renting a Sunfish or a zippy Water Sprite or for simply sunning yourself on the pretty beach; golfers might make the short trip by bus over to the nearby Golf Resort for 18 holes on the splendid Palm or Magnolia courses. Return to the park between 5 and 6 P.M., and grab a quick bite at The Tomorrowland Terrace. Then see American Journeys, If You Had Wings and, if time permits, Mission to Mars and Space Mountain, all nearby. By 8 P.M., head over to Main Street to stake a claim to a segment of curb for the 9 P.M. Main Street Electrical Parade. Watch the Fantasy in the Sky fireworks after the parade. If your youngsters are old enough to stay up until midnight, watch the Electrical Water Pageant on the Seven Seas Lagoon after the fireworks. Otherwise, proceed immediately to the Haunted Mansion in Liberty Square and Big Thunder Mountain Railroad in Frontierland.

The rest of the year, during the seasons in which the park closes early, follow this program after breakfast: Visit the Jungle Cruise and Pirates of the Caribbean, in Adventureland; Big Thunder Mountain Railroad and Country Bear Jamboree, in Frontierland; and the Hall of Presidents and the Haunted Mansion, in Liberty Square. Then lunch at Pinocchio Village Haus or the Lancer's Inn, in Fantasyland. Go to Peter Pan's Flight and It's A Small World, in Fantasyland; American Journeys and If You Had Wings, in Tomorrowland; the Haunted Mansion, in Liberty Square; and Big Thunder Mountain Railroad, in Frontierland. Then, having made reservations before leaving home, go to the 7:30 P.M. performance (including dinner) of the Hoop-Dee-Doo Musical Revue, in Pioneer Hall in Fort Wilderness. Afterwards, remain at Fort Wilderness to see the Electrical Water Pageant.

• Devote the second day of your visit to Epcot Center. Arrive about half an hour before the official park opening, and queue up at the gate. While waiting, choose a restaurant for dinner, based on our descriptions in the *Good Meals, Great Times* chapter of this guide (The Good Turn restaurant, in The Land, is particularly convenient to our Epcot Center assault plan). Then when the gates open send the speediest member of your party off to Earth Station to reserve an early dinner seating time there, preferably around 5 or 5:30 P.M. Then begin visiting the attractions in Future World that you were unable to see during your first evening. Around 9:30 A.M., leave Future World and walk reasonably quickly first to France, to see the lovely *Impressions de France* film, and then head over to The American Adventure and then to China. Next head for Mexico and stop at the pleasant Cantina de San Angel for lunch. Afterwards, reverse the direction of your route around World Showcase, and stop at the pavilions you missed the first time around. Even if you hate shopping, look into Germany's arts-and-crafts and toy shops. Also be sure to look in on the entertainers who perform around Italy, the puppeteers on the Promenade, the rice-candy sculptor and the dolls in the Mitsukoshi store in Japan, and the street players at the United Kingdom. For a midafternoon snack, stop at the U.K. pavilion's Country Manor, buy a box of crackers or cookies, and then head for the Refreshment Outpost for a cold drink with which to eat them. Then go back to Future World and explore CommuniCore East and the Trans-Center. Remember to allot a full 20 minutes for the walk to your dining spot. The uncrowded hours after dinner should be spent catching up with any attractions missed during previous attempts.

• On the third day, spend the morning in the Magic Kingdom seeing any attractions missed previously; be sure to arrive early. Then around noon take the bus from the Transportation and Ticket Center to Walt Disney World Village for lunch at the Fisherman's Deck or the Steerman's Quarters, aboard the *Empress Lilly* riverboat restaurant. Spend an hour or so looking around in the shops at Walt Disney World Shopping Village, or hire a Water Sprite for a spin on

the nearby waterways. If you're in the mood, it's fun just to sit in the shade at Cap'n Jack's and savor the delightfully frosty strawberry margaritas, a WDW specialty. Later, return to Epcot Center, and spend more time in CommuniCore East or West or browsing through the World Showcase shops until the crowds thin out. Then explore any attractions you haven't yet visited, or go back to those you particularly liked. During busy seasons, if your stamina permits, it's possible to cap a WDW stay with the Main Street Electrical Parade in the Magic Kingdom.

Four-day visit: Especially for first-time visitors, four days is the wisest length of time to devote to Walt Disney World. If you are staying in one of the WDW-owned resorts, the best value in admission media is the five-day World Passport.

• Before leaving home for WDW, make reservations for the Hoop-Dee-Doo Revue and for the Empress Room (if you decide on it for your third evening's dinner).

• On the evening of the day you arrive at WDW, head for Epcot Center and follow the schedule described for the first evening of a two-day visit.

• On the first full day, tour the Magic Kingdom as outlined in our suggestions for the first full day of a three-day visit. During busy seasons, however, visit Discovery Island in the afternoon.

• The second complete day, proceed to and through Epcot Center according to our suggestions for the second day of a three-day visit.

• On the third full day, spend the morning in the Magic Kingdom seeing any attractions you may have missed previously. Be sure to arrive before the park opens, then leave the Magic Kingdom around 11 A.M. For lunch, enjoy either the buffet at the Golf Resort Hotel (don't miss the French fried ice cream for dessert) or the one at the Polynesian Village Resort Hotel. Spend the afternoon pursuing either of the resorts' activities as described in our *Sports* chapter. For the unathletically inclined, try the Village Restaurant, in WDW Village, and an afternoon of shopping there instead. In the evening visit Fort Wilderness (during busy seasons), taking in the 7:30 P.M. or 10 P.M. Hoop-Dee-Doo Revue and the 9:45 P.M. Electrical Water Pageant (from the nearby beach); the rest of the year, head for the *Empress Lilly*'s Baton Rouge Lounge for drinks and entertainment, and for dinner, eat at either the Fisherman's Deck, the Steerman's Quarters or, if children are not along, the elegant Empress Room.

• On the fourth full day, have an 8 A.M. breakfast with the characters at the Contemporary Resort Hotel, then spend the morning at River Country, and go biking or canoeing at Fort Wilderness in the afternoon. Our alternate suggestions for the day are: Head for Epcot Center early in the morning, make reservations for an early dinner, head immediately to the Boulangerie Pâtisserie in France and enjoy pastry and coffee, spend a couple of hours at Epcot Center, go to the beach at the Contemporary Resort or River Country in the afternoon, or go boating or play tennis or golf at one of the resorts. Whichever plan you choose, return to the Magic Kingdom or River Country in the evening, when they're open late, or during the rest of the year, try the Campfire Program or the Marshmallow Marsh excursion at Fort Wilderness.

Five-day visit: Follow our program as outlined above for the four-day visit. On the next day, spend the morning until about 11 A.M. in Epcot Center or the Magic Kingdom, then spend the rest of the day at Sea World or Cypress Gardens. Have lunch first in WDW or later on at Al E. Gator's, in the Florida Festival opposite Sea World. Make a dinner reservation for an Epcot Center meal first thing in the morning, or try one of the other WDW restaurants—the Gulf Coast Room at the Contemporary Resort for something a little special or the Trophy Room at the Golf Resort Hotel if you haven't yet sampled the special French fried ice cream. Or, having reserved in advance, take in one of the other dinner shows, either "Broadway at the Top" at the Contemporary Resort Hotel or the luau at the Polynesian Village Resort Hotel.

For visits of six days and longer: To our program described for five-day visits, travelers without children should head for the charming town of Winter Park, a half hour's drive north of Walt Disney World, have lunch at Two Flights Up, stop for ice cream at the East India Ice Cream Company, and dine at one of the Orlando area restaurants described in our Orlando chapter. However, if offspring are in tow, head straight for Busch Gardens in Tampa and the nearby Gulf of Mexico beach towns, like Clearwater and St. Petersburg, or drive to Cape Canaveral and the Atlantic coast beaches to the east.

DO YOU NEED A CAR? Not if you're staying at a Walt Disney World resort. Public transportation within the World gets guests from point to point almost as quickly as a private car, and sometimes more so. And there's no parking problem. It's also possible to get to WDW resorts from Orlando Airport without a car—American Sightseeing shuttles operate about every 45 minutes around the clock, serving on-property hotels as well as WDW Village Hotel Plaza accommodations, Florida Center hotels, and hotels on U.S.-192. (Call for reservations: 859-2250 in Orlando; 933-1709 in Kissimmee.) Also those lodging outside the World can usually get to and from WDW via their own hotels' bus service (which most hotels offer). Limos and cabs are also available, but a car is a must for taking in Orlando area restaurants and attractions outside WDW.

INFORMATION SOURCES: For details about other things to see and do in Central Florida, contact the Florida Division of Tourism; 126 Van Buren St.; Tallahassee, FL 32301; 904-488-5606. To find out about the area directly around Orlando, contact the Greater Orlando Chamber of Commerce, Tourism Development/Visitor Inquiries; Box 1234; Orlando, FL 32802; 425-1234. And for general information about Walt Disney World, write the Walt Disney World Co.; Box 40; Lake Buena Vista, FL 32830; 824-4321.

Upon arrival at Walt Disney World, a variety of other information sources are available.

First, tune into the WDW radio stations after entering the grounds—1030 on the AM dial inbound to the Magic Kingdom and 810 approaching Epcot Center. (Helpful information is broadcast to guests departing from the Magic Kingdom on 1200, and from Epcot Center on 900.)

At check-in, guests at all WDW-owned resorts—that is, the Contemporary Resort, the Golf Resort, the Polynesian Village, Fort Wilderness, and the Walt Disney World Village—area villas—are given copies of *Your Guide to the Magic Kingdom* and the Epcot Center guide at no charge, plus the latest *Walt Disney World Vacation Guide,* detailing a variety of activities inside the World. In addition, all guests except those camping out at Fort Wilderness can tune to Channel 5 on their hotel-room television sets to see a filmed overview of all WDW attractions—a complete orientation tour of the property which is essential viewing for all first-time visitors. It's broadcast continuously. Guests at Walt Disney World Village Hotel Plaza establishments will see a similar program on Channel 7. (The latter gives somewhat more emphasis to the dining rooms and lounges at these lodging places, which, though located on WDW property, are neither Disney-owned nor Disney-operated.) For further information, guests at WDW properties can watch the daily program *Around the World Today,* which provides operating hours, name entertainers that are currently performing, special events, weather forecasts, and other useful information, on Channel 10. (This program is not shown outside WDW-owned lodging places.) For additional information, guests at WDW resorts should contact Guest Services. To do this, those staying at the Contemporary Resort, the Polynesian Village, and the Golf Resort should touch "1" on their room phones or house phones; Fort Wilderness campers should stop at the Pioneer Hall Information and Ticket Window or call extension 2788 or touch "1" from the phones at the comfort stations located at the center of each campground loop area; and guests at Walt Disney World Village—area villas should call 828-2382. After 11 P.M., guests at all these WDW resort properties should call their respective front desks.

Day visitors: All day visitors—that is, those staying off the property, as well as those living in the Orlando area—receive a toll plaza handout at the Toll Plaza detailing admission prices and other useful information. When purchasing one-day admission media at either the TTC or at Epcot Center, guests receive a copy of either the Epcot Center guide or the Magic Kingdom guide depending upon which park they have chosen to visit. Guests who purchase multi-day admission media receive both guides. City Hall (in the Magic Kingdom) and Earth Station (in Epcot Center) distribute extra copies of these guides at no charge.

Some hotels off the property—but not all of them—show their own version of the WDW resorts' Channel 5 orientation film; this attempts to give visitors an overview of all Central Florida attractions (WDW among them), rather than concentrating on the World.

For further information, phone WDW Information at 824-4321.

WHAT TO PACK: Walt Disney World is not so casual that all you need to bring is a bathing suit, but except for the dinner show at the Top of the World and dinner at the Empress Room aboard the *Empress Lilly* riverboat restaurant and at the Lake Buena Vista Club in Walt Disney World Village, where jackets are necessary for men, casual clothing is the rule. That means anything from T-shirts and cutoffs in the daytime to slacks or dresses in the evening. This is also true at Epcot Center full-service restaurants. Men commonly wear sport jackets for dinner in fancier restaurants, but seldom ties. Bathing suits are a must, and a spare one is useful, as are the right togs for any other sports you might want to pursue. On the tennis courts, tennis whites are appropriate, though not required. Guests should bring lightweight sweaters even in summer—to wear indoors when the air-conditioning gets too frigid. From November through March, warmer clothing is a must for evening wear. Always pack something to keep you comfortable should the weather turn unseasonably warm or cool. Especially in summer, lightweight rain gear and a folding umbrella come in handy.

And the most important item of clothing of all? Well-broken-in walking shoes.

RESERVATIONS

Walt Disney World vacations go most smoothly when details are planned well ahead of time. Procrastinators may find no room at the inn, or no space left for a show that they wanted to see. Golf starting times, tennis courts, and other sporting activities, as well as dinner reservations and other special affairs, also should be reserved in advance.

Central Reservations Office: Many arrangements are handled by the Central Reservations Office (CRO); the phone number is 824-8000 or, for speakers of French or Spanish, 824-7900.

When calling, expect the phone to ring for a couple of minutes (up to five or even ten minutes during some very busy periods) before being answered. This is to avoid putting callers, most of whom are phoning long distance, on hold. The telephone system is handled by a computer that automatically puts calls in order, so don't hang up.

Have a pencil and paper close at hand when calling, to jot down dates and the number of your reservation.

Room reservations: It is especially important to book accommodations in advance—up to two years in order to have your first choice of dates for visits during holiday periods, and 12 to 18 months ahead to get your pick of dates for a mid-summer visit. Even during other times of year, it's necessary to call six to nine months before arrival, and even then it may not be possible to get space in the precise resort you've selected, or the exact number of nights you wanted.

When Central Reservations can't accommodate your first preference, don't despair. Cancellations do come up. There are waiting lists for guests who have managed to reserve at least one evening of the multi-night stay that they had originally requested. Visitors who were not able to arrange for a room at all may sometimes get one by calling later on. There is also a very slim chance of snagging space, left vacant by the occasional early departure, on the day of arrival; you can contact Central Reservations or get help from Guest Relations (at City Hall, the Transportation and Ticket Center, Epcot Center, or at the individual hotel's front desk).

Eastern Airlines: As the "Official Airline of Walt Disney World," Eastern Airlines has a substantial number of rooms specifically allocated for its use. Eastern is, therefore, a very good means of access to hard-to-book Walt Disney World-owned hotel rooms. These rooms are available as part of Eastern packages, which also have the added attraction of saving visitors some money on air fares as well.

Reservations for supper seatings, dinner shows, and sporting activities: Some of these are handled by Central Reservations, while others are handled by the individual restaurants and sporting centers. It's always wise to make your plans and reserve your place as far in advance as WDW policy will allow. Just how far in advance may vary, depending on where you lodge. (See chart below.)

Package vacationers take note: Your packages cover only the *cost* of dinner shows and activities, *not the reservations that may be necessary to enjoy them. It's up to the individual traveler to make all the specific bookings.* (Eastern Airlines can, however, confirm reservations for the luau at the Polynesian Village for purchasers of its on-site packages.)

RESERVATION GUIDE

ACTIVITY	Phone for reservations (area code 305)	Advisability of reservations	How far in advance can reservations be made?		
			Guests in WDW hotels/villas	Guests at WDW Village Hotel Plaza establishments	Guests at off-property hotels
Sports					
Golf starting times—all courses	824-2270	Necessary from February through April; a good idea at other times	As far ahead as desired, the year round	As far ahead as desired, except for play between January 1 and April 30; then maximum five days ahead	
Walt Disney World Golf Studio, Golf Resort	824-2250	Necessary	.... No limit for any guest		
Private golf lessons, Golf Resort	824-2250	Necessary	.... No limit for any guest		
Private golf lessons, Lake Buena Vista course	828-3781	Necessary	.... No limit for any guest		
Tennis courts, Contemporary Resort Hotel	824-3578	Suggested	.... 24 hours in advance		
Tennis courts, Golf Resort	824-2288	Suggested	.... 24 hours in advance		
Tennis courts, Lake Buena Vista Club	828-3742	Suggested	.... 24 hours in advance		

ACTIVITY	Phone for reservations (area code 305)	Advisability of reservations	How far in advance can reservations be made?		
			Guests in WDW hotels/villas	Guests at WDW Village Hotel Plaza establishments	Guests at off-property hotels
Tennis lessons, private and group, at the Contemporary Resort and at Lake Buena Vista Club	824-3578	Necessary	.... No limit for any guest		
Trail rides, Fort Wilderness	824-2734	Necessary	.... Up to 7 days for all		
Fishing trips, Fort Wilderness	824-2757	Necessary	Three days in advance	.... Resort guests only	
Massages, Olympia Health Spa, Contemporary Resort Hotel	824-3410	Necessary	Up to three months, but a day or two is sufficient	.... Resort guests only	
Good Meals					
Empress Room, *Empress Lilly* Riverboat, Walt Disney World Shopping Village	828-3900	Necessary	.... 30 days		
Lake Buena Vista Club	828-3735	Necessary	.... 30 days		
Gulf Coast Room, Contemporary Resort Hotel	824-3684	Requested	.... 14 days		
Papeete Bay Verandah, Polynesian Village Resort Hotel	824-1391	Requested	.... 7 days		
Tangaroa Terrace, Polynesian Village Resort Hotel	824-1360	Suggested	.... No limit for any guest		
Trophy Room, Golf Resort Hotel	824-1484	Suggested; available for dinner only	.... 30 days		
Epcot Center full-service restaurants	Available in person only; see box on p. 163	Necessary	.... On day of dining only		
Great Times					
Top of the World Dinner Show, Contemporary Resort Hotel	824-8000	Necessary	.... 30 days for all		
Hoop-Dee-Doo Musical Revue, Pioneer Hall, Fort Wilderness	824-8000	Necessary	Upon receipt of confirmed reservations	45 days*	30 days
Polynesian Revue, Polynesian Village Resort Hotel	824-8000	Necessary	Upon receipt of confirmed reservations	45 days*	30 days
Breakfast à la Disney, *Empress Lilly*	824-8000	Necessary	Upon receipt of confirmed reservations	45 days*	30 days
Minnie's Menehune Character Breakfast, Polynesian Village Resort Hotel	824-8000	Necessary	Upon receipt of confirmed reservations	45 days*	30 days
Dinner à la Disney, Golf Resort Hotel	824-8000	Necessary	Upon receipt of confirmed reservations	45 days*	30 days
Marshmallow Marsh Excursion, Fort Wilderness	824-2788	Necessary	Four days	.... Resort guests only	
Sunday Brunches					
Papeete Bay, Polynesian Village Resort Hotel	824-1391	Required	.... No limit for any guest		
Trophy Room, Golf Resort Hotel	824-1484	Required	.... 30 days		
Lake Buena Vista Club	828-3735	Requested	.... 14 days		
Top of the World, Contemporary Resort Hotel	824-3611	Required	.... 7 days		

*only if hotel reservations have been made through CRO; otherwise, 30 days

HOW TO GET THERE

The preponderance of visitors who come to Walt Disney World arrive by car. This is a by-product of perceived economy—though this is not always the case—and also because a Walt Disney World holiday is usually part of a somewhat broader tour around Central Florida.

BY CAR

Here are some suggested routes to WDW from the downtown areas of several major metropolitan areas, as recommended by the American Automobile Association.

Figure on driving 350 to 400 miles a day—a reasonable distance that won't wear you down so much that you can't enjoy your stay.

Atlanta: I-75 south, Florida Turnpike south, U.S.-27 south, Rte. 192 east. Total mileage: 438.

Baltimore: I-95 south, I-4 west, Rte. 192 west. Total mileage: 929.

Boston: Massachusetts Turnpike, I-86 south to Hartford, I-84 west, I-684 south, 287 west, Garden State Parkway south, New Jersey Turnpike south to the Delaware Memorial Bridge, I-95 south (through the Harbor Tunnel), I-4 west, Rte. 192 west. Total mileage: 1,352.

Buffalo: I-90, I-79, Rte. 19, West Virginia Turnpike, I-77 south, I-20 west, I-26 south, I-95 south, I-4 west, Rte. 192 west. Total mileage: 1,320.

Chicago: I-65 to Nashville, I-24 to Chattanooga, I-75 south, Florida Turnpike south, U.S.-27 south, Rte. 192 east. Total mileage: 1,190.

Cincinnati: I-75 south, Florida Turnpike south, U.S.-27 south, Rte. 192 east. Total mileage: 949.

Cleveland: I-77 south, I-20 west, I-26 south, I-95 south, I-4 west, Rte. 192 west. Total mileage: 1,166.

Dallas: I-20 east to Shreveport, Rte. 1 to Alexandria, U.S.-71 south, U.S.-190 east, I-10 east, I-12 east, I-10 east, I-75 south, Florida Turnpike east, U.S.-27 south, Rte. 192 east. Total mileage: 1,076.

Detroit: I-75 south, Florida Turnpike south, U.S.-27 south, Rte. 192 east. Total mileage: 1,225.

Indianapolis: I-65 south to Nashville, I-24 to Chattanooga, I-75 south, Florida Turnpike south, Rte. 192 east. Total mileage: 1,008.

Louisville: I-65 south to Nashville, I-24 to Chattanooga, I-75 south, Florida Turnpike south, U.S.-27 south, Rte. 192 east. Total mileage: 717.

Minneapolis: I-94 east, I-90 south, I-294 south, I-90 east, I-65 south to Indianapolis, I-465 south, I-65 south to Nashville, I-24 south to Chattanooga, I-75 south, Florida Turnpike south, U.S.-27 south, Rte. 192 east. Total mileage: 1,524.

New York City: Lincoln Tunnel to New Jersey Turnpike, south to Delaware Memorial Bridge, I-95 south (through Harbor Tunnel), I-4 west, Rte. 192 west. Total mileage: 1,126.

Pittsburgh: I-79 south, U.S.-19 south, West Virginia Turnpike south, I-77 south to Columbia (S.C.), I-20 west, I-26 south, I-95 south, I-4 west, Rte. 192 west. Total mileage: 1,093.

Philadelphia: I-95 south (through Harbor Tunnel), I-4 west, Rte. 192 west. Total mileage: 1,027.

Richmond: I-95 south, I-4 west, Rte. 192 west. Total mileage: 776.

Toronto: Queen Elizabeth Way south, I-90 south, I-290 south, I-79 south, U.S.-19 south, West Virginia Turnpike south, I-77 south to Columbia (S.C.), I-20 west, I-26 south, I-95 south, I-4 west, Rte. 192 west. Total mileage: 1,307.

FROM THE AIRPORT

Take Route 528 (also known as the Beeline Expressway, a toll road) going west, to I-4 west until you reach the appropriate Walt Disney World exit (there are 3 in all). The total distance is 28 miles.

AUTOMOBILE CLUBS: Reputable national automobile clubs can offer help with en route breakdowns; insurance that covers personal injury, accidents, arrest, bail bond, and lawyers' fees for defense of contested traffic cases; and travel planning services—not only advice, but also free maps and route-mapping. Programs vary from one club to the next; fees range from about $25 to $50 a year.

Among the leading clubs are the following:

Allstate Motor Club; 30 Allstate Plaza; Northbrook, IL 60066; 312-291-5461.
American Automobile Association; 8111 Gatehouse Rd.; Falls Church, VA 22047; 703-222-6000.
Amoco Motor Club; PO Box 9049; Des Moines, IA 50369; 800-334-3300; 800-372-7721 in Iowa.
Ford Auto Club; PO Box 224688; Dallas, TX 75222; 800-348-5220.
Gulf Auto Club; PO Box 660461; Dallas, TX 75266; 800-348-5126.
JTX Travel Club Inc.; PO Box 13901; Philadelphia, PA 19101; 800-523-1965; 800-262-5213 from Pennsylvania.
Montgomery Ward Auto Club; 2020 Dempster St.; Evanston, IL 60202; 800-621-5151 and 800-572-5577 in Illinois.
Motor Club of America; 484 Central Ave.; Newark, NJ 07107; 201-733-1234.
United States Auto Club Motoring Division; PO Box 660460; Dallas, TX 75266; 800-348-5058.

FREE MAPS AND ROUTINGS: Those who don't belong to an automobile or travel club can get free maps from state tourist boards or from:

The Mobil Travel Service; 106 Hi-Lane Rd.; Richmond, KY 40475.
The Texaco Travel Service; Box 1459; Houston, TX 77001.

Also excellent is *Rand McNally's Road Atlas* (about $5.95 in bookstores).

BY BUS

Relatively few vacationers come to Walt Disney World by bus. But it makes sense to consider this means of transportation if you're traveling just a short distance or have plenty of time, if there are only two or three in your party, or if cost is a major consideration—bus travel is extremely economical.

Both Greyhound and Trailways provide frequent direct service into Orlando; some buses deposit their passengers on the very threshold of the Magic Kingdom and at the entrance to Epcot Center (where there are lockers in which luggage can be stored until the end of the day). From there, taxis and limousines provided by the various area hotels and motels provide transportation to the lodging place that you have selected. For further information, phone Greyhound at 305-843-7720 or Trailways at 305-422-7107.

Sample Travel Times

Jacksonville, Florida.... 3½ hours
Tallahassee, Florida.... about 5½ hours
Atlanta, Georgia....... about 11 hours
Charleston,
  South Carolina...... about 20 hours

BY TRAIN

Amtrak serves the Orlando area twice daily from New York City. The trip takes about 24 hours and costs in the neighborhood of $215 round-trip. En route stops are made in Washington, D.C., Virginia, North Carolina, South Carolina, and Georgia. (Special discounted fares are sometimes available; it's a good idea to check.)

Amtrak also offers Auto Train service. The overnight trains depart on Sundays, Wednesdays, and Fridays from Lorton, Virginia, 20 miles south of Washington, D.C., and travel directly to Sanford, Florida, just 21 miles northeast of Orlando. The auto trains make the trip back north on Tuesdays, Thursdays, and Saturdays. Departure time is 4:30 P.M. and arrival time is 9:30 A.M. in both directions. The fare is $200 per car, $130 per adult, and $98 for children ages 2 through 11. The fare includes two meals and some entertainment. Sleeping accommodations cost extra. Special excursion fares are often offered, so be sure to inquire.

For reservations and schedule information, contact Amtrak Distribution Center; Box 7717; Itasca, IL 60143; 800-USA-RAIL.

BY AIR

The Orlando airport that arriving travelers encountered in the early 1970s is a far cry from the sleek, new, multimillion-dollar facility that greets vacationers today. Orlando International Airport now is equipped to handle the millions of visitors who flock to Central Florida each year. Shuttle trains transport passengers to and from the central terminal, and there is a WDW information center where arriving guests can find out what's going on during their stay—and departing travelers can buy T-shirts and other Disney merchandise that they may have forgotten to acquire on the property.

There are more than a dozen airlines offering direct flights from all parts of the country. Eastern Airlines alone—the "Official Airline of Walt Disney World"—carries more than one and a half million passengers into Orlando annually, on nonstop flights from 19 cities, direct flights (not including a change of planes) and connecting flights from 70 more—so many that more than 20 ticketing positions, 10 gates, its own baggage claim area, and a special desk to serve Eastern's tour-package purchasers are required to handle them all. Over the years, Eastern's special style of service, with special meals and "Fun Flight" gift kits for youngsters, has grown up around the flourishing Walt Disney World/Central Florida trade.

The airline you decide to fly will depend in large part on where you live, when you'll be traveling, and which airline can get you there when you want to go, for the price you want to pay. Remember, direct flights—those whose lure is that they do not include a change of planes—are not always the swiftest way to get from point to point. If your itinerary requires several stops, it might be wise to investigate all of the possible connection alternatives.

THE WINGS OF THE WORLD

As the "Official Airline of Walt Disney World," Eastern Airlines not only has its own attraction, If You Had Wings, in the Magic Kingdom, but also its own ticket offices right on the property—one right inside its Magic Kingdom attraction, the other on the first-floor lobby of the Contemporary Resort Hotel. The close Disney-Eastern relationship also means that when guests make a reservation at a Walt Disney World hotel, the Central Reservations Office also can arrange for an Eastern representative to call and help with flight arrangements. It couldn't be easier. Eastern's passengers also benefit from the tie by being able to fly on the only airline that is able to offer packages that include lodgings at the Contemporary Resort, the Polynesian Village, and the Golf Resort. It is not an insignificant advantage.

DISCOVERING THE LOWEST AIR FARE

Gone are the days when it always cost a finite number of dollars to get from point A to point B, so it's more important than ever before to shop around.

Find out the names of all the airlines that serve your destination, then call them all—more than once if your route is complex. Tell the agent how many people there are in your party, and emphasize that you're interested in economy. The more flexible you can be in your dates and duration of stay, the more money you're likely to save. Fares are usually lowest on highly competitive, heavily traveled routes; if you live halfway between two airports—one a major city, the other relatively untraveled—you may do better from one than from the other. Check both.

- Watch the newspapers for ads announcing new promotional fares.
- When it's necessary to change planes en route, it's best to stick with one airline; the agent will know his or her own company's routing—and its discounted fares—better than those offered by other carriers. (For the same reason, smart travelers book all of a trip through the carrier they'll be using most.)
- Fly when other people don't—at night; on weekends on routes that usually serve business travelers; or midweek to and from vacation destinations.
- Plan ahead. Most carriers guarantee their fares—which means that you won't have to pay extra to use a valid ticket even if fares go up after you buy it. (But if your ticket has to be rewritten due to a change in dates or times of flights, you'll probably have to pay any new fare.) So pick up and pay for your ticket as soon as possible—before fares go up.

WHICH AIRLINE FLIES FROM YOUR CITY?

You can fly directly to Orlando—that is, without changing planes—from about 50 different cities, on more than a dozen airlines. Schedules do change from time to time, and flights occasionally are dropped or new ones added. This was the operative nonstop / direct / same-airline connecting service at press time:

City	Airlines
Akron/Canton, OH	PI, AL
Albany, NY	EA, AL
Albuquerque, NM	EA, AA, TW, DL
Alexandria, LA	DL
Allentown/Bethlehem/Easton, PA	EA, AL
Amarillo, TX	AA, DL
Asheville, NC	PI
Atlanta, GA	EA, DL, RC, NW
Augusta, GA	DL
Austin, TX	EA, AA, DL, CO
Baltimore, MD	EA, AL, PI, DL
Bangor, ME	DL
Baton Rouge, LA	DL
Beaumont/Pt. Arthur, TX	EA, CO
Binghamton, NY	AL
Birmingham, AL	EA, RC, DL
Bismarck, ND	NW, RC
Boise, ID	UA
Boston, MA	EA, DL, AL, NI, PI
Brainerd, MN	RC
Buffalo, NY	EA, AL, UA, PA
Burbank, CA	AA, RC
Burlington, VT	AL
Cedar Rapids/Iowa City, IA	OZ
Champaign, IL	PI, OZ
Charleston, SC	EA, PI, DL
Charleston, WV	PI
Charlotte, NC	EA, PI, DL
Charlottesville, VA	PI
Chattanooga, TN	EA, DL, RC
Chicago, IL	EA, DL, UA, OZ, TW, RC, PI, NW
Cincinnati, OH	RC, DL, PI
Cleveland, OH	EA, UA, DL, PI, AL, OZ
Columbia, MO	OZ
Columbia, SC	EA, PI, DL
Columbus, GA	DL
Columbus, MS	RC
Columbus, OH	EA, DL
Corpus Christi, TX	EA, AA, CO
Dallas/Ft. Worth, TX	EA, AA, DL, OZ
Dayton, OH	DL, PI
Denver, CO	EA, UA, DL, TW, OZ, CO, AA, PI, NW
Des Moines, IA	OZ, UA, AA, TW
Detroit, MI	EA, NW, DL, RC, TW, OZ, PA, PI
Duluth/Superior, WI	RC
Eau Claire, WI	RC
Elmira, NY	AL
El Paso, TX	EA, DL, AA
Evansville, IN	EA
Fargo, ND	NW, RC
Fayetteville, NC	PI
Flint, MI	PI

City	Airlines
Ft. Lauderdale, FL	GO, ZO, RC, DL, TW, NI
Ft. Myers, FL	EA, PT, UA, PA
Ft. Wayne, IN	PI, DL
Fresno, CA	UA
Grand Forks, ND	NW, RC
Grand Rapids, MI	PI, RC, NW
Greensboro/Highpoint/Winston-Salem, NC	EA, DL, PI
Greenville, MS	RC
Greenville/Spartanburg, SC	EA, DL, PI
Harlingen, TX	AA
Harrisburg, PA	AL
Hartford, CT/Springfield, MA	EA, DL, QS, AL
Hibbing, MN	RC
Houston, TX	EA, RC, CO, DL, AA
Huntington, WV	AL, PI
Huntsville/Decatur, AL	EA, RC
Indianapolis, IN	EA, DL, OZ, TW, ZO
Int'l Falls, MN	RC
Ithaca, NY	AL
Jackson, MS	EA, DL
Jacksonville, FL	PT, OZ, GO
Jacksonville, SC	PI
Jefferson City, MO	OZ
Kansas City, MO	EA, QS, DL, RC, TW, OZ, CO, UA, AA
Key West, FL	PT
Kinston, NC	PI
Knoxville, TN	EA, DL
Lansing, MI	PI, RC
Las Vegas, NV	EA, QS, OZ, AA, DL, UA, RC
Lexington/Frankfort, KY	DL, PI
Lincoln, NE	UA
Little Rock, AR	DL, QS
Long Island MacArthur, NY	QS
Los Angeles, CA	EA, DL, CO, NW, AA, UA, RC
Louisville, KY	EA, DL, PI, ZO
Lubbock, TX	AA, DL
Lynchburg, VA	PI
Madison, WI	NW, OZ
McAllen, TX	CO
Melbourne, FL	EA
Memphis, TN	RC, DL
Miami, FL	EA, RC, PI, PA, DL, ZO
Midland/Odessa, TX	AA
Milwaukee, WI	EA, NW, OZ, RC
Minneapolis/St. Paul, MN	EA, OZ, RC, NW, DL, AA, UA
Mobile, AL	EA, DL, RC
Moline, IL	OZ
Monroe, LA	DL, RC
Montgomery, AL	RC, DL
Montreal, Que.	EA, DL
Myrtle Beach, SC	PI
Nashville, TN	EA, RC, DL, PI, ZO
New Orleans, LA	EA, RC, DL, QS, PA, NT
New York, NY	EA, AL, DL, PA, PI, TW, QS, NY
Norfolk/Virginia Beach, VA	EA, PI, DL, ZO
Ocala, FL	AL
Oklahoma City, OK	EA, AA, TW, DL, CO, QS
Omaha, NB	EA, OZ, TW, UA, RC, CO
Ontario, CA	EA, AA, UA, DL
Panama City, FL	RC, NT
Pensacola, FL	EA, NT
Peoria, IL	TW, OZ
Philadelphia, PA	EA, DL, PI, AL, NI, PA
Phoenix, AZ	EA, DL, RC, AA, UA, CO
Pittsburgh, PA	EA, AL, DL, PI, NI
Portland, ME	DL
Portland, OR	EA, DL, NW, UA, AA
Providence, RI	EA, AL, DL, PA
Raleigh/Durham, NC	EA, PI, DL
Reno, NV	EA, UA, AA
Richmond, VA	EA, PI, DL, ZO
Roanoke, VA	PI
Rochester, NY	EA, UA, AL, PA
Sacramento, CA	UA, AA
Saginaw, MI	RC, UA
St. Louis, MO	EA, OZ, TW, DL, RC
Salisbury, MD	PI
Salt Lake City, UT	EA, DL, UA, AA, RC
San Antonio, TX	EA, AA, DL, CO
San Diego, CA	EA, DL, UA, QS, OZ, CO, AA
San Francisco, CA	EA, DL, NW, RC, AA, UA, CO
San Jose, CA	AA, UA
Sarasota/Bradenton, FL	EA, RC, PT
Savannah, GA	EA, DL
Seattle/Tacoma, WA	EA, AA, RC, UA, NW, DL
Shreveport, LA	AA, DL
Sioux Falls, SD	UA, OZ, RC
South Bend, IN	PI
Spokane, WA	NW, UA
Springfield, IL	OZ
Springfield, MO	OZ
Syracuse, NY	EA, AL, PA
Tallahassee, FL	EA, PT, RC
Tampa/St. Petersburg, FL	EA, DL, NW, RC, UA, ZO
Toledo, OH	PI, TW, DL
Toronto, Ont.	EA, RC
Tri-City Airport, TN	PI
Tucson, AZ	EA, AA, RC
Tulsa, OK	OZ, AA, DL, TW, RC, CO, QS
Vancouver, BC	UA
Vero Beach, FL	AL
Washington, DC	EA, PA, AL, PI, DL, RC
Wausau, WI	RC
West Palm Beach, FL	DL, AL, UA, TW, GO, PA
Wichita, KS	RC, TW, AA
Wilkes-Barre/Scranton, PA	EA, PI, AL
Williamsport, PA	AL
Wilmington, NC	PI

ABBREVIATIONS—AA: American. AL: US Air or Allegheny Commuter. CO: Continental. DL: Delta. EA: Eastern. GO: Trans Air. NI: American Int'l Airways. NT: Air New Orleans. NW: Northwest. NY: New York Air. OZ: Ozark. PA: Pan American. PI: Piedmont. PT: PBA. QS: Northeastern Int'l Airways. RC: Republic. TW: Trans World. UA: United. ZO: Florida Express.

TOUGH QUESTIONS

SHOULD YOU BUY A PACKAGE?

The sheer number of diverse packages offering vacations in Central Florida is enough to bewilder even the savviest traveler. Still, these packages offer significant advantages: the opportunity to purchase a vacation that's completely organized in advance, and that will generally cost less than the same package elements purchased separately. (Eastern Airlines' "Super 7" packages, for example, can cost less than the round-trip economy airfare from certain cities, though they also include accommodations, a rental car with unlimited mileage for a week, and a three-day World Passport that offers admission to both the Magic Kingdom and Epcot Center.)

The main difference among the various package offerings—aside from cost—is the matter of lodging in on-site hotels versus off-property accommodations. Eastern Airlines and American Express packages offer lodgings in Walt Disney World's own on-site hotels, and Walt Disney World itself offers on-site "World Adventure" packages for visitors staying five, six, or seven nights. The Walt Disney World package is perfect for "top of the line" visitors who don't mind spending a little extra money to obtain a package that includes virtually everything. This is the first time that the Disney organization has offered such an all-inclusive Walt Disney World vacation (though it does not include transportation to the site). Eastern Airlines' packages, by contrast, are more economical and include the added attraction of low-cost air transportation—plus accommodations at the Contemporary Resort, Polynesian Village, or Golf Resort. Eastern also offers even less expensive package plans that utilize the hotels at Walt Disney World Village Hotel Plaza and certain off-site properties. Your budget, the length of your planned stay at Walt Disney World, and the other Central Florida travel plans should determine which package is best for you.

Appraising the value of any package depends entirely on your specific needs, so check the elements of each package carefully to see how closely they fulfill your requirements. The various sections of this book describe the activities and attractions available in and around Walt Disney World, and once you've determined which of these are most appealing, call Walt Disney World, the airlines that fly between your city and Orlando, or a qualified travel agent to find a package that comes closest to your ideal.

Don't pick a package that includes elements you don't want or won't use; chances are that you'll be paying for them. And remember that while extras like welcome cocktails sound attractive, their cash value is negligible. Also note that some packages announce as attractive selling points certain services that are available to *every* Walt Disney World guest.

On the other hand, there's real value in certain other elements, such as transportation to the Walt Disney World property and discounts on meals. Some of the Eastern Airlines and Walt Disney World Travel Company packages also include meals with the Disney characters, tennis lessons, golf greens fees, court rentals or boat rentals, and the like.

SHOULD YOU USE A TRAVEL AGENT?

Our answer has to be an unqualified "maybe," since there have been some complaints from travelers who found their travel agents less than eager to book Walt Disney World accommodations. The reason is hardly obscure: no direct commissions are paid to travel agents by Walt Disney World for booking rooms in the Walt Disney-owned villas or hotels—the Contemporary Resort, the Polynesian Village, and the Golf Resort. Travel agents are generally far more enthusiastic about plans involving Walt Disney World Village Hotel Plaza hotels—Viscount Hotel, Howard Johnson's, Royal Plaza, Americana Dutch Resort, the Hilton, and Buena Vista Palace—and off-site accommodations. Agents can be first-class sources for the packages created by the Walt Disney Travel Company, which are Disney endorsed and assure a purchaser of good value. Eastern Airlines and American Express also pay commissions on their package arrangements, which include both on-site and off-site accommodations.

HOW TO CUT TRAVEL COSTS

Between general inflation and the rising cost of gasoline, vacations are not getting any less expensive. Yet scrapping the annual family getaway is no answer. It's better to simply prune the vacation budget in three main areas:

Food: Get hot meals in cafeterias instead of waitress-service restaurants. Visit fancier establishments at lunchtime rather than dinner. (The very same entrees usually cost less then.) Carry sandwich fixings and have lunches alfresco when possible. Look for lodging places with kitchen facilities: The savings on food, especially for families, may be more than the extra accommodations expense.

Lodging: The chief rule of thumb here is not to pay for more than you need. Budget chains such as Days Inns and Days Lodges, Susse Chalet Motor Lodges and Inns, Imperial 400 Motor Inns, Passport Inns and Downtowners, Red Roof Inns, Family Inns of America, and Motel 6's can prove economical, though they may not offer many frills. (The best single guide to their whereabouts from coast to coast is the *National Directory of Budget Motels*, revised annually and available for $3.95 plus $1 postage and handling from Pilot Books; 103 Cooper St.; Babylon, NY 11702.)

If swimming pools and other amenities matter, consider the nonbudget chain establishments that have them—but remember that cutoff ages (above which there is a charge for children sharing parents' room) do vary. At Holiday Inns, children age 12 and under always stay free; some properties allow teenagers age 19 and under to stay free, so check at the individual hotels for the policy there. Quality Inns charge for youngsters over 16; Rodeways charge for young people 17 or older; and Sheratons, Howard Johnson's, and Marriotts charge for kids when they reach age 18. At Ramada Inns, the cutoff age is 19. Get prices for Orlando hostelries in advance, then calculate the exact costs for your whole family.

Depending on the number of people in your party, guest houses and tourist homes may or may not be a good buy. Since these establishments usually levy substantial extra charges for more than two people, regardless of their ages, rooms that are inexpensive for two can prove costly for a family. Consult *The Great American Guest House Book* published by Burt Franklin & Co. ($8.95) and *Bed and Breakfast USA* published by E.P. Dutton ($6.95) for locations and prices. Also look into the AAA Bed and Breakfast of Florida (Box 1316; Winter Park, FL 32790; 628-3233). They represent B & B's in the WDW area.

Also consider sharing accommodations with family or friends. It's often possible to rent a resort condominium or house large enough to accommodate two families for much less than twice what each would pay for a single cramped hotel room. At Walt Disney World, couples can reap savings by this sort of doubling up—with no loss of privacy and some bonus in space. (See the chart "Rates at WDW-owned Properties" for details.)

Transportation: Comparative shopping is vital. Consider transportation needs at your destination, then figure the total transportation cost. Calculate the cost of driving based on your car's mileage, current gasoline prices, the distance you expect to cover, and the cost of accommodations and food en route, then figure what you'll pay by bus, plane, or train. Don't fail to add in the cost of getting to and from the airport or terminal, and the cost of renting a car (if necessary) in Orlando. And remember that special low fares that are economical for couples can sometimes prove less advantageous for families.

HOW TO GET

During the designing of the Magic Kingdom, one of the most important steps was the making of a scale model. Then, using a small periscope-like device with a rectangular viewing screen, designers looked at the model from the same viewpoint that today's visitors see the finished product through their cameras. So if the scenery hereabouts makes you instinctively want to reach for your camera, it's because it was laid out to do so. In fact, some 150,000,000 photos are snapped here every year.

Of course, there are limitations to what any camera can do. No camera can capture all the life of Epcot Center in quite the same way that it's perceived when the colors crowd your peripheral vision and no camera can depict the charm of the Magic Kingdom when the boom-boom-boom of the drums of an approaching marching band assails your ears.

Nonetheless, there are so many other wonderful images to be snatched all over WDW that just about any camera in good working order can get them for you, so long as you use the right techniques. Here are some hints:

• Don't shoot from closer than 4 feet from your subject, and don't try for a flash picture more than 12 feet away. The former will probably turn out fuzzy, and the latter likely will prove dark. Note that flash attachments can't illuminate a subject more than a dozen feet distant. (Important: Flash photography is prohibited inside attractions at Epcot Center and the Magic Kingdom.)

• Fill the frame with as much of the subject as possible. Especially when shooting people, remember that the larger the subject appears in the picture, the more interesting it will be.

• Hold the camera steady as you *gently* squeeze the shutter.

• Don't shoot into the sun. The camera's electric eye will assume that there's more light on the subject than there actually is, and the image will turn out too dark in the snapshot. Instead, position yourself so that light is falling directly on your subject—coming from behind you or from the side.

• Check the camera's batteries and battery contacts regularly.

• Use film that is fresh. When purchasing film, check the expiration date stamped on the bottom of the box. Keep the film as cool as possible; don't leave it in a hot car for long periods of time.

• Keep the camera clean. Blow dust off the lens and then wipe it with a soft tissue. Blow dust out of the inside of the camera.

• When taking movies or using videotape cameras, note that they'll be more effective if you pick a theme such as "A Walk Down Main Street," "A Stroll Through France," or the like. Don't shoot into the sun, and make sure that all subject matter is evenly lighted. Pan very slowly and smoothly, and give every scene plenty of time—at least five seconds. Don't use the zoom lens too often; it can be distracting.

• If you suspect that your camera isn't functioning correctly, visit the Kodak Camera Center on the east side of Main Street near Town Square in the Magic Kingdom or, at Epcot Center, the Camera Center near Spaceship Earth, or the Camera Center at Journey Into Imagination.

Rental cameras: One of the best deals in the Magic Kingdom is the free camera rental offered at the Kodak Camera Center. You must leave a deposit (cash, American Express, or MasterCard) of $50 for a Kodak Instant or Disc camera. At Epcot Center, rental cameras are available at the Camera Center near Spaceship Earth. The deposit is refundable, all you pay for is the film.

Camera repairs: Those of a minor nature can be handled by the Kodak Camera Center in the Magic Kingdom or at the Camera Center near Spaceship Earth and Journey Into Imagination at Epcot Center.

Film processing: Exposed film can be left for processing at Mickey's Film Express, at the Camera Center in the Magic Kingdom, or at Fort Wilderness or the hotels. Processing takes seven to ten days. At Epcot Center, drop off film at the Camera Center near Spaceship Earth before 7 P.M. and pick it up after 1 P.M. the following day; or leave film after 7 P.M. and it will be available the next day after 8 P.M.

THE BEST PHOTOS

WHERE TO BUY FILM

Walt Disney World is one of the largest retail outlets in the world for postcards and film.

In the Magic Kingdom
Main Street—Camera Center; Emporium
Adventureland—Tropic Toppers
Frontierland—Frontier Trading Post
Liberty Square—Heritage House
Fantasyland—Royal Candy Shoppe; Film, Photo & Information Kiosk

In Epcot Center
Future World—All merchandise locations (best stock at the Camera Center)
World Showcase—At least one shop in each pavilion (often stashed under the counter)

In the Hotels
Contemporary Resort—Plaza Gifts & Sundries
Golf Resort—Golf Gifts and Sundries
Polynesian Village—News from Civilization

At Fort Wilderness
Settlement and Meadow Trading Posts

At Walt Disney World Shopping Village
Village Gifts and Sundries

PHOTOGRAPHY IN EPCOT CENTER: Kodak has designated a series of about a dozen particularly scenic picture spots which are identified by plaques throughout the park.

THE MAGIC KINGDOM'S BLUE RIBBON PHOTO SPOTS: Certain locations in the Magic Kingdom seem made for family photos:
- The bridge by the Crystal Palace, with Cinderella Castle in the background.
- Anywhere right in front of the Castle.
- The Milk Cart in Town Square, at the top of Main Street.
- Fuente de la Fortuna, the fountain opposite Pirates of the Caribbean, next to the stage where the steel drum band usually plays, in Adventureland.
- In front of the Singing Drums, opposite the Enchanted Tiki Birds pavilion, in Adventureland. The drums start beating every four or five minutes.
- The stocks in Liberty Square.
- On the Barrel Bridge at Tom Sawyer Island.
- With the characters when they make their daily appearances in the Castle Forecourt or in front of City Hall. The character breakfasts or dinners are also good bets.
- Outside the Magic Kingdom, near the topiaries on the main entrance road.

HOW TO PHOTOGRAPH FIREWORKS: You need a camera with a manually adjustable aperture and shutter speed. Set your camera on a tripod, or arrange to brace it in some other way; set the aperture at f/8 and the shutter speed at B; and hold the lens open for three to five seconds at each burst. (Cover the lens with your hand between explosions.)

HOW TO PHOTOGRAPH THE MAIN STREET ELECTRICAL PARADE: Using an adjustable camera with a normal or wide-angle lens, open the aperture as wide as possible to f/1.4 or f/2.8, and shoot around 1/15 or 1/30 second, using fast films such as Kodacolor 400 (for prints), Ektachrome 160 Tungsten, or Ektachrome 400 Daylight (faster, though it yellows color slightly). To get an artistic blur, slowly pan with the camera as the float moves past. No tripod is necessary, though a steady hand assures best results.

HINTS ON TRAVELING

Tell youngsters that a Walt Disney World vacation is in the works and the response is apt to be nothing less than overwhelming—and the journey to the park is likely to be fraught with "Are-we-there-yets?" recurring like a stuck record.

En Route: Certain ploys can quiet this refrain. Get older children involved in planning every leg of the trip, and set up a series of intermediate goals to which they can look forward. Younger children can anticipate discovering the contents of a pint-sized suitcase packed with familiar games and toys, plus a few surprises.

In addition, it's smart to take along snacks to keep things peaceful when stomachs start rumbling and food is miles away. Above all, and especially if the trip is by car, take it easy, and allow time for plenty of breaks en route.

Those who fly should schedule travel for off-peak hours, when the chances are better that extra seats will be available. When the plane is taking off and landing, babies should be given bottles, pacifiers, or even thumbs to promote swallowing and clear ears; a piece of gum or hard candy will provide the same relief for a small child. Newborn babies (those only a couple of weeks old) should not be taken aloft, since their lungs may not be able to adjust to the altitude. For finicky young eaters, request special meals when reserving seats. Eastern Airlines offers a kiddie repast called a Fun Flight Meal—fruit, milk, and cereal for breakfast; and an all-beef hot dog, potato chips, chocolate milk, cookies, a banana, raisins, and a special Walt Disney lollipop for lunch or dinner. The meal comes in a box decorated with Disney characters, and is a special treat for kids. Remember, these meals must be ordered when your plane reservations are made. In addition, snacks for youngsters under age two can be arranged on request. Eastern also offers terrific packages of goodies for young travelers (ask for Eastern's Fun Flight Bag of diversions, like playing cards and coloring books).

Budget watchers should pay careful attention to motel rate structures (see page 25 for ideas) when reserving accommodations. Also, some charge for cots, which other motels might bring in at no charge. Note that some hostelries outside the World *seem* a lot less expensive than the WDW resorts—until the actual costs for everything for a whole family are computed. Sometimes airfares that sound inexpensive actually cost more for a family; sometimes air packages cut costs. So check carefully.

At Walt Disney World: This vacationland ranks among the easiest spots on earth for traveling families with children. Older youngsters don't need to be driven around, and the general supervision is such that kids are hard pressed to get into trouble. All the resorts, plus Fort Wilderness and the Villa Center in the Walt Disney World Village villa area, have at least a small room full of pinball machines and video games, much to the satisfaction of kids of all ages; the one at the Contemporary Resort Hotel is positively vast. And all the hotels have playgrounds; the one at the Polynesian Village is particularly nifty, with its thatched-roof treehouse, climbing rings, and offbeat slide.

And both the Polynesian Village and the Contemporary Resort (but not the Golf Resort) have child-care facilities. In-room babysitters can be summoned to all resort hotels and villas; contact the Guest Services desk. And there is also a center known as Kindercare, suitable for youngsters aged 2 through 12; parents may drop off their children anytime after 6 P.M. For details and availability, phone 827-KIDS.

WITH CHILDREN

Nor is there any cause for excessive hand-holding inside the Magic Kingdom or Epcot Center; with older youngsters, it's enough to establish a specific meeting place and a meeting time (allowing a little latitude, just in case). If there are younger children along, it's not a bad idea to stop at City Hall or the Baby Center next to the Crystal Palace to pick up a special name tag to facilitate a reunion in case the family gets separated. Aunt Polly's on Tom Sawyer Island is a good bet for lunch; while adults in the party are sipping lemonade, the kids can be bouncing across the Barrel Bridge and exploring every nook and cranny on the island.

Strollers are available for rent for a nominal fee (small deposit required) at the Stroller Shop on the east side of Main Street at the entrance to the Magic Kingdom and at the Stroller and Wheelchair Rentals Shop on the east side of the Entrance Plaza and at the France pavilion in Epcot Center. If your stroller disappears, as often happens while you're inside an attraction, a replacement may be obtained at Space Port (the shop of contemporary decorative gifts) in Tomorrowland; at the Trading Post in Frontierland; at Tinkerbell Toy Shop in Fantasyland; and at the France, Germany, and United Kingdom pavilions in Epcot Center.

The Baby Care Centers at the Magic Kingdom and Epcot Center can be helpful in many ways to mothers with young children. There are low-lighted rooms with comfortable rocking chairs and love seats for nursing mothers and a cheerful feeding room. There are highchairs, and bibs and plastic spoons are also available. The Baby Care Centers have facilities for changing infants, preparing formulas, and warming bottles. Disposable diapers and nurser bags, pull-on rubber pants, baby bottles with nipples, formula (*Similac*, *Isomil*, and *Enfamil*), teethers, pacifiers, prepared cereal, juices, and strained and junior baby food in a limited selection, are available for sale on the spot at a nominal cost. The decor of the whole place is soothing, the atmosphere is such that it seems a million miles away from the Magic Kingdom or Epcot Center, and the guest books list more wonderful children's names than many a baby name book—as more than one expectant mother has noted. A stop for diaper changing makes a good break for child and mother alike, though changing areas are available in most ladies' rest-rooms as well.

A variety of other baby care supplies can be purchased at the Baby Care Center in Epcot Center and the Stroller Shop on Main Street. Pampers are sold, though not displayed, in the Children's Books section of the Emporium on Main Street in the Magic Kingdom and at Gateway and the Centorium in Epcot Center.

Lost Children: That the security force inside the Magic Kingdom is far more careful than the happy appearance of things indicates is a welcome thought on those rare instances when a child suddenly disappears or fails to show up on schedule. If this happens to you, check the lost children's log books in the Baby Care Center and at City Hall in the Magic Kingdom and at Earth Station and the Baby Care Center behind the Odyssey Restaurant in Epcot Center. Every Disney employee knows where they are—and what to do if a lost-looking child suddenly starts to call for his or her mommy. There are no paging systems in either park, but in very serious emergencies an all-points-bulletin can be put out among employees.

HELPFUL HINTS

HINTS FOR OLDER TRAVELERS

Walt Disney World can overwhelm an elderly traveler not accustomed to unfamiliar places; Epcot Center takes in immense distances, and the Magic Kingdom can be disorienting because of the profusion of sights and sounds, nooks and crannies. The heat, particularly in summer, can be hard to take. Yet with the proper planning and precautions, all of WDW can be just as delightful for older visitors as for kids. Here are a few suggestions:

• Join a tour. Of the several organizations that specialize in group trips for older travelers, only one—the National Council of Senior Citizens (925 15 St. N.W.; Washington, DC 20005)—offers a tour to WDW often enough to mention (and even these are arranged only when interest warrants). Note that visitors who do come with a group bus tour should be sure to allow plenty of time to take the monorail or the ferry back to the bus parking area at the Transportation and Ticket Center or at Epcot Center—usually about half an hour—and should avoid queuing up when time begins to grow short.

Inside the Magic Kingdom or Epcot Center, group tours—among the best buys in the World—are offered by Guest Relations. These four-hour guided walks take in the whole park; the price, which is about $4 more than a one-day ticket, includes admission, the services of the guide, and visits to various attractions in all the "lands." For details and availability, phone 824-4633.

• Schedule visits for off-peak seasons and hours when the crowds will not be discouraging. Also, note that special values are available during Young at Heart Days on selected dates in the fall. Call 824-4321 for details.

• Read all Walt Disney World literature carefully before arrival so that things are familiar.

• In the parks, don't be timid about asking for directions or advice. Disney employees are always happy to help out.

• Eat early or late, to avoid mealtime crowds. In the Magic Kingdom, stop in more sedate restaurants such as the Crystal Palace, the Town Square Cafe, or King Stefan's in Cinderella Castle. Or take the monorail to the still calmer Polynesian Village or the Contemporary Resort, to lunch in one of the full-service restaurants there, or make a trip through one of the buffet lines. In Epcot Center, the Odyssey Restaurant in Future World is an especially restful counter service spot for lunch for those who did not make reservations in one of the full-service restaurants.

• Don't try to save money by scrimping on food. Traveling takes energy, and only a good meal can provide it.

• Protect yourself from the sun. Wear a hat, and slather on the sunscreen. (And don't forget to cover legs, which are easily sunburned by light rays reflected from pavements.)

• Don't become overheated. Take frequent rest stops in the shade, and get out of the mid-afternoon heat by stopping for a snack in an air-conditioned restaurant. Avoid standing in line at Frontierland's Big Thunder and at Fantasyland's 20,000 Leagues in midafternoon; parts of these queues are unprotected from the sun, and can be very hot. In Epcot Center, spend the hot midafternoon hours in the TransCenter in the World of Motion and in CommuniCore East and West in Future World and avoid the uncovered outdoor queues at all the Future World pavilions and at World Showcase attractions like *O Canada!*, *Impressions de France*, and *El Rio del Tiempo: Sail the River of Time*. Don't underestimate the distances at Epcot Center: You may need to walk as much as two miles in the course of a day. Taking that slowly and in short increments, this is not too ominous. But if you are not strong enough to cover that distance, be sure to rent a wheelchair at the outset of your visit. The buses that circumnavigate World Showcase Lagoon and the two launches that make regular crossings can help you cover the distances—but only when there are no long queues. It is better to walk between pavilions, resting frequently en route, than to wait 15 or 20 minutes for a ride in a bus or boat: neither stops directly in front of all pavilions, and there's still a need to walk to your ultimate destination.

• Above all, don't push yourself. Half the fun of the Magic Kingdom and Epcot Center—the part that younger travelers often miss—is just sitting under a shade tree on a park bench, watching the people go by.

LOST ADULTS

Occasionally, traveling companions do get separated in the press of the crowds or someone fails to show up at an appointed meeting spot. So it's good to know that Guest Relations maintains message books at Earth Station in Epcot Center and at City Hall in the Magic Kingdom.

FOR THE HANDICAPPED

Walt Disney World gets high marks among handicapped travelers because of the attention that has been paid to their special needs. Special parking is available for guests visiting the Magic Kingdom or Epcot Center; get directions at either of the Auto

HINTS FOR SINGLE TRAVELERS

Walt Disney World does not exactly attract the young swinging singles crowd, so those on the lookout for romantic encounters probably would do better elsewhere. But solo travelers who travel alone for the freedom and the fun of it can have as enjoyable a time at Walt Disney World as they would anywhere else.

WDW employees are generally a friendly lot, and entertaining to talk to; chatting with a painter about the perpetual repainting of Main Street woodwork, talking to the animal keepers on Discovery Island, or discussing life abroad with one of the young World Showcase employees born and educated in the country the pavilion represents, a single traveler usually learns more about the ways of the World than any group member. Other visitors that might be encountered in the course of a day are away from their own home base as well, and are apt to be just that much less standoffish.

Single women will not find the bars and lounges in WDW hotels off-limits (as they might in their real world counterparts). Sitting at the U-shaped bar at the Baton Rouge Lounge can be particular fun. In Epcot Center, the same relaxed atmosphere prevails in the Rose & Crown Pub in the United Kingdom pavilion and the Matsunoma Lounge in Japan, both in World Showcase. Another good way to meet people (albeit a somewhat older crowd) is to sign up for one of Guest Relations' Guided Walking Tours of the Magic Kingdom or Epcot Center. The Biergarten in World Showcase's Germany pavilion and the Teppanyaki Dining Rooms in Japan's Mitsukoshi Restaurant are especially convivial

since several parties are seated together at one large table. River Country, the hotel swimming pools and beaches, and (for those with the inclination) the Giraffe disco at the Royal Plaza Hotel at Walt Disney World Village Hotel Plaza are also good bets for meeting people.

A note for budget watchers: Rates at all WDW resort hotels and those at Walt Disney World Village Hotel Plaza, and at some others in the Orlando area, are the same whether one or two persons occupy a room. Similarly, the Walt Disney World Village villas are priced per unit, regardless of the number of people who sleep there.

Plazas upon entering. From the TTC, the Magic Kingdom is accessible either by ferry or by monorail (though the former is preferable, since the slant of the ramp to the monorails makes holding a wheelchair a bit taxing when there are any waiting lines at all). All WDW monorail stations are accessible to wheelchairs except the one at the Contemporary Resort, which can be reached only by escalator. Special "handicap vans," with motorized platforms that lift wheelchairs inside, are available, too. To request one, day guests should inquire at the Guest Relations Window at the TTC or at Epcot Center Entrance Plaza or in City Hall in the Magic Kingdom or Earth Station at Epcot Center. Resort guests should also contact Guest Services in their hotel. Count on at least 20 minutes between the request and pick-up.

In the Magic Kingdom, wheelchairs are available for rent at the Stroller Shop, on the right-hand side of the souvenir area, just past the turnstiles. In Epcot Center, the rental area is just inside the turnstiles on the left as you enter. A "guidebook for disabled guests" will prove beneficial throughout your visit and may be obtained at wheelchair rental locations, City Hall in the Magic Kingdom, and Earth Station in Epcot Center. Most restrooms in the parks have extra-wide cubicles with wall bars for people in wheelchairs. Furthermore, most attractions are accessible to guests who can be lifted to and from their chairs and many can accommodate guests who must remain in their wheelchairs at all times.

Outside the Magic Kingdom and Epcot Center, all WDW resort hotels are easily explored by wheelchair. The Polynesian Village is the most convenient for vacationers in wheelchairs. The monorail is easy to get to; and there are 3 special first-floor units with grab rails next to the bathtubs and wider automatic entrance doors. In that building, the Oahu, there are even Braille characters on the elevators.

In the Walt Disney World Village villa area, some units are accessible to wheelchairs and some are not; the best bets are the planned-for-the-purpose units in the Fairway Villas. The Fleetwood Trailers at Fort Wilderness would be difficult to manage because of stairway access and narrow interior spaces.

In River Country, life jackets are available for the handicapped. (No other flotation devices are permitted here.)

For blind guests, a tape recorder and cassette that describes the Magic Kingdom and Epcot Center in terms of smells and sounds is available. A small refundable deposit (about $5) is required for cassette use. Seeing eye dogs are permitted in both parks. In Epcot Center, personal translator units that amplify attraction sound tracks for the benefit of the hearing impaired are available at Earth Station. The $5 deposit is refundable upon the return of the unit. Guests who use telecommunications devices for the deaf (TDDs) can call 824-4101 for WDW information.

Tours: The Society for the Advancement of Travel for the Handicapped (26 Court St.; Brooklyn, NY 11242; 212-858-5483) has a number of member travel agents who are knowledgeable about tours for the handicapped and can help arrange individual and group tours. Send a self-addressed, stamped envelope to receive a copy of their listings. Among the organizations that sponsor trips for the handicapped and offer tours to WDW are:

- Flying Wheels Travel; Box 382; 143 W. Bridge St.; Owatonna, MN 55060; 507-451-5005.
- Evergreen Travel Service; 19505 L 44th Ave. W.; Lynnwood, WA 98036; 206-776-1184.
- Powers Travel Agency; 2445 S. Telegraph Rd.; Dearborn, MI 48124; 313-562-1700.

All of these organizations can also arrange trips for individuals.

Books: One of the best books we know for general hints on travel by the handicapped is *Access to the World* by Louise Weiss (available from Facts on File; 460 Park Ave. S.; New York, NY 10016; $14.95).

Traveling by car: Hertz, Avis, and National all have a limited quantity of hand-control cars for rent in the Orlando area; call well in advance to reserve them.

Traveling by plane: Airlines have not always been as helpful in dealing with handicapped travelers as they are now. Occasionally, vacationers can go into the aircraft in their own chair—providing the chair is narrow and the plane's aisles are wide; more often, travelers transfer to a narrower airline chair at the door of the aircraft, while their own chair is sent down to the luggage compartment. Wheelchair passengers are usually pre-boarded and then deplaned after other passengers. If you are not taking your own wheelchair along and have a tight connection to make, be sure to advise the airlines' attendants well in advance. Similarly, if a passenger wishes to utilize an airline's wheelchair at a connecting point or destination, that wheelchair service should be ordered at the time that flight reservations are being made.

Allow plenty of time to make all your arrangements, and don't fail to alert all airline personnel to your special needs.

Policies on motorized wheelchairs vary, depending on the airline and the type of chair; check with carriers in advance. Seeing eye dogs are always allowed aboard aircraft (though some carriers may require them to be muzzled), but arrangements should be made at the time reservations are made so that a bulkhead seat may be requested.

For general information on traveling by air, get copies of "Air Travelers' Fly Rights" (available for $2.75 from the Government Printing Office, Washington, DC; include the stock number 003-006-00106-5) and "Access Travel: Airports" (available for $1.25 from the National Clearing House of Rehabilitation Training Materials; 115 Old USDA Bldg.; Stillwater, OK 74078; include code number 108-X).

Traveling by train: Whether riding with or without reservations, it's wise to phone in advance to arrange for one of the special seats that Amtrak maintains for handicapped travelers. Wheelchairs are available at major Amtrak stations, some 400 in all, including Orlando. New cars have special seats and specially equipped bathrooms and sleeping compartments; older equipment has also been refurbished to accommodate handicapped travelers. Blind and handicapped passengers get a 25 percent discount on normal round-trip economy fares, though companions must pay full fare. Seeing eye and hearing ear dogs may ride with passengers at no extra charge.

Battery-powered, standard-size wheelchairs are permitted in coaches. Fuel-powered and oversize chairs must be stored in the baggage car for the duration of the trip. Always be sure to phone the train stations and reservations center well before your departure date to arrange for any special facilities or services you may need. The free booklet "Access Amtrak" details services for elderly and handicapped travelers. To get a copy, write the Amtrak Distribution Center; Box 7717; Itasca, IL 60143.

Traveling by bus: Both Greyhound and Trailways have implemented plans that allow a handicapped vacationer and a companion (to help with boarding and disembarking) to travel together on a single adult ticket; all that's required is a doctor's written statement of the necessity of such aid. Both bus companies carry nonmotorized folding wheelchairs at no additional charge. Motorized wheelchairs are not accepted by either company.

And remember to plan in advance. Allow plenty of time, and at each step of the way, inform air, bus, train, and hotel personnel of your special needs.

OTHER INFORMATION

BARBERS: The most amusing place to get a haircut is the old-fashioned Harmony Barber Shop (824-6550), tucked away at the end of the flower-filled cul-de-sac just off the west side of Main Street in the Magic Kingdom; the Disney books on hand are terrific, and the "Dapper Dans," the park's own barbershop quartet, can often be heard here. Moustache cups and other nostalgic shaving items are for sale.

Outside the Magic Kingdom, visit the Captain's Chair on the third floor of the Contemporary Resort (824-4311) or the Alii Nui Barber Shop on the first floor of the Great Ceremonial House at the Polynesian Village (824-1400).

BEAUTY SHOPS: Shampoos, sets, coloring, waving, manicuring and wig-setting are available at the Pretty Wahine Beauty Shop in the Polynesian Village (824-1396) and the American Beauty Shoppe on the third floor of the Contemporary Resort (824-3413); the manicurist at the Contemporary Resort's shop has held the hands of many a Walt Disney World executive, and can provide some fascinating insights into the workings of the park.

CAR CARE: Auto and travel club members probably will want to call their local club-sponsored towing service in the event of problems; anyone else can phone the Disney Car Care Center (824-4813), located on Floridian Way near the Magic Kingdom Main Entrance Toll Plaza. Though routine maintenance work is probably best done by mechanics who know your car well—before leaving home—the Disney Car Care Center is a good place for gas and repairs in a pinch. Disney personnel here will chauffeur guests to their day's WDW destination, and arrange for later pickup when requested.

It's also reassuring to know that WDW breakdowns don't mean disaster. All WDW roads are patrolled constantly by security cars that can radio for help if needed, and all parking lots are patrolled by two trucks with jumper cables.

CHURCH SERVICES: Vacations are a good time to broaden the family's religious experience. A variety of services are held around Walt Disney World on weekends.

Protestant: 9 A.M. on Sunday at Luau Cove at the Polynesian Village; and at the Royal Plaza in Walt Disney World Village Hotel Plaza.

Catholic: 8 and 10:15 A.M. on Sunday at Luau Cove at the Polynesian Village; 6 P.M. on Saturday and 8 A.M. on Sunday at the Royal Plaza in Walt Disney World Village Hotel Plaza.

In Orlando, there are services at St. James Cathedral (215 N. Orange Ave.) at 4 P.M. on Saturday, and, on Sunday, at 7:30, 9, 10:30 A.M. and noon, and a youth mass is held at 6 P.M. Phone 422-2005 for details.

In Kissimmee, there are services at the Holy Redeemer Catholic Church (1603 N. Thacker Ave.) on Saturday at 6 P.M. and on Sunday at 7:30, 9, 10:30 A.M., and noon. Daily masses are said at 7:30 and 9 A.M. Phone 846-3700 for details.

Jewish: There are services at 8:15 P.M. on Friday and at 9 A.M. on Saturday at the Congregation Ohev Shalom (5015 Goddard Ave.) in Orlando. Phone 298-4650 for details.

Kosher dinners are available at any time at the Contemporary Resort Hotel, the Polynesian Village, the Golf Resort, Fort Wilderness, and Walt Disney World Shopping Village- area restaurants. Given two weeks' notice (or sometimes less), it's possible to order veal, roast chicken, Salisbury steak, turkey, or roasted or broiled beef to eat at any location in the World, except the Magic Kingdom. Cost is around $10.

Note also that most airlines also offer special meals conforming to dietary codes. Order them when making reservations.

MAIL: Postcards are for sale at many spots in the resorts and around the Magic Kingdom, among them at the Card Shop on the west side of Main Street. Postage stamps can be purchased at the front desk at the three WDW hotels, at the trading posts at Fort Wilderness, at City Hall on Main Street, and at Earth Station at Epcot Center. The old-fashioned olive-drab mailboxes that punctuate Main Street are no longer official U.S. post boxes, but letters can be mailed there for later pickup by Disney employees and subsequent transportaion to the Lake Buena Vista post office. Postmarks read "Lake Buena Vista," *not* "Walt Disney World." All window services are available at the Lake Buena Vista post office, including postal money order and stamp sale, registry, and certification. The post office is located at the Reception Center at WDW Village.

Read'n & Rite'n in Walt Disney World Shopping Village sells attractive stationery and note pads. Postage stamps also are available here as well as at Village Gifts and Sundries.

Mail may be addressed to guests c/o their hotel at Walt Disney World; Box 40; Lake Buena Vista, FL 32830.

Don't forget to arrange for mail at home to be held by the post office.

LOST AND FOUND: The extensive indexing system maintained by Walt Disney World's Lost and Found department is impressive, especially when a prize possession turns up missing, whether it's false teeth or a camera. (Both have been lost in the past; the dentures were never claimed.) To see just how it works, the first thing to do is to report the loss on the proper forms at City Hall, at the Guest Relations window on the east end of the Transportation and Ticket Center, at Epcot Center Entrance Plaza, or the Guest Services desks in the first floor lobby at the Contemporary Resort or the main lobbies at the Polynesian Village and the Golf Resort; at Fort Wilderness, phone ext. 7-2726 from a comfort station telephone; from outside the campground, phone 824-2726.

Items lost in the Magic Kingdom can be claimed on the day of the loss at City Hall, and thereafter at the main Lost and Found station at the Transportation and Ticket Center. Articles found at Epcot Center remain at the Epcot Center Lost and Found for several days before being delivered to the main Lost and Found. Items lost in the hotels and at Walt Disney World Shopping Village are kept in those locations for three months before being sent to the Transportation and Ticket Center station. Keep checking; the phone number is 824-4245.

Articles not claimed by the owner may be claimed by the finder—an added incentive for visitors to turn over valuable items to Lost and Found.

POCKET PAGERS: Three types of devices are available to WDW guests to signal a telephone call or message. They are available at the three WDW hotels, Fort Wilderness Outpost, the Lake Buena Vista reception center, and the Hotel Royal Plaza.

GIFT CERTIFICATES: Available at the Guest Services Center at WDW Village, guest services desks at the three WDW hotels, and at Guest Relations windows in the parks.

DRINKING LAWS: In Florida, drinking is legal at 19. There are many bars and lounges all over the World; minors are permitted to accompany their parents, but are prohibited from sitting or standing at the bar. There's no drinking in the Magic Kingdom (where even the piña coladas are nonalcoholic), but alcoholic beverages are available at restaurants in Epcot Center and WDW Village.

By the bottle: Liquor is sold in full-size and mini bottles at Village Spirits at Walt Disney World Shopping Village, the trading posts in Fort Wilderness, at Trader Jack's on the second floor of the Great Ceremonial House at the Polynesian Village, at Golf Gifts and Sundries in the lobby at the Golf Resort, and at Spirit World on the Grand Canyon Concourse in the Contemporary Resort. Liquor also may be purchased from Room Service at the resorts.

LOCKERS: There are coin-operated lockers underneath the Main Street Railroad Station in the Magic Kingdom and at two locations at the Transportation and Ticket Center—next to Lost and Found on the west end and beside the bus parking lot on the east side. Lockers are also available at Epcot Center at the Bus Information Center in the bus parking lot, just outside the main Entrance Plaza, and in an area to the right of Earth Station as you face World Showcase Lagoon. Cost is 25¢ per day for the regular size, 50¢ for the larger ones. Items too big to fit into the latter can be checked at the Guest Relations windows at the TTC, at City Hall inside the Magic Kingdom, or in the package pick-up area or in the storage area near the bus parking lot at Epcot Center.

PLANT-SITTING: Plants do not fare well in the heat of a closed-up car for a day. Those who have purchased greenery at Walt Disney World Shopping Village, or brought a favorite fern from home, will be grateful to know that their horticultural wonders can be accommodated by the kennels at Fort Wilderness or at the TTC. There's no charge.

MEDICAL MATTERS: For travelers with chronic health problems, it's a good idea to carry copies of all prescriptions and to get names of local doctors from hometown physicians. However, Walt Disney World is equipped to deal with many types of medical emergencies. In the Magic Kingdom, next to the Crystal Palace, there's a First Aid Center staffed by a registered nurse; there are others at Epcot Center, one in Future World and one in World Showcase (during holidays and summer months, at the TTC and River Country as well). Serious emergencies can be reported to Orange Vista Hospital on the edge of the property.

The most common malady? Not sensitive stomachs upset by rides, but simple *sunburn*. So be forewarned. Wear a hat, and slather on sufficient sunblock or sunscreen, especially during the spring and summer.

For diabetics: Walt Disney World resorts provide refrigeration services for insulin; the villas and the Fleetwood Trailers at Fort Wilderness have their own refrigerators.

Prescriptions: These cannot be filled on the property. The closest pharmacies are located in Kissimmee on Route 192, about 10 miles from the WDW Auto Plaza.

MONEY: Cash, traveler's checks, personal checks, the American Express Card (the official credit card of WDW), and MasterCard are accepted as payment for all admission media. Checks must bear the guest's name and address, be drawn on a U.S. bank, and be accompanied by the proper identification—a valid driver's license and a current major credit card such as American Express, Visa, MasterCard, Diners Club, or Carte Blanche. Fast food restaurants in the Magic Kingdom and Epcot Center operate on a cash-only basis.

For charges at sit-down restaurants and shops inside the theme park, however, and for all other charges throughout Walt Disney World, American Express and MasterCard credit cards are accepted. WDW resort guests may use the WDW resort IDs that each member of a party receives upon check-in to cover purchases in shops, lounge and restaurant charges, and recreational fees incurred inside WDW (but outside the Magic Kingdom). At Epcot Center, guests can use IDs to charge meals at table-service restaurants. These cards are not valid for charges made past check-out time on the last day of the guest's stay.

Wiring money: Friends and relatives at home can send money to WDW guests through Western Union offices at WDW in the Contemporary Resort (824-3456), in Kissimmee (847-4838), and in Orlando (841-4733).

The Sun Bank: This institution (which has an old-fashioned branch on Main Street inside the Magic Kingdom, a branch in Epcot Center to the left of the turnstiles as you enter, and another in Walt Disney World Shopping Village) can:

• Give cash advances on MasterCard and Visa credit cards, with a $50 minimum in amounts as large as a guest's credit limit permits.

• Cash and sell traveler's checks and provide refunds for lost American Express and Bank of America traveler's checks.

• Cash personal checks of up to $1,000 for American Express cardholders upon presentation of their cards (part payable in cash and the rest in American Express traveler's checks).

• Cash personal checks for up to $25 upon presentation of a driver's license and a major credit card for other guests.

• Help with wire transfers of money from a guest's own bank to the Sun Bank.

• Exchange most foreign currency for dollars.

The Sun Bank branches in the Magic

Kingdom and Epcot Center are open from 9 A.M. to 4 P.M. daily; phone 824-5767 for further information. The Sun Bank in Walt Disney World Village at Lake Buena Vista is open from 9 A.M. to 4 P.M. on weekdays (until 6 P.M. on Thursday); drive-in teller windows are open from 8 A.M. to 6 P.M. on weekdays. Phone 828-6100.

Traveler's checks: Even the most careful of vacationers occasionally loses a wallet, and traveler's checks can take the sting out of that loss. Which type a traveler should buy is not so much a function of which is most easily refunded (because in the U.S., and at Walt Disney World in particular, all the major traveler's check offerers can come through with emergency funds in a pinch), as of which costs less. It's a good idea, therefore, to look for special promotions by banks at home in the months preceding a vacation, and check to see which of the six major brands—American Express, MasterCard, Visa, Thomas Cook, Citicorp, and Bank of America—are available free.

While at WDW, American Express checks can be purchased at the Sun Bank and at the American Express cardmembers' check dispenser located there as well. The machine automatically vends traveler's checks when you feed it an American Express card and punch in an identification number that has been obtained from the company in advance.

Don't fail to sign checks in the proper place as soon as they are purchased. And stash the receipt bearing the check numbers in a separate place from the checks themselves, along with one piece of identification such as a duplicate driver's license or spare credit card. These will speed the refund process should your checks get lost.

Foreign currency exchange: This can be done at the Guest Relations windows (to the right as you face the ticket windows at the Transportation and Ticket Center and to the right of the turnstiles as you enter Epcot Center), or at City Hall, or Earth Station, or, from 9 A.M. to 4 P.M. daily, at the Sun Bank in Town Square inside the Magic Kingdom or at the Epcot Center branch. Currency can be exchanged at all WDW resort hotels at other times. The Sun Bank in Walt Disney World Shopping Village also exchanges foreign currency.

SHOPPING FOR NECESSITIES: Almost all everyday needs can be satisfied right on the property. Plaza Gifts and Sundries on the Grand Canyon Concourse in the Contemporary Resort, Village Gifts & Sundries on the second floor of the Polynesian Village, Golf Gifts and Sundries in the lobby of the Golf Resort, and the Meadow and Settlement trading posts at Fort Wilderness all stock a limited number of brands of a wide variety of toiletries; a broader selection is available at the Walt Disney World Village shopping area at Gifts and Sundries. In addition, a number of over-the-counter health aids, plus many other useful items, can be purchased in the Books and Records section of the Emporium on Main Street in the Magic Kingdom; they're kept behind the counter, so it's necessary to ask for the supplies you want. Aspirin and suntan lotion are also available at Mickey's Mart in Tomorrowland.

In Epcot Center, sundries are available in at least one shop in each of the World Showcase pavilions and at all the retail outlets in Future World (except the Kodak camera sales kiosk at Journey Into Imagination). Here, too, you'll have to request what you need, since items are not on display.

Reading matter: Newspapers, magazines, bestsellers, and paperbacks are available in a limited selection at Spirit World on the Grand Canyon Concourse of the Contemporary Resort, at News from Civilization on the first floor at the Polynesian Village, at Golf Gifts and Sundries in the lobby at the Golf Resort, and at Village Gifts and Sundries at the Shopping Village. Most carry the daily papers from Orlando and Miami, and the *Wall Street Journal*, and, on Sundays, the *New York Times* and the *Chicago Tribune*.

A larger stock of paperbacks and hardcover books is available at Read'n & Rite'n in Walt Disney World Village. The Emporium on Main Street in the Magic Kingdom has a good selection of children's books.

Epcot Center offers an interesting selection as well. Books related to the themes of Future World pavilions are available in the Centorium. In World Showcase, Plume et Palette (in the France pavilion) stocks books on food and the U.K.'s Toy Soldier stocks children's books.

Cigarettes: Smoking items are widely available all over WDW, and Main Street provides a special tobacco store, the Tobacconist, which stocks a variety of smoker's aids. It's worth a stop if only to pick up a book of matches; these have particularly handsome covers.

Cigarettes also can be purchased inside the Magic Kingdom at Tropic Toppers in Adventureland, at the Trading Post in Frontierland, at the Royal Candy Shoppe in Fantasyland, at Heritage House in Liberty Square, and at Mickey's Mart in Tomorrowland. In addition, there are cigarette vending machines in the Columbia Harbour House in Liberty Square; at King Stefan's in Cinderella Castle and the Pinocchio Village Haus in Fantasyland; in Tomorrowland Terrace; and in the Mile Long Bar in Frontierland.

In Epcot Center, cigarettes are available in Future World retail locations and in at least one shop in each World Showcase pavilion. In addition, His Lordship in the U.K. pavilion stocks a selection of British tobaccos, the Les Halles area in the France pavilion offers French cigarettes, and Der Bücherwurm in the Germany pavilion sells their German counterparts.

In the hotels, you can buy cigarettes at Spirit World on the Grand Canyon Concourse in the Contemporary Resort, at News From Civilization on the first floor of the Great Ceremonial House at the Polynesian Village, and at Golf Gifts and Sundries in the lobby of the Golf Resort. In addition, there are vending machines in all the hotels. At Fort Wilderness, they are for sale in the Meadow and Settlement trading posts. At WDW Village, they are sold at Village Gifts and Sundries and the Gourmet Pantry.

PETS: No pets are allowed in the Magic Kingdom, Epcot Center, or at the WDW resorts. Travelers who bring a pet along can lodge it in one of three attractive air-conditioned kennels—the Walt Disney World Kennel Club, adjoining the Transportation and Ticket Center; the Epcot Center Kennel Club to the left of the Epcot Center Entrance Plaza; and the Fort Wilderness Kennel and Livery, at the campground entrance, next to a huge field where pet owners often take their animals out for a run. In busy season, try to arrive before the 9 to 10 A.M. morning rush hour, and note that the Kennel Clubs close an hour after the Magic Kingdom and Epcot Center.

Bears, cougars, and ocelots have all been accommodated by the WDW kennels, and exotic pets may be accepted—if a bit reluctantly. However, owners themselves must put the more unusual animals into the kennel's cages; and snakes, rabbits, birds, turtles, hamsters, and other animals unsuited (because of size) to cat- and dog-sized cages must be accompanied by their own escape-proof accommodations.

Advance reservations are not accepted. WDW resort guests and guests at WDW Village Hotel Plaza may board their pets overnight in either the TTC or Fort Wilderness kennels. Cost is about $4.50 for overnight stays, including food; $3.50 for a day stay, without food. Only pets of WDW resort guests may be boarded overnight.

Never leave pets in a car.

Also, bring along your pet's certificate of vaccination, since Florida law requires proof of immunization for animals involved in biting accidents.

Outside Walt Disney World: A number of hotels in the Orlando and Kissimmee area permit pets. For specific information, phone the Greater Orlando Chamber of Commerce, 425-1234.

TIPPING: Walt Disney World is not one of those places where bellmen stick out their hands even before they put down your luggage. Instead, they seem genuinely glad to help out. Oddly enough, however, this pleasant attitude seems to discourage tipping at the same time it arouses the sentiments that make most travelers want to reach for their wallets.

Lack of ostentatious need does not mean that tips are any less valued at WDW than they would be at any other good resort hotel—the standard 50 to 75 cents per bag is appropriate for lugging luggage. Gratuities of 15 to 18 percent are also customary at full-service restaurants all over WDW. At the posh Empress Room, a service charge of 20 percent of the food and drink bill is automatically added to the check.

Gratuities are not required in fast food restaurants or at the attractions, but in the beauty shops, it's usual to leave a tip of about 15 percent of the total bill, and at the spa, to acknowledge the services of the masseur with a tip of $3 to $5.

Cabdrivers in the Orlando area expect a 15 percent tip. Baggage handlers at bus and train stations and at the airport expect at least 50 cents per bag.

TELEPHONE: The folks at home can reach resort guests at the following numbers: 824-1000 for the Contemporary Resort; 824-2200 at the Golf Resort; 824-2000 at the Polynesian Village; 824-6993 at Lake Buena Vista–area villas; and 824-2900 at Fort Wilderness.

Public telephones in the Orlando area cost 25 cents. Those in Walt Disney World still cost only a dime.

TIME AND WEATHER PHONE: In the Orlando area, the number is 422-1611.

TRANSPORTATION AND ACCOMMODATIONS

41 Getting Oriented
42 Getting Around
46 WDW Resorts
60 Other Accommodations

Misconceptions about Walt Disney World (like the impression that it's located in the middle of downtown Orlando), and about the surrounding region (like the idea that the park is located on one or another of Florida's coasts), seem to abound. The fact is that Walt Disney World is situated virtually in the center of Florida, and, despite perhaps the most prevalent of nonresident misconceptions, nowhere near Miami or Miami Beach.

But the popularity of Walt Disney World has made the region around Orlando one of the world's major tourist centers, and everything from new airline facilities to a very efficient network of roads and state highways now brings visitors to the area literally by the tens of thousands.

There's no doubt, however, that confusion about getting around the Walt Disney World region is prevalent and may be exceeded only by the dilemma concerning which sort of specific accommodation is most appropriate for a given family's needs. Just the accommodations facilities that are operated by Walt Disney World itself range from futuristic high-rise towers to treehouses buried deep in piney woods. In between are resorts echoing images of the South Pacific and efficient trailer-type facilities in a nearly perfectly maintained campground. And that doesn't include a sports resort and villas that provide extraordinary luxury. What follows should help any traveler sort out his preferences.

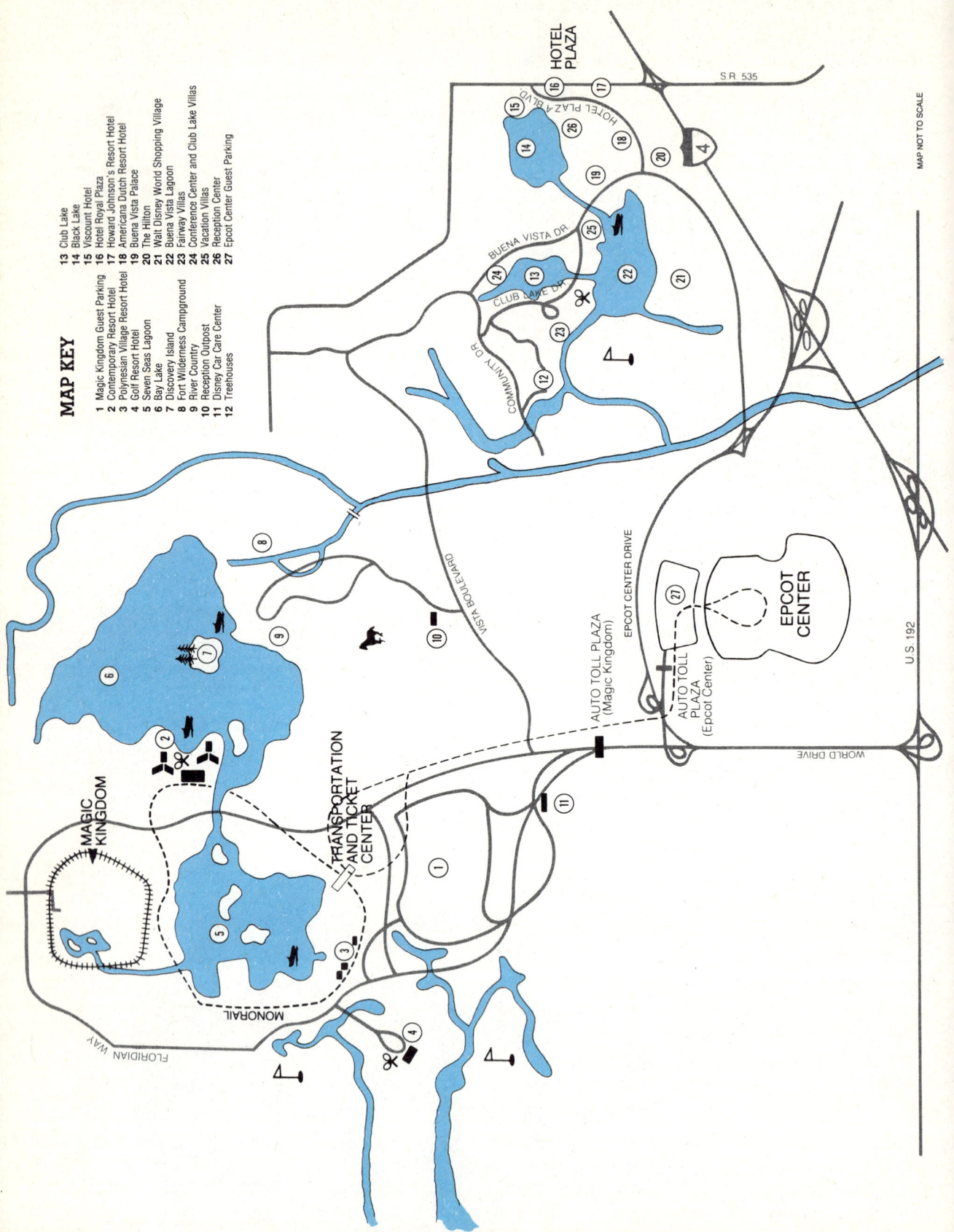

GETTING ORIENTED

Orlando, the Central Florida city of over 120,000 residents, is the municipality with which Walt Disney World is most closely associated. It is not, however, the closest urban community to WDW. That honor belongs to Kissimmee, a far smaller community of 17,000 people located just southeast of the World. Many newish motels are located here, though there are far more in Orlando proper, to the north.

Most of the area's better restaurants are found in Orlando, or in adjacent communities like Winter Park (on its northeastern extremity), Maitland (west of Winter Park), and Altamonte Springs (west of Maitland). Haines City, home of Circus World, is about 8 miles south of WDW's southern border, and Winter Haven, home of Cypress Gardens (described in the *Orlando* chapter), is about 12 miles southwest.

ORLANDO-AREA HIGHWAYS: The most important Orlando traffic artery is I-4, which runs diagonally through the area from southwest to northeast, cutting through the southern half of Walt Disney World, then angles on toward Orlando and Winter Park, ending near Daytona Beach at I-95, which runs north and south along the coast. All the city's other important highways intersect I-4. From south to north, these include U.S.-192, which takes an east-west course that crosses the WDW entrance road and leads into downtown Kissimmee on the east; S.R.-528 (aka the Bee Line Expressway), which shoots eastward from I-4; S.R.-435, also known as Kirkman Road, which runs north and south and intersects International Drive, where many motels catering to WDW visitors are located; U.S.-17-92-441 (aka Orange Blossom Trail), which runs due north and south, paralleling Kirkman Road on the east; and U.S.-50 (aka Colonial Drive), which runs due east and west.

GETTING AROUND INSIDE WALT DISNEY WORLD: The 43-square-mile tract that is Walt Disney World is roughly rectangular. I-4 runs through its southern half from southwest to northeast; there are now three highway exits within WDW. The Magic Kingdom, the Polynesian Village, Contemporary Resort and Golf Resort hotels, and Fort Wilderness are all located in the property's northern third. They are located off the Main Entrance Road, a route that is accessible via U.S.-192, which extends due east and west from the more southerly of WDW's trio of I-4 exits. The U.S.-192 exit is four miles from the Toll Plaza, the immediate gateway to the parking lots. The Main Entrance Road is about a mile from the I-4 exit, so that the parking lots are about five miles from the Interstate. Walt Disney World Village also has its own exit off I-4 (marked "Lake Buena Vista"), four miles from the one for the Main Entrance. The Walt Disney World Shopping Village parking lots are located about a mile from I-4. The newest exit off I-4 (between the two described above) leads to Epcot Center. Note that many off-property hotels offer free shuttle-bus service to WDW.

There are also a number of roads *inside* the World. In some cases, it is possible to drive from place to place inside the World. Bus transportation is also provided from most points to most other points, and is available to most guests. At the northernmost end of the World, an elevated monorail train operates along a circular route, making stops at the Polynesian Village and Contemporary Resort hotels and at the Magic Kingdom and the TTC; an extension of the monorail system also goes to Epcot Center. Motor launches and cruisers from those first three points call at Fort Wilderness and Discovery Island.

> ### GETTING AROUND WDW
>
> The WDW transportation system moves an amazing number of guests. The system is somewhat complicated, however, and can be confusing to a first-time visitor, so the following charts and lists are designed to help you get to your destination most directly. First, there's a chart on pages 42 and 43 that specifically routes you from one part of the World to another. There's also a list that describes the types of identification and admission media that are required to gain access to the different transportation systems. Finally, there is a table (on page 44) that shows the routes, destinations, operating hours, and frequency of the various transportation modes. For ease of identification, all bus and watercraft routes are identified by various colored pennants/flags and are listed by color on the following pages.

HOW TO GET WHERE YOU'RE GOING

From: \ To:	Contemporary Resort Hotel	Polynesian Village Resort Hotel	Golf Resort Hotel	Fort Wilderness Campground	WDW Village Villas
Magic Kingdom	Monorail Alternative: Ferry to TTC, then gold-flagged bus	Monorail Alternative: Ferry to TTC, then green-flagged bus	Monorail to Polynesian Village, then green-flagged bus Alternative: Ferry to TTC, then green-flagged bus	Green-flagged watercraft Alternative: Ferry or monorail to TTC, then blue-flagged bus	Monorail or ferry to TTC, then green-and-gold-flagged bus with "MK"
Contemporary Resort Hotel		Monorail Alternative: Gold-flagged bus to TTC, then green-flagged bus	Monorail to Polynesian Village, then green-flagged bus Alternative: Gold-flagged bus to TTC, then green-flagged bus	Blue-flagged watercraft Alternative: Monorail or gold-flagged bus to TTC, then blue-flagged bus	Monorail or gold-flagged bus to TTC, then green-and-gold-flagged bus with "MK"
Polynesian Village Resort Hotel	Monorail Alternative: Green-flagged bus to TTC, then gold-flagged bus		Green-flagged bus	Gold-flagged watercraft Alternative: Monorail or green-flagged bus to TTC, then blue-flagged bus	Monorail or green-flagged bus to TTC, then green-and-gold-flagged bus with "MK"
Golf Resort Hotel	Green-flagged bus to Polynesian Village, then monorail Alternative: Green-flagged bus to TTC, then gold-flagged bus	Green-flagged bus		Green-flagged bus to TTC, then blue-flagged bus Alternative: Green-flagged bus to Polynesian Village, then gold-flagged watercraft	Green-flagged bus to TTC, then green-and-gold-flagged bus with "MK"
Fort Wilderness Campground	Blue-flagged watercraft Alternative: Blue-flagged bus to TTC, then gold-flagged bus or monorail	Gold-flagged watercraft Alternative: Blue-flagged bus to TTC, then green-flagged bus or monorail	Blue-flagged bus to TTC, then green-flagged bus Alternative: Gold-flagged watercraft to Polynesian Village, then green-flagged bus		Blue-flagged bus to TTC, then green-and-gold-flagged bus with "MK"
Walt Disney World Shopping Village	Red-flagged bus to TTC, then gold-flagged bus or monorail	Red-flagged bus to TTC, then green-flagged bus or monorail	Red-flagged bus to TTC, then green-flagged bus	Red-flagged bus to TTC, then blue-flagged bus	Green-and-gold-flagged bus with "V"
Walt Disney World Village Hotel Plaza	Red-and-white-flagged bus to TTC, then gold-flagged bus or monorail	Red-and-white-flagged bus to TTC, then green-flagged bus or monorail	Red-and-white-flagged bus to TTC, then green-flagged bus	Red-and-white-flagged bus to TTC, then blue-flagged bus	Blue-and-white-flagged bus to Shopping Village, then green-and-gold-flagged bus with "V"
Transportation and Ticket Center (TTC)	Monorail Alternative: Gold-flagged bus	Monorail Alternative: Green-flagged bus	Green-flagged bus	Blue-flagged bus	Green-and-gold-flagged bus with "MK"
WDW Village Villas	Green-and-gold-flagged bus with "MK" to TTC, then monorail or gold-flagged bus	Green-and-gold-flagged bus with "MK" to TTC, then monorail or green-flagged bus	Green-and-gold-flagged bus with "MK" to TTC, then green-flagged bus	Green-and-gold-flagged bus with "MK" to TTC, then blue-flagged bus	
Epcot Center	Monorail or red-flagged bus to TTC, then monorail or gold-flagged bus	Monorail or red-flagged bus to TTC, then monorail or green-flagged bus	Monorail or red-flagged bus to TTC, then green-flagged bus	Monorail or red-flagged bus to TTC, then blue-flagged bus	Green-and-gold-flagged bus with "EC"

INSIDE WALT DISNEY WORLD

Walt Disney World Shopping Village	Walt Disney World Village Hotel Plaza	Magic Kingdom	Transportation and Ticket Center	Epcot Center
Monorail or ferry to TTC, then red-flagged bus	Monorail or ferry to TTC, then red-and-white-flagged bus		Monorail or ferry	Monorail or ferry to TTC, then red-flagged bus or monorail
Monorail or gold-flagged bus to TTC, then red-flagged bus	Monorail or gold-flagged bus to TTC, then red-and-white-flagged bus	Monorail Alternative: Gold-flagged bus to TTC, then ferry	Monorail Alternative: Gold-flagged bus	Monorail or gold-flagged bus to TTC, then red-flagged bus or monorail
Monorail or green-flagged bus to TTC, then red-flagged bus	Monorail or green-flagged bus to TTC, then red-and-white-flagged bus	Monorail Alternative: Green-flagged bus to TTC, then ferry	Monorail Alternative: Green-flagged bus	Monorail or green-flagged bus to TTC, then red-flagged bus or monorail
Green-flagged bus to TTC, then red-flagged bus	Green-flagged bus to TTC, then red-and-white-flagged bus	Green-flagged bus to Polynesian Village, then monorail Alternative: Green-flagged bus to TTC, then ferry	Green-flagged bus	Green-flagged bus to TTC, then red-flagged bus or monorail
Blue-flagged bus to TTC, then red-flagged bus	Blue-flagged bus to TTC, then red-and-white-flagged bus	Green-flagged watercraft Alternative: Blue-flagged bus to TTC, then ferry or monorail	Blue-flagged bus	Blue-flagged bus to TTC, then red-flagged bus or monorail
	Blue-and-white-flagged bus	Red-flagged bus to TTC, then monorail or ferry	Red-flagged bus	Red-flagged bus
Blue-and-white-flagged bus		Red-and-white-flagged bus to TTC, then monorail or ferry	Red-and-white-flagged bus	Silver-and-red-flagged bus
Red-flagged bus	Red-and-white-flagged bus	Monorail or ferry		Red-flagged bus or monorail
Green-and-gold-flagged bus with "V"	Green-and-gold-flagged bus with "V" to Shopping Village, then blue-and-white-flagged bus	Green-and-gold-flagged bus with "MK" to TTC, then monorail or ferry	Green-and-gold-flagged bus with "MK"	Green-and-gold-flagged bus with "EC"
Red-flagged bus	Silver-and-red-flagged bus	Monorail or red-flagged bus to TTC, then ferry or monorail	Monorail or red-flagged bus	

TRANSPORTATION ID REQUIREMENTS

Within WDW there are several different types of identification and/or admission media that are required for use of the various forms of transportation. The following list explains what sort of card, ticket, or World Passport permits use of each:

- WDW-owned resort identification card allows a guest unlimited use of any part of the WDW transportation system (including buses, monorails, and watercraft).
- WDW Village Hotel Plaza hotel identification card allows unlimited use of the bus transportation system (primarily red-and-white-flagged buses, silver-and-red-flagged buses, and blue-and-white-flagged buses, as well as connecting buses at the TTC).
- Valid 1-day Magic Kingdom ticket permits a guest to use the ferries and monorails running between the TTC and the Magic Kingdom entrance (Note: Valid 1-day Epcot Center ticket does not allow guests to use the WDW transportation system).
- Three-, Four-, and Five-Day World Passports and One-Year Passports allow guests unlimited use of the WDW transportation system.
- River Country, Discovery Island, and Pioneer Hall tickets allow guests the use of blue-flagged buses from the TTC, blue-flagged watercraft from the Contemporary Resort, green-flagged watercraft from the Magic Kingdom, and gold-flagged watercraft from the Polynesian Village on the way to and from River Country, Discovery Island, and Pioneer Hall. Guests with these tickets also may take buses from the Polynesian Village and Contemporary Resort hotels to the TTC and then transfer to blue-flagged buses. For further information, call 824-4457.

A WDW Transportation Ticket (around $2) entitles the bearer to unlimited use of all WDW transportation systems for one day.

WDW TRANSPORTATION ROUTES

Route	Destinations	Hours of Operation	Frequency
Blue-flagged bus	Fort Wilderness—TTC	7 A.M. to 2 A.M.	every 15 minutes
Green-flagged bus	Polynesian Village—Golf Resort—TTC	7 A.M. to 2 A.M.	every 15 minutes
Gold-flagged bus	Contemporary Resort—TTC	7 A.M. to 2 A.M.	every 15 minutes
Green-and-gold-flagged bus/MK	TTC—WDW Village resort villas	8 A.M. to 2 A.M.	every 20 minutes
Green-and-gold-flagged bus/EC	Epcot Center—WDW Village resort villas	8 A.M. to 2 A.M.	every 20 minutes
Green-and-gold-flagged bus/V	WDW Shopping Village—WDW Village resort villas	8 A.M. to 2 A.M.	every 20 minutes
Red-flagged bus	WDW Shopping Village—TTC	8 A.M. to 2 A.M.	every 20 minutes
Red-and-white-flagged bus*	WDW Village Hotel Plaza—TTC	8 A.M. to 2 A.M.	every 20 minutes
Blue-and-white-flagged bus*	WDW Shopping Village—WDW Village Hotel Plaza	8 A.M. to 11 P.M.	every 20 minutes
Silver-and-red-flagged bus*	Epcot Center—WDW Village Hotel Plaza	8 A.M. to 2 A.M.	every 20 minutes
Blue-flagged watercraft	Contemporary Resort—Discovery Island—Fort Wilderness	9 A.M. to midnight	every 20 minutes
Green-flagged watercraft	Magic Kingdom—Fort Wilderness (includes a stop at Discovery Island when it's open)	One half hour prior to Magic Kingdom opening to park closing	every 20 minutes
Gold-flagged watercraft	Polynesian Village—Fort Wilderness—Discovery Island	Hours depend on Discovery Island and River Country hours	every 20 minutes
Magic Kingdom ferry	TTC—Magic Kingdom entrance	One half hour prior to Magic Kingdom opening to one hour after park closing	every 10 minutes
Magic Kingdom express monorail	TTC—Magic Kingdom entrance	One half hour prior to Magic Kingdom opening to one hour after closing	every 10 minutes
Magic Kingdom local monorail	Contemporary Resort—TTC—Polynesian Village—Magic Kingdom entrance	From the hotels, beginning at 7:30 A.M. and until one hour after park closing or 11 P.M. if park closes early	every 10 minutes
Epcot Center monorail	TTC—Epcot Center monorail station	One hour prior to Epcot Center opening to one hour after park closing	every 10 minutes

*At press time, plans were being made to replace the buses on these routes with red-and-white-flagged buses with "MK," "EC," or "V" designations, depending upon destination.

ACCOMMODATIONS

Orlando and environs have literally thousands of hotel and motel rooms. Few of these, however, whether inside or outside the World, are of a design much beyond the standard Anywhere, USA motel/modern decor, usually with two standard double beds, shag carpeting, simulated wood paneling, color television, and private bathroom.

The biggest differences among groups of accommodations seem to be the power of the shower, the size and thickness of the towels, the dimensions of the room and the adjacent bathroom, the quality of the furnishings, the recreational facilities, the landscaping of the surrounding grounds, and the hotel's location.

Yet in practice, no two are really exactly alike. The differences often are subtle enough, however, that the overall impression is one of unending sameness.

Basically, Walt Disney World–area accommodations fall into two main categories: those owned by WDW and those not owned by the company.

All of the former are located inside the World. Rates are higher than at most other motels in the area, but the convenience is so much greater, the quality of the facilities so far superior, and the additional benefits available to an on-property guest so extensive—closed circuit TV announcing WDW events, a free copy of Walt Disney World News, and the best possible access to Guest Services personnel—that the extra expense is not at all unreasonable. Resort guests, for instance, can reserve tee-off times on the golf courses and places at most of the dinner shows as soon as room reservations are confirmed. They have unlimited access to transportation within the World. The cost of admission media, as well as River Country and Discovery Island tickets, and green fees and tennis court usage charges, are lower for guests at resorts on WDW property. (The benefits for guests are so extensive that you should be wary of travel agents who encourage you to stay elsewhere for reasons other than a major difference in price. Since the Disney properties do not pay direct travel agent commissions—as the establishments at the Walt Disney World Village Hotel Plaza and those outside Walt Disney World do—it could be that your agent's advice is influenced by financial considerations.)

Locations of the non-Disney properties are quite scattered. Some are located within the WDW boundaries at Walt Disney World Village Hotel Plaza. The rest are located completely off the property, primarily in Kissimmee, along U.S.-192 (which runs east and west) intersecting the WDW entrance road, and along International Drive (off S.R.-435 at the Orlando city limits). The U.S.-192 establishments are closer to the WDW main entrance—usually only a few miles away, depending on the individual hostelry. But International Drive, some ten miles from the WDW main gates, is a more pleasant place to stay, thanks to its array of sidewalk-connected lodging places, restaurants, and other minor attractions. Its proximity to still more of the same in Orlando, just a few miles farther north, constitutes an additional benefit.

In choosing a place to stay, you first must decide how much money you want to spend. If your budget permits, try to get reservations at a Disney property. If not, select accommodations outside the World based on what you can afford and on the guidelines given here.

Remember, when examining rate sheets for the best buy for your family, to examine carefully the cutoff age at which children accompanying you (and staying in the same room) will be billed as extra adults. Those with large families should note that villa-type accommodations, which may seem more expensive at first glance, can actually prove less costly in the long run by eliminating the necessity of hiring an additional hotel room—in addition to providing cooking facilities that can provide big savings on meals.

WDW—OWNED RESORT PROPERTIES

If what you can afford to spend on accommodations approaches the cost of WDW properties, you'll do well to spend the extra money, and to plan far enough ahead to be sure to get one of the rooms here—and to keep trying in hopes of getting a cancellation if you don't secure a reservation the first time around.

In general, rooms at the three hotels—the Contemporary Resort, the Polynesian Village, and the Golf Resort—are quite large and can accommodate up to five without difficulty since they were designed expressly with a fair-size family in mind. Most rooms have patios or balconies. And considering the incredibly high occupancy rate here, it's astonishing that things look so fresh. Even the rooms without views have views, if only across the gardens at masses of lovely flowers.

The villa accommodations at Walt Disney World Village, which can accommodate larger groups, are also good for families, especially those who want to cook some of their own meals "at home." Like the hotel accommodations, the villas aren't pretentiously luxurious, but the basics are all there. In fact, some of the utensils and fixtures found in a villa kitchen may be better than those you're using at home. In addition, there are beds that don't sag, big thick towels (and plenty of them), and wisely laid-out bathrooms.

Each resort and villa complex has its own character, and one may hold more appeal for you than another. The Contemporary Resort and the Polynesian Village are right on the monorail and are the most centrally located and most bustling; youngsters love them because there are always other kids around to meet. The Golf Resort, off the monorail and just a bit off the main WDW track, offers a quieter atmosphere and only a slightly less convenient location. The villa accommodations at Walt Disney World Village are remote enough from the heart of things so that you will probably want a car in which to get around—or you can use the WDW buses to get from place to place. But the Lake Buena Vista Club, with its golf course and tennis courts (described in *Sports*), and the *Empress Lilly* riverboat restaurant are just a short distance away. So for a longer Walt Disney World vacation, one that will not involve spending every day in the Magic Kingdom, the Walt Disney World Village accommodations are probably a good bet. Their proximity to Epcot Center makes them especially convenient for visits there.

Plans for increasing the number of rooms at the Polynesian Village Resort, the Golf Resort, and the Club Lake Villas are under way; there will be approximately 500 additional rooms available when making reservations for visits during the latter half of 1985.

CONTEMPORARY RESORT

Watching the monorail trains disappear into this hotel's enormous, 15-story, A-frame tower never fails to amaze onlookers. The sleek trains look like long spaceships docking as they slide inside or the sight may bring to mind the story of Jonah being swallowed up by the whale. (Note that wheelchair guests cannot board the monorail here.)

Passengers, for their part, are impressed by the cavernous lobby, with its tiers of balconies and, at its center, designer Mary Blair's huge 90-foot-high, floor-to-ceiling, tile mural depicting Indian children, stylized flowers, birds, trees, and other scenes from the Southwest. (Look carefully and you may be able to spot the five-legged goat.)

This imposing establishment is the largest of the WDW properties, boasting over 1,046 rooms in its Tower and the two garden wings that flank it on either side. The hotel has six shops, six complete restaurants, two snack bars, four lounges, large meeting rooms (described in *Meetings and Conventions*), a marina, a beach, a health club, and more. The larger of the hotel's pair of swimming pools, measuring a generous 20 by 25 meters, is a delight for lap swimmers—the best in the World for that purpose. And the Fiesta Fun Center—a vast room full of pinball and other electronic games that's open around the clock—is lively until the wee hours of the morning. For many youngsters, just the presence of this room is reason enough to lodge here. The activity that these installations generate gives the place an urban feeling that is not found elsewhere in WDW: desk clerks who have also done duty at the Polynesian Village and the Golf Resort note that guests arriving at the Contemporary Resort seem more tense and irritable, exhibiting greater anxiety and a defeated-before-they-start mood that Disney personnel surmise is directly related to the environment. Certainly, the place can be a bit intimidating, and the hotel is not to everyone's taste. But you can't deny the Contemporary Resort's vitality, and the sense it gives of being right in the heart of things can prove irresistible.

ROOMS: The hotel's guest rooms are almost evenly apportioned between the Tower and the North and South Garden Wings flanking it on either side. Rooms in the Tower boast exciting views of Bay Lake or the Magic Kingdom, and cost more than the rooms in the garden wings. From rooms on the Bay Lake side, guests can watch the sun rise through the eerie early-morning mists; in the evening, they can watch the Electrical Water Pageant (described in *Good Meals, Great Times*) from their own terrace. Rooms on the Magic Kingdom side, on the other hand, have fine views of the sun setting behind Cinderella Castle (and the Central Florida sunsets are real dazzlers) and of the fireworks exploding around the Castle just after 10 P.M. on nights when the park is open until midnight. Access to Tower rooms is by elevator, and the elevators used to be slower than molasses in winter and every trip up and down was a chore. But new, speedy elevators—ones that can talk—make comings and goings much more of a breeze.

All rooms can accommodate up to five (plus one additional child under three). Some units have king-size beds; the rest have two queens. Adjoining and connecting rooms both may be requested, but they cannot be guaranteed.

Bathrooms in the Contemporary Resort are particularly well laid out. Not only are they extremely large, but they also have double sinks, a bathtub with a shower head, and a separate shower stall.

Suites: Several varieties are available. In the Tower, they come with a Bay Lake or Magic Kingdom view, either with one bedroom (and two queen-size beds and two double sleep sofas, to accommodate up to eight), or with two bedrooms (to accommodate up to twelve). Garden Wing suites are available in three types—third-floor Bay Lake–view studio suites that accommodate two, in a parlor and an only slightly separated sleeping area fitted out with a king-size bed; Bay Lake–view one-bedroom suites on the second floor, which sleep up to six in a bedroom, with a king-size bed and a parlor furnished with two double sleep sofas; and garden-view suites, which can accommodate up to seven in the bedroom, which has a pair of queen-size beds, and a parlor furnished with two sleep sofas. (For price information, see the chart "Rates at WDW-Owned Properties" in this chapter.)

WHERE TO EAT: Most of the hotel's restaurants are located on the Grand Canyon Concourse on the fourth floor, but there are also restaurants on the fifteenth and second floors, and snack spots beside the marina and in the first-floor Fiesta Fun Center. Special children's menus are generally available at these restaurants. The meal-by-meal specialties of these facilities are described in some detail in the *Good Meals, Great Times* chapter. Here is a brief synopsis:

Terrace Buffeteria: On the Grand Canyon Concourse, this establishment serves breakfast, lunch, and dinner daily.

Terrace Cafe: On the Grand Canyon Concourse. Features a character breakfast daily and a bountiful, all-you-can-eat Italian buffet every evening; one of the World's best buys. No reservations.

Pueblo Room: On the Grand Canyon Concourse, tucked away behind Coconino Cove. Breakfast, lunch, and dinner are offered. At breakfast, the menu is composed of fairly standard offerings; at lunch, there are salads, hearty sandwiches, and hamburgers; with dinners featuring an assortment of fairly straightforward meat, chicken, and seafood dishes. Reservations are accepted for dinner.

Outer Rim: On the Grand Canyon Concourse, opposite the Terrace Cafe, with a good view over Bay Lake. Dinner is the only meal usually served here. No reservations.

Gulf Coast Room: One of Walt Disney World's continental restaurants, this one is on the second floor of the hotel and has a subdued, relaxed atmosphere that seems worlds away from the other areas of the Contemporary Resort. Dinner is the only meal served. (Jackets are required.) Children might not find the leisurely pace of the service to their taste, but it's possible to send them off to the Fiesta Fun Center Snack Bar. Reservations are requested; phone 824-3684.

Top of the World: This lovely room boasts superb views from the hotel's 15th floor. There's a bountiful, all-you-can-eat buffet for breakfast, lunch, and brunch (on Sunday), and a dinner show, Broadway at the Top. The setting is unique in the World. After dark, the golden spires of Cinderella Castle glitter under the floodlights, and the white lights edging the rooflines of Main Street wink and twinkle like distant fireflies. Reservations are required for the dinner shows; phone the CRO at 824-8000. For Sunday brunch reservations, call 824-3611.

Fiesta Fun Center Snack Bar: On the first floor; serves light fare until midnight.

Dock Inn: The snack stand at the marina behind the hotel.

WHERE TO DRINK: The no-liquor policy in the Magic Kingdom notwithstanding, tippling is one of the pleasantest pastimes at Walt Disney World, thanks to the settings of many of the bars and lounges and the array of specialty drinks. The Contemporary Resort is no exception.

Monorail Club Car: Near the escalators on the Grand Canyon Concourse, this long, skinny barroom overlooking Bay Lake is a cozy, companionable sort of place for serious drinking. No entertainment but the company you bring.

Coconino Cove: On the Grand Canyon Concourse, just outside the Pueblo Room. Guests waiting to be seated there can have drinks and Mexican-style snacks; there's entertainment nightly.

Top of the World Lounge: Adjoining the Top of the World Restaurant, this spacious, high-ceilinged room offers superb views over the Magic Kingdom. While listening to the dinner show's entertainment just out of sight, it's possible to gaze across the night toward Cinderella Castle. This is a good spot to watch the sunset and, when the park is open until midnight, the fireworks. Dash out onto the more easterly of the two observation decks nearby at 10:05 to see the Electrical Water Pageant blipping and bleeping and glittering on Bay Lake far below.

Sand Bar: Beside the marina, serving a variety of mixed drinks. The specialty is a nifty ice cream piña colada.

ROOM SERVICE: A wide range of offerings suitable for breakfast, lunch, dinner, and snacks can be ordered; consult room service menus for serving times.

Note, however, that room service is generally very slow. To prevent disappointment, pre-order room service breakfasts the night before, using the card hanging from the doorknob; for other meals, count on phoning in an order a couple of hours before you want to be served. When the food finally does arrive, it comes with a smile and, in the morning, with a newspaper.

WHAT TO DO: All by itself, the Contemporary Resort boasts more activities and recreational facilities than many large resorts; it would not be difficult to have a first-class holiday without ever leaving the premises.

Boat rentals: Sailboats, pedal boats, and pontoon boats, as well as the zippy little motorcraft known as Water Sprites, are all available for rent at the Contemporary Resort marina, near the beach. (See *Sports* for details.)

Water Skiing: Boats with driver and skis can be hired at the hotel marina. (For details, see *Sports*.)

Swimming: There are two main pools here, the big 20-by-25-meter main pool, and the round teen splash pool, deep in the center and shallow on the outside. A toddler's pool is located near the North Wing, and swimming is permitted in the roped-off area of Bay Lake beside the beach. The bottom is delightfully sandy. (For hours, see *Sports*.)

Volleyball: Nets are set up on the beach.

Children's playground: Located near the North Garden Wing.

Jogging: The Fort Wilderness Exercise Trail is only a short run away. Inquire at the desk for directions, and pay careful attention so that you don't miss the turnoff—it's the first road to the left after you pass under the Water Bridge.

Fiesta Fun Center: On the first floor of the hotel, this is one of the World's great indoor recreational facilities, the biggest and most varied of all the Disney hotels' mechanical games rooms, boasting everything from ping pong to skee ball and a couple of different kinds of air hockey, not to mention Asteroids and Space Invaders and all the other current favorites of the pinball-and-electronic-games-playing set. Worth at least a look.

Movies: Three different Disney movies are shown daily (late afternoons and in the early evening) in the theater at the Fiesta Fun Center. A good place to pass a rainy day—or just to get off your feet.

Shopping: The fourth-floor Grand Canyon Concourse is full of shops that are not only several cuts above those found in other Orlando-area hotels, but are also interesting enough to make browsing here an amusing way to weather a late-afternoon thundershower. The Fantasia Shop sells kids' stuff and Walt Disney–themed merchandise (china figurines of Mickey Mouse, Minnie, the Cheshire Cat, the Mad Hatter, the White Rabbit, Pluto, and company; T-shirts and sweat shirts; and stuffed animals). Plaza Gifts and Sundries, which adjoins it, is the place for baby food and Pampers, sun hats, and other items, including fresh flowers; and Spirit World, next door, has a selection of newspapers, magazines, books, snack foods, and liquor—just what's needed for a cocktail party on your terrace or aboard a pontoon boat hired at the marina. On the opposite side of the Concourse, the Contemporary Woman offers a range of good-quality women's clothing in all price ranges (and plenty of bathing suits), and the adjoining Contemporary Man stocks casual and beach wear for men. Even tuxedo rentals are available.

The adjacent Kingdom Jewels, Ltd., displays men's and women's jewelry from around the globe.

TRANSPORTATION: The Contemporary Resort is connected to the Transportation and Ticket Center (TTC) by gold-flagged buses, which operate every 10 to 15 minutes from 7 A.M. until 2 A.M. The monorail trains, which glide into the hotel with roughly the same frequency, stop just above the Grand Canyon Concourse, inside the atrium area of the Tower; they make stops at the Polynesian Village (from which point you can board a bus to the Golf Resort), the Magic Kingdom, and the TTC. From the TTC, Epcot Center can be reached by red-flagged bus or by monorail.

Blue-flagged watercraft also travel regularly from the marina to Fort Wilderness and Discovery Island.

POLYNESIAN VILLAGE RESORT

The Polynesian Village is as close an approximation of the real thing as Walt Disney World Village's *Empress Lilly* riverboat restaurant is an evocation of a genuine stern-wheeler. The vegetation is as lush as anywhere in the World; the architecture speaks of the tropics; and the atmosphere is more subdued than that of even the relatively placid Golf Resort. *Aitea-Peatea,* promises the hotel's motto: "There will be another day tomorrow just like today." Here, that's a pleasant thought.

The mood is set by a three-story high garden that occupies most of the lobby. To call the construction at the center a fountain is to do it a grave injustice; it's more like a waterfall that a wanderer might suddenly come upon in the jungle. The water cascades over craggy volcanic rocks. Coconut palms tower over 250 square feet of some 75 different species of tropical and subtropical plants—1,500 anthuriums, banana trees, ferns, gardenias, orchids, and other greens. The climatic conditions are nearly perfect, so that everything looks verdant year round.

The structure that contains this mass of greenery, the so-called Great Ceremonial House, is the central building in the Polynesian Village complex. The front desk, the shops, and most of the restaurants are located here. Flanking the Great Ceremonial House on either side are nine 2- and 3-story "longhouses" named for various Pacific islands. These structures house the resort's 636 rooms. On the east side, there is the Tangaroa Terrace restaurant, the resident snack bar, in a building that also houses the game room; on the west, there is Luau Cove, where the Polynesian Revue (described in *Good Meals, Great Times*) is presented nightly. A marina is located just west of the Great Ceremonial House, and a powdery white-sand beach borders the resort property on the north. The fact that the monorail makes stops at this resort makes it a very convenient place to stay; in fact, it's just a couple of minutes' ride to the Magic Kingdom—the next stop down the line. But because the accommodations are so scattered, and because the hotel is not quite as large as the Contemporary Resort, things seldom feel as hectic, and the Polynesian Village has a loyal following among second- and third-time Walt Disney World visitors. That, coupled with the appeal of the theme as conveyed by the hotel's name, makes the Polynesian Village rooms sell out quickly, and it's the most difficult of the Disney-owned hotels in which to get a reservation.

ROOMS: These are located in the nine longhouses. Many rooms have a balcony or a patio, and most have a view of either the Seven Seas Lagoon or of one of the swimming pools; those in the Oahu longhouse, the most easterly of the group, are the largest. Most have two queen-size beds, and, as at the Contemporary Resort, all rooms can accommodate five (plus a sixth under age three). Adjoining rooms may be requested, though they cannot be guaranteed. (The Oahu longhouse has some specially equipped bathrooms for handicapped visitors.)

Suites are available to accommodate from four to six. Most have a king-size bed in the bedroom and one or two sleep sofas in the parlor. All are located in the Bali Hai longhouse.

WHERE TO EAT: Some of the more interesting Walt Disney World eating spots are located at the Polynesian Village. (See *Good Meals, Great Times* for more details.)

South Seas Dining Room: Located on the first floor of the Great Ceremonial House. Dinner is served buffet-style at this smallish room and it is the current site of the Minnie's Menehune character breakfast that is held daily.

Papeete Bay Verandah: On the second floor of the Great Ceremonial House, Papeete Bay serves sit-down dinners daily, breakfast and lunch buffets

Monday through Saturday, and a massive brunch buffet on Sunday. The room is large and open, and offers fine views across the Seven Seas Lagoon all the way to Cinderella Castle. After dark, Polynesian dancers and a small combo entertain quietly. Reservations are requested for dinner and Sunday brunch; phone 824-1391.

Coral Isle Cafe: On the second floor of the Great Ceremonial House, around the corner from Papeete Bay. This standard coffee shop (with faintly South Seas decor) serves the usual assortment of breakfast items each morning, and does a booming business at lunch and dinner. A good bet when you want a no-fuss meal.

Tangaroa Terrace: This sprawling establishment, on the eastern edge of the property near the Oahu longhouse, has never been as heavily patronized as some of the other Polynesian Village restaurants because of its somewhat remote location. Increasingly, however, good word-of-mouth is spreading, and the restaurant's popularity seems to be rising. Reservations are requested at dinner; phone 824-1361.

Barefoot Snack Bar: In the lobby level of the Great Ceremonial House, this is a good spot for continental breakfasts and for snacks during the rest of the day.

Tangaroa Snack Isle: Most guests discover this snack bar on their way to Tangaroa Terrace, the game room, or the East Pool—to which it is extremely convenient.

WHERE TO DRINK: The resort's Polynesian theme has inspired a whole raft of deceptively potent potables like Seven Seas (fruit juice, grenadine, orange curaçao, and rum), Chi Chis (a standard piña colada made with vodka instead of rum), and WDW piña coladas (which include orange juice in addition to rum, pineapple, and coconut cream). There's even a special Polynesian Village non-alcoholic treat—the pink Lei-Lani, a delicious orange juice and strawberry mixture. These drinks are specialties at Polynesian Village lounges, listed below, but can also be ordered elsewhere in WDW. (Details about individual drink menus can be found in the *Good Meals, Great Times* chapter.)

Barefoot Bar: Adjoining the Swimming Pool Lagoon.

Tambu Lounge: Cozy and clublike, this lounge adjoins the Papeete Bay Verandah. A good spot for quiet conversation.

Captain Cook's Hideaway: Off the lobby of the Great Ceremonial House, this small, dark nook also has entertainment nightly.

ROOM SERVICE: It should be noted that while a variety of tempting specialties is available, there is usually a considerable wait between the placing of an order and its arrival. Allow about an hour, and be sure to fill out the card on your doorknob specifying your breakfast desires *the night before*. If this doesn't dampen your enthusiasm for breakfast in your room, the fact that the delicious banana-stuffed French toast is served only in the restaurants might do the trick.

WHAT TO DO: A wide range of activities is available at the Polynesian Village, just as at the Contemporary Resort.

Boat rentals: Sailboats, speedy little Water Sprites, pedal boats, pontoon boats, and outrigger canoes (requiring eight to paddle) are available for rent at the Polynesian Village marina. And waterskiing is available.

Swimming: There are two main pools here, the elliptical East Pool, in the shadow of the Oahu, Tonga, Hawaii, Bora Bora, and Maui longhouses, and the larger free-form Swimming Pool Lagoon, closer to the marina and the beach. This pool is framed by a large cluster of boulders that forms a water slide much beloved by youngsters; to get to the ladder that takes you to the top, you must duck underneath a waterfall. For swimming laps, the large pool at the Contemporary Resort is best. Toddlers have their own shallow areas in both Polynesian Village pools. Swimming is also permitted in the roped-off areas of the Seven Seas Lagoon (when there's a lifeguard on duty).

Children's playground: Located near the Great Ceremonial House, this assemblage of kid stuff features a small, low, thatch-roofed treehouse affair with an assortment of apparatus for climbing and sliding.

Jogging: The Fort Wilderness Exercise Trail and the roads around the Golf Resort are just a short jog away. Ask for directions at the front desk.

Game room: Moana Mickey's Fun Hut, while not as large as the Contemporary Resort's Fiesta Fun Center, usually manages to keep youngsters occupied. Located alongside the Tangaroa Snack Isle.

Shopping: News from Civilization, on the first floor of the Great Ceremonial House, is the only place in Walt Disney World where you can buy a grass skirt, and for that reason alone it's worth a special trip, though most of the other merchandise there—with the exception of a few handsome shells—is of the utilitarian variety—daily newspapers, magazines, tobacco, film, and gifts. Robinson Crusoe Esq., right nearby, sells casual sportswear and swimwear for men, while the Polynesian Princess stocks an appealing assortment of brightly colored resort fashions, bathing suits, and hot-weather accessories. Upstairs, Village Gifts & Sundries sells gift items, souvenirs, and miscellaneous items; Trader Jack's Grog Hut has food, liquor, wine, beer, and other fixings for an impromptu party; and Village Florist can make up a bouquet or a fruit basket to be delivered to your room on request.

TRANSPORTATION: The Polynesian Village is located right on the monorail line, just one stop away from the Magic Kingdom. The entrance is on the second floor of the Great Ceremonial House.

Green-flagged buses, which circulate between the Polynesian Village, the Golf Resort, and the Transportation and Ticket Center, stop at the traffic island in front of the hotel. From the TTC, Epcot Center is accessible by monorail or by red-flagged bus.

Gold-flagged watercraft make regular trips from the Polynesian Village's marina to Fort Wilderness and Discovery Island. Schedule depends on River Country and Discovery Island hours of operation.

GOLF RESORT HOTEL

This 151-room establishment, originally built as a golf clubhouse and later enlarged, is not the hotel that first-time visitors usually choose. "But I don't play golf," they often say. "And besides, it's not on the monorail." Consequently, when there are any empty rooms available in any of the WDW resort hotels, chances are they'll be at the Golf Resort.

Yet guests who stay there for that reason often return enthusiastically on their next visit. For the lack of attachment to the monorail route makes the Golf Resort the most serene of all the Disney-owned hotels. What's more, there aren't so many day guests wandering all over just to see what a Disney hotel is like.

Though the rooms here look about the same as those at the two sister Disney hotels, they're actually a few feet larger. Decorated in subdued earth tones, the Golf Resort also has a pleasantly relaxed atmosphere—more akin to that of the Walt Disney World Village Villas. But the Golf Resort is miles more convenient: buses make the short trip between the Golf Resort, the Polynesian Village, and the Transportation and Ticket Center every ten minutes or so.

WHERE TO EAT: The Trophy Room, the hotel's single full-service restaurant, also happens to rank among the most pleasant spots in the World for a meal. Many Disney executives come here for lunch, because even when there are lines at the Polynesian Village and the Contemporary Resort, the Trophy Room will usually be fairly quiet. Also, the food is quite good. At breakfast and lunch, there are immense all-you-can-eat buffets; at dinner, there is a full, diverse menu. An early sit-down Dinner à la Disney is featured nightly with visits by favorite characters. Sunday brunch buffets are also offered. Reservations are suggested; phone 824-1484.

For snacks, there's the Sand Trap at poolside.

WHERE TO DRINK: The Players' Gallery, adjoining the Trophy Room with a view over the Magnolia golf course, serves an assortment of specialty drinks and cocktails—Double Eagles (Kahlua, Amaretto, and brandy blended with cream), Lateral Hazards (sangría, triple sec, and rum), Strawberry Colada Bogeys (rum, strawberries, pineapple juice, and cream of coconut), and Duffer's Delight (brandy, triple sec, and orange juice). Beer and piña coladas are available at the Sand Trap at poolside.

ROOM SERVICE: Here, too, it's necessary to plan well in advance when you want to eat in. For breakfast, fill out the pre-order card on your doorknob, and hang it outside your room before retiring.

ROOMS: These are located in a three-story wing behind the lobby area. All have patios or balconies and views of woods or the golf courses; can accommodate up to five (plus a sixth under age three); and have two queen-size beds and a sleep sofa. (No king-size beds are available here.) Adjoining rooms can be requested but are not guaranteed. (There are no special room provisions for handicapped guests here, but the hotel is accessible to all visitors.)

Two suites, each with two queen-size beds and two sleep sofas, are available as well; they can accommodate up to seven. (For complete price information, see the chart "Rates at WDW-owned Properties" later on in this chapter.)

WHAT TO DO: The Golf Resort is landlocked, so when you decide to go boating, you've got to head for the Contemporary Resort or the Polynesian Village. But there are plenty of other activities.

Game room: There's a small one located on the lobby level in the guest-room area.

Golf: There are two par-72, Joe Lee–designed, championship courses—the tree-dotted Magnolia, to the north of the hotel, which plays from 5,485 (ladies) to 7,253 (championship) yards; and, south of the hotel, the Palm, ranked by *Golf Digest* magazine among the United States' top hundred courses—shorter and tighter, with more wooded fairways and nine water hazards, playing from 5,398 to 6,917 yards. Each course has its own driving range. The Wee Links, a 6-hole, 1,525-yard experimental junior layout, occupies a 25-acre corner near the Magnolia. (See *Sports* for details.)

Shopping: The Pro Shop stocks men's and women's golf and tennis togs and gear, some emblazoned with Mickey and Minnie emblems. Golf Gifts and Sundries sells souvenirs, books and magazines, daily newspapers, liquor, tobacco, film, toiletries, and a little bit of a lot of other things.

Swimming: The Golf Resort has its own 60-foot-long swimming pool. For beach action, head for the Polynesian Village.

Tennis: There are two courts tucked away behind the hotel. These are open from 8 A.M. to 10 P.M. daily, and are lighted for night play. (For more information, and for details about fees and court reservations, see *Sports*.)

TRANSPORTATION: The green-flagged bus makes regular trips from the Golf Resort to the Polynesian Village and then on to the Transportation and Ticket Center (TTC). To get to the Magic Kingdom or the Contemporary Resort, it's quickest to take the monorail from the second-floor lobby at the Polynesian Village; to get to Walt Disney World Village or Epcot Center, stay on the bus until you get to the TTC, and then change for the red-flagged bus. To get to Fort Wilderness, change to the blue-flagged bus.

SPECIAL ROOM REQUESTS

The Central Reservations Office (824-8000) can accept *requests* for a particular view or location, but although they will try, they cannot guarantee that the resort will be able to fulfill your request.

WALT DISNEY WORLD VILLAGE VILLAS

The area near Walt Disney World Shopping Village is dotted with exceptionally attractive villa-type accommodations, many fitted out with fully equipped kitchens and many other amenities. Some may cost more than individual guest rooms at the three resort hotels, but they accommodate more people as well. For families of more than five (who might otherwise need to rent an extra hotel room), this is the most economical way to stay hereabouts. Smaller families can generally come out even by cooking some of their own meals in their villa.

Aside from the delights of having more space, the villas are exceptionally quiet and secluded; the pace is definitely more relaxed and the atmosphere very low-key. They are conveniently located with respect to Epcot Center and River Country, but less so in relation to everything else in the World.

TYPES OF VILLAS: There are four major types of villas, each one in several sizes. Most have kitchens.

Check in and check out for the Vacation Villas, the Treehouse Villas, and the Fairway Villas at the Reception Center on Hotel Plaza Boulevard, between Americana Dutch Resort Hotel and the Viscount Hotel at Walt Disney World Village Hotel Plaza. Those staying at the Club Lake Villas should check in and out at the Walt Disney World Conference Center.

Vacation Villas: Located about five minutes' walk from the Lake Buena Vista Club, these villas, which are fairly formal in feeling, have cathedral-height living-room ceilings; in some, one of the walls is dramatically mirrored. One- and two-bedroom models are available. One-bedroom units can accommodate four, plus an additional child under three; there's a king-size bed in the bedroom and a queen-size sleep sofa in the living room. Two-bedroom units, which can accommodate up to six, plus a seventh guest under age 13, have a king-size bed (or two twins) in each bedroom, and a queen-size sleep sofa in the living room.

The Villa Center in the center of the Vacation Villas is the main recreation area. In addition to the 50-by-30-foot swimming pool, there are bicycle and electric-cart rentals, a laundry, snack bar, and electronic games and pinball machines. Another swimming pool, this one measuring 65 by 30 feet, is located closer to Walt Disney World Shopping Village.

Club Lake Villas: Located slightly northeast of the Vacation Villas area, these units are handsomely done in sophisticated fabrics in reds and blues. The smallest one-bedroom units have a roughly L-shaped configuration, with a special wet-bar equipped sitting area that is just far enough removed from the sleeping area (with its two queen-size beds) that business travelers who invite their compatriots in for a nightcap don't feel as if they're entertaining in the bedroom. While the layout was drawn up with special care to the needs of those attending conferences at the Walt Disney World Conference Center, it works equally well in providing families with a bit more privacy than they get in the rooms at the three WDW resort hotels. (The single disadvantage for families is the size of the bathrooms—small.) Note that these units, which cost about the same as rooms at the resort hotels, do not have full kitchens—only a small refrigerator and a sink.

For the largest rooms, take a one-bedroom suite, which sleeps five and includes a Jacuzzi. One-bedroom units have two queen-size beds upstairs and a sleep sofa downstairs, and are priced at a level just slightly higher than the two-bedroom Fairway Villas, Vacation Villas, and Treehouse Villas, all of which sleep at least six.

The Club Lake Villas are all within a ten-minute walk of the Lake Buena Vista Club, across Club Lake, where a 65-by-30-foot swimming pool, golf course, three tennis courts, and restaurants are located.

Fairway Villas: These cedar-sided, slant-roofed, two-bedroom units, located near the tenth, eleventh, seventeenth, and eighteenth fairways of the Lake Buena Vista Club Golf Course, are among the World's most attractive accommodations, bar none, with cathedral ceilings, rough-hewn walls, large windows, contemporary-styled furniture, and an overall feeling of vast spaciousness. They can sleep six, plus a child under 12. Some units for the handicapped are available.

Joggers can loop through the shady Treehouse area or venture forth along Fairway Drive, alongside the golf course, and into the Club Lake Villas area; the nearest swimming pool is the 65-by-30-footer at the Lake Buena Vista Club, within walking distance of some units, a short drive from others.

Treehouse Villas: When you lodge in one of these octagonal, two-bedroom houses-on-stilts scattered along a barbell-shaped roadway at the western edge of the villa area, you go to sleep at night to a cacophony of crickets and wake up to a chorus of bird songs. You're literally in the woods, alongside some of the winding WDW canals, and you feel a million miles from the rest of the WDW property and all its hubbub. Upstairs is the small (but modern) kitchen, with a breakfast bar; the living room (where the television and a sleep sofa are located); two bedrooms (each with a queen-size bed) and two bathrooms; the whole floor is surrounded by a deck where you can eat or just sit and look out into the trees. Downstairs, there's a den and a utility room equipped with a washer and dryer. The canals offer some of the World's best fishing, mainly for bass, and the roadways—shady, flat, and untrafficked as they are—are terrific for jogging. The nearest swimming pool is the 65-by-30-footer at the Lake Buena Vista Club.

Grand Vista Suites: A quartet of ultraluxurious two- and three-bedroom homes—originally designed as model homes for a development project that has been abandoned for the moment—is available for rent in the Vacation Villa area. Bed turndown service and daily newspaper deliveries are provided, refrigerators are stocked with staples when you arrive, and the furniture is first class. (For complete price information, see the chart "Rates at WDW-owned Properties" later on in this chapter.)

WHERE TO EAT: None of the four villa complexes has its own restaurant. But this is not a problem, except for guests lodging in the kitchenless one-bedroom Club Lake Villas, who may want to travel to the Lake Buena Vista Club or to Walt Disney World Shopping Village. (Electric carts that hold four people are available for rent at $15 for each 24 hours.) For breakfast, the options include the Lake Buena Vista Club's main dining room or (for continental breakfasts only) the snack bar downstairs; or, at Walt Disney World Shopping Village, the Verandah Restaurant (where there's a character breakfast) or the pastry window at the Gourmet Pantry (which opens at 9:30 A.M.). For lunch and dinner, the selections are broader. (See *Good Meals, Great Times* for more details.)

Groceries: The Gourmet Pantry stocks staples of all sorts, as well as delicacies from around the globe, and good meat, poultry, and fresh green vegetables. Purchases can be delivered to your villa at no charge; if you can't be home to receive them, arrangements can be made for the delivery person to be let in so that perishables can be stashed in the refrigerator. It's also possible to order by phone. Touch "3" on your room telephone (before 2 P.M.), or dial 824-6993 when calling from elsewhere.

WHERE TO DRINK: The Villa area's most convenient drinking spot is the Lake Buena Vista Club's lounge. Otherwise, for liquid refreshment, head for Walt Disney World Shopping Village—Cap'n Jack's Oyster Bar, the Village Lounge, or, aboard the *Empress Lilly* riverboat restaurant, the Promenade Lounge or the Starboard Lounge, or the exceptionally lively Baton Rouge Lounge. (For details about these, see *Good Meals, Great Times* and *Everything Else in the World*.)

ROOM SERVICE: Room service is not available at Walt Disney World Village Villas.

WHAT DO DO: In addition to boating, shopping, and fishing at Walt Disney World Shopping Village (discussed in more detail in *Sports* and *Everything Else in the World*), you can also enjoy a variety of activities in and around the villas themselves.

Biking: The meandering, relatively untrafficked, and quite scenic roads around the Walt Disney World Village Villas, not to mention the eight miles of bike paths there, can make for an enjoyable hour or two of pedaling. Tandems and ordinary two-wheelers are both available for rent at the Villa Center. (See *Sports* for fees.)

Game room: A small arcade with electronic games and pinball machines is located in the Villa Center near the Vacation Villas.

Golf: The par-72 Lake Buena Vista Club course plays from 5,359 to 6,655 yards, and is the shortest of the Disney courses; it's more like the Magnolia than the Palm, and doesn't have the latter's water hazards. There are also practice tees and a driving range, and private lessons (with or without video replay) are available here as well; head pro Rina Ritson, the first woman golf pro ever to hold the top position at a major golf club, is a first-class instructor. First-class clubs, shoes, and balls can be rented at the Pro Shop. (For fees and starting information, see *Sports*.)

Swimming: There are three pools in the Villa area—two near the Vacation Villas (one at the Villa Center, the other close to the shores of the Buena Vista Lagoon) and the third at the Lake Buena Vista Club. Still, they're small; the best for swimming laps is at the Contemporary Resort Hotel.

Tennis: There are three courts, bordered by the woods and a section of the golf course, at the Lake Buena Vista Club (open 8 A.M. to 10 P.M. daily; lighted for play after dark). Racquets can be rented for a nominal fee; you must buy your own balls. (For fee information, see *Sports*.)

TRANSPORTATION: Green-and-gold-flagged buses have designations such as "EC," "MK," or "V" on the front indicating which goes to Epcot Center, the Magic Kingdom, or the Village. All of these circulate through the Villa areas, making pickups at bus stops located at regular intervals along the roadways; they arrive every 15 to 20 minutes.

Another option: A $15-a-day electric golf cart can get you from your villa to the WDW Shopping Village or the Lake Buena Vista Club. Or rent a bike. Either can be rented at the Villa Center.

FORT WILDERNESS CAMPGROUND RESORT

The very existence of this 650-acre, canal-crossed expanse of cypress and pines, laced by pleasant blacktop roadways, always surprises visitors who come to WDW expecting the Magic Kingdom and nothing more. If they've heard about Fort Wilderness at all, they often confuse it with the park's Frontierland section.

But the Fort Wilderness atmosphere is relaxed and not at all frenetic. In one corner, a group of kids may be battling it out at tetherball, and on the playing fields there are often a couple of energetic touch football games in progress. In the mornings, the campground smells sweetly of dew-wetted pines, then of frying bacon. In the evening, the heat and stillness of the afternoon gives way to dinnertime bustle, and fish and steaks are thrown onto grills as next-door neighbors organize get-togethers. Later on, little clumps of teens and preteens gather alongside the trading posts or at Pioneer Hall, where Fort Wilderness's electronic-games-and-pinball arcade is located. Fort Wilderness also has a marina and a beach, a nature trail, and a number of waterways where fishing, canoeing, and paddleboating are popular; these and other recreational possibilities make Fort Wilderness one of the livelier places to be in WDW.

And you can enjoy the Fort Wilderness experience even if you don't have your own camping gear. Among the 828 campsites, there also are a number of air-conditioned trailers available for rent, complete with kitchen utensils, dishes, linens, color television, daily maid service, and enough other amenities that the woods all around are the only reminders of the fact that you're camping out. The cost is comparable to that of some of the least expensive of the rooms at the resort hotels. (But those don't have kitchens and so don't offer the money-saving option of cooking a few meals "at home.")

CAMPSITES: Fort Wilderness has 828 campsites, ranging in length from 25 to 65 feet, spaced throughout 21 camping loops. Some of them are set up for tent campers, and most of the rest are rented to trailer campers. Each site has a 110/220-volt electric outlet, barbecue grill, and picnic table. Most offer a sanitary-disposal hookup; all loops have at least one comfort station equipped with rest rooms, private showers, an ice machine, telephones, and a laundry room. The per-site fee allows for occupancy by up to seven people.

The various campground areas are designated by numbers. The 100, 200, 300, 400, and 500 loops are the closest to the beach, the Settlement Trading Post, and Pioneer Hall. The 1500, 1600, 1700, 1800, and 1900 loops are farthest away from the beach and many other Fort Wilderness activities, but they have the heaviest foliage and are quieter and more private.

RENTAL TRAILERS: It used to be that the 250 Fleetwood Travel Trailers scattered through the camping loops at Fort Wilderness were taken only by people who wanted hotel rooms and couldn't get a reservation. Now—mainly as a result of good word-of-mouth—almost every booking is specifically requested. Lodging here provides all the advantages of a villa—and woodsy surroundings to boot.

Trailers are 35 feet long, sleep four adults and 2 children, and come equipped with pots and pans, dishes, and all the basic kitchen equipment. There's a bedroom at one end with a double bed (and, in some trailers, bunk beds); a sofa-bedded living room at the other end with a color TV; and a kitchen and complete bathroom in the center. The bathroom is not the sort of makeshift setup you might expect, but instead compares favorably with, say, a bathroom in the Club Lake Villas or the Treehouses.

Note: No extra camping equipment is allowed on the site; all guests must be accommodated in the rental trailer. (For complete price information, see the chart "Rates at WDW-owned Properties" later on in this chapter.)

WHERE TO EAT: Most people cook their own; groceries and supplies are available at the Meadow and Settlement trading posts (open from 8 A.M. to 10 P.M. in winter, to 11 P.M. in summer). Deli-style sandwiches can be concocted there for carry-out; you can eat them at your own site, on the beach, or at tables just outside River Country.

When you want to go out, there's the Trail's End Cafe, an informal, log-walled, beam-ceilinged cafeteria inside Pioneer Hall, where home-style fare is served. Beer and sangría are also available.

Snacks: The Campfire Snack Bar, in Pioneer Hall, is at the center of the campground and serves hamburgers, cheeseburgers, hot dogs, and the like, from about 11 A.M. until 6 P.M. (and until 9 P.M. during the summer). Down on the shores of Bay Lake, the Beach Shack offers snacks and sodas.

Pizza: Served nightly at Pioneer Hall from 9 P.M. to 12:30 A.M., along with soft drinks, beer, and sangría. Silent movies are shown here then, and a sing-along is staged every night.

WHERE TO DRINK: Beer and sangría are served in Pioneer Hall. Otherwise, take a blue-flagged watercraft to the Contemporary Resort or a gold-flagged watercraft to the Polynesian Village. Be sure to check the operating hours before boarding, however, so you don't miss the last trip back. Or, if you have a car, make the short drive to the *Empress Lilly* riverboat restaurant, Cap'n Jack's, or the Village Lounge ($5 minimum except for dinner guests at the Village Restaurant) at Walt Disney World Shopping Village.

FAMILY ENTERTAINMENT AFTER DARK: In addition to the sing-along and silent movies at Pioneer Hall, there's the Hoop-Dee-Doo Musical Revue, presented three times nightly at 5, 7:30, and 10 P.M.; reservations are required and are so hard to come by that they need to be made well in advance through the WDW Central Reservations Office (824-8000). Cancellations do occur, however. Fort Wilderness guests who can't get a reservation the first time around can have their names added to a waiting list by presenting themselves at the Pioneer Hall Ticket Window before the show.

There's also a nightly campfire program held at the center of the campground, near the Meadow Trading Post. A sing-along (featuring Chip 'n' Dale) and Disney movies and cartoons are the main goings-on (free). The Marshmallow Marsh Excursion (scheduled during the summer months), which begins at the campfire, includes more singing, a marshmallow roast, and a canoe excursion to a secluded lakeside spot from which, at 9:45 P.M., you also can see the Electrical Water Pageant—a procession of waterborne floats, during which an assortment of sea creatures is outlined in a galaxy of tiny colored lights. This can also be viewed from the Fort Wilderness Beach; don't miss it. (For more details, see *Everything Else in the World* and *Good Meals, Great Times*.)

WHAT TO DO: There are more on-site activities at Fort Wilderness than at almost any other area in the World, outside the Magic Kingdom. For golf, of course, it's necessary to travel to the Golf Resort or the Lake Buena Vista Club; for tennis, the Contemporary Resort is most accessible—just a short ride across Bay Lake in the blue-flagged watercraft from the Fort Wilderness marina.

Though it has no swimming pool, Fort Wilderness does have a 315-foot-long, 175-foot-wide beach for swimming in Bay Lake. You can rent tandems, Sting Rays, and other two-wheelers at the Bike Barn for afternoon bicycle excursions or as reliable transportation around the campground. Visits to the Petting Farm, the blacksmith shop, and the horse barn near Fort Wilderness are amusing. Boating is popular; rentals are available at the marina. Canoes can be hired at the Bike Barn. Baseball, basketball, checkers, electric-cart rentals, fishing (on your own in the canals or on organized morning or afternoon angling excursions), horseback riding (on guided trail rides), horseshoes, jogging on the 2.3-mile exercise course, softball, tetherball, volleyball, and water skiing are also available. Or you can just go out for a stroll along the 1½-mile-long Wilderness Swamp Trail, near Marshmallow Marsh. All of these activities are described in detail in *Everything Else in the World* and *Sports*. There's also a games arcade in Pioneer Hall.

River Country, a major attraction in its own right, with a separate admission charge, is also located at Fort Wilderness; the features of this watery playground—a WDW must right along with the Magic Kingdom—are discussed in detail in *Everything Else in the World*.

TRANSPORTATION: Trams and buses circulating at 7-minute intervals provide transportation within the campground, while buses and watercraft connect Fort Wilderness to the rest of the World. To get to the Polynesian Village, the Contemporary Resort, or the Magic Kingdom, watercraft (which have regular departures from the Fort Wilderness marina) provide the most efficient transportation during their operating hours. At other times, and to get to Walt Disney World Shopping Village, take the blue-flagged bus from the Fort Wilderness bus stop, near the Settlement Trading Post and Pioneer Hall, to the Transportation and Ticket Center. This bus operates at regular intervals. Change to the red-flagged bus for Walt Disney World Shopping Village and Epcot Center; the gold-flagged bus for the Contemporary Resort; or the green-flagged bus for the Polynesian Village and the Golf Resort. (For information on watercraft and bus operating hours and frequencies, see the preceding chart under *Transportation* in this chapter.)

Fort Wilderness guests headed for the Polynesian Revue can take special black-flagged buses, which provide service to the Polynesian Village, scheduled for arrival at the Polynesian Village in time for the show. Black-flagged buses also make pickups at the Polynesian Village for guests bound for the Hoop-Dee-Doo Musical Revue at Pioneer Hall. For schedules, inquire at Guest Services.

PRACTICAL MATTERS

The Walt Disney World-owned hotels and villas have some important operating procedures that first-time guests don't always take seriously—much to their later dismay.

Deposit requirements: Deposits equal to one night's lodging (or campsite rental) are required within 21 days of the time that a reservation is made. Personal checks, traveler's checks, cashier's checks, and money orders are acceptable forms of payment. To have deposit charges billed to an American Express or MasterCard account, send your card number, its expiration date, the bank number (for MasterCard), and your signature. Deposits will be fully refunded if you cancel your reservation at least five days before your scheduled arrival. Reservations are automatically cancelled if deposits are not received by the deadline. (Reservations booked less than 30 days prior to arrival will receive special instructions for deposits and such.)

Check-in and check-out times: While not unique in the Orlando area, the early check-out time (11 A.M. at all WDW lodging places) is almost invariably too early for most WDW guests, while the late check-in times (3 P.M. in the resort hotels, 4 P.M. in the villas) are often painfully late. Even more frustrating is the fact that (except in slow seasons, when the Disney-owned hotels may not be entirely sold out from night to night), these are rules to which all the reservations clerks rigidly adhere. Desk clerks do try to accommodate a guest when possible, but it seldom is.

There is only limited storage space at the hotels, so when you try to check in and your room is not ready, store luggage in the trunk of your car, get your resort ID cards, and then head off to the Magic Kingdom or Epcot Center for the day. (Changing rooms are not abundant; if you don't want to do your sight-seeing in your traveling clothes, you can change in a hotel rest room.)

Payment methods: Hotel bills may be paid with American Express and MasterCard credit cards, with traveler's checks or cash, and with personal checks. Checks must bear the guest's name and address, be drawn on a U.S. bank, and be accompanied by proper identification—that is, a valid driver's license or a government-issued passport, and a major credit card such as American Express, Carte Blanche, Diners Club, MasterCard, or Visa.

ALL ABOUT WDW RESORT ID CARDS

Issued on arrival at WDW-owned resorts, these unprepossessing little squares of cardboard are among resort guests' most valuable possessions while in WDW. They entitle you to:

- Unlimited transportation by bus, monorail, and watercraft.
- Use of many of the roadways within Walt Disney World.
- Charge privileges: the cards may be used to cover purchases (up to certain account limits) in shops, lounge and restaurant charges, and recreational fees incurred anywhere in WDW—except the Magic Kingdom. At Epcot Center, guests may use their IDs to charge meals at full-service restaurants.

Note: ID cards are valid for use of the transportation facilities through the end of the last day of your stay, but are not valid for charging past check-out time.

RATES AT WDW-OWNED PROPERTIES

	Charge for single or double occupancy	Charge for additional occupants	Charge for cots	Room capacity	Types of beds	Check out/check in times
Contemporary Resort Hotel Rooms	$105 to $130 in Garden Wings; $140 in Tower with Bay Lake or Magic Kingdom view	No charge for those under 18; $15 per additional adult	None	Five, plus one additional occupant under age three	Two queen beds. Some king-sized beds available	11 A.M./3 P.M.
Suites	$240 to $300 in Garden Wings; $300 to $420 in Tower	None	None	Seven to twelve	Most have two queen beds and two sleep sofas	11 A.M./3 P.M.
Polynesian Village Resort Hotel Rooms	$105 to $120 without lagoon view; $130 with lagoon view	No charge for those under 18; $15 per additional adult	None	Five, plus one additional occupant under age three	Two queen beds. Some king-sized beds available	11 A.M./3 P.M.

Accommodation	Price	Extra Adult Charge	Cribs/Cots	Maximum Occupancy	Bed Configuration	Check-in/Check-out
Suites	$325 to $345, all in Bali Hai longhouse	None	None	Four to eight	King-sized beds in bedroom and one or two sleep sofas in parlor, usually	11 A.M./3 P.M.
Golf Resort Hotel Rooms	$105 with woodland view, $120 with pool or golf course view, $130 with pool access	No charge for those under 18; $15 per additional adult	None	Five, plus one additional occupant under age three	Two queen beds and a sleep sofa in all rooms; no king-sized beds available	11 A.M./3 P.M.
Suites	$240	None	No cots available; no charge for cribs	Up to seven	Two queen-sized beds and two sleep sofas	11 A.M./3 P.M.
Club Lake Villas One-bedroom	$100	None	No cots available; no charge for cribs	Five, plus one additional occupant under age three	Two queen-sized beds and one double sleep sofa	11 A.M./4 P.M.
One-bedroom suite	$170	None	No cots available; no charge for cribs	Five	Two queen-sized beds upstairs, one sleep sofa downstairs	11 A.M./4 P.M.
Fairway Villas	$150	None	No cots available; no charge for cribs	Six, plus one additional occupant under age twelve	One queen-sized bed in one bedroom, two double beds (or another queen) in the other, one double sleep sofa in living room	11 A.M./4 P.M.
Vacation Villas One-bedroom	$130	None	None	Four, plus one additional occupant under age three	One king-sized bed in bedroom, queen sleep sofa in living room	11 A.M./4 P.M.
Two-bedroom	$150	None	None	Six, plus one additional occupant under age twelve	King-sized bed (or two twins) in each bedroom, queen sleep sofa in living room	11 A.M./4 P.M.
Grand Vista Suites Two-bedroom	$400	None	None	Six	3 kings; 2 queens & 2 twins; or 1 king & 2 queens	11 A.M./4 P.M.
Three-bedroom	$475	None	None	Eight	1 king, 2 queens, & 2 twins	11 A.M./4 P.M.
Treehouse Villas	$150	None	No cots available; no charge for cribs	Six	One queen-sized bed in each bedroom, plus sleep sofa in living room	11 A.M./4 P.M.
Fleetwood Trailers at Fort Wilderness Campground	$105	None	No cots available; no charge for cribs	Four, for those in 1200 and 1300 loops	One double bed in bedroom, queen-sized sleep sofa in living room	11 A.M./3 P.M.
	$105	None	No cots available; no charge for cribs	Six, for those in 600, 700, 800, 1100, and 2100 loops	One double bed and bunk beds in bedroom, queen-sized sleep sofa in living room	11 A.M./3 P.M.

Campsites: Preferred loops 100, 200, 300, 400, & 500 with full hookups ($30 per night); loops 900, 1000, 1400, 1600, 1700, 1800, & 1900 with full hookups ($25 per night); and loops 1500 & 2000 with electrical and water hookups only ($25 per night).

Effective Jan. 1, 1985. Prices subject to change.

WDW VILLAGE

The six hotels here—Americana Dutch Resort Hotel, the Viscount Hotel, the Royal Plaza, the Howard Johnson's, the Buena Vista Palace, and the new Hilton—occupy a unique position among non-Disney-owned Orlando-area accommodations. They are actually located inside the boundaries of Walt Disney World, which makes them especially convenient. Their guests enjoy certain privileges similar to those of guests at WDW-owned properties, such as reduced prices for World Passports, bus transportation direct to the TTC and to Epcot Center, and the possibility of making reservations for dinner shows before bookings are accepted from the general public. Guests can also use the tennis and golf facilities at the Lake Buena Vista Club. WDW Central Reservations (824-8000) can take your bookings for WDW Hotel Plaza hotels (they're also included in several Walt Disney Travel Co. and Eastern Airlines packages), and most of these hotels have toll-free numbers that can be called at no charge.

AMERICANA DUTCH RESORT HOTEL: This gleaming white hotel, its 614 rooms installed in a 19-story tower and two wings, has had its share of problems, but the former erratic level of operation and maintenance now seems to have been improved. Most of the carpets are blue, the bedspreads white, and the rocking chairs and the wallpaper blue and white; other rooms have been redecorated in a blue-and-tan scheme. Each room has a Mickey Mouse combination lamp-telephone. Restaurants include the Flying Dutchman, which serves breakfast, lunch, and dinner; and the new Only Steak, which serves dinner only. (For details on these, see *Good Meals, Great Times*.) There's entertainment and dancing in The Hague Lounge; the Nightwatch Lounge is the hotel's cozy just-for-drinking spot. Two lighted tennis courts, racquetball and shuffleboard courts, a putting green, a playground, and a game room are also available. Rates range from $80 to $99 for two year round ($6 for cots). There are currently no rooms specially equipped for handicapped travelers. More information: Americana Dutch Resort Hotel; 1850 Hotel Plaza Blvd.; Lake Buena Vista, FL 32830; 828-4444 (toll-free 800-228-3278).

VISCOUNT HOTEL: This tri-arc hotel-tower has 325 spacious rooms and suites. All rooms were recently redecorated and have two queen-size beds, color TV, AM/FM radio, in-room coffee service, and private balconies offering very pretty views of the Central Florida countryside. The game room, pool, and playground are especially appreciated by youngsters. There's one restaurant, the Palm Grill, which serves breakfast, lunch, and dinner, and the new Ice Cream Parlor features pizza and light snacks. The Top of the Tower Lounge on the 18th floor offers a panoramic look out over Walt Disney World. Rates are $89 low season (the months of January and

HOTEL PLAZA

September), $110 the rest of the year (no additional charge for children under 17 sharing parents room; $6 for rollaways). There are six rooms for handicapped travelers. More information: The Viscount Hotel; 2000 Hotel Plaza Blvd.; Box 22205; Lake Buena Vista, FL 32830; 828-2424.

HOTEL ROYAL PLAZA: Offers 400 rooms in a 17-story high rise and two-story garden-style wings. Each room has its own balcony and safe deposit box. A comprehensive $5.5 million program of improvements was completed in 1984, giving a fresh, new look to guest rooms, dining rooms, and the lobby. In addition, two celebrity suites were created and named for stars Michael Jackson and Bob Hope. For on-site recreation, there's a pool, a Jacuzzi, a game room, shuffleboard courts near the pool, putting green, four tennis courts, and special children's programs.

Dining includes El Cid, specializing in continental cuisine, and the Knight's Table Coffee Shop. There are two lounges—La Cantina, serving shrimp, crab, and fresh oysters along with cocktails, and Giraffe, a popular spot that features top 40 live entertainment and attracts an energetic young local crowd (many of them Disney employees). A barbershop, beauty salon, and a one-day film-developing service are also available on the premises. "Superior" rooms on the hotel's lower floors run $95 per night; "premium" rooms with preferred views cost $110; "deluxe" rooms on the middle floors go for $122; and "preferred deluxe" poolside and tower rooms are $130. Room rates apply for up to five in a room using existing beds. Handicapped visitors should note that first-floor rooms have wider doors, however there are no grab rails in bathrooms. More information: Hotel Royal Plaza; 1905 Hotel Plaza Blvd.; Lake Buena Vista, FL 32830; 828-2828 (toll-free 800-327-2990; from Florida 800-432-2920).

HOWARD JOHNSON'S RESORT HOTEL: A handsome establishment with 323 rooms located in a 14-story tower and a 6-story annex building. Tower rooms surround a plant-filled atrium and are reached by glass-walled elevators. There are two swimming pools—plus a kiddie pool—and the hotel has its own game room. The Howard Johnson's Restaurant on the premises was enlarged and renovated in 1984 and it's open around the clock. Five special rooms are equipped with wider doors and grab rails for handicapped guests. Rates range from $80 to $100 year round (no additional charge for children under 18; $8 for cots). More information: Howard Johnson's Resort Hotel; Box 22204; Lake Buena Vista, FL 32830; 828-8888 (toll-free 800-654-2000).

BUENA VISTA PALACE: This is the largest of the Walt Disney World Hotel Plaza properties. It's actually a cluster of towers (one of them, at 27 stories, is the tallest in Central Florida) boasting mirrored, multi-faceted facades, and a contemporary interior. Every one of the 870 rooms (including suites) has its own private patio or balcony, ceiling fan, air-conditioning, and remote-control color TV. Most rooms and suites can glimpse Epcot Center's Spaceship Earth. Each has at least two telephones—one in the bathroom and a push-button Mickey Mouse telephone at bedside. Three guest rooms have hot tubs. There are two swimming pools, a kiddie pool, a health spa, four tennis courts, a huge game room, and a marina where mini speedboats, paddleboats, and other craft can be rented. The hotel also features 24-hour room service, Disney-run gift and sundry shops, and a self-service laundry. Aida Grey of Beverly Hills operates a fine beauty salon for men and women.

Eating spots include the Watercress Cafe, the hotel's water's-edge restaurant (open 24 hours); Arthur's 27, an elegant rooftop dining room offering an ambitious menu (reservations essential); and The Outback Restaurant, which is accessible via a glass-enclosed private elevator. The adjacent Laughing Kookaburra Lounge offers live entertainment and 99 brands of beer from around the world. Unfortunately, noise from these restaurants tends to flow through the atriums and penetrate the solid oak doors, so if serenity and silence matter to you, choose accommodations in either the 5-story tower or the 27-story tower, neither of which has an atrium. Rooms range from $98 to $150 per night (no charge for additional persons using existing beds). Six rooms are equipped for handicapped guests. More information: Buena Vista Palace; 1900 Buena Vista Dr.; Lake Buena Vista, FL 32830; 827-2727 (toll-free 800-327-2990; from Florida 800-432-2920).

THE HILTON: Located directly across the street from Walt Disney World Village, this is the newest Hotel Plaza property. It features a state-of-the-art digital telephone system that adjusts air-conditioning, controls the television set, and contacts the valet, room service, and operators with just the touch of a key. The 814 rooms are tastefully decorated in mauve, peach, and earth-tone color schemes. The hotel is set on 23 acres and features three restaurants and two lounges. The American Vineyards offers American regional cuisine; County Fair serves breakfast, lunch, and dinner; and the Pool Terrace Broiler and Bar offers light snacks, hamburgers, hot dogs, fresh fruits, and sandwiches. Recreational activities include two lighted tennis courts, a swimming pool, and a health club. Guests traveling with children will appreciate the Youth Hotel, a hotel-within-a-hotel that has been designed to accommodate children from 3 to 12 years of age while their parents are away from the Hilton. There are overnight facilities and a video room and play area, as well as scheduled recreational activities supervised by a trained staff. Rates range from $110 to $140, with the higher prices prevailing for rooms on the higher floors. More information: Hilton at Walt Disney World Village; Box 22781; 1751 Hotel Plaza Blvd.; Lake Buena Vista, FL 32830; 827-4000.

U.S.-192 ACCOMMODATIONS

The motels along this four-lane divided highway, which intersects I-4 in the community of Kissimmee, are closer to the WDW main gate than those along Orlando's International Drive, but the area itself is far less attractive and lacks International Drive's abundance of eating places. Still, the accommodations here can't be faulted for convenience, and on stays of short duration, that may be a consideration.

HOLIDAY INN-MAIN GATE EAST: Situated 2½ miles from the WDW main gate, this 512-room property is not the most attractive of the local inns, yet it can easily be counted among the best-looking in its price range—about $47 to $65, depending on the season, and the facilities are somewhat broader than those you usually get for that kind of money. For instance, there are two lighted tennis courts, and in a somewhat perfunctorily landscaped courtyard at the center of each of the squares where the 512 rooms are located, there are two Olympic-size swimming pools. A children's dinner theater (open to youngsters 4'10" and under) operates every evening; grown-ups can park kids there and eat elsewhere in peace if they desire. Drinks in the Mason Jar Buffet and at the pool bar are served in Mason jars that you can keep. A few rooms are equipped for handicapped travelers. Details: Holiday Inn-Main Gate East; 5678 E. Space Coast Pkwy.; Kissimmee, FL 32741; 396-4488 (toll-free 800-HOLIDAY).

HYATT ORLANDO: This hotel, the closest non-Disney-owned resort to the WDW main gate, is large, with some 950 rooms grouped in four clusters of buildings so complexly arranged that it takes many people a couple of days to find their way around. But it's one of the few hotels outside WDW that can even begin to compete with the Disney properties in terms of service, facilities, and amenities. The tastefully decorated rooms, with their sophisticated, subdued coloring and sleek modern furniture, are a cut above even Disney's. Each guest room has color TV, AM/FM radio, and in-room movie capacity, and there are three tennis courts and a 1.3 mile jogging-and-exercise trail right on the property. The game room here stands out, even in a town full of terrific competitors. Each of the four clusters has its own medium-size swimming pool and an innovative playground. There are also several restaurants—Limey Jim's, whose continental-style menu makes it some Orlando residents' favorite destination for a night on the town; the Big Bicycle Buffet, pleasant and informal, serving meals buffet-style; and Gatsby's, the multileveled, intriguingly designed coffee shop. The Bus Stop Deli serves snacks and light sandwiches from morning until late evening, and Limey Jim's Pub and Show Lounge has entertainment every night except Sunday. The gift shops may not excite you the way those in the Disney hotels can, but there are plenty of them. The hotel provides shuttle service to WDW for a minimal fee. Room rates are high—$67 to $87 per room, $175 to $340 for suites. Facilities for handicapped travelers are available. Details: Hyatt Orlando; 6375 Space Coast Pkwy.; Kissimmee, FL 32741; 396-1234 (toll-free 800-228-9000).

KING'S MOTEL: There are a handful of nonchain establishments on U.S. 192 as you head toward downtown Kissimmee and away from Walt Disney World. This 96-room establishment is among the better ones. Its small rectangular pool sits on the shore of a lake, and boats can be rented at the motel office (or you can fish from the dock). In addition to standard motel rooms, efficiencies accommodating four or six also are available. Many units have lake views. Rates are a reasonable $37 to $46. Handicapped travelers should note that while doors are wide enough for wheelchairs, bathrooms lack grab rails. Details: King's Motel; 4836 W. Space Coast Pkwy.; Kissimmee, FL 32741; 396-4762 (toll-free 800-327-9071; 800-432-9928 from Florida).

KNIGHTS INN: The royal purple, crushed-velvet bedspreads of this establishment (down the road from the Holiday Inn-Main Gate East) may take some getting used to, but this small hostelry offers an excellent choice of rooms—standard two double-bed ones; efficiency apartments (fitted out with a bed, a sofa bed, and a completely furnished kitchen); and two deluxe rooms (equipped with just one bed and a sofa). Both smoking and nonsmoking units are available in every style. The pool is small, but everything is on one story, and you can park right outside your door; it seldom happens that someone else parks in your space. Rates are about $42 to $46 for two (no charge for children under 18). All rooms are accessible to wheelchair travelers. Details: Knights Inn; 2800 Poinciana Blvd.; Kissimmee, FL 32741; 396-8186.

RAMADA RESORT KISSIMMEE: Attractive landscaping makes this 386-room establishment, just west of I-4, another very pleasant spot. There are two medium-size, heated swimming pools—rectangular to make for good lap swimming; plus a pair of lighted tennis courts; an excellent game room (with 30 electronic machines); and two restaurants—the elegant Mayan Restaurant and the Café Terrace, where breakfasts and family-style lunches and dinners are served daily. The Mayan Lounge has entertainment nightly except Sunday. Rates are about $50 to $80, depending on the season. The hotel has two rooms for the handicapped. Details: Ramada Resort Kissimmee; 2950 Reedy Creek Blvd.; Kissimmee, FL 32741; 396-4466 (toll-free 800-327-9127; 800-432-9195 from Florida).

DAYS LODGE–192 EAST: As a rule, establishments in this chain offer the best value for your lodging dollar in the WDW area, and this 615-room property is a good case in point. There are three swimming pools, and each unit is an apartment, complete with a bedroom, kitchen, and a living room with a sofa bed—ideal for a family that has had it with the togetherness of two double-bed rooms. The price for all this is only about $55 to $78, depending on the season—a very good buy indeed, especially after you consider the additional savings available from fixing some of your own meals. There are no special facilities for handicapped travelers. Details: Days Lodge; 5820 Space Coast Pkwy.; Kissimmee, FL 32741; 396-7900 (toll-free 800-327-9126).

SHERATON–LAKESIDE INN: One of a pair of fancy resorts on U.S. 192, the Sheraton-Lakeside, located west of I-4 (not far from the Ramada Resort Hotel), has 652 rooms arranged in several buildings around two good-size trapezoidal swimming pools and along the shores of Black Lake, where guests go paddle boating (though swimming is not permitted). Playgrounds are located poolside, and there are four tennis courts and a good miniature golf course as well. Restaurants include Max's Deli, which serves high-piled sandwiches to eat at lakeview tables; Sadie's Seafood Saloon, which offers fresh Florida fish and crustaceans; and the Cafe Lakeside, the hotel's main dining room. The cost, about $60 to $80 per couple (no charge for children under 17), is lower than at the Hyatt Orlando and the WDW hotels, and there are enough amenities to make this a fairly good deal. Wide doors and ramps make most of the hotel accessible to wheelchair-bound travelers. Details: Sheraton-Lakeside Inn; 7711 U.S. 192 West; Kissimmee, FL 32741; 828-8250 (toll-free 800-325-3535).

CAMPING OUTSIDE WALT DISNEY WORLD

The lush, cypress-hung woods of WDW's Fort Wilderness are not duplicated at any other Orlando-area campground. But not everyone can get a reservation at Fort Wilderness, and in any case, not everyone wants to spend the money. If you fall into one of these groups, consider some of the other local campgrounds. Most offer planned activities, swimming pools, hot showers, and other amenities.

JOHN FOWLER'S PORT O' CALL RV RESORT: This campground is big, with some 488 sites, and it has an expansive list of activities and facilities: fishing, shuffleboard, a playground, a game room, and a large swimming pool with a water slide built into the rocks, very much like the one at WDW's own Polynesian Village. And you can't beat the location, just five miles east of the main gates. But there's not much shade. Rates are about $18 for two adults and children under 12 the year round, $2 per additional adult per night, including all hookups. Tenters are welcome. Details: John Fowler's Port O' Call; 5195 U.S. 192; Kissimmee, FL 32741; 396-0110 (toll-free 800-327-9120, or 800-432-0766 from Florida).

ORANGE GROVE CAMPGROUND: Though not the biggest or fanciest of Orlando-area campgrounds, this one does boast plenty of shade—as much as the 700 citrus trees on the site can provide. There's also an oversized rectangular swimming pool, a game room, playground, horseshoe and shuffleboard courts, and, in winter, an activities program that includes bingo, movies, and crafts. There are 192 sites. Two people pay $13 (for sites with water and electric hookups) or $16 (for those with sewage hookups as well). There's an additional charge of $1 for each of the next three guests. Tenters are welcome. Located five miles east of WDW. Details: Orange Grove Campground; 2425 Old Vineland Rd.; Kissimmee, FL 32741; 396-6655.

YOGI BEAR'S JELLYSTONE PARK CAMPGROUNDS: There are three Yogi Bear campground locations in the WDW area: 8555 W. Space Coast Pkwy.; Kissimmee, FL 32741 (396-1311; 800-327-7115); 9200 Turkey Lake Rd.; Orlando, FL 32819 (351-4394; 800-327-7115); and Rte. 1, Box 2000; Apopka, FL 32703 (889-3048; 800-558-2954). The three sites offer similar facilities including a swimming pool, boating and fishing facilities, and a mini golf course. Rates range from about $13 for tenters to about $18 for full hookups.

FLORIDA CENTER ACCOMMODATIONS

This area, ten miles north of the WDW main gates—a 15-minute drive—is the best developed of the several areas where guests not staying in WDW-owned properties usually lodge. It comprises Sand Lake Road (S.R. 528A), which intersects I-4 (and runs eastward all the way to the airport); International Drive, the sidewalk-bordered boulevard that runs roughly northward off Sand Lake Road; and Kirkman Road (S.R. 435), which heads north off Sand Lake Road.

The densest concentration of lodging and eating places is on International Drive. Most of the best-known motel chains are represented here, and many restaurant chains also have branches: Arby's, Baskin Robbins, Burger King, Cork and Cleaver, Denny's, Dino's Pizza, International House of Pancakes, Long John Silver's, McDonald's, Perkins Cake and Steak, Pizza Inn, Pizza Hut, Steak and Ale, Wendy's, and Western Sizzlin' among them. Bennigan's, a somewhat tonier chain with a restaurant here, is known among some Disney employees for its particularly good "happy hours."

Most of these facilities on Sand Lake and Kirkman Roads are clustered close to their intersections with International Drive. The city's more interesting restaurants are too far away to reach on foot, however, and the cost of shuttle transportation for a family of four is so close to that of renting a car that it seems pointless not to do so.

It's also worth noting that the distance to the WDW main gates from here (you have to figure an hour from Main Street to your hotel swimming pool) is such that leaving the Magic Kingdom for a rest at your hotel—a good idea, especially in the heat of summer—is not always practical unless the park is open late and you can muster the energy to go early, stay for a few hours, and then return after dinner to savor the nighttime delights of the park for a few hours more. This takes stamina; young children may not always have it.

The area is, however, one of the livelier places to lodge outside WDW. Florida Center is also relatively accessible to downtown Orlando (ten to fifteen minutes' drive away), and Winter Park (about 20 minutes from parking space to parking space), where there are more than a dozen interesting little shops and nearly as many intriguing restaurants, including one of the most pleasant ice cream parlors around.

A selection of some of the more attractive properties (in a variety of price ranges) follows:

RAMADA COURT OF FLAGS: This lively, 820-room establishment in the Kirkman Road area of Florida Center has facilities for meetings of up to a thousand people, but the family trade wasn't forgotten either, and the place is as bright and cheery and appealing as any in the area, especially considering the price. Rooms are arranged in four 4-story buildings. There are three swimming pools—two small round ones and another that is shamrock-shaped (but large enough for swimming laps); and they all have plenty of palm trees and chairs. There are two tennis courts nearby that are lighted for night play. The somewhat secluded location, inside a complex of hotels where the roads are little used, off busy Kirkman Road, makes for good (if unshaded) jogging. The children's playground is nothing out of the ordinary. Doubles cost $43 to $66, depending on the location (no additional charge for children under 18; $9 per cot). This is a little more than the neighboring Caravan Resort Inn and considerably less than the Sheraton–Twin Towers complex nearby (which does a big convention business)—but a better choice than either. (The Howard Johnson's, the fourth in the Kirkman Road quartet, has some rooms that are less expensive than any offered at the Court of Flags, and if price is a prime consideration, it is your best bet.) Pet owners are permitted to bring animals inside, but only after paying a $50 deposit. Details: Ramada Court of Flags Hotel; 5715 Major Blvd.; Orlando, FL 32819; 351-3340 (toll-free 800-327-0721; from Florida, 800-432-1171).

DAYS INN-LAKESIDE: In all, there are seventeen Days Inns in the Orlando area, and they have played host to more WDW guests than any other chain because they provide especially good value for a traveler's lodging dollar. Facilities include swimming pools and sometimes game rooms; other economical attractions are a "kids eat free" plan where youngsters 12 and under dine free when accompanied by a registered adult guest. The 720-room complex on Sand Lake Road, one of the largest of the chain, is located on the shores of Spring Lake, and the view from many of the rooms is particularly attractive. There are three swimming pools here, plus laundry facilities, a playground, and a restaurant-and-cafeteria. Room rates are currently $39 from May through December, and vary only slightly the rest of the year ($5 extra per additional occupant under 18). Single rates, which cost $4 less, are even more economical. There are no special facilities for the handicapped. Details: Days Inn; 7335 Sand Lake Rd.; Orlando, FL 32819; 351-1900 (toll-free 800-325-2525).

HILTON INN FLORIDA CENTER: Comparable to the Marriott (described below), this 400-room establishment has a restaurant and a deli, two large swimming pools (one of them Olympic-size and under an open-air pavilion), a well-kept (but hardly huge) game room with about a dozen machines, and a large convention center. This means a certain amount of hubbub that may not appeal to all family vacationers, but the hotel itself is quite pleasant.

Rates are $55 to $89 during busy seasons; off-season rates are $45 to $79. No charge for up to three children, regardless of age, sharing accommodations with parents. Cribs and rollaway beds are free, and an entire section of the hotel was designed with handicapped travelers in mind. Details: Hilton Inn Florida Center; 7400 International Dr.; Orlando, FL 32819; 351-4600 (toll-free 800-327-1363; from Florida, 800-332-4600).

HOLIDAY INN-INTERNATIONAL DRIVE: This 650-room property's 13 tropically landscaped acres are occupied by six buildings—a 14-story tower, a 5-story annex, and four other buildings two stories high. There is a free-form pool (with a water slide and a landscaped island in the center), a playground, an excellent game room that looks appropriately Space Age, and shuffleboard and volleyball courts. There are two restaurants—Gomba Joe's, which serves Italian and American specialties every evening, and the Pipers Restaurant, one of the handsomest of area coffee shops, with its blond-wood Windsor chairs and glassed-in alcove overlooking the swimming pool. Twelve special rooms for the handicapped are available. Every room has a digital clock-radio, a smoke detector, and a color television set wired to receive Home Box Office. Rates for doubles in the hotel are about $60 to $75 (no charge for children 18 and under; rollaways $6). Details: Holiday Inn-International Drive; 6515 International Dr.; Orlando, FL 32819; 351-3500 (toll-free 800-465-4329).

COMFORT INN: The rates—about $26 to $36 for doubles, depending on the season (with no charge for children under 17 sharing their parents' quarters)—are low enough that you wouldn't expect fancy accommodations, but the establishment is quite pleasant and well-kept. The 160 rooms are arranged in four 2-story wings that wrap around a small (but tidy) pool. Entrances to the rooms are in hallways inside; there's no at-door parking. Ground-floor rooms are suitable for handicapped travelers. Denny's Restaurant, open around the clock, is next door. Details: Comfort Inn; 5825 International Dr.; Orlando, FL 32809; 351-4100 (toll-free 800-327-1367).

ORLANDO MARRIOTT INN: Located at the corner of Sand Lake Road and International Drive, near the exit to I-4, this is one of the choicest of the lodging spots outside the World. It's not cheap—the appeal is primarily to businessmen and vacationers willing to pay for WDW-level accommodations but unable to get a reservation—though there is value here. The Marriott has three outdoor pools—one quite large and dogleg-shaped, another barbell-shaped and relatively small, and the third Olympic-size—near the four lighted tennis courts. The 1,079 smartly decorated guest rooms are arranged in some 16 2-story, cream-colored, stucco-walled "villas" scattered around grounds that are handsomely landscaped with ferns, palms, and all manner of other tropical vegetation. (You'll even find some lagoons, canals, and waterfalls.) Rooms can be opened up to form spacious quarters with one or two bedrooms, living room (or third bedroom), two or three baths, and a full apartment-size kitchen. Rates are $80 to $90 in high season, about $10 less the rest of the year. Two rooms for the handicapped are available. Details: Orlando Marriott Inn; 8001 International Dr.; Orlando, FL 32819; 351-2420 (toll-free 800-228-9290).

QUALITY INN INTERNATIONAL: Adjoining Morrison's Cafeteria, this 729-room property is extremely pleasant, if not fancy. Quite well-kept rooms are in two-story structures flanking the reception building, with the newest rooms located in two 6-story additions. Two Y-shaped pools are perfect for a few laps. And there's also a game room. The Family Restaurant is ornamented with pretty antiques. There's good value here: rates are about $36 to $45 for two during the summer and over the Christmas holidays, $29 to $39 from September until mid-December, with no extra charge for children under 17 occupying the same room as their parents. Some facilities for the handicapped are available. Details: Quality Inn International; 7600 International Dr.; Orlando, FL 32819; 351-1600 (toll-free 800-228-5151).

SHERATON WORLD: Particularly attractive and situated off to itself, well south of Sand Lake Road, just a stroll from Sea World, this 807-room establishment has three good-size swimming pools, three game rooms, five lighted tennis courts, and a miniature golf course. The surrounding area is undeveloped and is ideal for early-morning jogging. Several rooms are suitable for the handicapped. Rates are particularly reasonable: $64 to $89 (no charge for youngsters under 18 when accompanied by an adult). Details: Sheraton World; 10100 International Dr.; Orlando, FL 32809; 352-1100 (toll-free 800-325-3535).

MISCELLANEOUS

The following establishments are located outside the U.S. 192 and Florida Center/International Drive areas. Each of the ten has appealing features that make it stand out among Orlando-area hostelries.

HARLEY HOTEL OF ORLANDO: Lodging in downtown Orlando puts vacationers close to some of the more interesting local restaurants, and the Harley—one of the best among the Greater Orlando–area hotels—is the establishment of choice. You're only a few minutes' drive from Winter Park—a fact best appreciated when, at the end of a long day of sight-seeing, you can have a late meal there. And you're only a couple of minutes from Rosie O'Grady's, a lively Orlando night spot. On the other hand, you are not quite as close to the Magic Kingdom. But driving the 17 miles or so to the WDW main gate early in the day is not difficult. Adults traveling without children will especially enjoy the atmosphere at this hotel, which is one of the few in the Orlando area that doesn't cater primarily to a family crowd. The Cafe on the Park, the hotel's restaurant, is lovely, with its rosy salmon-pink color scheme and its fine view out over Lake Eola and the municipal fountain at its center. The hotel's swimming pool, which shares the view, is also an especially relaxing place to be. And the guest rooms' handsome decor warrants special mention. Rates are $58 to $98. Some rooms are equipped for handicapped travelers. Details: Harley Hotel of Orlando; 151 E. Washington St.; Orlando, FL 32801; 841-3220 (toll-free 800-321-2323).

BEST WESTERN WORLD INN: Located on the edge of WDW's 27,400 acres, next to the Orange Vista Hospital, this pleasant 245-room stopping place is a good bet among off-property establishments. Though slightly farther from the WDW main gate than some of the U.S. 192 lodging places, the World Inn is still quite close, and it's only a couple of minutes' drive from Walt Disney World Shopping Village and all of its excellent restaurants (described at length in *Good Meals, Great Times*). There's a fine rectangular swimming pool (good for laps) and a kid's pool; and the peaceful country roads nearby, not to mention the WDW roads around the Shopping Village and the WDW Village villas, are fine for jogging. Free shuttle buses make round trips to WDW's Transportation and Ticket Center two or three times daily. The hotel's lounge has nightly entertainment and a "happy hour" that attracts many Disney employees. Doubles cost from $55 to $70, depending on the season (with no additional charge for children under 17). The hotel has no special facilities for the handicapped. Details: Best Western World Inn; I-4 and Rte. 535; Box 22095; Lake Buena Vista, FL 32830; 239-4646 (toll-free 800-327-6954; 800-432-0769 from Florida).

GRENELEFE GOLF AND TENNIS RESORT: Located some 22 miles from the WDW main gate, this 950-acre resort—a fine destination in its own right with its three 18-hole golf courses, its 13 tennis courts, golf and tennis instruction programs, its lakefront marina, beach, pools, saunas, Jacuzzis, and 1.6-mile-long fitness course—is primarily of interest to those who want to add a visit to the Magic Kingdom to the beginning or end of a vacation in a country club–like atmosphere that is less oriented to the family trade than WDW's own resorts—not to mention lots less frenetic. The 900-odd rooms here are located in clusters of buildings scattered along winding drives next to the fairways of the golf courses; some are like standard hotel rooms, with one or two double beds, while one- and two-bedroom parlor suites with fully equipped kitchens are also available. The program of golf instruction, the Andy Bean Golf Studio, is particularly interesting: private,

ORLANDO RESERVATIONS

The Orlando Central Reservations Center can make finding accommodations in the area easier for travelers. Orlando Central represents from 20 to 25 hotels in various price ranges. For information and reservations, call 800-322-2220; 800-235-2220 in Florida.

ACCOMMODATIONS

semi-private, group, and playing lessons that use videotape recordings, as well as private lessons without video, are offered. There are three restaurants and three lounges. Cost is $75 for hotel rooms, $105 for suites with one bedroom, $180 for those with two bedrooms; during the summer season, prices are a bit lower. Grenelefe is a real bargain for WDW visitors in summer. Details: Grenelefe Golf and Tennis Resort; Grenelefe, FL 33844; 813-422-7511 (toll-free 800-237-9549; from Florida, 800-282-7875).

ORLANDO VACATION RESORT: Occupying 85 acres on U.S. 27 just over a mile from its intersection with U.S. 192 and close to eight miles from the WDW main gate, this 230-room establishment designed for active families stands out for its variety of recreational offerings, the most striking of which is tennis on the 17 courts. But the low rates ($42 in low season, $48 in high season; no additional charge for children under 17) also merit mention, especially since they include shuttle service (operated one or two times a day) to WDW's main gate. The resort's Misty Harbor Restaurant, designed around a New England theme, serves fine dinners; another eatery, the Greenhouse, is available for breakfast and lunch. There are minimal facilities for handicapped travelers. Details: Orlando Vacation Resort; Box 2527; Orlando, FL 32802; 656-8181 (toll-free 800-874-9064 from outside Florida).

PARK PLAZA: Orlando's closest approximation of a cozy country inn occupies a prominent location on Park Avenue in Winter Park. The guest rooms don't quite measure up to the lobby, but with their thick carpet, subdued color scheme, and polished wooden moldings, they're attractive enough—particularly the two-room suite ($90 nightly), with its sitting area and balcony. Smaller rooms, more suitable for one, could be cramped for two; they're available with courtyard or parkside views at $60 to $80 nightly. Continental breakfast in your room is included in the rates. No children under five are permitted—but this is not basically set up for families because of the size of the rooms and bathrooms. (Nor is the hotel set up for handicapped travelers.) The distance from Walt Disney World, a half-hour's drive or so, makes it a good choice only for those who don't plan to spend a great deal of time in the World. Details: Park Plaza; 307 Park Ave. S.; Winter Park, FL 32789; 647-1072.

LANGFORD RESORT HOTEL: This esteemed 220-room hotel is set on its own tree-shaded grounds, just off the beaten path in the ritzy community of Winter Park. The Park Avenue shopping district is a block away, but the hubbub of commerce (what little hubbub is allowed in the exclusive shops there) never reaches the guests at Langford—even those lounging by the side of the Olympic-size pool. A recent addition here is the health spa. It has two dining rooms, the Anchor Room and the Empire Room Supper Club; the latter has a show every night (except Sunday) that includes plenty of opportunities for ballroom dancing. Rates are $50 to $55 a night for a single; $60 to $70 for a double. Details: Langford Resort Hotel; 300 E. New England Ave.; Winter Park, FL 32789; 644-3400.

WYNDHAM HOTEL AT SEA WORLD: This $86 million hotel located directly across the street from Sea World was scheduled to open just as we went to press. It was expected to offer 782 guest rooms and has been designed as a convention facility with a 17,600-sq.-ft. main ballroom, a smaller ballroom, and 23 other convention and meeting rooms. Each guest room will have individual climate controls, color TV, radio, telephone, and either two double beds or one king-size bed. The rooms are built around a 60,000-sq.-ft. atrium and will be reached by six glass-enclosed elevators. There will be three restaurants (a continental dining spot, a cafeteria, and an outdoor café), and recreational facilities include a swimming pool, five lighted tennis courts, and a health club. Rates will be $95 to $140. Details: Wyndham Hotel at Sea World; 6677 Sea Harbor Dr.; Orlando, FL 32821; 351-6695 (toll-free 800-331-6600).

ORLANDO PLAZA: The city's first all-suite hotel, slated to open in October 1984, is located near the Convention Center and features a seven-story atrium with a waterfall and piano lounge below. Each of the 246 suites includes a bedroom, living room, dressing area, bathroom, and wet bar. Guests will also receive a complimentary deluxe buffet breakfast. Recreational facilities include an indoor/outdoor pool, whirlpool, steam room, sauna, and an exercise center. Rates are $85 to $95. Details: Orlando Plaza; 8250 Jamaican Court; Orlando, FL 32819; 325-8250 (toll-free 800-327-9797).

HYATT REGENCY GRAND CYPRESS: The new Florida flagship property of the Hyatt chain, this $110 million hotel is the centerpiece of a 730-acre resort. Directly adjacent to the Lake Buena Vista area and just three miles from Epcot Center, the 18-story building is T-shaped with three wings of guest rooms

---

SHORT-TERM RENTALS

Apartment, condominium, and bed-and-breakfast accommodations can be arranged locally. For a list of availabilities, write Tourism Development; Orlando Area Chamber of Commerce; Box 1234; Orlando, FL 32802; 425-1234.

off the 200-foot atrium lobby. There are 750 rooms (75 are suites) and each has air-conditioning, a ceiling fan, color television, and one king-size or two double beds. Three of the suites are multilevel and include a sleeping loft, bar, grand piano, and private spa with sauna or Jacuzzi. The 11th floor has been designated the Regency Club, and guests receive a complimentary breakfast buffet and the convenience of a concierge. (There are also three concierges in the lobby for other hotel guests.) There's a half-acre, free-form swimming pool with 12 waterfalls and a 45-foot water slide. (Most of the pool is not heated, however, so be sure to test the water before diving in.) The 21-acre lake is a perfect place to try out one of the sailboats, windsurfers, canoes, or paddleboats available for rent. The tennis complex features 10 courts, and there are racquetball, shuffleboard, and volleyball courts as well. There are also a children's playground, walking and jogging trails, and a health club. The 18-hole, Jack Nicklaus–designed golf course stands out among the facilities. The superb 7,054-yard, par-72 course features two Scottish-style shared greens, grassy dunes, and elevated tees. The course is currently open to hotel guests only, and the green fee for a round will set you back $50.

The hotel has three restaurants and three lounges, plus a poolside bar. Cascade, the main dining room, serves breakfast, lunch, and dinner; Hemingway's offers a touch of Key West, specializing in seafood; and La Coquina is the more formal dining spot. There are also extensive meeting and convention facilities. Ten guest rooms are designed for handicapped travelers. Rates range from $105 to $145; suites begin at $200. Details: Hyatt Regency Grand Cypress; One Grand Cypress Blvd.; Box 22156; Orlando, FL 32830; 239-1234 (toll-free 800-228-9000).

SONESTA VILLAGE HOTEL: Something a little different in the Orlando area, this complex features 170 one- and two-bedroom villas (another 500 units are expected to be built during the next two years). Each beautifully decorated villa features a living room, dining room, two bathrooms, and a fully equipped kitchen. The complex is set on 97 acres facing 300-acre Sand Lake. The hotel currently offers two tennis courts, four whirlpools, a swimming pool, health club, and golf privileges at nearby courses (Cypress Creek and the three WDW courses). The hotel expects to feature a restaurant, general store, gift shop, and meeting space early in 1985. There's full maid service daily and complimentary transportation to The Marketplace, a shopping center with a grocery store, specialty shops, and restaurants. Rates for a one-bedroom villa are $90; two-bedroom units are $120. Details: Sonesta Village Hotel; 10000 Turkey Lake Rd.; Orlando, FL 32819; 352-8051 (toll-free 800-343-7170).

DAYS INNS

The locations of the seventeen members of this economical chain in the Orlando/WDW area are as follows: 12799 Apopka-Vineland Rd.; Lake Buena Vista 32830 (239-4441); 7980 Space Coast Pkwy., Kissimmee 32741 (396-1000); 5840 Space Coast Pkwy., Kissimmee 32741 (396-7969); 5820 Space Coast Pkwy., Kissimmee 32741 (396-7900); 2095 E. Space Coast Pkwy., Kissimmee 32741 (846-7136); 7200 Sand Lake Rd., Orlando 32819 (351-1900); 7200 International Dr., Orlando 32809 (351-1200); 9990 International Dr., Orlando 32811 (352-8700); 1221 W. Landstreet Rd., Orlando 32809 (859-7700); 2323 McCoy Rd., Orlando 32809 (859-6100); 2500 W. 33rd St., Orlando 32809 (841-3731); 1600 W. 33rd St., Orlando 32809 (423-7646); 720 S. Orange Blossom Trail, Orlando 32805 (843-3410); 650 Lee Rd., Orlando 32810 (628-2727); 235 S. Wymore Rd., Orlando 32701 (862-2800); 450 Douglas Ave., Altamonte Springs 32701 (862-7111); and I-4 & S.R. 46, Sanford 32771 (323-6500). For reservations, call toll-free 800-325-2525.

THE MAGIC KINGDOM

73 Lay of the Lands
91 Shopping
98 Entertainment
102 Special Tips

Though occupying just 98 acres of Walt Disney World's 27,400 total acres, the Magic Kingdom is a very special part of the World. Few who have traveled the four miles from the main highway to see it are disappointed, and even the most blasé travelers manage a smile. Every day is like a great fair. The sight of the soaring spires of Cinderella Castle, the gleaming woodwork of the Main Street shops, the tiny white lights that edge their rooflines after dark, and the crescendo of music that follows the parades never fail to have their effect. Even when the crowds are thick and the weather is at its warmest, a visitor who has toured this wonderland dozens of times still can look around and think once again how satisfying this place is for the spirit.

The delight that most guests experience on first sight of the Magic Kingdom can quickly disappear when disorientation sets in, however. There are so many nooks and crannies, so many bends to every pathway, and so many sights and sounds clamoring for attention—not to mention over 45 attractions and adventures and the dozens of shops and restaurants—that it's too easy to wander aimlessly and miss the best that the Magic Kingdom has to offer. So we earnestly suggest that you peruse this chapter carefully before you make your own visit.

At the same time, it's also interesting to learn a little about how the Magic Kingdom works. This wonderland started out as little more than swampland. When the Seven Seas Lagoon was dredged, the leftover soil was used to build up the level of the Magic Kingdom site, to provide proper drainage, to supply dry land on which to plant trees and flowers, and to accommodate a vast subterranean system of rooms and hallways where the magic of the Magic Kingdom is manufactured. One vast room of the underground warren is given over solely to computers, used in everything from food planning to the timing of the presidents' nods in Liberty Square's Hall of Presidents. Another area houses a photo library and darkrooms. Yet another whole network of rooms houses the world's largest working wardrobe, where the thousands of costumes worn by the young Magic Kingdom hosts and hostesses hang on dozens and dozens of racks. The place looks like the world's gaudiest department store. Another room is given over solely to the wig department. And that's only the beginning.

Every land has a theme, which is carried through from the hosts' and hostesses' costumes to the food served in the restaurants, the merchandise in the shops, and even the design of the trash bins. Thousands of details contribute to the effects; paying attention to these small touches makes any visit more enjoyable.

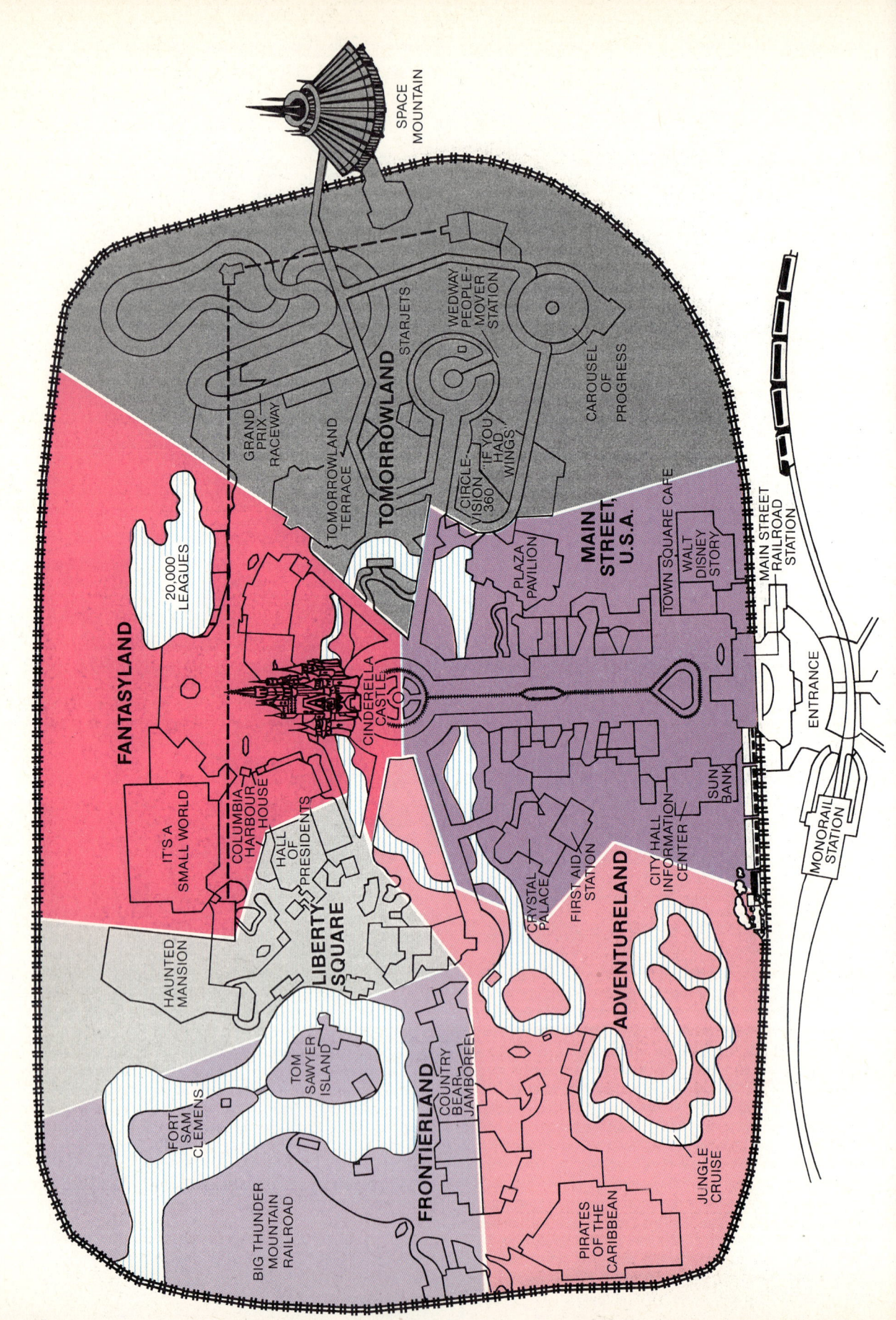

HOW TO GET TO THE MAGIC KINGDOM

From the Contemporary Resort Hotel or the Polynesian Village: The monorail is the easiest way to go.

From the Golf Resort: Take the green-flagged bus in front of the hotel to the Polynesian Village, walk through the lobby to the second floor, and then out to the monorail boarding area.

From Epcot Center: Take the monorail or the red-flagged bus to the TTC, then there's another monorail or a ferry.

From Walt Disney World Village: Guests at the resort villas can take green-and-gold-flagged buses labeled "MK" from bus stops located at frequent intervals throughout the villa area to the TTC, then the monorail or ferry. Guests coming from the Shopping Village take the red-flagged bus to the TTC, then the monorail or ferry.

From Fort Wilderness: Blue-flagged buses make the trip from the campground to the TTC; depending on the location of your campsite, it may be easier to take one of the green-flagged boats that call at the dock.

From the hotels at Walt Disney World Village Hotel Plaza: Take the red-and-white-flagged buses that stop at the front door of your hotel. Because WDW's private roads are off limits to all but guests at WDW-owned establishments, guests who are staying at one of the six Hotel Plaza properties and who want to drive must go out onto I-4, drive 4½ miles west, then enter the park via the Toll Plaza along with other day visitors; this can mean grappling with traffic (see "When to Arrive," below), so in most cases it's more efficient to take the bus—even though it may mean a wait at both ends.

From Orlando or Kissimmee: Follow the signs for Walt Disney World on I-4, take the U.S. 192 west turnoff, and proceed to the Toll Plaza. Go straight ahead and then turn left into the parking lots. Gray Line and Rabbit shuttle buses serve most hotels, but the per-person charges are so high relative to the low local car rental rates that it makes sense to drive. Some hotels have free shuttle service to WDW.

GETTING IN: One of Walt Disney's greatest disappointments was the fact that the citrus groves that originally rimmed the Disneyland site in Anaheim, California, soon gave way to unsightly commercial development. Finally, only the berm rimming the park protected it from surrounding eyesores. When planning Walt Disney World, he pledged to prevent a repeat of that situation, and set the Magic Kingdom some four miles from the nearest interstate highway.

From the Disney World exit off highway I-4, it's four miles to the Toll Plaza; from there, it's under a mile to the main entrance complex known as the Transportation and Ticket Center (TTC). Even then, the Magic Kingdom visitors have not completed their journey: there remains a five-minute ride by ferry across manmade Seven Seas Lagoon, or a slightly shorter trip by monorail around its shore. Each section of the trip—the drive from the I-4 exit to the Toll Plaza and then to the parking lot, then the lake crossing—serves to heighten the suspense, and by removing guests from the workaday world, to prepare them for the visual delights that follow.

TRANSPORTATION COSTS: Parking in the Magic Kingdom lots costs $1 (free to guests at WDW-owned resorts, upon presentation of their IDs). Most WDW buses provide transportation to most visitors at no extra charge. Gold-, green-, and blue-flagged buses are courtesy vehicles. To ride the red-and-white-flagged bus between Walt Disney World Village Hotel Plaza and the Transportation and Ticket Center, and to board the red-flagged bus between Walt Disney World Shopping Village and the Transportation and Ticket Center, it is necessary to show an ID card from a Hotel Plaza establishment or a WDW-owned property; all multi-day World Passports will also get you onto the buses. (For details on the bus and monorail system, see *Transportation and Accommodations*.)

WHEN TO ARRIVE: Especially during the busy summer and holiday seasons—when the highways leading to the Toll Plaza can look like a Los Angeles freeway during rush hour, and when there are long queues at WDW monorails and ferries—it's advisable to plan on reaching the park by 7:30 or 8 A.M. Eat breakfast at your hotel, if you will—or wait and eat inside the park. Or if this just seems too early, wait until later—about 1 P.M.—or even later than that during the seasons when the park is open late. During less congested periods, when the park closes at 7 P.M., plan to arrive around 10 A.M.

PARKING: After passing through the Toll Plaza, drive straight ahead and bear left for the parking lots. Parking attendants will direct you to a spot in one of a dozen areas. Each lot is named for a Disney character—Daisy, Donald, Sneezy, Bashful, Grumpy, Happy, Goofy, Pluto, Chip & Dale, Minnie, Sleepy, and Dopey. Minnie, Sleepy, and Dopey are within walking distance of the Transportation and Ticket Center

(TTC); other lots are served continuously by tractor-drawn trams that make periodic stops to pick up and discharge passengers.

When leaving your car, note the name of your section and your aisle number; there is a spot for noting this information on the back of your parking ticket. Roll up all windows and lock all doors. Also, do not leave your pet in the car! The Walt Disney World Kennel Club—which is air-conditioned, far more comfortable for the animal, and far safer for him—is conveniently located right at the TTC.

Guests who leave the park at midday for their hotels should keep their parking tickets; the tickets are good for reentry to the parking area throughout the day.

FERRY VS. MONORAIL: Once you've bought your admission ticket or Passport and made your way through the TTC turnstiles, it's necessary to decide whether to travel to the Magic Kingdom by ferry or by monorail.

The monorails make the trip in a bit less than the five minutes required by the ferries—but the latter often will get you there more quickly in the busier season, because long lines can form at the monorails; most people just simply don't make the short extra walk to the ferry landing. When there's no line for the monorail, it's your best choice.

Wheelchair vacationers should note that while the monorails are accessible, the ramp leading to the boarding area is a bit steep.

Guests staying at the Golf Resort may take a bus to the Polynesian Village, where they can join guests from that resort and from the Contemporary Resort Hotel on the monorail, which links the two hotels directly to the Magic Kingdom.

ADMISSION MEDIA: A one-day ticket provides admission to the Magic Kingdom, plus unlimited access to all its rides, shows, and attractions. (If you want to spend a second day inside the Magic Kingdom, simply buy another one-day ticket.)

Three-, four-, and five-day World Passports are also available. These allow you not only admission to the Magic Kingdom and unlimited use of all the rides, shows, and attractions there, but also admission to Epcot Center, unlimited use of the attractions there, and unlimited use of the transportation system inside Walt Disney World.

Those who last visited WDW when the old system of coupons and general admission tickets (now completely phased out) was in effect may redeem up to $5 of unused ride coupons at special ticket exchange booths at the Transportation and Ticket Center (TTC); the value of those coupons turned in can be applied to the cost of a new ticket or Passport. Check at City Hall on Main Street for further information.

Passports may be purchased at the TTC and at many local resorts and hotels, including WDW-owned establishments.

World Passports by mail: Send a check or money order in the exact amount to:

Admissions; Walt Disney World;
Box 40; Lake Buena Vista, FL 32830

Remember to include your return address. Allow at least 15 *working* days for ticket requests to be processed.

Buying World Passports at the airport: Admission media may also be purchased at the guest services counter of "Walt Disney World On Parade" at Orlando International Airport.

Guided tours: Four-hour guided walking tours of the Magic Kingdom are available. These include the services of a guide and admission to attractions during your tour of all "lands" in the Magic Kingdom. These tours are terrific for first-time visitors, especially those without a great sense of direction, and the cost is quite reasonable ($4 for adults and $2 for children in addition to price of admission media). For details, call Guest Relations (at 824-4633), or inquire at the Transportation and Ticket Center.

MONEY MATTERS: WDW resort guests who buy their Passports at WDW resorts may charge them to their rooms by using their resort IDs. At the TTC, cash, traveler's checks, personal checks, or American Express cards are accepted as payment for all admission media; personal checks must be imprinted with your name and address and must be accompanied by a driver's license and a major credit card (that is, American Express, Visa, MasterCard, Diners Club, or Carte Blanche).

At sit-down restaurants and for merchandise: American Express and MasterCard are accepted, as are cash and traveler's checks. WDW resort identification cards are not accepted as payment for food and merchandise purchases inside the Magic Kingdom.

At fast-food restaurants: No credit cards are accepted at fast-food eating spots. You must pay cash; traveler's checks are also accepted.

ADMISSION PRICES

A Guests at WDW-Owned Resorts/Villas and WDW Village Hotel Plaza
B Other Guests

	A	B
ONE-DAY TICKET		
Adult	$18	$18
Child*	$15	$15
THREE-DAY WORLD PASSPORT		
Adult	$41	$42
Child*	$33	$34
FOUR-DAY WORLD PASSPORT		
Adult	$50	$52
Child*	$40	$42
FIVE-DAY WORLD PASSPORT		
Adult	$59	$62
Child*	$47	$50

The cost of a **ONE-YEAR WORLD PASSPORT** is $125 for adults and $100 for children.

*3 through 12 years of age

Prices subject to change

THE LAY OF THE LANDS

Not long ago, one Magic Kingdom visitor spent an entire day in Tomorrowland—thinking it was the full extent of the place. To avoid having a similar experience, it's essential to understand the lay of all the lands *before* you arrive on Main Street.

There are six sections, or "lands," in the Magic Kingdom—Main Street, U.S.A.; Adventureland; Frontierland; Liberty Square; Fantasyland; and Tomorrowland. The monorail stations and ferry docks at which all guests arrive are just outside the Magic Kingdom gates; just inside them is Town Square, at the head of Main Street, which runs straight to Cinderella Castle. The area in front of the Castle is known as the Central Plaza, or, more aptly, the Hub. It is surrounded by small canals, the Hub Waterways, which are crossed by bridges to enter each of the lands. The first bridge to your left goes to Adventureland; the next, to Liberty Square and Frontierland. On your right, the first bridge heads to Tomorrowland, the second to Fantasyland. The end points of the avenues leading to the lands are linked by a roadway that is roughly circular, so that the layout of the Magic Kingdom resembles a wheel. All of the attractions, restaurants, and shops are arranged in various buildings along the rim of the wheel and along its spokes.

In theory, it couldn't be simpler; in practice, it's all too easy to get confused because of the many bends and curves in the pathways, the many entrances to each shop and restaurant, and the somewhat angular placement and architecture of many of the buildings. But if you keep mental notes of your own route, losing your bearings becomes fairly difficult. If you still manage to get confused, however, any park employee can help set you straight—and there are information booths prominently located in each land.

A note on north, south, east, and west: when you stand at the Magic Kingdom entrance and face Cinderella Castle, you're looking north. Main Street is straight ahead, with Fantasyland beyond the Castle. Adventureland, Liberty Square, and Frontierland are to the west (your left). Tomorrowland flanks the Hub on the east.

MAIN STREET, U.S.A.

This is the Disney version of turn-of-the-century small-town Main Streets all over the country—freshly painted, full of curlicued gingerbread moldings and pretty details and, with its baskets of hanging plants and genuine-looking gaslights, a showplace both in the bright light of high noon and after nightfall, when the tiny lights edging all the rooflines are flicked on.

What's particularly amazing is that all the variety of furbelows and frills that a real Main Street would have enjoyed as a result of normal growth have been assimilated into the Disney version. Most of the structures along the thoroughfare are given over to shops, and each one is different, from the wallpaper and layout of displays to the flooring material, the style of chandeliers, and even the lighting level. Some emporiums are big and bustling, others are relatively quiet and orderly; some are spacious and airy, others are cozy and dark. Floors are made of black-and-white tile, or of wide-oak planks set in with wooden pegs; some are covered with Victorian-patterned carpet. Where wallpapers are used, they are striped, or gaudily flowered; in contrast, some walls are paneled in subdued mahogany or oak. In one shop, you find a potbellied stove; others boast slowly turning ceiling fans. The effect is far more sophisticated than first-time visitors probably would have imagined, and it doesn't really matter that some of the "wood" is fiberglass.

Inside and outside, maintenance and housekeeping are superb. White-suited sanitation men patrol the street to pick up litter and quickly shovel up any droppings from the horses who pull the trolley cars from Town Square to the Hub. The pavement, like all in the Magic Kingdom, is washed down every night with fire hoses. There's one crew of maintenance men whose sole job is to change the little white lights around the roofs; another crew devotes itself to keeping the woodwork painted. As soon as these men have worked their way as far as the Hub, they start all over again at Town Square. Epoxy, acrylic, and more ordinary varieties of paints are used, depending on the area to be painted. The greenish, horse-shaped, cast-iron hitching posts are repainted 20 times a year on the average—and totally scraped down each time. It's no wonder the painters who visit here marvel at the quality of work they see.

Visitors from outside the United States find all these details so fascinating that it takes them a good deal longer than the 40 minutes spent by the average guest to get from one end of Main Street to the other. There are only four real "attractions" along Main Street, and they are relatively minor compared to the really big deals such as Tomorrowland's Space Mountain and Frontierland's Big Thunder Mountain Railroad. But each and every shop has its own quota of merchandise that is meant as much for fun and show as for sale—the monster masks at the House of Magic, for instance, or the large Hummel figurine at Cup'n Saucer. It's also entertaining to stand and just watch the candlemakers at the Wonderland of Wax; the magicians at the House of Magic; the cake-decorators turning frosting into roses at the Sara Lee Bakery; and the cooks stirring up batches of peanut brittle at the Confectionery. The windows at the Emporium and the Mickey tableaux in the Christmas Shop and the House of Magic are also musts.

While walking along the street, note the names on the second-story windows. Above Crystal Arts, you can see the names of Roy Disney, Walt's brother, and Patty Disney; above the Shadow Box, those of Ron Miller, who married Walt's daughter Diane and is now president of Walt Disney Productions, and Dick Nunis, who heads Outdoor Recreation (the company's theme parks division). Above the House of Magic are the names of Ted Crowell, WDW's vice-president of facilities, who, among other things, is responsible for maintenance and for the World's own electric generating plants, and John de Cuir, the Disney artist in charge of the production of the paintings filmed for the Hall of Presidents show. Card Walker, the "practitioner of Psychiatry and Justice of the Peace" mentioned nearby, is the company's Chairman of the Executive Committee. Other names, as well as those on signs elsewhere in the Magic Kingdom, are also those of real people connected with the company.

Finally, some advice. Before heading toward the Castle, stop at City Hall and inquire about the times and places that live entertainments are scheduled to take place all around the park that day and night. Also, do your shopping in the early afternoon, rather than at day's end when the shops are jammed; purchases can be stored in lockers under the Walt Disney World Railroad's depot, or, in the case of very large items, behind the desk at City Hall.

PENNY ARCADE: Scarcely a motel in Orlando lacks its blipping, bleeping, squeaking room full of electronic games; the one at the Contemporary Resort ranks among the largest in the country. The Magic Kingdom also has its games room—but here on Victorian Main Street, in addition to the modern machines, there are authentic old-time games—a Kiss-O-Meter, tests of strength, and an antique football game.

In addition, in the center of the front section of the arcade, there are a number of machines that show very early "moving pictures"—that is, stacks of cards on a roller that can be turned to flip the cards and thereby "animate" the images they contain. There are two types of viewing devices—Mute-o-scopes, first introduced around 1900, whose rollers must be turned by hand, and Cail-o-scopes, developed about a decade later. These are turned automatically. Both of these are worth your while. Most stories here are comedies; the humor is broad and slapstick—good for at least a smile (if not a roar) and as amusing comments on the changing ideas about what tickles a funny bone. On the Cail-o-scopes, you can see such stories as *Yes, We Have No Bananas*, in which a suitor slips on a banana peel and is ridiculed; *Tough Competition*, in which sailors come to blows over a pretty girl; *Texas Rangers*, where the good guy lassoes the robber; and *Run Out of Town*, in which one unfortunate man has paint dumped on him, falls into a manhole, is knocked over by a car, sits on a freshly painted bench, and knocks over a paint bucket—all in a single day. During *A Raid On A Watermelon Patch*, two fellows do and are discovered. *Oh Teacher* concerns the antics of a teacher's pest. *Brigitte On A Bike* shows a real sourpuss taking a tumble; it might be subtitled, "Or The Trials of Riding In A Long Skirt." Particularly interesting is

Captain Kidd's Treasure, in which a pirate lass shows knees, bare arms, and ankles. The display of skin—which would rate a solid G today—must have looked positively risqué three quarters of a century ago.

Among the Cail-o-scopes, the best are probably *Expecting*, which is a funny cartoon about people waiting, and *Knock Out*, which documents a World's Heavyweight Boxing Championship between Joe Louis and German fighter Max Schmeling; but some of the others are also worth a peek—and the cost is only a penny.

While you're looking, you can be pumping the big coin-operated antique band organ against the Arcade's south wall; its ringing tones almost block out the clatter and clacks of the pinball and electronic games machines (at least when it's not out of order; it's as temperamental as a prima donna, and even the ministrations of the resident musical-instrument caretaker can't always keep it singing). Before leaving, also note the paintings that hang on the walls. They depict a roadster race, the Wright Brothers and an early flying machine, a Victorian-era amusement arcade, and a rural Illinois river valley scene. All of these were created for the film that precedes the chief executives' roll call in Liberty Square's Hall of Presidents.

MAIN STREET CINEMA: The beauty of this prominent attraction on Main Street is that most vacationers bypass it in their rush to get to 20,000 Leagues Under The Sea in Fantasyland or Pirates of the Caribbean in Adventureland, or other thrill-a-minute attractions. Yet on a steamy summer afternoon—when everyone else is standing in line for these blockbusters—this air-conditioned theater is a fine place to relax. Five short silent films are shown here simultaneously: an early film version of Robert Louis Stevenson's *Dr. Jekyll and Mr. Hyde*; Thomas A. Edison's *The Great Train Robbery*; *The Rounders*, starring Fatty Arbuckle and a balletic Charlie Chaplin in a vignette about two wayward husbands and their wailing wives; *Crashing Through*, a steamy melodrama about baby-napping in Poker Flat, starring one Ford Sterling; and *Steamboat Willie*, the first sound cartoon, in which a little mouse named Mickey, making his film debut, meets Minnie and then makes beautiful music on (among other instruments) a cow's udder, a feat which drew one of the film's biggest laughs at the time of its November 1928 release.

WALT DISNEY WORLD RAILROAD: The best introduction to the layout of the Magic Kingdom, the 1½-mile, 15-minute journey on this rail line is as much a must for the first-time visitor as it is for railroad buffs. For the former, it offers an excellent orientation, as it passes through Adventureland and Frontierland and skirts Fantasyland and Tomorrowland. En route, viewers see alligators and other Audio-Animatronics animals, and pass an Indian settlement, as well as the flooded mining town glimpsed on the fly from the cars at the runaway Big Thunder Mountain Railroad. Aficionados of railroadiana may remember that Disney himself was among their number and perhaps, during the early years of television, saw films of him circling his own backyard in a one-eighth-scale train named for his wife, Lilly Belle. The Walt Disney World Railroad also has a *Lilly Belle* among its quartet of locomotives. All of these were built in the United States around the turn of the last century and later were taken down to Mexico to haul freight and passengers in the Yucatan, where Disney scouts found them in 1969; the United Railways of Yucatan was using them to carry sugar cane.

Brought north once again, they were completely overhauled, and even the smallest parts were reworked or replaced. New boilers and fiberglass cabs were built, along with new tenders and tanks. (The cast-iron wheels, side rods, frames, and parts of the hardware, however, are original.) Originally designed to burn coal or wood, then converted by the Mexicans to use oil, they now consume diesel fuel—considerably less dirty than either of the former fuels.

The *Lilly Belle* is a Mogul-type engine, with two small front wheels and six drive wheels, while the *Roy O. Disney* is an American Standard eight-wheeler (with four small wheels forward and four drive wheels), and the *Walter E. Disney* and the *Roger Broggie* (named for a Disney imagineer who shared Walt Disney's enthusiasm for antique trains) are both two-wheelers, with four small forward wheels and six large drive wheels.

THE WALT DISNEY STORY: Housed in the yellow building on the east side of Town Square, this film tells the story of the boy from Marceline, Missouri, who built a Kingdom around a mouse. Walt himself narrates part of the presentation, which includes some rare film footage. Well worth your while.

In the waiting area outside the screening room, there are a number of exhibits dealing with Walt Disney, his honors, and his life: letters from Harry Truman, Dwight Eisenhower, Richard Nixon, U Thant, Winston Churchill, Dag Hammarskjold, and Leopold Stokowski; posters from old Disney movies, photos of the Mouseketeers (and a real Mouseketeer hat), Zorro's cape, and—among the other medals and honors—the Oscar presented for *Snow White and the Seven Dwarfs*, the familiar tall golden figure with seven miniature versions arranged alongside. Note the photo of Walt Disney with Stan Laurel and Oliver Hardy against the wall to your right as you pass through the turnstiles.

OLD-FASHIONED VEHICLES: A number of these can be seen traveling up and down Main Street—horseless carriages and jitneys patterned after turn-of-the-century vehicles (but fitted out with Jeep transmissions and special mufflers that make the putt-putt-putting sound); double-decker buses; a spiffy scarlet fire engine, which can be seen in the Firehouse adjoining City Hall when not in operation; and a troop of trolleys drawn by Belgians and Percherons, two strong breeds of horses that once pulled plows in Europe. These animals—aged between six and ten, weighing in at about a ton each, and shoed with plastic (easier on their feet)—pull the trolley the length of Main Street about two dozen times during each of their three to four working days; afterward, they're sent back to their homes at the barn at the Fort Wilderness Campground.

CINDERELLA CASTLE

Just as the courtly little mouse named Mickey stands for all the joy and merriment in the whole of Walt Disney World, the many-spired Cinderella Castle, childhood's storybook castle made real, represents the hopes and dreams of those youthful years when anything seems possible.

This Castle is different from Disneyland's Sleeping Beauty Castle: Measuring some 180 feet in height, the Florida castle is more than a hundred feet taller; and with its slender towers and lacy filigree work, it's also more graceful, taking its inspiration not only from the architecture of twelfth- and thirteenth-century France, the country where Charles Perrault's classic fairytale originated, but also from the mad Bavarian King Ludwig's castle at Neuschwanstein, and from the designs prepared some three decades ago for the motion-picture version of Perrault's story—and the imaginations of a whole troupe of creative Disney imagineers who have collectively spent several lifetimes turning fantasies into reality.

Unlike real European castles, this one is not made of granite, but of steel beams, fiberglass, and some 500 gallons of paint. There are no dungeons underneath it, but rather service tunnels for the Magic Kingdom's day-to-day operations. In the Castle's upper reaches there are broadcast facilities, security rooms, and the like; toward the top, there's the apartment originally meant for members of the Disney family (but never occupied).

When mounting the curving staircase to the parapet-level restaurant King Stefan's Banquet Hall, or when passing through the Castle's main gateway—or as seen by night from the Contemporary Resort's observation deck, with fireworks exploding all around those slender towers—the Castle looks as if it had come straight out of some never-never land of make-believe.

The mosaic murals: The elaborate murals in the five panels beneath the Castle's archway-entrance rank as one of the true wonders of the World. Measuring some 15 feet high and 10 feet wide, these creations of the Disney artist Dorothea Redmond, crafted by the mosaicist Hanns-Joachim Scharff, tell the familiar story of a little cinder girl, a hardhearted stepmother, two ugly stepsisters, a fairy godmother, a pumpkin transformed, a handsome prince, a certain glass slipper, and one of childhood's happiest happily-ever-afters, using a million bits of Italian glass in some 500 different colors, plus real silver and 14-carat gold. The renderings of the stepsisters and of the many small woodland animals are particularly faithful to images from the Disney film; but every passerby has favorite sections. Don't fail to stop and look.

Coats of arms: The one above the Castle on the north wall belongs to the Disneys. Others belonging to assorted Disney executives hang in the waiting hall just inside the door to King Stefan's; the hostess keeps a book behind the desk that details which belong to whom for any interested party to see. Some of the same names show up as on the second-story windows of the Main Street shops.

ADVENTURELAND

Adventureland seems to have even more atmosphere than the other lands. That may be a result of its neat separation from the rest of the Magic Kingdom, by the bridge over Main Street on the one end, and by a gallery-like structure where it merges with Frontierland on the other; or possibly it's because of the abundance of landscaping. There are Canary Island date palms, the small Cape Sable palms, as well as Pigmy date species, and more. On the Adventureland Bridge alone, visitors will see Cape honeysuckle from South Africa, flame vines from Mexico, bougainvillea from Brazil, Chinese hibiscus, hanging sword ferns, spider plants, and Australian tree ferns, to name just a few. It's hard to imagine that just over ten years ago, the landscape of this little piece of real estate was as bare and flat as that flanking the WDW entrance road.

As for the architecture, even though it derives from such diverse areas as the Caribbean, Polynesia, and Southeast Asia, there's a strong sense of being in a single place, a nowhere-in-particular that is both exotic and distinctly foreign, smacking of island idylls and tropical splendor. Shops offer imports from India, Thailand, Hong Kong, Africa, and the Caribbean islands. The Adventureland Veranda serves food cooked in the Magic Kingdom's most exotic style (never mind that it happens to be simple Chinese fare).

Strolling away from Main Street, you hear the beating of drums, the squawk of a couple of parrots, the regular boom of cannon. Paces quicken. And the wonders you soon encounter do not disappoint.

TROPICAL SERENADE (ENCHANTED TIKI BIRDS): The first of the Audio-Animatronics attractions, the one that laid the foundation for attractions such as *Great Moments With Mr. Lincoln* at the 1964-65 New York World's Fair, this one, introduced at Disneyland in 1963, features four emcees—José, Michael, Pierre, and Fritz—plus some 225 birds, flowers, and Tiki god statues singing and whistling up a tropical storm with such animation that even the most blasé folks can't help but smile. Presented by the Florida Citrus Growers.

PIRATES OF THE CARIBBEAN: One of the very best of the Magic Kingdom's adventures, this cruise through a series of sets depicting a pirate raid on a Caribbean town—a Disneyland original added to WDW's Magic Kingdom, in revised form, because of popular demand—remains strangely uncrowded in the afternoons, even when guests are lining up at Frontierland's Big Thunder and Liberty Square's Haunted Mansion, which resemble Pirates in attention to detail. Here there are flowerpots that explode and mend themselves, drunken pigs whose legs actually twitch in the porkers' soporific contentment, chickens that look for all the world like the real thing (even when seen at close range); the observant will note that the leg of one swashbuckler, dangled over the edge of a bridge, is actually hairy. Each pirate's face has remarkable personality, and the rendition of "Yo-Ho-Yo-Ho"—the attraction's theme song—makes what is actually a rather brutal scenario into something that comes across as good fun.

Before entering the plaza-queue area, be sure to stop and give a nod to the parrot in the pirate costume sitting near the Pirates of the Caribbean sign.

JUNGLE CRUISE: Inspired in part by the 1955 documentary *The African Lion*, this ten-minute cruise adventure is one of the crowning achievements of Magic Kingdom landscape artists for the way it takes guests through landscapes as diverse as a Southeast Asian jungle, the Nile valley, the African veldt, and Amazon rain forest. Along the way, passengers encounter zebras and giraffes, impalas, lions, vultures, and headhunters; they see elephants bathing and tour a Cambodian temple—and listen to the funny spiel delivered by the boatman. For most passengers, this is all just in fun. Gardeners, however, are especially impressed by the variety of species coexisting in such a small area. To keep some of the more sensitive of subtropical specimens alive, 100 gas-fired heaters and electric fans concealed in the rocks pump hot air into the jungle at the rate of 25 million BTUs per hour when temperatures fall to 36° F. This adventure, which is best enjoyed by daylight, is one of the Magic Kingdom's most popular attractions, and it does tend to be crowded from late morning until late afternoon, so plan accordingly.

SWISS FAMILY ISLAND TREEHOUSE: "Everything we need right at our fingertips" was how John Mills, playing the father in Disney's 1960 remake of the classic novel *Swiss Family Robinson*, described the treehouse that he and two of his three sons constructed to house the family after the ship transporting them to America was wrecked in a storm. When given a chance—several adventures later—to leave the island, all but one son decided to stay on. That decision is not hard to understand after a tour of the Magic Kingdom's version of the Robinsons' banyan-tree home. This is everybody's idea of the perfect treehouse, with its many levels and many comforts—patchwork quilts, lovely mahogany furniture, candles stuck in an abalone shell, even running water in every room. (The system is ingenious.)

The Spanish moss draping the branches is real; the tree itself—unofficially christened *Disneyodendron eximus*, which translates roughly as "out-of-the-ordinary Disney tree"—was constructed by the props department. Some statistics: the roots, which are concrete, poke 42 feet into the ground; and some 800,000 leaves and flowers (vinyl) grow on 600-odd branches, which stretch some 90 feet in diameter. "Boy, Dad sure went out on a limb for that one," quipped a Disney props worker's son on hearing of his father's task.

FRONTIERLAND

With the Rivers of America lapping up at its borders, and Big Thunder Mountain rising toward the rear, even higher than Cinderella Castle at the center of the park, this re-creation of the American Frontier encompasses the area from New England to the Southwest, from the 1770s to the 1880s. Hosts and hostesses wear denim, calf-length cut-offs, long skirts, or similar garb. The shops, restaurants, and attractions have unpainted barnboard siding, or stone or clapboard walls, and outside there are a few of the kind of wooden sidewalks down which Marshall Matt Dillon used to stride.

Near Pecos Bill the landscape seems desertlike (even on humid summer days), with mesquite providing shade, and Peruvian pepper trees nearby; the latter's twisted branches boast clusters of bright red berries in fall and winter. Jerusalem thorns blossom with sweet-smelling yellow flowers in the spring. Century plants and Spanish bayonets also can be seen. Farther down the Frontierland avenue, slash pines provide some shade, along with other evergreens of a variety known as cajeput, which can be recognized by its spongy, light-colored bark and white flowers.

DIAMOND HORSESHOE REVUE: The half-hour-long show presented in this re-creation of a Western dance hall-saloon is the kind of thing that makes sophisticated folk laugh despite themselves. As at the Hoop-Dee-Doo Musical Revue, which takes place nightly at Fort Wilderness's Pioneer Hall, the jokes range from corny to absolutely preposterous, yet seldom fall flat, thanks to the enthusiastic, energetic efforts of the talented crew of singers, dancers, ventriloquists, and comedians who perform here several times each day. As at the Hoop-Dee-Doo Musical Revue, reservations are necessary: here they must be made in person at the saloon's porch on the morning of the day of the performance. Since they are dispensed on a first-come-first-served basis, it's essential to show up within an hour of park opening. Those who arrive too late may be able to snag a cancellation by showing up at the door a half hour or so before seating time, which is 40 minutes before the entertainment begins; but you can't count on it. Presented by Del Monte.

COUNTRY BEAR JAMBOREE: An occasional determined sophisticate will remain impervious to the charms of this country-and-western hoedown (aka, informally, the Teddy Bear Jamboree) in Frontierland's big stone-walled Grizzly Hall. But most guests call it one of the Magic Kingdom's best attractions. Ostensibly concocted by one Ursus H. Bear after an especially inspiring season of hibernation, it is performed mainly by a cast of close to 20 life-size Audio-Animatronics bruins, with results more believable than almost anywhere else in the park outside the Hall of Presidents. Henry, the debonair, seven-foot-tall master of ceremonies, introduces the Five Bear Rugs (a C&W plinking group made up of Zeke, Zeb, Ted, Fred, and Tennessee); a big-bodied, tiny-headed pianist named Gomer; the girthy Trixie, the Tampa Temptation, who laments her transformation from cubby to chubby in particularly plaintive C&W tones; the feather boa-wrapped, long-lashed Teddi Barra; the three little bears in blue—Bubbles, Bunny, and Beulah (singing a little like the Andrews Sisters); and assorted other bruins, including Terrence, the shank shaker; Wendell, the overbearing baritone; Liver Lips McGrowl; and Big Al, who demonstrates such force of personality as he deadpans his way through "Blood on the Saddle" that he nearly stops the show. The fact that Big Al postcards are hot sellers at souvenir stands throughout the park ought to convey some idea of his popularity.

Since the Country Bear Jamboree is a top attraction, lines can get quite long during busy periods. They usually seem longer than they are, however, and it's worth noting that huge bunches of people are admitted all at once so that once a line starts moving, it dwindles fast. Seats in the rear of the house are just as good as seats toward the front, if not a little better. In fact, the only marginal seats in the house are those on the far right-hand side, where Teddi Barra's one-in-a-million face can't be seen. When entering the auditorium, hostesses always request that you slide all the way to your right. Consequently, it's best not to try to be the first one in, but instead to tarry a bit so as to have the pick of center seats.

TOM SAWYER ISLAND: Opened in April of 1973, this small landfall in the middle of the Rivers of America has hills to scramble up, a working windmill, Harper's Mill, with an owl in the rafters and a perpetually creaky water wheel, and a pitch-black (and scary) cave in which kids can get lost.

There are oaks, pines, and sycamores here, red maples and elms, and a number of small plants—dwarf azaleas; firethorn, an evergreen shrub that sprouts bright red berries in December; Brazilian pepper trees, which also grow berries at the end of the year; and American holly plants, which acquire their masses of berries in fall. Dirt paths wind this way and that, and it's easy to get disoriented, especially the first time around. There also are two bridges—an old-fashioned swing bridge and a so-called barrel bridge, which floats atop some lashed-together steel drums. When one person bounces, everybody lurches—and all but the most chicken-hearted laugh. Both bridges can easily be missed, so keep your eyes peeled and ask for directions if the path eludes you.

Across the bridge is Fort Sam Clemens, where there is a guardhouse in which the figure of a ratty-looking drunk is Audio-Animatronically snoring off his last bender, accompanied by a mangy-looking dog, chickens, and a pair of horses. On the second floor of the fort, there are close to a dozen air guns for youngsters to trigger into ceaseless cacophony. This area gives a fine view across the Rivers of America to Big Thunder Mountain. Keep poking around, and near the refreshment stand you'll find the twisting, dark, and occasionally scary escape tunnel out of the fort. Walk along the pathway on the banks of the Rivers of America, and you're back at the bridges.

The whole island seems as rugged as backwoods Missouri, and probably as a result, it actually feels a lot more remote than it is, enough to be able to provide some welcome respite from the bustle of the Magic Kingdom. One particularly pleasant way to pass an hour here is over lemonade and a sandwich on the porch at Aunt Polly's. While adults in the party are giving their feet some rest, watching the sternwheelers plying the Rivers of America, kids can go out and burn up some more energy. Rest rooms are located at the refreshment stand in the fort and at the main raft landing. Note that this attraction closes at dusk.

WALT DISNEY WORLD RAILROAD: The old-fashioned steam trains also pick up and discharge passengers at the depot in Frontierland. There's seldom a waiting line, and the breezy, open-sided passenger cars are good places to cool off from the heat of summer afternoons, for putting up your feet, and for getting from Frontierland to Main Street without expending too much energy. The vegetable-like plants in front of the depot, flowering cabbage, are edible but not tasty—and are mainly ornamental; the trees flanking this Victorian station are laurel oaks, and, behind it, towering slash pines, long-leaf pines, and evergreen elms.

BIG THUNDER MOUNTAIN RAILROAD: This attraction, located partly inside the 197-foot-high redstone mountain that pokes into the sky behind the Tom Sawyer Island rafts landing, is something of a cross between Tomorrowland's Space Mountain (an honest-to-goodness roller coaster) and Adventureland's Pirates of the Caribbean (a tame but very exciting and scenic boat tour). As any true coaster buff could tell you, this three-minute ride is a relatively mild one, despite the posted warnings; the thrills are there, but the experience is not so extreme that you'll be left with a determination never to subject yourself to it again. The pleasant rush of adrenaline that comes with some of the swoops and curves, as well as the attractive scenery along the 2,780 feet of track, gives most visitors the opposite reaction. There are the bats, the phosphorescent pools and waterfalls, and best of all, Tumbleweed, the flooded mining town (best seen to your right during one of the uphill climbs). There are some 20 Audio-Animatronics figures here—including real-looking chickens, donkeys, possums, a goat, and a rainmaker, clad in long underwear, whose name is Professor Cumulus Isobar. Careful observers will note a party still going on in a not-yet-sunken second-story room of a saloon, whose weathered look (like that of some other sections of the Magic Kingdom) derives from a judicious mixture of plant food and paint. The $300,000 worth of real antique mining equipment sprinkled around the attraction's 2.5 acres—an ore-hauling wagon, a double-stamp ore crusher, a wooden mining flume, and an old ball mill used to extract gold from ore—were picked up at auctions all over the Southwest, at something less than bargain prices, since the high price of gold and the resulting profitability of small-scale mining operations had boosted demand by genuine miners themselves. As with Pirates of the Caribbean, every trip yields new sights, and even a second or third trip in a matter of days is as amusing as the first time around.

The summit of the mountain, whose name refers to an old Indian legend about a certain sacred mountain in Wyoming that would thunder whenever white men took out its gold, is entirely Disney-made. It was in the planning for some 15 years and under construction for two, and required some 650 tons of steel, 4,675 tons of cement, and 16,000 gallons of paint; hundreds of rock-makers contributed, applying multiple coats of cement and paint, throwing stones at the mountain, kicking dirt on it, and banging on it with sticks and picks to make the whole thing resemble the rocks of Monument Valley, Utah—that is, as if Mother Nature herself had created it. Design was largely by Tony Baxter, a Disney imagineer who started his career with the company with a job at a Disney ice-cream parlor while in high school. (His name now can be seen on one of the doors in the unloading and boarding area.) The area inside the mountain that does not house the tunnels of the ride itself is occupied by the machinery that makes the ride go—pumps, electronic equipment, and part of the computer that runs the show. The total cost was about $17 million, which, give or take a few million, was as much as it cost to build all of California's Disneyland in 1955. Incidentally, that park's version of the attraction, which opened in 1979, is similar, but lacks the flash-flood scene and a few other details.

Note on timing: Certain aspects of the ride are more convincing after dark. Optimally, you should experience it first at night, then have a second go-round by the light of day. Since the trip is extremely popular, plan to take it in during the 9 P.M. running of the Main Street Electrical Parade (in season), or just before park closing, when the lines are generally shorter. By day, go early in the morning or around dinnertime.

LIBERTY SQUARE

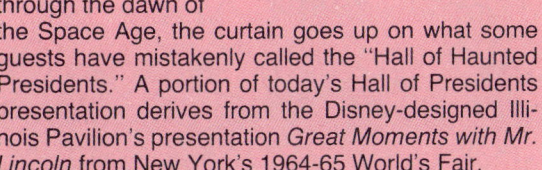

The transition between Frontierland on one side and Fantasyland on the other is so smooth that it's hard to say just when you arrive, yet ultimately there's no mistaking the location. The small buildings are clapboard or brick and topped with weather vanes; the decorative moldings are Federal or Georgian in style; the glass is sometimes wavy, and there are flower boxes on shop windows, bright-colored gardens, neatly trimmed borders of Japanese yew, and masses of azaleas in a number of varieties— George Tabor azaleas, which blossom white and pink in March and May; redwing-hybrid Kurume azaleas, which boast red blossoms in winter; southern charms, which from February to April turn rosy pink; and more. There are a number of good shops, most notably the Yankee Trader, Mlle. Lafayette's Parfumerie, and Olde World Antiques; plus two of the park's most popular attractions—Haunted Mansion and the Hall of Presidents—and the Liberty Tree Tavern, one of the few Magic Kingdom restaurants to offer waitress service, and one of just two to take reservations (though only at dinner). Liberty Square also is home of one of the most delightful nooks in all the Magic Kingdom—the small, secluded area just behind the Silversmith Shop near the Fife and Drum. There are tables with umbrellas, plenty of benches, and big trees to provide shade—and the sound of the crowds seems a million miles away.

THE LIBERTY TREE: Not an attraction per se, this 130-year-old live oak (*Quercus virginiana*)—which recalls trees all over the colonies, on which the Sons of Liberty used to hang lanterns after the Boston Tea Party of 1773—was found on the southern edge of WDW's 27,400 acres, and then moved to its present site in one of the more complex of the Magic Kingdom's landscaping operations. Since the tree was so large (weighing an estimated 35 tons, with a root ball that measured some 18 by 16 by 4 feet around), lifting it by cable was out of the question—the cable would have sliced through the bark and into the trunk's tender cambium layer, injuring the tree. Instead, two holes were drilled horizontally through the sturdiest section of the trunk; the holes were fitted with dowels, and a 100-ton crane lifted the tree by these rods, which were subsequently removed and replaced by the original wood plugs. Unfortunately, these had become contaminated, and an infection set in and rotted out a portion of the inside of the trunk. To save the tree, the plugs again were removed, the holes were filled with cement, diseased areas cleaned out, and a young *Quercus virginiana* was grafted onto the tree at its base, where it grows even today. Careful observers will be able to spot the plugs and the portions of the trunk that were damaged. The thirteen lanterns hanging on the branches represent the thirteen original states.

HALL OF PRESIDENTS: This is not one of those thrill-a-minute attractions, like the Pirates of the Caribbean or the Country Bear Jamboree; it's long on patriotism and short on humor. But the detail certainly is fascinating. After a film (presented on a sweeping 70 mm screen) discusses the importance of the Constitution from the time of its framing through the dawn of the Space Age, the curtain goes up on what some guests have mistakenly called the "Hall of Haunted Presidents." A portion of today's Hall of Presidents presentation derives from the Disney-designed Illinois Pavilion's presentation *Great Moments with Mr. Lincoln* from New York's 1964-65 World's Fair.

At the Magic Kingdom show, Lincoln's remarks are prefaced by a roll call of all 39 American presidents, including Ronald Reagan, who debuted in 1981. Each chief executive responds with a nod; careful observers will note the others swaying and nodding, fidgeting, and even whispering to each other during the proceedings.

Costumes were created by two famous film tailors who were coaxed out of retirement. Not only are the styles those of the period in which each president lived, but so are the tailoring techniques and the fabrics. Some had to be specially woven for the purpose. Each figure has at least one change of clothes, and jewelry, shoes, hair texture, and even George Washington's chair are all re-created exactly as indicated by the results of careful research using paintings, diaries, newspapers, and government archives. The observant should be able to see the brace on Franklin Delano Roosevelt's leg. The effect is so lifelike that the figures look almost real, even at close range.

The paintings in the waiting area outside the hall are just a few of the 85 created for the pre roll–call film—in the style of the period during which the event depicted took place—by a dozen artists working under the direction of the Academy Award–winning artist John De Cuir. Other paintings can be seen in Main Street's Penny Arcade and Liberty Square's Liberty Tree Tavern and Columbia Harbour House.

LIBERTY SQUARE RIVERBOATS: The *Admiral Joe Fowler* and the *Richard F. Irvine*, built in drydock at WDW and named for two key Disney designers, are real steamboats. Their boilers turn water into steam, which is then piped to the engine, which drives the paddle wheel that propels the boats. They are not the real article in one respect, however: they move through the half-mile-long, seven-foot-deep Rivers of America on an underwater rail. The ride is more pleasant than thrilling, but it's good for beating the heat on steamy afternoons. En route, a variety of props creates a sort of Wild West effect: moose, deer, cabins on fire, and the like. (Many of these are also visible from the Walt Disney World Railroad.)

parts were expunged and a pleasant voice-over keeps things from getting too serious. Even then, the experience that's left is among the Magic Kingdom's best. Special effect is piled upon special effect, and just when you think you've seen it all, there's something new: the raven who appears over and over again; the bats' eyes on the wallpaper; the plaque that reads "Tomb, Sweet Tomb"; the suit of armor that comes alive; the horrible transparent specter in the attic; the terrified cemetery watchman and his mangy mutt; the ghostly teapot pouring ghostly tea; the difficult-to-identify flying objects above the image in the crystal ball (which is actually of a woman who works in the wardrobe department).

Best seats are in front or rear and center, so that you can see both river banks equally well.

The trees framing the entrance to Riverboat Landing, which bear crinkly blossoms of bright red throughout much of the year, are crepe myrtles; these can also be seen in other areas of the park.

MIKE FINK KEEL BOATS: Named for a riverboat captain who lived from 1770 to 1823 and once met up with Davy Crockett, the pair of squat, oddly shaped Mike Fink Keel Boats—*Bertha Mae* and the *Gullywhumper*—also traverse the Rivers of America. Since they take in the same scenery as the Liberty Square Riverboats (though from a slightly different angle), you wouldn't want to do both in the same day.

HAUNTED MANSION: Those who expect to get the daylights scared out of them inside this big old house, modeled on those built by the Dutch in the Hudson River Valley in the 18th century, will be a tad disappointed. In deference to the number of small children and other easily frightened souls who tour the Magic Kingdom every day, the most terrifying

In the portrait hall (which you enter after passing through the mansion's front doors), it's amusing to speculate: is the ceiling moving up—or is the floor descending? It's one way here, and another way at the New Orleans–style Haunted Mansion in Disneyland.

At both places, one of the biggest jobs of the maintenance crews is not cleaning up, but keeping things nice and dirty. Since each mansion's attic is littered with some 200 trunks, chairs, dress forms, shovels, harps, rugs, and assorted other knick-knacks, it requires a good deal of dust. This is purchased from a West Coast firm by the five-pound bagful and distributed by a device that looks as if it were meant to spread grass seed. Local legend has it that enough has been used since the park's 1971 opening to bury the mansion. Cobwebs are bought in liquid form and strung up by a secret process.

When waiting to enter, be sure to note the amusing inscriptions on the tombstones in the overgrown cemetery.

FANTASYLAND

Walt Disney called this a "timeless land of enchantment," and his successors term it "the happiest land of all"—and it is, for some. Although it's not precisely a kiddieland, it is the home of a number of rides that are particularly well-liked by younger children. The nursery-song cadences of "It's A Small World" appeal to them, as do the bright colors of the trash baskets, the flowers, and the tentlike rooftops; and they delight in the fairy-tale architecture and ambience, reminiscent of a king's castle's courtyard during a particularly lively fair. Fantasyland is also one of the most heavily trafficked areas of the park.

CINDERELLA'S GOLDEN CARROUSEL: Not everything in the Magic Kingdom is a Disney version of the real article. This carrousel, discovered at the now-defunct Maplewood, New Jersey, Olympic Park, was built for the Detroit Palace Garden Park (also long gone) by Italian-born wood-carvers of the Philadelphia Toboggan Company back in 1917, toward the end of the golden century of carrousel-building that began around 1825 (when the Common Council of Manhattan Island, New York, granted one John Sears a permit to "establish a covered circus for a Flying Horse Establishment"). "Liberty"—as the Philadelphia Toboggan Company's red, white, and blue creation was called during that patriotic era—originally featured 72 horses on an oversized moving platform measuring 60 feet in diameter, plus several stationary chariots. During the Disney refurbishing, these were removed, and many were replaced with additional horses made of fiberglass. Also, the original horses' legs, which were arranged in a rather decorous pose, were ingeniously rearranged to make the steeds look like real chargers. (Careful examination seems to reveal some of the cracks by which this change was effected.) Also, for the wooden canopy above the horses, Disney artists hand-painted 18 separate scenes (each measuring about two by three feet) with images of the little cinder girl from Charles Perrault's fairy tale and Disney's 1950 film. Additionally, the original mechanical wooden parts were replaced by metal ones; the thick layer of paint that had obscured some of the finer points of the original carving was stripped away, and the horses were repainted. The painting alone required about 48 hours per horse. All the horses are white, Disney spokespeople will tell you, because all the riders are good guys!

While waiting to mount the carrousel's steeds, it's worthwhile to take the time to study the animals carefully. One is festooned with yellow roses, another carries a quiver of Indian arrows, and yet another sports a portrait of Eric the Red on its back. No two are exactly alike. The band organ, which plays favorite music from Disney studios (such as the Oscar-winning "When You Wish Upon A Star," "Zip-a-dee-doo-dah," and "Chim-Chim-Cheree"), was made in one of Italy's most famous factories.

SNOW WHITE'S SCARY ADVENTURES: This attraction near the carrousel retells the scary part of the Grimm Brothers' fairy tale, which Walt Disney made into the world's first full-length animated feature in 1937 and 1938. Though basically a ride for kids, Snow White's Scary Adventures features two skeletons and plenty of spooky darkness; also, the wicked witch—evil, long-nosed, and practically toothless—appears more than once with such suddenness and menace that some youngsters end up really frightened. At the end, the hag dumps a rock on the passengers; the stars you see are among the attraction's best special effects.

MAD TEA PARTY: The theme of this ride—in a group of oversized pastel-colored teacups that whirl and spin as wildly as many carnivals' Tubs of Fun—derives from a scene in the Disney studio's 1951 production of Lewis Carroll's novel *Alice in Wonderland*. During the sequence in question, the Mad Hatter hosts a tea party for his un-birthday. Unlike many of the other rides in Fantasyland, this attraction is not strictly for the younger children; the 9-to-20-crowd seems to like it best. Be sure to note the soused mouse that pops out of the teapot at the center of the platform full of teacups.

DUMBO, THE FLYING ELEPHANT: This is purely and simply a kiddie ride—though personages as varied as Romanian gymnast Nadia Comaneci and Muhammad Ali have loved it. The character of the flying elephant was developed for the 1941 film release of *Dumbo*, one of the shortest of Disney's animated features and one of the best, starring a baby elephant born with inordinately large ears and an ability to fly that is discovered after he accidentally drinks a bucket of champagne. The mouse that sits atop the mirrored ball in the middle of the circle of the ride's flying elephants is the faithful Timothy Mouse, who in the film becomes Dumbo's manager after the circus folk who had once laughed at the flying elephant hire him to be a star.

SKYWAY TO TOMORROWLAND: Entered from near Peter Pan's Flight, this aerial tram transports guests one-way to Tomorrowland. En route it's possible to see the clear aquamarine pool traversed by Captain Nemo's ship, the striped tent tops of Cinderella's Golden Carrousel, Tomorrowland's Grand Prix, and the not-so-wonderful rooftops of the buildings where many Magic Kingdom adventures actually take place. This attraction is best boarded at its Tomorrowland terminus, where the lines are usually shorter.

PETER PAN'S FLIGHT: The inspiration for this attraction was the Scottish writer Sir James M. Barrie's play about the boy who wouldn't grow up, which appeared as a Disney movie in 1953. Riding in flying versions of Captain Hook's ornate ship—which are suspended from an overhead rail once they leave the boarding area—visitors swoop and soar through a series of scenes that tell the story of how Wendy, Michael, and John get sprinkled with pixie dust and, heading for "the second star to the right and straight on till morning," fly off to Never-Never-Land with Tinkerbell; and meet Princess Tiger Lilly, the evil Captain Hook, his jolly-looking sidekick Mr. Smee, and the crocodile—who has already made off with one of Hook's hands and is on the verge of getting the rest of him as you sail out into daylight. As in the movie, one of the most beautiful scenes—one that makes this attraction a treat for adults as well as for littler folk—is the sight of nighttime London, dark blue and speckled with twinkling yellow lights, complete with the Thames, Big Ben, London Bridge, and vehicles that really move on the streets. The song that accompanies the trip is "You Can Fly, You Can Fly, You Can Fly" by Sammy Cahn and Sammy Fain.

IT'S A SMALL WORLD: Originally created for New York's 1964–1965 World's Fair, with a tunefully singsong melody written by Richard M. and Robert B. Sherman (the Academy Award–winning composers of the music for *Mary Poppins*, among other Disney scores), this favorite of young children and senior citizens involves a boat trip through several large rooms where stylized Audio-Animatronics dolls— wooden soldiers, cancan dancers, balloonists, chess pieces, Tower of London guards in scarlet beefeater uniforms, bagpipers and leprechauns, gooseherds, little Dutch kids in wooden shoes, Don Quixote and a goatherd, yodelers and gondoliers, houri dancers, dancers from Greece and Thailand, snake charmers, Japanese kite flyers, hippos and giraffes and frogs, hyenas, monkeys, and elephants, hip-twitching Polynesians, surfers, and even dolphins—sing and dance to a melody that will run through your head for hours after you float out of their wonderland. Of the two queues that are usually found here, the one to the left is almost always shorter. Presented by Kodak.

20,000 LEAGUES UNDER THE SEA: Jules Verne, on whose novel Disney based the 1954 release that provides the theme for this attraction, described the Machiavellian Captain Nemo's ship as an undersea monster, with headlights that appeared as eyes in the dark water. The 61-foot-long, 58-ton, 38-passenger craft that ply the beautiful, blue Fantasyland lagoon are far too handsome to fit the description, but—at least on the outside—they bear a remarkable resemblance to the craft piloted by the nefarious Nemo toward Vulcania. In the course of the trip, visitors tour an 11½-million-gallon pool filled with sea grass, kelp, giant fishes, clams, seahorses, coral, icebergs, and rock formations fashioned of fiberglass, plastic, steel, stucco, and epoxy paint. The ship's course passes by the lost city of Atlantis and under a rather attractive "polar ice cap"; as in the film, passengers listen to Nemo playing the organ, and endure an attack by a giant squid. The special effects aren't the Magic Kingdom's best, and the queues outside move rather slowly—so don't line up unless it's not too busy.

Incidentally, the nautical flags above the entrance—which now spell out the word "Leagues" in the attraction's name—read S-E-U-G-A-E-L when the park first opened. A Navy visitor pointed out the mistake. The queue area, which is done up with Disney-made rocks, is meant to resemble the volcanic boulders that would have been found on Nemo's Vulcania. The area is also graced by a large Senegal date palm and a Southern magnolia, which were so heavy that the ceiling of the Magic Kingdom basement down below had to be specially reinforced to support them. The cliffs into which the submarines disappear, on the far side of the lagoon, conceal the backstage area where much of the scenery is set up; a better view of the layout is available from the Skyway above.

MR. TOAD'S WILD RIDE: Wild in name only, this attraction is based on the October 1949 Disney release *The Adventures of Ichabod and Mr. Toad*, which itself derives from Kenneth Grahame's classic novel *The Wind in the Willows*. It seems that a gang of weasels has tricked that memorable man-about-town Mr. J. Thaddeus Toad into trading the deed to his ancestral mansion for a stolen motorcar. In the attraction, flivvers modeled on this very car take guests zigging and zagging along the road to Nowhere in Particular, through dark rooms painted in neon colors and illuminated by black lights where the redoubtable Mr. Toad is trying to get out of the scrape. In the process, you crash through a fireplace, narrowly miss being struck by a falling suit of armor, go hurtling through haystacks and barn doors and into a coop full of squawking chickens, then ride down a railroad track on a collision course with a huge locomotive. Some of this is scary enough that some small children end up momentarily frightened. By and large, though, this is a ride for kids.

TOMORROWLAND

With its vast expanse of concrete, Tomorrowland offers a picture of the future that is a little less than wonderful, since the architecture looks a bit too much like yesterday's version of Tomorrow: As Disney planners have discovered, it isn't easy to portray a future that persists in becoming the present. Mission to the Moon, for instance, became Mission to Mars in 1975, when the earth's lunar neighbor began to seem almost as close-to-home as the neighborhood McDonald's. But the extreme forms into which many of the trees and bushes have been pruned do look vaguely futuristic. Note the ligustrums between the Grand Prix Raceway and the Tomorrowland Terrace—shrubs that have been shaped into single-trunked trees topped with spheres; the oleanders, another type of shrub pruned like a tree, located in raised planters near the Carousel of Progress; and many others. One of the most interesting of the plantings, the ligustrum near Tomorrowland Terrace—which looks a bit like an octopus balancing many green trays—was found by a Disney landscape artist in the 1960s on the front lawn of a Sarasota home whose owner was persuaded to give up her pet for a check and a promise to repair any damages incurred in the transplanting operation. (Eventually, that meant not only fixing the lawn, but also repaving the lady's driveway.)

Also, Space Mountain—which anchors this land at its eastern edge (with the bulky contours of the Contemporary Resort Hotel rising just beyond)—has a shape that seems almost timeless. Though this attraction is usually very crowded in the afternoon, most others—high-capacity adventures that they are—may require no waits then, so Tomorrowland is a good area to visit during a busy time on one of the Magic Kingdom's busier days.

SPACE MOUNTAIN: Rising to a height of over 150 feet and extending some 300 feet in diameter, this gleaming white steel and concrete cone (shaped vaguely like Japan's Mount Fuji) houses an attraction that most people call a roller coaster. Actually, it bears the same sort of resemblance to the traditional thrill ride that the Magic Kingdom does to the garden variety of theme park. It's the Disney version—a roller coaster and then some. While the 2-minute–38-second ride does not exactly duplicate a trip into outer space, there are some truly phenomenal and quite lovely special effects—shooting stars and strobe-like flashing lights among them; and the whole ride takes place in an outer-space–like darkness that gets progressively inkier—and scarier—as the journey progresses. The eight-passenger rockets that roar through this blackness attain a maximum speed of just over 28 miles per hour. Just how terrifying this actually is to any given passenger depends on his or her level of tolerance. In general, the Space Mountain trip seems to inspire in lovers of thrill rides an immediate desire to go again; it's just wild enough to send eyeglasses, purses, wallets, and even an occasional set of false teeth plummeting to the bottom of the track (and turbulent enough to upset the stomachs of those so unwise as to ride it immediately after eating)—but not so harrowing that passengers shake and the weakened knees persist for more than a minute or two after "touch-down." Those in a quandary about whether or not to line up can get a preview from the WEDway PeopleMover described below; and those who decide to pass after hearing the shrieks and the clatter of the cars from the queue area have their own special exit.

After experiencing the space journey, it's interesting to note some statistics: the mountain itself—which occupies a 10-acre site and contains 4,508,500 cubic feet, enough to accommodate a small skyscraper—is composed of 72 pre-stressed concrete beams cast nearby, then hoisted into place by mammoth cranes. Each rib weighs 74 tons, and measures 117 feet in length and, in width, 4 feet at the top and 13 feet at the bottom. With the work lights on, the interior of Space Mountain looks humdrum and almost commercially common, with its tangled array of track and supporting scaffolding. Some of the shooting stars are produced quite simply, by aiming a beam of light at a mirrored globe; and

legend has it that the meteors visible to guests in the queue area are actually projections of chocolate chip cookies! The whole ride is controlled by a Nova-2 computer (with another Nova-2 in backup) and is monitored on a board full of dials and a battery of closed-circuit television screens by Disney hosts and hostesses sitting in a control room (whose eerie blue glow is another striking feature of the queue area). As a result, any guest caught disobeying posted rules will be seen—and his or her rocket stopped so that the offender can be escorted out of the park. Children under seven must be accompanied by an adult; no children under three are permitted; and as the many signs at the attraction warn, "You must be in Good Health, and Free from Heart Conditions, Motion Sickness, Weak Back, or Other Physical Limitations" to ride. It is also suggested that expectant mothers pass up the trip. Presented by RCA.

Home of Future Living: The moving sidewalk that takes guests out of Space Mountain also carries them past scenes in which some of the Magic Kingdom's less-sophisticated Audio-Animatronics figures demonstrate the uses of the electronic media in the future, in business and in the home. Far more interesting are the RCA Broadcast Systems ($70,000 to $80,000 each) that allow guests to see themselves on television—in living color.

SKYWAY TO FANTASYLAND: This aerial cable car takes guests from Tomorrowland to a point near Peter Pan's Flight in Fantasyland. The trip takes five minutes, and the cable car—built by Von Roll, Ltd., of Bern, Switzerland, then shipped to Miami and on to Orlando—is notable for being the nation's first conveyance of a type able to make a 90-degree turn. If you're going to ride the Skyway, this is the place to get on: The lines at the Fantasyland end are usually much longer.

STARJETS: Towering high over Tomorrowland, this is purely and simply a thrill ride and ought to delight anyone who loves Space Mountain, but doesn't necessarily want to get in line all over again.

WEDWAY PEOPLEMOVER: Boarded near the StarJets, these small, five-car trains move at a speed of about ten miles per hour along close to a mile of track, alongside or through most of the major attractions in Tomorrowland. If you have any doubts about riding Space Mountain, a trip on the PeopleMover—which travels through the queue area inside and offers a view of the rockets as they hurtle through the darkness—will probably help you make your decision. Just as important, from an intellectual standpoint, is the fact that the WEDway PeopleMover shows off an innovative means of transportation operated by a linear induction motor that has no moving parts, uses little power, and emits no pollution. Presented by the Edison Electric Institute.

MISSION TO MARS: After a pre-flight briefing in a room styled to look like Mission Control, and a narration by an Audio-Animatronics flight engineer who looks just like the father in the Carousel of Progress family, guests enter a round cabin for a simulated trip to Mars that was developed in cooperation with NASA. Seats tilt and shake, sub-audible sound waves are sent out, and oversized speakers let out great roars and hisses that sound like a washing machine during the spin cycle; corny though the idea is, the realization is okay. The attraction is located opposite CircleVision 360 (below). Films screened during the flight, some developed from photos taken during the Mariner Nine space program, show a section of Mars's surface called Mariner Valley and its 40-mile-wide Olympus Mons, the universe's largest known volcano. The best viewing is from the third and fourth rows. Presented by McDonnell Douglas Corp.

CAROUSEL OF PROGRESS: First seen at New York's World's Fair of 1964–1965 and moved here in 1975, this 22-minute show features a number of tableaux starring an Audio-Animatronics family, and demonstrates the great improvements in American life that have come about as the result of increased use of electricity. The sheet music for the song "Now Is the Time" is almost always available at the entrance at no charge.

IF YOU HAD WINGS: Located behind CircleVision 360 (described below), this five-minute-long adventure takes guests along a track where, to the accompaniment of the very catchy song that gives the attraction its name, some 83 projectors show scenes of the tropics (a waterfall in a Trinidadian tropical forest, a bluer-than-blue Caribbean sea, a Mexican marketplace, and the like). Most of these effects are a bit tame, but the next-to-last shot, which features some you-are-there film taken from speeding planes and cars, is the sort of footage that makes you want to go all over again—something that is blessedly easy to do, since the lines here are usually minimal. The attraction's sponsor, Eastern Airlines (the Official Airline of Walt Disney World), maintains an airline-ticket office at the exit.

CIRCLEVISION 360 "AMERICAN JOURNEYS": This 21-minute film, the first attraction on the far right just over the Tomorrowland Bridge, is a travel film like few others. Instead of showing only what's in front, it also lets viewers see what's behind and to either side, thanks to an unusual filming technique that involves nine 35mm cameras mounted in a circle on a pole-like affair. Part of the footage was filmed by a ground crew of seven who did their shooting from a station wagon; the rest was taken from a modified B-25 bomber plane emblazoned with the face of Mickey Mouse himself. Both crews spent two months on the road and brought back 200,000 feet of film, which was edited down to 17,000 feet. This footage is shown in the big theater by an equally innovative arrangement of nine projectors, nine 20-by-30-foot screens, and 12 channels of sound reproduced through nine different speakers, plus six others, affixed to the ceiling, which carry the narration. Consequently, the experience is really impressive (and a few of the flight scenes are realistic enough to make some guests airsick). The journey includes stops at London's Tower Bridge and the Thames River, Copenhagen's Tivoli Gardens, Paris's Notre Dame Cathedral, the Swiss Alps, Germany's castles on the Rhine, Vienna (to hear the celebrated Vienna Boys' Choir), Rome's ancient Colosseum, a bull ring in Madrid, Jerusalem's Wailing Wall, the Sahara Desert, the Valley of the Nile (to see the Pyramids and the Sphinx), the big-game country of Africa, India's Taj Mahal, Hong Kong Harbor (aboard a Chinese junk), and more. The grand finale involves a tour of the United States, from San Francisco Bay to the Statue of Liberty. The attraction can accommodate up to 3,700 people an hour, so don't be discouraged if you see a crowd outside; it disappears every 20 minutes or so. This is generally one of a handful of spots where the queues on a busy afternoon are the least discouraging. Presented by Black and Decker.

GRAND PRIX RACEWAY: The little cars that *vroom* down the four 2,760-foot-long tracks at this attraction opposite the Tomorrowland Terrace provide most of the background noise in Tomorrowland—and that's another grim thought about the future. Older kids and teenagers love the ride and will spend as many hours driving the Mark VII-model gasoline-powered cars as they can; one 87-year-old grandmother comes here just to watch. Like true sports cars, the vehicles—which cost about $6,000 each—have rack-and-pinion steering and disc brakes; unlike most sports cars, these run on a track. Nonetheless, even expert drivers have a hard time keeping them going in a straight line until the technique is mastered: just steer all the way to the right, or all the way to the left, and you've got it made. One lap around the track takes about five minutes, and the cars (which are manufactured by a Disney company called MAPO, short for Mary Poppins) can travel at a maximum speed of about 7 miles per hour. You must be at least 4'4" to ride. Presented by Goodyear.

SHOPS IN THE MAGIC KINGDOM

No one travels all the way to the Magic Kingdom just to go shopping. But as many a first-time visitor has learned with some surprise, shopping is one of the most enjoyable pastimes there. Donald Duck key chains and Mickey Mouse lapel pins, Alice-in-Wonderland dresses for little girls and Walt Disney World sweat shirts, and other Disney souvenir items make up a large portion of the merchandise you see on display. Most of this Disney merchandise has been custom-made for the park and is not available elsewhere.

But the Magic Kingdom's boutiques and stores stock much more than just Disneyana, and it's possible to buy antiques and silver-plated tea services, escargot holders and cookbooks, mock pirate hats and toy frontier rifles, 14-carat gold charms and filigreed costume jewelry in Main Street shops that also sell magic tricks and film, peanut brittle and Droste chocolate apples. In Adventureland, you can buy imported items from around the world—hand-carved elephant statues from Africa, inlaid marble boxes from India, batik dresses from Indonesia, and much more. Shops stock items that complement the themes of the various lands (and so, in Tomorrowland, one finds contemporary wall hangings and futuristic-looking table lamps). Every store offers a selection of items from the inexpensive to the costly: in Tinkerbell Toy Shop in Fantasyland, for instance, kids can beg for a $5 windup toy after requests for the larger-than-life-sized $350 stuffed animals are denied. In the Cup 'n' Saucer, a china shop on Main Street, a four-foot-high Hummel figurine costs thousands of dollars; a music box in the shape of the Taj Mahal can be seen in Adventureland's Magic Carpet. And in many shops, you can watch craftsmen at work—peanut brittle being poured in the Main Street Confectionery, perfume being mixed at Mlle. Lafayette's Parfumerie in Liberty Square, a glass blower in Main Street's Crystal Arts and Adventureland's La Princesa de Cristal, and the like.

Consequently, there's no need to spend a fortune to have a good time. Budget-watchers should note, though, that the temptation to nickel-and-dime yourself into penury is very strong, and you need to be careful. It's a good idea to set a spending limit for each member of your party in advance—and try to stick to it.

MAIN STREET

EAST SIDE

STROLLER SHOP: Just after the turnstiles into the Magic Kingdom, to the right as you face Cinderella Castle. Strollers and wheelchairs can be rented here, and assorted souvenirs purchased.

THE CHAPEAU: This Town Square shop is the place to buy Mouseketeer ears and have them monogrammed, and to shop for visors, straw hats, derbies, top hats, and other headgear. The shop sells individually decorated ladies' hats—fun to try on, if not necessarily worth the investment.

KODAK CAMERA CENTER: Gleaming glass-fronted mahogany cases show off the Canon, Minolta, Pentax, Nikon, and the other 35mm, instant-load, quick-developing cameras for sale at this high-ceilinged shop near Town Square. Flash cubes, film, and other photo supplies are also available, and very minor repairs can be made. Cameras are available for rent (a deposit is required).

You can also have an 8-by-10 Kodak portrait taken in old-fashioned costumes that look for all the world like something a favorite grandmother would have worn—except that the back of the costumes are treated like hospital gowns; sitters pose on the rear end of a caboose. Even if you decide not to spend the money, it's amusing just to stand and watch other guests lining up to say "cheese."

MAIN STREET CONFECTIONERY: The store is an old-fashioned pink-and-white paradise, a delight at any time of day, but especially when the cooks in the shop's glass-walled kitchen are pouring peanut brittle onto a huge tabletop to cool, and the candy is sending up clouds of scent that you could swear was being fanned right out into the street. Some 18 to 20 batches are made each day. The sweet product is for sale in small bags, along with pastilles, jellied candies by Davidson of Dundee, and jelly beans, marshmallow peanuts and nougats, mints and kisses, rock candy, and dozens of other nemeses for a sweet tooth. When your stomach is growling, this is a good place to grab a snack.

THE CUP 'N' SAUCER: Fine china and other gift items—china birds and figurines, swans, china flowers, Dresden and Lladro figurines, and all manner of pretty teacups, Disney character figurines, and Wedgwood stoneware—priced at $1 to $13,000—are the stock-in-trade of this airy establishment. The most expensive item, at last look, was a giant Hummel statue, depicting ruddy-cheeked peasant children in an apple tree; at least peek at it, even if it is a bit rich for most pocketbooks.

HOLIDAY CORNER: The warm wax that the candlemakers use to produce snow men, decorative candles, and other creations-with-wicks perfumes this area of the Holiday Corner, behind the Cup 'n' Saucer (the china shop). Fun to watch, even if you're not out to buy. There's also a wide selection of Christmas items—including tree-top dolls and souvenir ornaments.

DISNEY & COMPANY: The wallpaper at this shop on Center Street (the cul-de-sac just off Main) is bright and Victorian, the floors are parquet, and the woodwork elaborate; and old-fashioned ceiling fans twirl slowly overhead. This character shop offers sweat shirts and T-shirts, hats and bags, pens and pencils, stuffed animals, and other items by the dozen. The selection is not as vast as at the Emporium, but neither is Disney & Company quite so overwhelming.

UPTOWN JEWELERS: Not far from Disney & Company. The selection of good-quality and costume jewelry here is excellent, particularly for pins, necklaces, pendants, bracelets, and earrings with an old-fashioned look. One counter in the corner of the shop stocks wonderful souvenir charms in 14-carat gold and sterling silver: Tinkerbell, Cinderella Castle, and the Walt Disney World logo (a globe with mouse ears).

MARKET HOUSE: An old-fashioned spot, with displays of Smucker's jams and jellies in more varieties than supermarket shoppers would have imagined even existed, plus maple candy, pretzels, pickles, honeys, and all kinds of tea and snack items arranged in old-fashioned oak cases flanking a sturdy, black potbellied stove. The floors are oak and pegged, the lighting comes in part from brass lanterns dangling above the stove, and in one corner there's a real old-fashioned hand-crank telephone.

THE SHADOW BOX: Watching silhouette cutters snip black paper into the likenesses of children is one of Main Street's more fascinating diversions, and there's always a crowd on hand—some folks waiting their turn, some just inspecting the progress and the results. Framed silhouettes cost $3 to $4.

CRYSTAL ARTS: Cut-glass bowls and vases, urns and glasses, plates and shelves glitter in the mirror-backed glass cases of this high-ceilinged, brass-chandeliered emporium. An engraver or a glassblower is always at work by the bright light flooding through the big windows. The wares available at Adventureland's La Princesa de Cristal are similar.

forms made with moss and wire and planted with a kind of small-leafed vine that will cover completely in about six months. A must.

NEW CENTURY CLOCK SHOP: Clocks and watches in all shapes and sizes, not to mention Mickey Mouse watches in a variety of configurations, are displayed in the polished wood cases at this establishment adjoining the Emporium. There are clocks for the kitchen and clocks for the living room, clocks with chimes and clocks without them, alarm clocks for bedside tables and others for travel, digital watches and watches with hands, and even some pocket watches and a Mickey Mouse telephone—with rotary dial or Touch Tone. Purchases can be shipped on request. Presented by Elgin-Helbros.

WEST SIDE

NEWSSTAND: No newspapers are sold in the Magic Kingdom—even at its Newsstand, which is opposite the Stroller Shop, to your left as you face Cinderella Castle, just after you've passed through the turnstiles at the entrance to the Magic Kingdom. Character merchandise and souvenirs are for sale; the selection is fairly limited, but you can usually pick up items you've forgotten during your travels through the rest of the park.

THE EMPORIUM: Framed by a two-story-high portico, this Town Square landmark, the Magic Kingdom's largest gift shop, stocks a little bit of everything—flower pots and silk flowers, all kinds of candles, including some in animal shapes, some done up like hot dogs or ice cream sundaes; stuffed animals and toys; a doll-lover's array of Madame Alexander dolls, as well as five or six other kinds; and more. Everyone seems to have an armload of Walt Disney World T-shirts and sweat shirts, towels and handbags, Mouseketeer ears and other hats, and various items emblazoned with Mickey, Minnie, or Walt Disney World logos. The cash registers almost always seem to be busy, especially toward the end of the afternoon and before park closing. It's a good place to souvenir-shop, though, since it's only a few steps from lockers (under the train station) where purchases can be stowed. Don't forget to note the window displays, which usually feature Audio-Animatronics displays ranging from themes of the season to the most recent Disney movie.

THE GREENHOUSE: While inside the Emporium, it's sometimes hard to tell where this sprawling store ends and the next shop begins. The Greenhouse is the corner of the Emporium devoted to growing things. There are intriguing little clay pots for sale, some with fruits and vegetables molded onto the sides in relief, alongside some animal-shaped ceramic potters in bright colors; plus hundreds upon hundreds of lovely silk and plastic flowers that spill out into Center Street (and make the view from the Harmony Barber Shop next door particularly colorful). Guests who have come by car may be interested in buying one of the mock topiaries—animal-shaped

HARMONY BARBER SHOP: The setting is quaint and old-fashioned, worth a peek even if you've no need for a trim. Nostalgic shaving items and mustache cups are for sale.

HALLMARK CARD SHOP: Hallmark stocks this boutique near the Emporium on Main Street with cards, wrapping paper, and pretty party items, such as paper plates, napkins, and tablecloths.

HOUSE OF MAGIC: Magicians can make ordinary playing cards simply disappear, balls pass through cups, water pour out of a jug that looks empty, coins pass through solid sheets of rubber, and a wand turn into two silken handkerchiefs. Some believers can produce coins from thin air, or pour the milk from a whole pitcher into a thimble. This Main Street shop sells the kind of magician's tools that can turn everyday travelers into magicians, along with party-joke items such as phony arm casts, slimy reptiles, and similar stuff.

TOBACCONIST: The sign outside ranks among the Magic Kingdom's handsomest; the matchbooks given out with purchases are especially attractive; and the smell of all the pipe tobaccos is heavenly. Even nonsmokers will at least want to breeze through.

ADVENTURELAND

TRADERS OF TIMBUKTU: This shop is in a marketlike complex in the plaza opposite the Enchanted Tiki Birds, and displays a fine selection of the sort of handsome (but inexpensive) trinkets that travelers find while visiting the erstwhile Dark Continent—carved wooden giraffes and antelopes, ethnic jewelry (including carved bangles, wooden combs, and shark's tooth necklaces), dashikis, and khaki shirts. The great child-pleasers here are the plastic pith helmets.

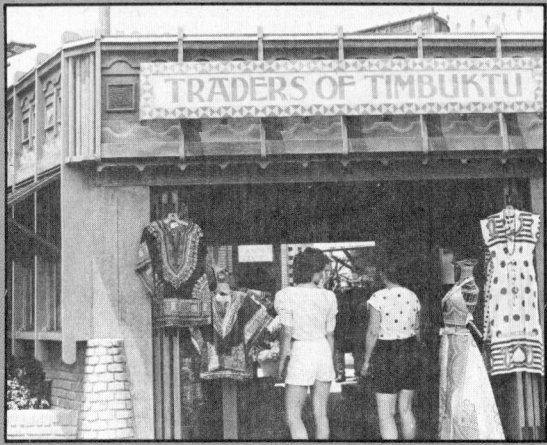

TIKI TROPIC SHOP: Hawaiian and Caribbean clothing—polyester caftans, terry rompers, and other such items, plus a fine assortment of bathing suits—is the specialty at this establishment located near Traders of Timbuktu, opposite the exit of Sunshine Tree Terrace.

THE MAGIC CARPET: Not all guests manage to wander into this tiny, low-ceilinged shop tucked away in Adventureland, near Traders of Timbuktu and the Sunshine Tree Terrace. But the showpiece here, a two-foot-high music box replica of India's onion-domed Taj Mahal, makes the fragrant shop well worth a detour, even if you don't flip over the other Middle Eastern and Asian imports (carved tea trays, cotton and silk dresses made in India, brass bells and baubles, leather items, jingle bells in three sizes, incense, and more) displayed on glass shelves against elaborate damask backdrops.

ORIENTAL IMPORTS: This shop, hung with silk-tasseled Oriental lanterns, stocks the sort of goods that merchants in Hong Kong sell in quantity: lovely satin change purses and eyeglass cases, slinky women's dresses, straw boxes made in China, Chinese-style hand-embroidered pajamas for kids, figurines, and hand-gilded and engraved copper plates, done by the so-called Chokin method, which was originally used to decorate Samurai warriors' helmets.

TROPIC TOPPERS: This simple shop near Traders of Timbuktu is the spot to find the kind of safari hats worn by the pilots at the Jungle Cruise. Assorted other straw hats and handbags as well as film and sundries and other knickknacks are for sale.

COLONEL HATHI'S SAFARI CLUB: This emporium near the entrance to the Swiss Family Treehouse, named after the elephant in the 1967 film *The Jungle Book*, smells sweetly of the rattan and straw goods that give it its tropical character. Merchandise here is all summer stuff: sunglasses and wind chimes, thongs and terry-cloth rompers, straw handbags and shells, coral bangles, palmetto fans, and the like.

LAFFITE'S PORTRAIT DECK: Hidden away near the Plaza del Sol Caribe, this is the Adventureland counterpart of the photography studio in Main Street's Camera Center. Here, though, instead of posing in the genteelest of Gay Nineties garb, you dress up as swashbucklers and pirate maids amid what look to be pieces of eight and chests brimful of pearls and precious jewels.

PIRATES OF THE CARIBBEAN PLAZA

HOUSE OF TREASURE: The only spot in the Magic Kingdom that sells pirates' hats, this swashbucklers' delight adjoins Pirates of the Caribbean on the west and stocks piratic merchandise—toy rifles and brass dolphins, a Pirate's Creed of Ethics printed on parchment, Jolly Roger flags, shell rings, old-looking maps, pirate dolls, and an assortment of books (one on how to build ships in bottles, others on whalers and frigates and men-of-war). There's as much for adults as for youngsters.

GOLDEN GALLEON: A real antique diver's helmet is the centerpiece of this neighbor of La Princesa de Cristal, a low-ceilinged, tile-floored shop full of golden treasures—handsome nautical items, globes and brass door knockers, brass cannons, ships' wheels, and a spyglass—not to mention nautical ready-to-wear fashions for men and women as well as comfortable, casual shoes.

LA PRINCESA DE CRISTAL: The cut-glass items, custom-engraved goblets and bowls, and blown-glass baubles sold at this emporium tucked away behind the snack stand called El Pirata y El Perico, opposite Pirates of the Caribbean, are about the same as those in Crystal Arts on Main Street—but the ceilings here are lower and beamed, and the floors are red tile instead of linoleum—so the feeling is totally different.

Warning to the squeamish: the sound made by the engravers is for all the world like fingers scraping on a chalkboard. Eek!

PLAZA DEL SOL CARIBE: This market next to the Pirates of the Caribbean sells candy and snacks, a variety of straw hats (including colorful oversized sombreros), piñatas, pottery, and artificial flowers.

FRONTIERLAND

FRONTIER TRADING POST: This is the place to outfit a youngster like a true son of the Great Frontier: cowboy hats and boots or feathered headdresses and moccasins, hefty brass belt buckles, sleeve garters, calico sunbonnets, sombreros, sheriff's badges, gold nugget jewelry, and reproduction pistols and rifles should do the trick. Also available are Western items like tom-toms, peace pipes, plastic toy horses, forts, Big Al stuffed bears, books on American folklore, and C. M. Russell paintings. Film and sundries are in stock, too. Don't miss the doll-sized model store against the rear wall at the eastern end of the emporium.

TRICORNERED HAT SHOPPE: This emporium offers hats of all descriptions (especially Western ones), plus feathered hatbands and leather goods. It's tucked away near the arcade leading to Adventureland, between the ornamental Frontierland stockade, alongside the Diamond Horseshoe Saloon.

LIBERTY SQUARE

OLDE WORLD ANTIQUES: One of the first of the Liberty Square shops that visitors pass after crossing the bridge from the Hub area in front of Cinderella Castle, this little, lace-curtained emporium stocks real antiques—grandfather clocks and rocking chairs, hutches, drop-leaf tables, and assorted decorative items in brass, pewter, copper, mahogany, oak, and pine—as well as some reproductions. Prices run into thousands of dollars, and bargains are nowhere to be found, but every item is in tip-top condition, and is tagged with a description of its origin, so the browsing is good.

MLLE. LAFAYETTE'S PARFUMERIE: Few spots in the Magic Kingdom smell quite as fragrant as this tiny neighbor of Olde World Antiques, where perfume blenders turn six basic fragrances into hundreds of different combinations, using an assortment of giant eyedroppers, tiny paper blotters, glass funnels, and graduated cylinders; the process is fun just to watch. Each formula is recorded so that guests can reorder at will. Those who decide to stick with traditional fragrances can shop for dozens of perfumes by makers as varied as Nina Ricci, Hermès, Worth, Patou, Chanel, Madame Rochas, Charles of the Ritz, and Myrurgia. Pretty glass atomizers are also available.

HERITAGE HOUSE: Among the Early American reproductions that predominate in the stock of this store next to the Hall of Presidents, youngsters may go for the parchment copies of famous American documents, while homeowners might snap up pewter plates and candlesticks, creweled items, wooden candlesticks and pepper mills, busts of the presidents, souvenir spoons, mugs in Early American motifs, wrought-iron knickknacks, or lovely enameled paintings of clipper ships. Most wonderful of all—more for grown-ups than for kids—are the dolls, the quaint and intensely personable creations of a Poughkeepsie, New York, doll maker: elegant ladies in Victorian garb, as well as characters from Early American life such as the chimney sweep, the peddler, the pottery vendor, the soap fat man carrying a tub of tallow.

YANKEE TRADER: No first-time visitor to the Magic Kingdom would expect to be able to buy stoneware soufflé dishes and espresso makers, cast-iron muffin tins and escargot holders. But this wonderfully fragrant shop, immediately to the right after you turn into the lane leading to the Haunted

Mansion, is crammed like a too-small kitchen cabinet with just these kitchen knickknacks, and more: cookie cutters and choppers, graters and spatulas, French-fry slicers, wooden-handled whisks, egg timers, and wall plaques made of dough, to name just a few of the sorts of items available here. Cookbooks are also for sale—not only the old favorites like *Joy of Cooking*, but also unusual volumes of historic recipes. The store is located near the archway-entrance to Fantasyland.

KEEL BOAT SHOPPE: This small shop, situated next to Mike Fink's Keel Boats, gives guests on their way to the Haunted Mansion a taste of things to come with a stock of horrific monster masks and assorted ghoulish goodies (in a more limited selection than at Fantasyland's Merlin's Magic Shop and Main Street's House of Magic).

SILVERSMITH: The sign above the entrance to this tiny shop adjoining Olde World Antiques (just next to the Liberty Square bridge to the Hub) reads "J. Tremain, Prop." That refers to the main character in the 1957 Disney film of the Esther Forbes novel about a silversmith's apprentice who joins the Boston Tea Party and helps hang the lights on the Liberty Tree during America's colonial days. At this low-ceilinged, plank-floored establishment, antiquey-looking cabinets display tongs and teaspoons, Revere-style bowls, tea sets, silver-coated roses, candelabra, and more—all in silver plate.

FANTASYLAND

THE KING'S GALLERY: Situated inside Cinderella Castle, near the entrance to King Stefan's Banquet Hall, this shop is one of the Magic Kingdom's best. The walls are dark and the ceilings beamed, and the stock includes a huge and imaginative selection of wonderful handmade dolls, music boxes, cuckoo clocks, Russian lacquer boxes, Spanish-made swords and leather handbags, German beer mugs with lids, chess sets, and more—very little of it at rock-bottom prices. Also here, practiced artisans demonstrate the art of Damascene, a form of metalworking originated by the inhabitants of Damascus in the sixth century A.D.; it is mastered today by only a handful of specialized craftsmen around the world. Painstakingly, these skilled workers dip steel pendants into acid to create tiny pores, then use a combination of sterling silver and 24-carat gold wire to outline butterflies and other intricate designs onto the acid-blackened steel.

MERLIN'S MAGIC SHOP: Another really wonderful place near the Cinderella Castle archway. In addition to ogre fangs, monster makeup, and all manner of bizarre masks costing up to $40 (some of them really horrific), the store stocks Chinese rings, cups and balls, and other staples of the magician's trade, plus magic books by Houdini and other masters of prestidigitation. There are party jokes as well: rubber fried eggs, bald-skull caps, bloodshot eyeballs-on-springs that pop out of the wearer's head, Slinkies, ventriloquists' dummies, fake scorpions and lizards, and other knickknacks much loved by youthful Magic Kingdom visitors.

DISNEYANA SHOP: This shop near Cinderella Castle, opposite Cinderella's Golden Carrousel, specializes in Disney collectibles such as limited edition Disney plates, cels from Disney movies, and other one-of-a-kind Disney items.

MAD HATTER: Another place to buy Mouseketeer ears and other souvenir hats and have your name embroidered on them on the spot. This shop was named for the Mad Hatter, who held the tea party for his un-birthday in Disney's 1951 film version of Lewis Carroll's classic *Alice in Wonderland*.

TINKERBELL TOY SHOP: One of the more wonderful boutiques in the Magic Kingdom, and a fine toy store by any standards. One of the sales counters is shaped like a section of a pirate ship, and behind the counter there's a velvet-cloaked Captain Hook and his cohort, Mr. Smee. For sale are stuffed animals, miniature model cars and trucks, character patches, windup toys and wooden toys, bar soap emblazoned with Disney scenes, Mickey and Minnie toys and clothing, Alice-in-Wonderland dresses, Snow White dresses (with Dopey on the skirt), and a positively marvelous array of Madame Alexander dolls. A must.

THE ARISTOCATS: Most of the lands have one store that specializes in Disney souvenirs; this stone-walled, vaguely Gothic shop alongside Merlin's Magic Shop, slightly to the northeast of Cinderella Castle, is Fantasyland's spot for Donald and Mickey key chains, sweat shirts and T-shirts, china Disney figurines, salt and pepper shakers, Donald Duck needlepoint kits, Minnie tote bags, tennis balls with a Mickey logo, and more.

THE ROYAL CANDY SHOPPE: This souvenir stand next to the Lancer's Inn sells assorted Disneyana, including Mickey Mouse back scratchers, key chains, and stuffed animals, plus a selection of jelly beans and peppermint sticks, Tootsie Rolls, lollipops, and other hard candy.

KODAK KIOSK: A convenient location to buy film and other photo supplies.

TOMORROWLAND

MICKEY'S MART: One of the best places in the Magic Kingdom for Disney-themed items, along with Main Street's Emporium.

SKYWAY STATION SHOP: A small spot tucked away near the Tomorrowland terminus of the Skyway to Fantasyland. Disney souvenirs are the stock-in-trade.

SPACE PORT: Sells the kind of contemporary decorative gifts that teens and pre-teens seem to love: futuristic toys, books, games, jewelry, and other such items. This is one of the Magic Kingdom's most popular shops.

WHERE TO BUY A RAINCOAT: The show doesn't stop just because of a storm. Instead, shops all over the Magic Kingdom stock raincoats to outfit guests who have left their own back home, at their hotel, or in the car. Among them are:
  Main Street: The Emporium
  Adventureland: Tropic Toppers
  Frontierland: Frontier Trading Post
  Fantasyland: Tinkerbell Toy Shop,
    Mad Hatter, AristoCats
      (also umbrellas)
  Tomorrowland: Mickey's Mart

MAIL-ORDER MICKEY: T-shirts, Mouseketeer ears, stuffed animals, and any other souvenir items for sale in Walt Disney World shops can be ordered by mail. For details, write:
  Mail Order Department
  Walt Disney World
  Box 40
  Lake Buena Vista, FL 32830
  Or call: 305-824-4718

WHERE TO EAT IN THE MAGIC KINGDOM

A complete listing of all Magic Kingdom eateries—full-service restaurants, fast food emporiums, snack shops, and food vendors—will be found together with all other WDW eating spots in the *Good Meals, Great Times* chapter.

HAPPENINGS AND LIVE ENTERTAINMENT

Before heading down to Main Street, check at City Hall to get times for live shows and other special Magic Kingdom happenings, as well as a schedule of entertainment at the resorts, WDW Village, and Epcot Center. Others may be encountered serendipitously in the course of the day, and occasionally shows scheduled for a given place or time may be changed or canceled at the last minute—but more often than not, the shows proceed as planned.

DAPPER DANS: Are likely to be encountered while you're strolling down Main Street. This barbershop quartet, its members clad in straw hats and striped vests, tap dance and let one-liners fly during their short four-part harmonic performances. Occasionally, they bring out their set of bamboo organ chimes.

WALT DISNEY WORLD MARCHING BAND: This concert band performs during the morning five days a week in Town Square and on occasion at the Fantasy Faire stage in Fantasyland.

REFRESHMENT CORNER PIANIST: Tickles the ivories of a snow-white upright at busy periods at this centrally located hamburgers-and-hot-dogs restaurant.

ALL-AMERICAN COLLEGE MARCHING BAND: Featuring college students from around the country. Performs on Fantasyland's Fantasy Faire stage only during the summer. Part of a 12-week summer program.

KIDS OF THE KINGDOM: Perform five days a week in the Castle Forecourt, in a show featuring lively singing and dancing to classic Disney tunes—plus appearances by Disney characters such as the portly Winnie the Pooh and Mickey Mouse himself.

FLAG RETREAT: Usually around 4:45 P.M., a small band and color guard march into Town Square, take down the American flag that flies from the flagpole there, then release a flock of snowy homing pigeons symbolic of the dove of peace. Watch carefully lest you miss them: as one wag quipped, these are union pigeons; they flap away toward their loft-home (behind the Castle) practically before you can say "Cinderella." The whole flight takes just 20 seconds. Some trivia: the carts in which the birds are transported are fashioned from authentic peddlers' carts bought in England for the 1971 film *Bedknobs and Broomsticks*.

J. P. AND THE SILVER STARS: Play familiar tunes on the instruments so well-known in the Caribbean Islands, steel drums—oil barrels whose sides have been cut to a foot or less from the bottom (which itself has been pounded hollow). On a stage near Adventureland's Pirates of the Caribbean.

HANDPICKED: Can occasionally be found fiddling and banjo-picking in the busy season in Frontierland and Liberty Square, near the Rivers of America.

DIAMOND HORSESHOE SALOON: A dance hall such as might have been found in nineteenth-century Missouri. Five times a day, there's a lively old-time saloon show with can-can dancers. Reservations are required; to get them, appear in person at the Diamond Horseshoe in the morning shortly after park opening.

FANTASY IN THE SKY: Even those rare recalcitrant souls who resist fireworks displays as though they were other people's home movies have little quarrel with this spectacular show, which is presented nightly when the park is open until midnight. The 150-odd shells that were mortarized over a 15-minute period when the program was first introduced are now ignited in a period of just four minutes—a rate of one shell every two seconds. They're detonated electrically, so that firings coincide perfectly with the announcer's voice on the P.A. system. The big symmetrical starburst shells are generally Japanese-made, while the ones whose explosions look as if they had been poured from a pitcher (with a concentrated area of particularly vivid color at the center) are of English manufacture.

FANTASY FOLLIES: This lively musical revue features the Disney characters in zany performing

roles backed up by two vocalists and a trio of musicians. Presented five times daily five days a week at the Fantasy Faire stage.

MARDI GRAS SOUND COMPANY AND "TOBASCO": Plays popular music and rock at the Tomorrowland Terrace.

BANJO KINGS: Play specialty songs and comic ditties from the Roaring Twenties on washboards and banjos, mostly on Main Street.

SHOW BIZ IS: This new show features singers, dancers, musicians, and Disney characters in a rollicking, fun-filled, 35-minute musical tour through the world of show business.

THE GREAT MAIN STREET ELECTRICAL PARADE

Since it premiered on June 9, 1977, this dazzler has been WDW's biggest hit. Featuring a million twinkling lights, some 100 performers, and nearly 30 floats, it is presented in busy seasons—usually during Easter, summer vacations, and when the park is open until midnight, usually at 9 and 11 P.M. each evening—and it's a little like all the world's best Christmas trees rolled into one, so undeniably, incredibly, supercalifragilisticexpialidociously spectacular that it's well worth enduring the Magic Kingdom's busiest periods to see. Part of the fascination is the presentation: one minute the lights are twinkling along the edges of the Main Street roofs; the next, as soon as the announcer heralds its arrival, everything is black. The crowds, already impatient, strain anxiously for a sight of the procession. And then it comes, aglitter with tiny colored lights, accompanied by some of the most tuneful music that ever graced a parade, the "Baroque Hoedown," written by Gershon Kingsley and Jean-Jacques Perrey. Heads nod and feet tap. Windows and eyeglasses reflect the sparkle of the lights. One by one the floats cruise by: Alice, atop her mushroom; Pinocchio, the marionette without strings; Pete, atop his dragon; and more. While the parade theme is piped over the park's P.A. system, each float carries radios that receive their own variations from a transmitter atop Cinderella Castle, and the floats' speakers broadcast these tunes. The combination creates a complex tapestry almost as grin-inspiring as the spectacle of the lights.

Where to catch the parade: Of all the spots along the route outlined in the first paragraph of this section, the single best vantage point for watching this stupendous procession is the very center of the platform of the Walt Disney World Railroad's depot. From there, it's possible to see the floats circling Town Square, and then you can get the effect of the whole stream of lights as the parade continues down Main Street and around the Hub. You're close enough to catch the glitter, but far enough away so that you don't see the framework that holds it all together. Unfortunately, only a couple of seats here have views that are not obstructed by trees.

The next-best viewing point is from the curbs on either side of Main Street. It's very crowded here, and you must claim your foot of curb as much as an hour before the parade (particularly for the busier 9 P.M. running). But there's something about seeing the show at its beginnings, on the edge of one of the quaintest avenues on earth, that enhances the experience enormously.

If you hate crowds, head for Pecos Bill's; park yourself on one of the restaurant's stools right next to the parade route.

Note that the 9 P.M. parade is always more crowded than the one at 11 P.M.

MORE GREAT PARADES

Every day in the Magic Kingdom feels like a celebration, from the moment the park opens until the last guest has gone home. But that's never more true than during one of the many parades that wend their way along the Magic Kingdom parade route daily—usually down Main Street, around the east half of the Hub, across Liberty Square Bridge, through Frontierland.

There's a daily character parade (held mid afternoon) where Mickey, Donald, and all their friends come out to greet the crowds.

HOLIDAY DOINGS

EASTER SUNDAY: A holiday show at Cinderella Castle and a promenade help make this holiday extra special.

FOURTH OF JULY CELEBRATION: The busiest day of the summer—and with reason: there's a dou-

ble-sized fireworks display, whose explosions light up the skies not only above Cinderella Castle, but those over the Seven Seas Lagoon.

CHRISTMAS: A Christmas tree—a real Douglas fir that is as perfect among trees as Main Street is among small-town thoroughfares—goes up in Town Square, and the entire Magic Kingdom is decked out as only Disney can do it. There are also special Christmas parades, shows, and carolers. The crowds, of course, are thick. But the scenery is beautiful, and the weather is fine (if chilly)—so it's no wonder that some veteran Magic Kingdom lovers call this the very best time of year.

NEW YEAR'S EVE CELEBRATION: With nearly 93,000 people streaming through the gates of the theme park, New Year's Eve Day of 1980 hosted the biggest crowd in Magic Kingdom history. And though the visitation rate was a little higher than in years past, it has always been true that on December 31, the throngs are practically body to body. For a celebration, that's fun. (On an introductory visit, it could be less delightful; first-timers take note.) There is a double-sized fireworks display, and the Main Street holiday decorations (including that almost surrealistically perfect Christmas tree presiding over Town Square) are still up. There's plenty of nip in the air as the evening wears on, so dress accordingly.

WHERE TO FIND THE CHARACTERS

They'll most often make appearances in front of City Hall, in the Castle Forecourt, and on the Fantasyland side of the Castle (picture taking is particularly good here); City Hall can give you approximate times. If you miss those appearances, try to catch the Character Show in Fantasyland. Again, City Hall will have the times.

TIPS FROM WDW VETERANS

- Study up before you arrive in the Magic Kingdom so that you're familiar with the layout and the things to see and do in the park. Special services are occasionally available to guests during slack seasons, so be sure to peruse any printed information you find in your room.
- Allow plenty of time, so that you can sample the Magic Kingdom in small bites. Trying to see it all in a day (or even just two) is like eating a rich ice cream sundae too quickly.
- Try to visit the park on a weekend in summer—and any day but Monday, Tuesday, or Wednesday (the busiest days) year round.
- Start out early. Most people arrive between 9:30 and 11:30, when the roads approaching the Toll Plaza and the parking lots are jammed. If you're coming at Easter, Christmas, or in summer, plan to arrive before 8:30 A.M., or wait until nightfall, when things are less crowded. Arrive very early, so as to be at the gates to the Magic Kingdom when they open, have breakfast at the Town Square Cafe or the Crystal Palace, and then be at the end of Main Street when the rest of the park opens.
- Organize your visit so that you don't hop around from area to area, for that wastes time. Plan to eat before 11 A.M. or after 2 P.M., and before 5 P.M. or after 8 P.M.
- Break up your day. Buy a River Country/Discovery Island ticket at the entrance to the Magic Kingdom and plan on heading for its beach when the crowds get thickest. Or take in Discovery Island. Or head back to your hotel, if it's not too far, for some swimming or other activities available there. Guests not staying at WDW's own resorts should be sure to have their hands stamped and hold on to their parking-ticket stubs, to avoid paying additional fees when returning.
- At busy times on busy days, take in the following not-so-packed attractions:

  Main Street: Walt Disney World Railroad, Main Street Cinema
  Adventureland: Pirates of the Caribbean
  Liberty Square: Liberty Square Riverboats
  Tomorrowland: Mission to Mars, WEDway PeopleMover, Carousel of Progress, If You Had Wings, CircleVision 360 "American Journeys"
  Fantasyland: It's A Small World (after 5 P.M.)

- Shop on Main Street in the early afternoon, not at day's end, when everybody else goes. Besides, the stores are good places to escape the afternoon heat.
- Many attractions have two lines. Before getting into the one on the right-hand side, look at the one to your left. Most of the time it will be less crowded, since most Magic Kingdom visitors automatically head for the one on the right.
- Wear your most comfortable shoes: You'll be spending a lot of time on your feet. (Note that no bare feet are permitted in the Magic Kingdom.)
- Don't take food into the Magic Kingdom. (There are, however, picnic facilities and lockers at the TTC.)
- If your party decides to split up, set a fixed meeting place and time that can't be confused. Avoid meeting in front of Cinderella Castle, since this area can become congested during showtimes and parades.
- If you have arranged to meet members of your group somewhere, don't get into a queue as the meeting time approaches.
- If you've a limited amount of time remaining before meeting the rest of your group, don't hesitate to ask a Disney employee for suggestions about things to do.

USEFUL STOPS

Cash: The Sun Bank, located in Town Square next to City Hall. Open seven days a week, from 9 A.M. to 4 P.M.

Tobacco: The prime outlet is the Tobacconist on the west side of Main Street.

Baby care needs: The Magic Kingdom Baby Care Center, at the Hub end of Main Street, next to the Crystal Palace Restaurant, is the best source. But disposable diapers and other infant paraphernalia are also available on request at other shops. This is a good area for nursing mothers. Sponsored by Gerber.

Strollers: For rent at the Stroller Shop, located to the right in the souvenir area near the turnstiles at the entrance to the Magic Kingdom.

Haircuts and shaves: At the Harmony Barber Shop on Center Street, the flower-filled cul-de-sac off the west side of Main Street. The barber chairs are heavy, curlicued metal, like the cash register—the real McCoy.

Postcards and stamps: The Hallmark Card Shop on the west side of Main Street is the prime source for postcards; stamps are sold at City Hall.

Mailboxes: Located up and down Main Street, they're olive-drab. An elaborate polished brass one can be found near the entrance to the Hallmark Card Shop. Postmarks read Lake Buena Vista, *not* Walt Disney World.

EPCOT CENTER

105 Getting In and Around
107 Future World
117 World Showcase
128 Hot Tips

Imagine a typical world's fair, with the requisite number of pavilions devoted to nations from all around the world and others depicting the most advanced state of modern technology. Then add the inevitable fast-food facilities and the obligatory souvenir stands. Got all that? Now imagine that same world's fair as the creators of the Magic Kingdoms in Disneyland and Walt Disney World might have created it, using every skill and resource at their considerable command, not to mention the sum of about one billion dollars. You now have some small inkling of what Epcot Center is all about.

Walt Disney suggested the idea back in October, 1966. "Epcot will be an experimental prototype community of tomorrow that will take its cue from the new ideas and new technologies that are now emerging from the creative centers of American industry." It would never be completed, he said, but would "always be introducing and testing and demonstrating new materials and systems." And it would be "a showcase to the world for the ingenuity and imagination of American free enterprise."

Walt Disney's dream has become a wonderful reality as his successors have used the ideas that inspired him to create a marvel of entertainment, a unique combination of pure imagination and innovative technological virtuosity.

There are two "entertainment worlds"—Future World and World Showcase. The former examines complex and often controversial concepts such as energy and transportation in ways that suddenly make them seem not only comprehensible but also downright appealing. In the latter, the nations of the earth are portrayed in all their dazzling variety, with the same extraordinary devotion to detail that makes the Magic Kingdom so enchanting. Appropriate entertainment and menus full of ethnic specialties enhance the experience: The food has been chosen for its intrinsic appeal to American taste, though in only a few instances have native cuisines been modified in any substantive way to make them most palatable. And the shops in each pavilion are stocked with merchandise that was actually made in the featured nation.

This chapter describes first Future World and then World Showcase. Both of these are huge and complicated complexes, and to get the most out of your visit read the following pages in their entirety before arriving. It's also wise to study our hints and tips on page 128.

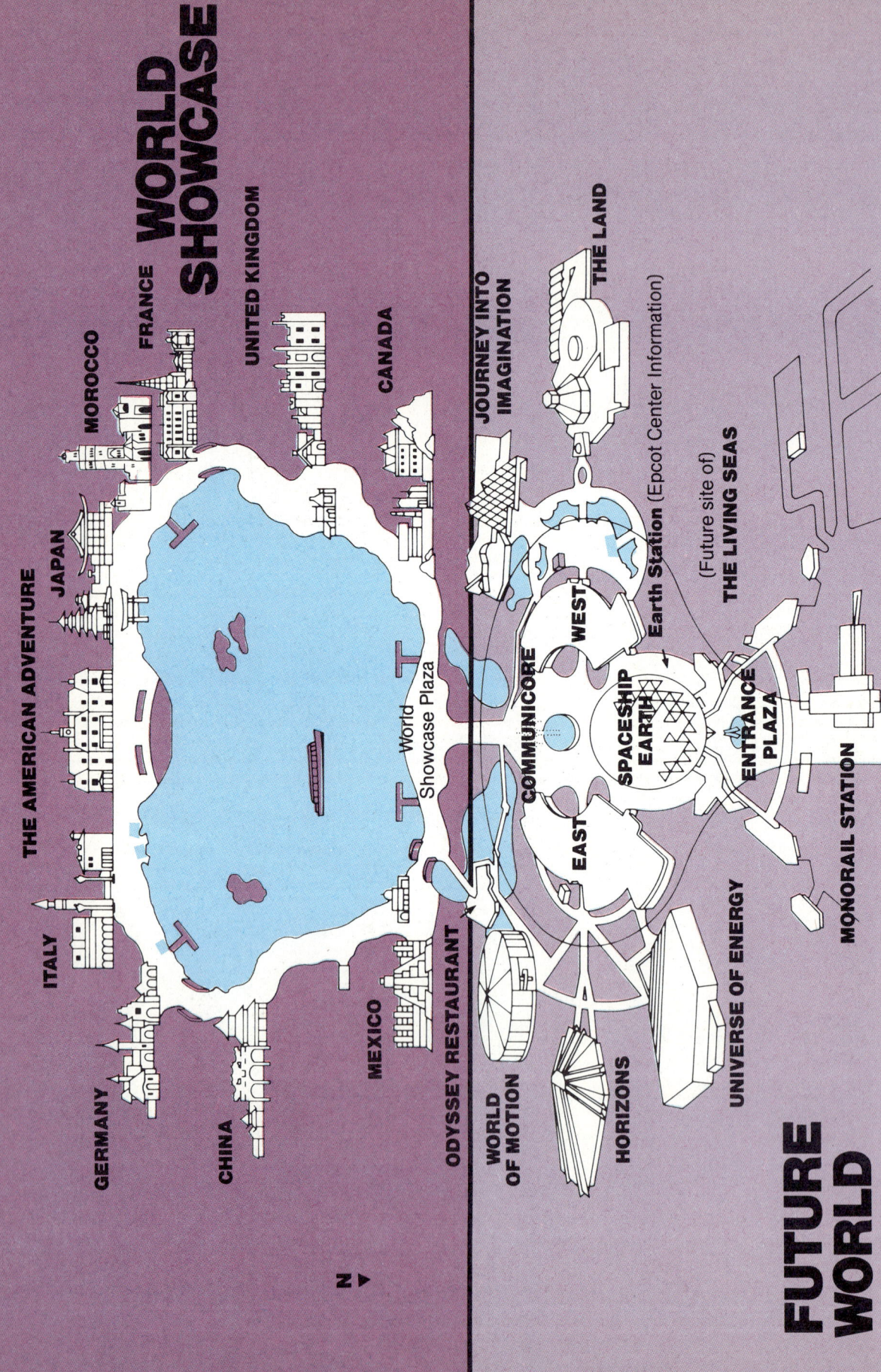

GETTING IN AND AROUND

TRANSPORTATION TO EPCOT CENTER: These WDW entertainment worlds are every bit as easy to get to as the Magic Kingdom.

By car: A new interchange (the third) was constructed on I-4 especially for Epcot Center visitors, about halfway between the exits for Route 535 and U.S. 192. Take this exit and follow the signs along Epcot Center Drive through Epcot Center's main gate. Epcot Center has its own 9,000-space parking lot; daily parking costs $1. Parking is free for Walt Disney World resort guests with proper identification. Trams carry visitors from their parking space right to the ticket booths.

By WDW monorail and bus: In general, allow about 30 minutes to get from one point to another whether you go by bus or by monorail. Contact WDW Information (824-4321) before you leave your room to confirm the following routes and for the latest operating schedules. (In general, monorail and bus schedules coordinate with Epcot Center operating hours, so there's little chance of ever being stranded.)

• From the Contemporary Resort or Polynesian Village Resort hotels, take the local hotel monorail to the TTC, walk down the ramp and across the platform, and board the TTC-Epcot Center monorail.

• From the Magic Kingdom, take the express monorail to the TTC, then walk down the ramp and up another ramp to board the TTC-Epcot Center monorail.

• From the Golf Resort, take the green-flagged bus to the TTC, then change to the TTC-Epcot Center monorail.

• From Fort Wilderness, take the blue-flagged bus to the TTC, then change to the TTC-Epcot Center monorail.

• From the WDW villas, take the green-and-gold-flagged bus with an "EC" on the front direct to Epcot Center.

• From WDW Shopping Village, take the red-flagged bus direct to Epcot Center.

• From WDW Village Hotel Plaza, take the silver-and-red-flagged bus direct to Epcot Center.

HOURS: Epcot Center is usually open from 9 A.M. to 8 P.M.; hours are extended during Washington's Birthday week, spring school breaks, summer months, and certain holidays. Occasionally, during busy periods, the park may open earlier or close later. Call 824-4321 for up-to-the-minute schedules.

GETTING ORIENTED: Epcot Center is shaped something like a giant hourglass. Future World fills up the northern bulb, while World Showcase occupies the southern half. In Future World, which is anchored on the north by the imposing "geosphere" known as Spaceship Earth, most pavilions are arranged around the bulb's perimeter. The exception is CommuniCore, which occupies the area at the center of the bulb. In World Showcase, pavilions are arranged around the edge of World Showcase Lagoon, with The American Adventure directly south of Spaceship Earth on the southernmost shore of the lake.

BABY CARE: Changing tables and facilities for nursing mothers can be found in the Baby Center, near the Odyssey Restaurant and next to World of Motion (in Future World) and Mexico (in World Showcase). Disposable diapers also are kept behind the counter at many merchandise locations in both worlds; just ask.

CAMERA NEEDS: A large Camera Center is located on the west side of the Entrance Plaza. A good variety of film is available, and several different types of cameras can be rented or purchased. There is a satellite camera shop in Journey Into Imagination. Film is available at many locations throughout World Showcase.

ENTERTAINMENT: There is some entertainment in Future World, and a broader spectrum of live performances in each pavilion in World Showcase.

The America Gardens Theatre and World Showcase Plaza are the two main stages for scheduled daily shows. (Check at the stages for exact times; the WorldKey Information Service at Earth Station also has details on shows and times.)

FIRST AID: Minor medical problems can be handled at First Aid, which is near the Odyssey Restaurant next to the World of Motion (in Future World) and Mexico (in World Showcase).

GETTING AROUND: Five 66-foot water taxis, the *FriendShip* boats, shuttle guests back and forth across World Showcase Lagoon. Docks are located at both sides of World Showcase Plaza, in front of

Germany, and near Morocco. Several double-decker buses, in styles once found all over New York City, London, and Berlin, can be boarded for a ride around the World Showcase Promenade, stopping at several points along the way.

HANDICAPPED VISITORS: Nearly all the attractions, shops, and restaurants in Epcot Center are completely barrier-free. Parking for handicapped guests is available; inquire at the Toll Plaza. The monorail platform is accessible via elevator. Wheelchairs can be rented at the Stroller and Wheelchair Rentals shop on the east side of the Entrance Plaza, at the Gift Stop on the west side, and at the France pavilion. A guidebook for handicapped visitors is available at Earth Station.

INFORMATION: In Future World, visit Earth Station, beside Spaceship Earth, to use the intriguing computer terminals of the WorldKey Information Service there. Hosts and hostesses also are on hand. In World Showcase, visit the WorldKey satellites in World Showcase Plaza and outside Germany.

LOCKERS: These can be found at the Bus Information Center in the bus parking lot, just outside the Entrance Plaza, and in a small area on the west side of the plaza, underneath Spaceship Earth.

LOST AND FOUND: Located on the west side of the Entrance Plaza.

MEMORABILIA: The Gateway, located alongside Spaceship Earth in the Entrance Plaza, and Centorium in Future World's CommuniCore are the two main sources for Epcot Center souvenirs. The Gift Stop and the Stroller and Wheelchair Rentals shop near the Entrance Plaza are good shopping spots, too. Souvenirs of the participating nations are found in each World Showcase pavilion.

MONEY MATTERS: Currency exchange and other banking services are available at the bank on the east side of the Entrance Plaza, just beyond the ticket booths. Both credit cards (American Express and MasterCard) and traveler's checks are accepted in shops and (with the exception of fast food locations, where you must pay with cash or traveler's checks only) in restaurants as well.

PACKAGE PICKUP: Cumbersome or heavy purchases can be transported free of charge (by Disney hosts or hostesses) to this small office on the west side of the Entrance Plaza for later pickup. Ask your salesperson how this is arranged.

THE GIFT STOP: Rental wheelchairs and strollers are available, and film, gift items, sundries, and tobacco are sold. Located near handicapped parking at the entrance to the park.

PETS: No pets are permitted in Epcot Center, but there is the Kennel Club just east of the Entrance Plaza. *Do not leave pets in the car.* The cost for boarding pets is $3.50 per day; pets may not be boarded overnight at the Epcot Center kennel.

STROLLER AND WHEELCHAIR RENTALS: Available in the shop of that name on the east side of the Entrance Plaza, as well as the Gift Stop, and at the France pavilion. Replacement strollers and wheelchairs are available in Germany, France, and the United Kingdom.

ADMISSION PRICES

A Guests at WDW-Owned Resorts/Villas and WDW Village Hotel Plaza
B Other Guests

	A	B
ONE-DAY TICKET		
Adult	$18	$18
Child*	$15	$15
THREE-DAY WORLD PASSPORT		
Adult	$41	$42
Child*	$33	$34
FOUR-DAY WORLD PASSPORT		
Adult	$50	$52
Child*	$40	$42
FIVE-DAY WORLD PASSPORT		
Adult	$59	$62
Child*	$47	$50

The cost of a **ONE-YEAR WORLD PASSPORT** is $125 for adults and $100 for children.

*3 through 12 years of age

Prices subject to change

ADMISSION: Tickets and Passports are available for one, three, four, and five days. The Disney organization defines a ticket as admission for one day only; other forms of admission media (for longer periods) are called Passports. One-day tickets may be used at either Epcot Center *or* in the Magic Kingdom, but not at both sites on the same day. Three-, four-, and five-day World Passports can be used at both Epcot Center *and* the Magic Kingdom on the same day; unlike one-day tickets, they include unlimited use of the transportation system inside Walt Disney World. There are no admission media for two-day visits; a two-day guest must buy two one-day tickets. Cash, traveler's checks, personal checks (with proper ID), American Express, and MasterCard can be used to pay for all admission media.

FUTURE WORLD

A mere listing of the basic themes covered by the Future World pavilions—agriculture, communications, energy, imagination, and transportation—tends to sound a tad academic, and perhaps even a little forbidding. But when these serious topics are presented with that special Disney flair, they become part of an experience that ranks among Walt Disney World's most exciting. Some of these subjects are explored in the course of lively and unusual Disney "adventures," involving a whole arsenal of remarkable motion pictures, special effects, and Audio-Animatronics figures so remarkable that it is hard to remain unmoved. Other themes come into play at hands-on exhibits full of touch-sensitive video screens, two-way televisions, computers that play special games, and other high-tech equipment that few people ever actually get a chance to experience in everyday life. Far from depicting the kind of sci-fi future seen in the Magic Kingdom's Tomorrowland, this look into the future seems far more practical and realistic. In addition, the basic elements of Future World are warm, attractive, and appealing in their own right, from the palm-dotted Entrance Plaza and the massive (but airy) glass-walled buildings of CommuniCore East and West to the stupendous fountain just past Spaceship Earth and that many-faceted "geosphere" that has rapidly become the universal symbol of Epcot Center.

There is so much to see and enjoy that it's hard to know just what to do first. Many guests simply stop at Spaceship Earth on their way into Epcot Center and proceed to wander at random from one pavilion to the next throughout the morning. As a result, many of the pavilions are frustratingly crowded in the morning—especially Spaceship Earth, which has its largest crowds before lunch.

A wise alternative is to choose one pavilion from those described below—or perhaps two, if you've arrived early enough to be there when the gates to Epcot Center open—and then to head for World Showcase, moving clockwise around the lagoon on one day of your visit and counterclockwise on the next. Then in the afternoon, when the majority of guests are lining up at World Showcase pavilions, return to Future World. World of Motion, Horizons, and the Universe of Energy, a five-minute walk from each other, have relatively few visitors during the afternoon; CommuniCore East and World of Motion's TransCenter are not only fascinating spots to pass the exceptionally busy hours after lunch, but also very cool refuges when high temperatures prevail outdoors. And although queues can be found at Journey Into Imagination and at The Land throughout most of the late morning and afternoon—not only for the several attractions that each one houses, but also at the pavilion entrances—the period from late afternoon through closing is usually peaceful.

GETTING ORIENTED

As one crosses the enormous Entrance Plaza, the gleaming silver ball straight ahead (and facing south) is Spaceship Earth (not to be confused with Earth Station, which is at its base). CommuniCore East (at left) and West (to the right) are the two large, crescent-shaped buildings that flank the large fountain just past Spaceship Earth. Universe of Energy, Horizons, and World of Motion lie to the left (east) of CommuniCore East; Journey Into Imagination and The Land are located to the right (west) of CommuniCore West. The World Showcase section of Epcot Center surrounds the shoreline of the large lagoon.

Future World pavilions are described here as a visitor encounters them while moving counterclockwise (from right around to the left, that's west to east around the area).

1. Spaceship Earth
2. CommuniCore West
3. The Land
4. Journey Into Imagination
5. World of Motion
6. Horizons
7. Universe of Energy
8. CommuniCore East

SPACESHIP EARTH

As it looms impressively just above the earth, this great faceted silver geosphere—visible on a clear day from an airplane flying along either Florida coast—looks a little bit like it's ready to blast off like the gigantic spaceship in *Close Encounters of the Third Kind*. It looks large from a distance, and seems even more immense when viewed from directly underneath. It's no surprise that most visitors simply stop beneath it and just gawk. The show inside, which explores man's continuing search for ever more efficient means of communication, remains one of Epcot Center's most visually compelling.

Weighing one million pounds, measuring 164 feet in diameter and 180 feet in height, and encompassing 2,200,000 cubic feet of space, this geosphere is held aloft by six legs supported by pylons sunk 100 feet into the ground. The distinctive sheen of its covering derives from a sort of quarter-inch-thick sandwich made of two anodized aluminum faces and a polyethylene core. This sheath is made up of 954 triangular panels, not all of equal size or shape.

107

A common misconception about Spaceship Earth is that it is a geodesic dome. Not so. The designers had to make up the word *geosphere* because the structure is unlike any other preexisting building. A geodesic dome is comprised of only half a sphere, while Spaceship Earth is completely round. Nor can it be compared to the similarly faceted creation that housed the U.S. pavilion at Montreal's Expo 67, which actually was only three quarters of a sphere. In fact, this extraordinarily large Disney creation is not even a perfect sphere; the steelworkers' requirements dictated its slightly uneven dimensions.

Presented by AT&T.

SPACESHIP EARTH SHOW: The noted science fiction writer Ray Bradbury, together with a number of consultants and advisers from the Smithsonian Institution, the Los Angeles area's prestigious Huntington Library, USC, and the University of Chicago (among others), collaborated with Disney designers in developing this memorable journey. It begins in an inky black time tunnel complete with a musty smell that suggests the ages, and continues through history from the days of Cro-Magnon Man (thirty or forty thousand years ago) to the present.

En route, an Egyptian temple shows off the pictorial representations of words and sounds known as hieroglyphics, which were first used around 3000 B.C., and hieratic writing, a form of script used to write on papyrus. A Phoenician scene set in the ninth century B.C. acknowledges civilization's debt to those tireless traders who introduced a 22-character alphabet (based on sounds) that put written communication, once the province of the intelligentsia alone, within the grasp of the entire public at large. The Roman system of roads, the Islamic empire, the efforts of 11th- and 12th-century Benedictine monks to hand-copy religious and classical manuscripts, the Gutenberg press, the Renaissance in Italy, and a number of the 20th century's inventions are all represented, and in most cases it's not necessary to be a history scholar to understand why. The Greek theater scene, whose meaning here may be not as widely understood as it should be, reminds viewers that it was the Greeks who refined the alphabet (by the addition of vowels) and then went on to use the language so expressively. Then, as now, theater was an important means of examining and transmitting the moral and social questions of the time.

The attraction features some remarkable special effects: the shooting stars and thunderbolts and dampness in the time tunnel at the start; the flickering candles in the scene where a monk (himself crafted with such precision and authenticity as to appear to be breathing) has nodded off; the smell of smoke coming from the fall of Rome, to name only a few.

And every scene is executed in remarkable detail. The symbols on the wall of that Egyptian temple really are hieroglyphics, and the contents of the letter being dictated by the pharoah was excerpted from a missive actually received by an agent of a ruler of the period. The actor in the Greek theater scene is delivering lines from Sophocles' *Oedipus Rex*. In the scene depicting the fall of Rome, the graffiti reproduces markings from the walls of Pompeii. In the Islamic scene, the quadrant—an instrument used in astronomy and navigation—is a copy of one from the tenth century. The type on Johann Gutenberg's press actually moves, and the page that the celebrated 15th-century printer is examining is a replica of one from a Bible in the collection of the above-mentioned Huntington Library. In the Renaissance scene, the book being read is Virgil's *Aeneid*; the musical instruments in that scene are a lute and a *lyra da braccio*, both replicas of real period pieces. In the 20th-century scenes, the steam-powered press is a reproduction of one that had been developed by William Bullock around 1863, notable because it used paper in continuous rolls rather than individual sheets.

Some visitors wonder as to the identity of the excerpts from the radio and television shows broadcast in this area. Take note: The former include *The Lone Ranger*, *The Shadow*, a commentary by Walter Winchell, and the Joe Louis–Max Schmeling 1938 rematch. It's the first round, and Schmeling, who had defeated Joe Louis for the first time in his career in a 1936 twelfth-round K.O., is on the mat. The referee is counting—and the crowds are going wild. Among the television programs are Walter Cronkite's reports from the March 10, 1964, New Hampshire Republican primaries, Walt Disney introducing *The Wonderful World of Color*, Ed Sullivan and the Harlem Globetrotters, the Colts versus Browns NFL championship game (1964), and *Ozzie and Harriet*, with David and Ricky Nelson. Film buffs may recognize clips from the movies *Girl Shy*, with Harold Lloyd (1924), *Top Hat* with Fred Astaire and Ginger Rogers (1935), and *20,000 Leagues Under the Sea* (1954).

All these sights are enough to keep necks craning and heads turning as the "time machines" wend their way upward. But the most dazzling scene is the ride's finale, when the vehicles arrive at the topmost point in the geosphere, and visitors gaze in awe into a vast inky dome full of what seem like thousands of tiny stars. These are projected by the "star ball," created by the Disney special effects department when it was discovered that the inside ceiling of the geosphere was too large for conventional planetarium equipment.

Note: The lines for this attraction are usually at their longest during the morning hours, and at their shortest just before park closing time.

THE GATEWAY AND CAMERA CENTER: These two shops are located quite near the entrance to Spaceship Earth. The former sells Epcot Center souvenirs—T-shirts, mugs, toys, etc.—as well as sun tan lotion, tissues, and the like. Film and various other Kodak products are sold at the Camera Center. Cameras are sold or rented here and same-day film processing is available.

EARTH STATION: The similarity of names between this area (just south of Spaceship Earth) and that of the attraction itself can be confusing to first-time visitors, and that's unfortunate because this area is one of the most vital parts of Epcot Center.

Not only is it the principal source of Epcot Center information, but it is also the spot to make dinner reservations via the easy-to-use touch-sensitive TV screens found in abundance at Epcot Center. For more specific details on making these reservations, see page 163. When the terminals are not being utilized to arrange tables for dinner, they can be used to get an overall picture of Epcot Center, to learn about each pavilion in considerable detail, and to discover nearly everything else that one could conceivably want to know about Epcot Center. If the system's electronic A-to-Z index to shops, restaurants, attractions, and services does not answer a question, it's possible to summon a specially trained human host or hostess, who will be able to hear and see the querying guest with the aid of a microphone and video camera unobtrusively placed adjacent to the screen. (Most of these WorldKey Information Service hosts and hostesses speak Spanish fluently; some speak other languages.)

Meanwhile, overhead, huge multifaceted screens provide an overview (albeit a somewhat cubistic one) of everything Epcot Center offers, while hosts and hostesses are on duty in person at two counters. They also keep records of any lost children who may be at the Baby Care Center at any given time, and maintain a notebook in which adults who have become separated from their families or friends can leave messages for each other.

COMMUNICORE WEST

This pavilion, the large crescent-shaped building located just west of the three-tiered fountain south of Earth Station (to your right while facing World Showcase Lagoon), is the setting not only for one of Future World's most attractive fast-food eateries but also for an exhibit known as FutureCom that is similar to the lively Epcot Computer Central in CommuniCore East.

Don't miss the gardenias on the fountain plaza side of the CommuniCore West breezeway. These fragrant bushes bloom about three times a year, from spring into summer.

FUTURECOM: How people gather information—via signs and satellites, newspapers and traffic lights, and ticker tape and telephones—is the topic here. Dominating the area is a sculpture known as the Information Fountain, made up of just about all imaginable forms of communication with which 20th-century denizens are bombarded: books and records, magazines, maps, TV screens, laser discs, signs, labels, seed catalogues, stock certificates, movie film, neon lights, and more.

Equally compelling are a couple of hands-on exhibits that show off new technology. At one bank of touch-sensitive TV screens, a visitor merely touches the machine to find out what's happening in his or her home state. Another exhibit demonstrates video teleconferencing; increasingly, businesses are using this device in lieu of flying their employees all over the country for meetings. At Epcot Center it gives visitors the chance to see themselves on TV.

Don't miss the Phraser: It actually speaks, in a curious monotone, the words that guests peck out on a typewriter keyboard, and it does so with remarkable accuracy—so long as the words follow standard rules of pronunciation.

Also amusing is an adjacent Network Control game, which, by giving visitors a chance to try their own hand, demonstrates how network controllers at the telephone companies manage the flow of long-distance telephone calls. The idea of the nearby Chip Cruiser game is to use "laser beams" to blast computer-control-room contaminants before they affect the service.

For preschoolers, there's a crawl-through maze—a 420× enlargement of a microprocessor chip. Adults find this as fascinating to look at as their offspring do to play inside.

Note: The Mickey Mouse clock in the Age of Information animated mural on FutureCom's east wall is one of the few reminders anywhere in Epcot Center of the pint-size character that built the World.

EPCOT OUTREACH: No single Epcot Center pavilion pretends to tell the whole story of the subject it covers, but since the addition of this information and resource center (to the northern half of CommuniCore West, the section closest to Spaceship Earth), no visitor can complain about a lack of fact-finding sources at Epcot Center. That's because EPCOT Outreach provides access to information from encyclopedias, periodicals, and wire services, via a computerized data service. A research librarian and a group of assistants can extract appropriate printed materials from the files at hand to answer any lingering questions that might remain. The topics covered? Anything and everything that's presented in either Future World or World Showcase.

Educators take note: The EPCOT Outreach area includes a teachers' lounge, with cubicles where instructors can view audio-visual materials. There also are areas in which to examine computer software, filmstrips, and videotapes. A special bonus are the lesson plans on Future World themes, geared to students from elementary through high school levels. They're available free just for the asking.

THE LAND

Occupying six acres, this enormous skylighted pavilion, Future World's largest, examines the nature of one of everybody's favorite topics—food. A film, *Symbiosis*, explores the creative partnerships between mankind and the land he inhabits. A boat ride takes a look at farming in the past and future. Guided tours give interested visitors the chance to learn more about the experimental agricultural techniques actually being practiced in the pavilion and nearby greenhouses, and to get ideas about applications in the garden. In addition, the subject of nutrition is touched upon in one of Future World's wackiest attractions, an Audio-Animatronics musical revue (called the Kitchen Kabaret) which was inspired by the Magic Kingdom's Country Bear Jamboree.

Also the home of two of Epcot Center's most interesting eating spots, The Land is understandably popular. Lengthy queues do build up, not only for the boat ride but also for entry to the pavilion itself, especially around 11 A.M. (Those with reservations for the guided tour or for a meal in The Good Turn restaurant are permitted to bypass the queue, by showing their reservation card, within 15 minutes of the time of their appointment.) The best plan is to visit the pavilion first thing in the morning, have a quick breakfast, and perhaps make reservations for lunch in The Good Turn. Or wait until afternoon, when—though there may be a wait for the boat ride—it probably won't be necessary to line up just to get inside. Count on spending two hours, longer if plans include eating here.

Presented by Kraft.

LISTEN TO THE LAND: This 13½-minute boat ride ventures into three ecological communities (rain forest, desert, and prairie) that covered much of the world before man arrived on the scene. It then cruises through a turn-of-the-century American farm and, finally, moves among growing areas full of live plants for a mind-expanding sample of innovative agricultural techniques. One of these newly developed methods features lettuce grown in rotating drums that simulate gravity in outer space, thereby demonstrating how food might be grown in space stations of the future. In an Aqua Cell area, fish and shrimp are raised in a controlled environment, and in the Desert Farm area, plants receive nutrients through a drip irrigation system that delivers just the right amount of water, and no more—important in an arid environment.

As fantastic and unreal as they appear, the plants on view in the experimental greenhouses are living. In contrast, those in the biomes (ecological communities) were manufactured in Disney studios out of flexible, lightweight plastic that simulates the cellulose found in real trees. The trunks and branches were molded from live specimens; the majestic sycamore in the farmhouse's front yard, for example, duplicates one that stands ouside a Burbank, California, car wash. Hundreds of thousands of polyethylene leaves, made in Hong Kong, were then snapped on. These are fire retardant, as are the blades of grass, which are made of glass fibers implanted into rubber mats. In the South American rain forest scene, the water on the leaves and trunks is supplied by a special drip system that provides a constant flow of moisture.

TOMORROW'S HARVEST TOUR: Guided tours take place daily every half hour between 9 A.M. and 4:30 P.M. They cover basically the same topics as the boat ride, but because they last 30 to 45 minutes, they can go into far more detail. And participants do have an opportunity to ask questions—and listen to what the home gardeners and farmers who commonly make up at least part of the tour groups have to say. Guides are all members of the agricultural operations staff, and all have degrees in some area of plant science. Reservations, which are required, must be made in person on the day of the tour near the Broccoli & Co. shop at the entrance to the Kitchen Kabaret on the pavilion's lower level; most places are filled by 10 A.M.

KITCHEN KABARET: Bonnie Appetit is the star of this zany show about good nutrition. Each of the four acts focuses on one of the main food groups—dairy products, fruits and vegetables, meats and proteins, and grains and cereals. But that is almost peripheral to the entertainment, presented by the Kitchen Krackpots Band, Mr. Dairy Goods and his Stars of the Milky Way, the Boogie Woogie Bak'ry Boy, the Cereal Sisters (Mairzy Oats, Rennie Rice, and Connie Corn), the Colander Combo, the Fiesta Fruit, and Mr. Hamm and that incurable punster Mr. Eggz, who joke up a corny storm. ("Cheese! I cheddar to think about it," says one. And: "Why was Chicken Little so upset when his mom fell asleep in a hot tub? His brother came out hard-boiled.") The characters are endearing, especially Mr. Broccoli, with his punk-rocker hairdo and pink-rimmed glasses, and the shop outside, Broccoli & Co., does a booming business in mementos bearing their likenesses.

SYMBIOSIS: Presented in the Harvest Theater (near The Land's entrance) on a 23-by-60-foot screen, this 18½-minute 70mm motion picture examines the delicate balance between technology's progress and environmental integrity, reinforcing the sound ideas behind some of the techniques seen in The Land's growing areas. There are some horror stories about the misuse of land, including tales of the pollution of lakes and streams throughout the world. But there also are some tremendously reassuring tales—the timely rescue of the Thames, Lake Constance, and Oregon's Willamette River from death-by-pollution, and sound forest management practices in Sweden, in Germany's Black Forest, and in the U.S.'s Pacific Northwest. Filming took place in about 30 nations around the world, and there is some terrific scenery. The breathtaking opening scene shows the magnificent rice terraces located near Banaue in the Philippines. Don't let the unfamiliar name of the film put you off: this is a highlight of any Epcot Center visit.

BROCCOLI & CO.: This little shop alongside the Kitchen Kabaret stocks merchandise bearing the images of Mr. Broccoli, Mr. Eggplant, the Colander

Combo, and all the other characters from the adjacent show—plastic mug-and-bowl sets and plush toys for the school-age crowd, magnetized plastic stick-ons to embellish the front of a refrigerator, place mats, and more.

JOURNEY INTO IMAGINATION

The oddly shaped glass pyramids that house Journey Into Imagination (as you face World Showcase Lagoon and then straight ahead to your right) are striking, but they pale by comparison with the experiences inside—which may be the most exciting of all at Epcot Center. Dreamfinder, a jolly red-headed professorial figure, who sports a carrot-colored beard and is accompanied by a purple baby dragon called Figment, is only one of the pavilion's delights. He appears in person outside and again when he escorts guests through the imagination world during a 14-minute ride inside.

There's also a 3-D movie so true-to-life that almost everyone in the audience reaches out to touch at least one of the images during every showing. Not to mention the electronic funhouse known as the Image Works. Or the quirky fountains outside—the Jellyfish Fountains that spurt streams of water that spread out at the top, look like their namesake sea creature for an instant, and then fall back to earth, or the Serpentine Fountains, which send out smooth streams of water that arc from one garden plot to another in the most astonishing fashion.

Plant lovers will recognize the sculpted trees in this garden as podocarpus—the same type that are planted in many other locations (but pruned to many different shapes) throughout Epcot Center.

Count on spending at least an hour and fifteen minutes at the very least at this pavilion—two hours wouldn't be too long at all. Note that the queue outside seems to be longest between around 10 A.M. and noon and remains fairly lengthy throughout most of the day. Early mornings and late evening are the least congested times to visit.

Presented by Kodak.

JOURNEY INTO IMAGINATION RIDE: It is here that Dreamfinder creates Figment out of a lizard's body, a crocodile's nose, a steer's horns, two big yellow eyes, two small wings, and a pinch of childish delight—and commences the visitor's journey into the world of imagination.

First-timers may not realize that the 14-minute ride doesn't present a random assortment of scenes that are handsome and scary by turns, but rather an organized exploration of how imagination works and the areas of life in which it functions.

First there is a visit to the Dreamport, the area of the mind to which the senses are constantly sending data to be stored for later use by the imagination. Subsequent scenes depict the way imagination suffuses the worlds of the visual arts, of literature, of the performing arts, and of science and technology. In the course of all this, laser beams dance, lightning crackles, and letters pour out of a giant typewriter like notes from an organ. The images are as fanciful as imagination itself.

It's interesting to note that the iridescent painting-in-progress on the wall in the visual arts scene—a so-called "polage" produced by refracting light through polarized filters—is the largest of its kind anywhere. The artist who executed the mural had previously done paintings no larger than four feet in height. Also, when you see flashing lights ahead about three quarters of the way through the ride, be sure to sit up straight and smile—your picture is being taken.

IMAGE WORKS: It's a rare Image Works visitor who doesn't experience at least some of the emotion experienced by one four-year-old girl who cried every time her parents tried to take her home. That's not surprising, because the Image Works is literally crammed with activities that give every visitor the chance to use his or her imagination and creative abilities.

For instance, at Dreamfinder's School of Drama, near the entrance to the Image Works, visitors have the opportunity to be in pictures. Five guests at a time step onto a small stage and, thanks to a new Chroma-Key video effects technique that involves foreground and background matting, perform in short video stories—"Daring Deputies and the Return of Sagebrush Sam," a Western; "Acrobatic Astronauts in Galactic Getaway," in a sci-fi setting; or "Enchanted Travelers—Wily Wizard and the Cranky King," a sort of fairy tale. Spectators and performers alike see the results as they happen via strategically placed video screens. It's *always* fun to watch the groups of senior citizens, teenagers, or families jumping crazily around on stage following on-screen instructions from Dreamfinder (and, in fact, having the time to spend more than just a few seconds watching these goings-on is sufficient reason to allot more time to your overall Epcot Center visit).

Not far from Dreamfinder's School of Drama is another especially lively area known as The Sensor, a sort of electronic maze whose various elements react to a visitor's presence by producing lights and sounds. Upon entering the Rainbow Corridor, you'll find a tunnel full of neon tubes in all the hues of the rainbow. Image Warp's pneumatically powered Mylar mirrors produce moving versions of old-style fun-house reflections in a room wackily illuminated by strobe lights. Then there's the Lumia—a plastic ball seven feet in diameter, inside which swirling patterns of light and color appear in response to the sounds of voices of different frequencies and intensities. At Stepping Tones, hexagonal splotches of colored light on the floor correspond to sounds—a drumroll, a flourish on the harp, a couple of chords sung by a men's chorus, a snippet of hoedown fiddling, and such—that are emitted when the area is trodden upon; the last red hexagon in the room, located in the farthest corner from the entrance, sends out the sound of a beautiful chord played on a harp. In fact, the first tones re-create the music heard in Close Encounters of the Third Kind. The floor was "orchestrated" by an avant-garde San Francisco Bay Area composer so that all possible combinations sound interesting at the very least—and the more the merrier.

Outside The Sensor maze, the Image Works offers the Lightwriter, which involves drawing geometric patterns with laser beams, and the Magic Palette, where a special stylus and a touch-sensitive control surface can be used to create all kinds of images, mostly in Day-Glo colors. People often queue up to try these, while huge kaleidoscopes nearby and the very unusual pin screens are practically overlooked. Manufacturing the latter involved putting thousands of straight pins through a screen illuminated with colored lights from below (visitors run their hands across the bottom, thereby creating sweeping patterns of color). Producing the pin screens, however, was not an easy task: because every straight pin had to be identical, and because production-line straight pins simply aren't made quite so precisely, the artist who worked on the project spent a month at the Dayville, Connecticut, pin factory to monitor pin production and thereby assure total uniformity.

The Electronic Philharmonic, one of the most amusing sections of the Image Works, allows guests to take turns conducting an orchestra. Here's how this works: Each patch of light on the console represents a group of instruments (strings, woodwinds, brass, percussion). Raising and lowering one's hand above that patch of light increases and decreases the volume of the sound produced by that section of the "orchestra"; by covering three out of four patches of light, it is theoretically possible to bring up only the strings or only the brass or only the percussion. This is very difficult to do alone, however, so it's wise to enlist a partner.

MAGIC JOURNEYS: This very special and quite spectacular 70mm 3-D motion picture, which is viewed while wearing purple-rimmed polarized eyeglasses, is one of the largest-format films of its type ever created. It is also remarkably realistic: when the screen fills with apple blossoms or a kite heads right at the audience, nearly everyone in the theater reaches out; when lightning strikes, people jump back in fright.

To get dramatic results like these, Disney cameramen developed a new system of 3-D photography, which some observers have called the most precise and versatile in existence today. Two synchronized cameras are used, one for each of the images that each visitor's eye sees. The amount of depth that the viewer perceives is determined by the distance between the cameras and the direction in which they are aimed. The new Disney system offers greater-than-ever control over both of these variables. The 18-minute film was directed by Murray Lerner, who won an Academy Award in 1981 for his documentary From Mao to Mozart: Isaac Stern in China.

CAMERA SALES AND RENTAL KIOSK: A limited selection of film is for sale here, along with a small selection of cameras, filters, cable releases, and other necessities of life for the traveling photographer.

WORLD OF MOTION

This wheel-shaped, stainless-steel-clad structure, 318 feet in diameter and about 60 feet high, presents the story of transportation past, present, and future through a whimsical show full of Audio-Animatronics figures (the most colorful since the hairy-legged Pirates of the Caribbean, in the Magic Kingdom) and a series of exhibits that look far into the future of transportation.

The tall trees on the plaza in front of the pavilion are eucalyptus: They were grown from seeds planted a dozen years ago. The tops are being pruned flat and the branches trimmed so that in a few years passengers on the monorail will look across a flat plane of treetops, while guests on the ground will be shaded by a spreading canopy of green.

Presented by General Motors.

WORLD OF MOTION SHOW: Chronicling man's passion for always getting somewhere just a little bit faster, this appealing, if rather unsophisticated, show reflects the eccentric humor of one of its chief designers—longtime Disney art director Ward Kimball, who also shares the credit for developing Jiminy Cricket. The 14½-minute ride-through attraction begins with a look back to the sometimes painful days when foot power was the only means of transportation. It then moves wackily forward through time as man tries out ostriches and zebras, dreams of magic carpets, invents the wheel, rides in chariots, and tinkers with flying machines, balloons, steam carriages, riverboats, stagecoaches, buckboards, airplanes, automobiles, and assorted other vehicles.

In the show's 22 scenes, about 150 Audio-Animatronics figures make their debut. (Actually, some of the faces of the "people" in the group are used several times because, since they wear different expressions, only the exceptionally keen of eye recognize the duplication.)

In order to lend verisimilitude to each scene, bicycles, streetlights, cars, carts, wagons, and trains were added as props—some of them genuine antiques and some of them reproductions. The Wells Fargo Stagecoach in the Western wagons scene is a 150-year-old item imported from Phoenix, Arizona, and then restored, along with several others unearthed in northern California. In the city scene, the telephone wire is the real thing (made around

---

WHERE TO EAT IN EPCOT CENTER

For all the details on restaurants in Epcot Center—including both Future World and World Showcase—plus information about how to obtain restaurant reservations where necessary, see the Good Meals, Great Times chapter that begins on page 153.

1920), and all of the early automobiles are authentic. Especially amusing is the final scene, which shows Americans enjoying the good life on the road in a trio of spiffy vintage cars that looked modern not too long ago.

The journey through the history of transportation is followed by trips through special "speedrooms" that provide a dizzying you-are-there feeling—similar to the ones in If You Had Wings, in the Magic Kingdom, except that the film was shot in a much larger format, 70mm—and through a breathtaking city of the future, where trainlike vehicles shoot through the air from skyscraper to skyscraper.

It's worth noting that this attraction is almost empty during the first half-hour after park opening; it usually is at its busiest from midmorning until around 4 P.M.

TRANSCENTER: Far from being just a showroom for the latest model GM cars, this area situated at the ride's exit contains entertaining exhibits about the 20th century's most important means of transportation. One section, called The Bird and the Robot, stars a cigar-puffing, Groucho Marx–like toucan bird originally built for Tokyo Disneyland's Enchanted Tiki Room, and a General Motors assembly-line robot whose dexterity and flexibility make it easy to understand how similar devices can be used for painting and welding a new car on the assembly line.

Then there's *The Water Engine*, an amusing animated film that explores possible alternatives to the internal combustion engine (including "Equus Cheapus"), and the "Dreamer's Workshop," an exhibit that shows off sleek prototype cars of the future like the Aero 2000, an experimental four-seat subcompact designed specifically for display at Epcot Center. Other areas demonstrate the torture test that GM vehicles must pass—locks flicking up and down, windows and visor mirrors and door handles opening and closing, keys turning, and more so as to make the TransCenter a fine place to spend time when you don't feel like queueing up at another ride-through attraction.

HORIZONS

For generations, visionaries have been making predictions about life in the future. Jules Verne forecast rockets that would fly like bullets. The 19th century French artist Albert Robida envisioned subways and dirigible taxis and sketched what life in Paris would be like in 1950. And in the Thirties, pulp science-fiction magazines circulated ideas about automatic barber chairs that would give their owners shoeshines and haircuts, about air conditioners that would pipe in alpine chills and tropical breezes, about robots that would do housework, and about suntan lamps and televisions.

The three-acre Horizons show, which draws on the wisdom of countless scientists, adds its own predictions in a pavilion located between Universe of Energy and World of Motion, just beyond CommuniCore East. After a nod to the visions of earlier centuries in a Looking Back at Tomorrow sequence, the pavilion's continuously moving, suspended, four-passenger vehicles convey guests into an OmniSphere. Here, on a pair of spectacular hemispherical screens (80 feet in diameter), projectors with special lenses show filmed scenes of the space shuttle launch and of growing crystals, together with animated sequences of life in a space colony, a DNA chain, computer chips, etc. All this is a prelude to a voyage through a series of sets demonstrating aspects of life in the future. In Nova Cite, the first destination, advanced transportation and communication systems, such as holographic telephones and trains that work by magnetic levitation, keep members of far-flung families in touch with one another. In the Mesa Verde sequence, voice-controlled robot harvesters and genetically engineered fruits and vegetables populate a once-arid desert. Overhead, "hoverlifts" with spinning blades function as automatic shade controls, and "helium lifters" drop their hooks, collect baskets of the harvest from the robots, and fly the produce off to market. In the future farmer's home, shown nearby, there's an electronic pantry that delivers food to the inhabitants at the push of a button and a home communications center where youngsters can study math (or other subjects) by computer. In the Sea Castle sequence, depicting a moveable—but otherwise islandlike—floating city in the Pacific, schoolchildren take underwater field trips to nearby mining and kelp-farming operations manned by robot devices. And in Brava Centauri, a free-floating colony in space, crystals are grown for use by computers back on Earth and colony inhabitants keep in shape in a health-and-recreation center that features games like zero-gravity basketball (seen in shadow along the rear wall), and rowing and bicycling in simulators that allow space folk the opportunity to pursue their favorite sport in any environment they choose. Boaters, for instance, may shoot the Colorado River's rapids in the Grand Canyon, or paddle a Louisiana bayou, or float through the canals of Venice. Home life is just like that on Earth, but with a couple of twists: When a boy newly arrived at the colony doesn't put on his shoes in the morning, he floats away. (They're magnetic shoes, designed for this zero-gravity environment.) And when the family gets together to celebrate a birthday, those who can't attend in person put in an appearance via a holographic telephone.

There's another fine experience at the ride's conclusion: visitors pick the journey's ending. Just push a button, and a special audience-polling device inside your vehicle delivers the 30-second experience that the majority of your fellow riders have requested. The car tilts back and vibrates, and the sound effects enhance the sensation of great speed created by fast-moving, close-up filmed visuals of travel on land, in the sea, and in space, not unlike those found in the speedrooms in the nearby World of Motion and, in the Magic Kingdom, in If You Had Wings.

Trivia buffs will be curious about the sources of the science-fiction clips presented in the Looking Back at

113

Tomorrow sequence. These include the films *Metropolis* (1926) and *Woman in the Moon* (1928) by the director Fritz Lang; *Mars and Beyond* and *Magic Highways U.S.A.*, shown on the *Disneyland* programs of the 1950s; and Woody Allen's *Sleeper*.

Presented by General Electric.

UNIVERSE OF ENERGY

When strolling through Future World toward World Showcase Plaza, it's easy to spot this pavilion's mirrored, asymmetrical pyramid off to the left. But the facade doesn't provide any clue at all to the 38 minutes of surprises in store for those who venture inside. One of the most technologically complex experiences at Epcot Center, the Energy show consists of three motion pictures and a ride-through attraction. Not one of these is exactly what you might expect.

The first film, seen when you enter the pavilion, examines types of energy used today. Its vivid images of falling water, leaping fire, burning coal, enormous piles of logs, sailing ships, jet engines, and beautiful yellow flowers are the makings of a fine photo essay—but there's a twist: the 14-by-90-foot projection surface is not at all a conventional flat motion picture screen but instead is made up of 100 solid triangular elements. These actually rotate on cue from a computer, in synchronization with the changing images, to produce what its creator (Czech filmmaker Emil Radok) described as a "kinetic mosaic."

The second film, shown in an adjoining area, is a 4½-minute animated feature depicting the eras in which today's fossil fuels were created. This film was photographed with the multiplane camera developed by the Disney organization over forty years ago, and the feeling of depth it gave to the forest scenes in famous films like *Bambi* and *Snow White* also enhances the cinemascape here.

But contrary to the expectations of some visitors, there's not an adorably Disneyesque creature in the show. The animals lumbering across the giant screen (which measures 32 feet by 155 feet, over half the length of a football field) are gigantic prehistoric beasts, and the landscape is an eerie one, full of volcanoes, exotic plants, and bizarre insects. Even more astonishing is the moment at the conclusion of the movie when the screen rises and suddenly the whole seating area of the auditorium begins to rotate, and then breaks up into six smaller sections that slowly move forward—usually to the accompaniment of a chorus of oohs and aahs from startled members of the audience.

Before very many people have even begun to grasp the transformation, the vehicles have embarked upon an odyssey through a three-dimensional re-creation of the primeval world suggested in the film, an otherworldly region of sulfur-scented air, eerie blue moonlight, unearthly fogs, and lava so ominously authentic that few visitors dare reach out and touch it—even when told that one of its main ingredients is a type of commercial food thickener.

Huge trees crowd the forest. Millipedes duel on a log to the left of the vehicles. Brontosauruses wallow in the lagoon out front. A lofty allosaurus battles dramatically with an armored stegosaurus a bit farther along, and an elasmosaurus bursts out of a tidal pool with frightening suddenness—all under the vulturelike gaze of winged creatures known as pteranodons. All of these were created only after months of research, including interviews with countless well-known paleobotanists and paleontologists. The Audio-Animatronics animals are the largest of their type ever to be fabricated, and the 250 prehistoric trees are the first ever to come off any production line. There are so many sounds, smells, and sights here that the time passes in a flash, and before you know it the vehicles have entered another theater.

Here a 12½-minute motion picture, shown on a 220° screen whose breadth intensifies the impact of every image, dramatizes sources of energy for the future. During the filming of the North Sea segment, temperatures dropped so low that the three 65mm cameras used in the filming—specially mounted to generate the almost seamless image projected on the curved screen—had to be taken indoors and defrosted before work could continue. Footage depicting the Space Shuttle's thunderous blast-off, so unusual that even NASA wanted a copy, serves as the film's grand finale and provides images that stay with you as you travel into another Energy adventure, a splendid computer animated light show of what looks like dancing laser beams.

Fully as intriguing as the whole Energy experience is the advanced technology behind it. The traveling vehicles measure 29 feet long and 18 feet wide, and weigh about 30,000 pounds when fully loaded with their complement of 87 passengers. Yet they are guided along the concrete floor using a guide wire only *one eighth inch thick*. And twelve to fifteen percent of the pavilion's required energy is generated by two acres of photovoltaic cells mounted on the roof.

In leaving the pavilion, home gardeners should note that the southern live oaks immediately to the east of the Universe of Energy (to your right as you face the entrance) are pruned to follow the slanted roofline of the pavilion. These trees were among a handful started from acorns for Hotel Plaza Boulevard (the broad street that runs down the center of Hotel Plaza) for Walt Disney World's opening over a decade ago; a quartet of their siblings, in an un-

pruned state, still can be seen in front of The American Adventure, in World Showcase.

Presented by Exxon.

COMMUNICORE EAST

Officially, CommuniCore—short for Community Core—is the central area of Future World, just beyond (south of) Earth Station. It is comprised of the two large crescent-shaped buildings to the left and right (east and west) and the fountain in the center. The entire complex, which explores the subject of present-day technology, ranks as one of the most interesting areas at Epcot Center.

EPCOT COMPUTER CENTRAL: Computers that talk and play games are the focus of this area located to the left of the fountain plaza entrance to the building. Within the area, there are several activity islands (described below).

Presented by Sperry.

SMRT-1: He looks like a little purple space man; he talks in a sweet little-boy voice; he has a great time playing simple guessing games with guests, whom he asks questions like "Is Lincoln buried in Grant's Tomb?" and "Were Huey, Dewey, and Louie the nephews of Donald Duck?"; and he chortles with considerable glee when someone flubs an answer.

None of this would be very remarkable if not for the fact that the questioner, SMRT-1, is a computer. To judge from the rapt faces that surround him throughout most of Epcot Center's operating hours, guests enjoy the games as much as he does. In fact, it's amusing just to watch, even if the time to spend waiting for a turn to talk back isn't in the day's program.

Note that the instructions relating to SMRT-1 aren't as crystal clear as they could be: Remember to push the button on the telephone set as soon as you arrive on the scene so that SMRT-1 will know you're there.

Rollercoaster: Via a bank of touch-sensitive video screens, this area makes the point that designing these thrill rides is the job of a computer. Players get the chance to build their own coaster using the parts that the computerized program provides—long and short rises, a loop-the-loop, a semi-spiral, and a big drop. The reward for a job well done: a simulated (and rather remarkably scary) ride on the finished product.

Backstage Magic: Accessible via a ramp along the north wall of Epcot Computer Central, this short show is designed to explain the evolution of computers, how they work, and how they are used at Walt Disney World, and to provide a glimpse of the role computers will be playing in the 21st century. It features an array of special effects that help bring computers to life.

Great America Census: It's difficult to say which aspect of this attraction is more compelling: the chance to use those amazing touch-sensitive TV screens, or the facts that are revealed about this nation in the course of the computers' guessing games. A list of topics appears on the screen at the start of the quiz, and guests choose the ones on which they'd most like to be questioned—The Fifty States, School Days, On the Farm, Communication Line, Home Sweet Home, Population Clock, etc. The answers reveal—among other interesting facts—that

there are approximately 12,000 centenarians alive in the United States today, that women in the 1800s had an average of seven children, that the citizens of Alaska have a higher average income than those of any other state, that Florida will be the fastest growing state during the rest of the century, and that more motorbikes are registered in Michigan than in any other state. Every time someone answers a question incorrectly, an obnoxious-sounding buzzer goes off, provoking embarrassed titters from the erring players—and a good deal of warmhearted sympathy from lookers-on.

Get Set Jet Game: The idea of this game, which aims to demonstrate the use of computers in some passenger-related sections of the aviation business, is to load the greatest possible number of passengers and luggage and to complete a required checklist of safety and maintenance precautions within 60 seconds. To accomplish this successfully requires considerable hand-eye coordination, but the game is amusing even for members of the all-thumbs crowd. The touch-sensitive video screens on which the game is played are located practically alongside those of the Great America Census.

Flag Game: Designed to illustrate the role of computers in manufacturing, this bank of touch-sensitive video screens (not too far from the ones described just above) gives players a chance to try to build an American flag. People with good hand-eye coordination usually can complete the assignment with flying colors—and the whole area is usually filled with the peppy patriotic music that celebrates their success so enthusiastically that it's hard to resist another go-round.

Central Reservations Office: A branch of the Central Reservations Office—which handles bookings for rooms in the Walt Disney World resorts as well as for dinner shows and an assortment of other special activities—is located in the corner of the room near SMRT-1.

AMERICAN EXPRESS TRAVELPORT: In this area (opposite Epcot Computer Central), touch-sensitive video screens, located in each of a handful of booths dubbed "vacation stations," provide the opportunity to preview vacations anywhere in the world, from Singapore to Mexico to France to the California coastline. Guests choose the region that interests them—or ask the machines to make suggestions—and then are shown short slide presentations about the destination they've selected. Further prompting elicits lodging, dining, and sight-seeing suggestions. The nearby American Express Travel Service office can sell traveler's checks, travel insurance, airplane tickets, tours and cruises, etc., and can arrange for car rentals and individual trips as well. Various services for American Express cardholders are also provided here.

Incidentally, the mysterious-looking 14-foot sphere near the entrance to the TravelPort was designed by the same artist who created the massive Lucite sculpture at the entrance to Future World.

Presented by American Express.

ENERGY EXCHANGE: Biomass, synthetic fuels, and solar, wind, nuclear, and mechanical energy are among the subjects explored here. But although the overall subject matter is serious, the exhibits are so diverting that it's entirely possible to spend an hour or more in the area without being aware of the passage of time. One display gives guests the opportunity to compare the amount of energy that they themselves can generate by pedaling a stationary bicycle, with the power contained in a gallon of gasoline. (Even pedaling at top speed, human beings come in a poor second.) In a related exhibit nearby, turning a crank lights a bulb, and a monitor tells how long it would take working at that rate to produce $1 worth of electricity.

Elsewhere, there are buttons to push to activate taped programs discussing hydropower, geothermal power, and wind power (and the new-style windmills). One bank of touch-sensitive video screens provides information about conserving energy in the home—about radiators and registers, the proper use of a fireplace and a wood-burning stove, air-conditioning, and other such stuff. Another set of screens answers queries on energy sources, energy conservation, and the energy outlook; it also solicits guest opinions about thought-provoking and sometimes controversial energy-related issues. A coal-mining display informs guests about different kinds of coal and shows samples; it also compares reserves of U.S. coal with the nation's other recoverable energy resources and with oil from the Middle East. There is a model of an offshore drilling platform and an exhibit that explains what a "guyed" platform is about. How wells are drilled, from hole making to processing drilling fluid and oil-shale rock, is one of the many other topics.

Presented by Exxon.

ELECTRONIC FORUM: Located in CommuniCore East (close to the lagoon), this attraction contains Future Choice Theater, Epcot Center's ongoing poll of guest opinions. It works this way: Visitors enter a

small theater whose seats are equipped with a number of push buttons. A moderator at the front of the room gives a brief account of an issue (often accompanied by videotapes or film clips that feature people who are authorities on the subject). The moderator then solicits individual opinions, and participants push the right button for the answer that is appropriate. The feelings of the audience are immediately flashed on a screen at the front of the room; often the responses are broken down by age group or sex.

Most people really enjoy themselves here, and better still, few ever have to wait more than the 20 minutes that each session takes to run its course. In any event, that time speeds by thanks to the exhibits outside the theater—a veritable armada of television sets showing regional news, national news, international news, sports news, weather, and foreign-language news. While one channel broadcasts live from the House of Representatives, others bring the news from French Canada, news from the Caribbean and South and Central America (in Spanish), and from Japan (in Japanese; sometimes the screen shows videotaped sessions of the Japanese legislature). As a backdrop, there's an exhibit that explains how the satellites responsible for this large selection of stations work. Eventually, live newscasts aimed for Disney Channel subscribers are expected to be broadcast from here.

CENTORIUM: This large, sleek shop, the most spacious in all of Epcot Center, stocks a vast selection of Epcot Center memorabilia—bumper stickers, watches, books, key chains, pennants, T-shirts, license plates, pencils, hats, visors, memo pads, and much more, plus a good selection of sci-fi and other books relating to the future. In addition, there are all kinds of items related to other areas of Future World, such as dolls that look like the little dragon Figment (one of the new Disney creations seen exclusively at Epcot Center). In anticipation of the upcoming Living Seas pavilion, seashells, sculptures of dolphins, plus sea creatures, sand dollars, and jewelry made out of seashells are among the wares.

Upstairs there are toy cars and elaborate models of all kinds of vehicles, plus computerized chess games and video games, and a whole raft of intriguing solar-powered items, electronic watches, tape players, fancy telephones, and television sets—all state-of-the-art items that are amusing to look at even when you've no intention of buying. Youngsters will particularly enjoy Centorium's round, glassed-in elevator.

WORLD SHOWCASE

Noble sentiments about the brotherhood of man and the fellowship of nations, which have motivated so many world's fairs in the past, also infuse World Showcase. But make no mistake about it: this half of Epcot Center, located to the south of Future World, is unlike any previous international exposition.

It is instead a group of pavilions that curve around World Showcase Lagoon (a body of water that, incidentally, is the size of 85 football fields) to demonstrate Disney conceptions about participating countries in remarkably realistic, consistently entertaining styles. You won't find the real Germany here; rather, the country's essence, much as a traveler returning from a visit might reconstruct what he or she saw. Shops, restaurants, and an occasional special attraction are all housed in a group of structures that is an artful pastiche of all the elements that give that nation's countryside and towns their distinctive flavor. Although occasional liberties have been taken when scale and proportion required, careful research governed the design of every nook and cranny.

In the shops, all wares on display (with the exception of books) were made in the country in whose pavilion they are offered for sale. The food closely approximates native cuisine, and the entertainment is as authentic as the Disney casting directors can make it, with native performers consistently featured. And craftspeople are occasionally on hand to demonstrate their art in the appropriate shops. Thanks to special Epcot Center cultural exchange programs and the personnel department's energetic efforts to recruit nationals from around Central Florida, nearly all the World Showcase staff members in restaurants, shops, and attractions were born in the countries the pavilions represent (or at least spent many years living there), and that contributes still more atmosphere. The ongoing efforts of the entertainment department mean that special festivities are always in the works and that new performers are continually making Epcot Center debuts.

Home gardeners should be sure to note the World Showcase landscaping: Each pavilion's plant material closely approximates what would be found in the featured nation. The 1.3-mile World Showcase Promenade, which links pavilions on the shores of the World Showcase Lagoon, has its own interesting vegetation, beginning in World Showcase Plaza with 75-foot Washingtonia fan palms, Arizona-California natives that were imported into Central Florida. Underneath them is a garden full of rosebushes, numbering among the more than 10,000 tree roses, teas, grandifloras, and miniatures planted throughout World Showcase. The Y-shaped trees nearby are callery pears, which can be seen in several other spots in World Showcase. Those encircling the lagoon on the Promenade are camphor trees, which should eventually grow to a height of 60 or 80 feet and about the same dimensions in breadth, to provide the walkway with abundant and welcome shade.

Note that World Showcase pavilions are at their least crowded from the time the park opens until about 11 A.M., and then again from 6 or 7 P.M. until park closing. So while most of the crowds are standing in line at Future World attractions, shows at World Showcase often are almost empty.

Pavilions are described here in the order that they would be encountered while moving counterclockwise (west to east) around the lagoon after leaving Future World.

CANADA

Celebrating the beauties of America's neighbor to the north, the area devoted to the Western Hemisphere's largest nation is complete with its own mountain, waterfall, rushing stream, rocky canyon, a mine, and a splendid garden massed with colorful flowers. There's even a totem pole, a trading post, and an elaborate, mansard-roofed hotel similar to ones built by the Canadian railroads as they pushed west around the turn of the century. All this is imaginatively arranged somewhat like a split-level house, with the section representing French Canada on top, and another devoted to the mountains alongside it and below. From a distance, the Hôtel du Canada, the main building here, looks like little more than a bump on the landscape—as does Epcot Center's single Canadian Rocky Mountain. But up close they both seem to tower as high as the real thing, thanks to a motion picture designers' technique known as forced perspective, which involves exaggerating the relative smallness of distant parts of a structure to make the totality appear taller than it really is.

The gardens were inspired by the Victoria, British Columbia, Butchart Gardens, a famous park created on the site of a limestone quarry. The hotel is modeled after Ottawa's Victorian-style *Château Laurier*.

Entertainment is provided by the Maple Leaf Brass Band, whose talented members do a comedy routine as they play, and by the Caledonia Bagpipe Band, featuring two pipers and a drummer.

Willow, birch, sweet gum, and maple trees can all be found in the Victoria Gardens; Canada's hemlocks are represented here by deodar cedars, a Himalaya native that can withstand torrid Florida summers with aplomb, while purple-leaf plum trees substitute for Japanese maples, another distinctively Canadian tree not well suited to the Epcot Center climate.

O CANADA!: This motion picture, presented in CircleVision 360 inside Canada's mountain, portrays the Canadian confederation in all its coast-to-coast splendor—the prairies and the plains, the sparkling shorelines and rivers, and the untouched snowfields and rocky mountainsides. The Royal Canadian Mounted Police also put in an appearance. The maritime provinces are all pictured, with their covered bridges and sailing ships, as is Montreal,

117

with its Old World cafés and imposing churches; the scene in the Cathédral de Notre Dame, with its organ booming and choirboys in attendance, is particularly stirring. The great outdoors gets equal play. In one scene, Canada geese take off all around the screen, and the beating of their wings is positively thunderous. Eagles, possums, mallards, bobcats, wolves, bears, deer, bison, and herds of reindeer were all filmed, along with steers being roped at a rodeo and the chuck wagon race that takes place every year at that great provincial fair known as the Calgary Stampede. Skiers in the vast and empty Bugaboos, dogsledders, and ice skaters are featured in the winter scenes; in a hockey game, the sound system almost perfectly conveys the scratch of skates on ice and the sharp whack of sticks against puck. And throughout, the motion picture conveys a sense of the vast size of Canada, providing a you-are-there feeling that makes all of this spectacular scenery still more memorable.

This is partly due to the filming technique, Circle-Vision 360. Also used in the Magic Kingdom's *American Journeys,* it involves a special five-foot-tall, 600-pound camera rig composed of nine individual 35mm cameras evenly arranged around a tubular shaft containing the motor that drives the mechanisms for all the cameras. In some scenes the rig was suspended from a helicopter; when depicting the precision-flying Canadian Snowbirds, Canada's answer to the U.S. Air Force's Thunderbirds, it was mounted on a B-25 bomber; in the Calgary sequence, it was placed in one of the racing buckboards; and in the reindeer roundup scene, which took place on the edge of the Arctic Ocean, it was concealed by burlap and hidden. Presented by Telecom Canada.

NORTHWEST MERCANTILE: The first shop to the left upon entering the pavilion's plaza on the way to the Hôtel du Canada, this emporium does a booming business in Canadian sheepskins, which are piled high just inside the entrance. Heavy lumberjack shirts, wild rice, maple syrup, and other wares that trappers might have purchased back in pioneering days round out the stock. Skeins of rope, tin scoops, lanterns, and a pair of antique ice skates hanging from the long beams overhead set the mood, together with the structure itself. That, like the adjacent Trading Post, is built of adze-hewn logs and ornamented by stone statues, masks, and paintings done in the style of the Ojibway Indians.

TRADING POST: Located to the rear of the plaza at the top of the steps, this shop (actually part of the Northwest Mercantile) is chockablock with Indian artifacts and assorted souvenirs—items like pewter collector's spoons, leather purses and satchels, small handmade brooms, hangings made of appliquéd felt, toy tomahawks, fur vests and moccasins, and sleek-lined sculptures (some made of marble and some carved in soapstone by the Inuit). The small teepees are made from the bark of deciduous trees, which can be gathered up only once a year when the tree goes dormant. These, like the carved coal pieces that are also sold here, are among several handcrafted Canadian items that are seldom seen elsewhere in the American market.

UNITED KINGDOM

In the space of only a few hundred feet, visitors to this pavilion stroll from an elegant London square to the edge of a canal in the rural countryside—via a bustling urban English street framed by buildings that constitute a veritable rhapsody of historic architectural styles. But one scene leads to the next so smoothly that nothing ever seems amiss. Here again, note the attention to detail: the half-timbered High Street structure that actually leans a bit, the hand-painted "smoke" stains that make the chimneys look as if they had been there for centuries. When a thatched roof is called for, it's right where it should be—though the roof may be made of plastic broom bristles because fire regulations prohibit the real thing. London plane trees, so common in British cities, are represented, and a sundial punctuates the Promenade. Off to the side is a pair of scarlet phone booths identical to those found in the U.K. And there are eight different architectural styles characteristic of the local streetscapes, from English Tudor and Georgian to English Victorian.

There is no single major special attraction in this pavilion; instead, it features a half-dozen fine shops and a pub that serves a selection of British-brewed beers and ales that would be the toast of any first-class establishment in London itself. There's also plenty of good entertainment, including an exuberant Pearly Band, whose members wear traditional clothing encrusted with white buttons; a talented lutenist-calligrapher who can be found with his pens or his instruments in the shops or the pub; and a group of comedians called the Renaissance Street Players, who, when not engaged in general clowning on the World Showcase Promenade, coax audience members into participating in their farcical and altogether entertaining (if unsophisticated) playlets.

Sharp-eyed visitors with an interest in horticultural matters will have a field day examining the landscaping here. The geometrically trimmed bush in front of The Toy Soldier shop is not an Irish yew, so common to the British Isles, but instead a podocarpus; Irish yews don't grow well in Florida. A podocarpus, left in its natural shape, also flanks the shop door just to the rear. A similar substitution had to be made for the London plane tree, also not suited to the Epcot Center climate; its replacement, crowding the half-timbered walls of the Country Manor, is a western sycamore, which looks nearly identical and belongs to the same genus. Don't miss the perennial-and-herb garden next to Anne Hathaway's cottage (to the left of the entrance to The Tea Caddy as you face it), and the small path that leads to the garden courtyard to the rear of the shops.

THE TOY SOLDIER: All the necessities are here for such beloved youthful pastimes as bathtub sailing (boats and windup ducks), playing house (knitting sets, sampler kits, tiny pots and pans), creating works of art (finger paints, "colouring" books), and just having a good time (Matchbox and Corgi toys, Tower of London models, a complete line of Sasha dolls, and such).

No toy shop is complete without temptations for adults, and this one is no exception: There are elegant dolls designed expressly for collectors, and some personable Highland character dolls dressed as fishermen and crofters and other figures out of British folk life. Big spenders may also succumb to one of the most wonderful hobbyhorses ever—a sleek, blond-maned steed fabricated of layers of carved, laminated woods.

Be sure to notice the display at the shop's Promenade entrance—a miniature, glitter-strewn medieval banquet hall peopled by royalty and nobles, musicians, jesters, and a host of other court figures. On the windows downstairs are the heraldic crests for eight of the U.K.'s principal cities, plus those for the three nations that make up the U.K. (Scotland, England, and Northern Ireland—but not Wales, which is a principality). In addition, there are the three crosses that, combined, make up the Union Jack—the crosses of St. Andrew, St. George, and St. Patrick.

Outside, the shop resembles a stone manor built during the last half of the 16th century; the Scottish stepped gable parapet and the round turrets are inspired by Scotland's Abbotsford Manor, where the novelist Sir Walter Scott lived for a period, wrote his most famous romances, and died in 1832.

HIS LORDSHIP: This shop looks like a set for a child's fantasy of the days of King Arthur, with its high rafters decked out with bright banners, its vast fireplace (and crossed swords above), and its immense wrought-iron chandelier. Brass knockers, hourglasses, whistles, keys, bowls, and clocks; "pub mugs" and limited-edition chess sets; canes and blackthorn walking sticks; pewter; and a whole range of British tobaccos and smoking devices are the stock in trade at this emporium adjoining The Toy Soldier.

PRINGLE OF SCOTLAND: On a sweltering summer day in Central Florida, trying on lamb's wool and cashmere may not hold terrific appeal. But the huge selection of styles and colors in men's and women's sweaters, knitted by Scotland's most famous maker, may well prove too enticing. Tam o' shanters, socks, hats, ties, scarves, mittens, and kilts complete the offerings, and woolen cloth in the Anderson, Black Stewart, Black Watch, Cockburn, Douglas, Green Douglas, Lindsay, Menzies, and Mackinnon plaids can be measured out using a gleaming brass meterstick embedded in the handsome marble counter. Don't fail to look at the fascinating tartan map on the wall near the entrance to His Lordship; this identifies plaids from Glen Burn and Gordon to Langtree and St. Lawrence.

THE QUEEN'S TABLE: Sponsored by the Royal Doulton china makers, this shop opposite Pringle of Scotland may be one of the loveliest in Epcot Center. That's particularly true of the elegant Adams Room, embellished with elaborate moldings, hung with a chandelier made of Waterford crystal, and painted in cream and robin's egg blue in a geometric pattern designed to match the subtly hued carpet. The setting is a perfect background for the selection of superbly crafted collector's statuettes. The detail is almost photographically perfect, and the prices, which range from around $400 to $12,000, are correspondingly high.

But the Royal Doulton shop does not deal exclusively in the largely unaffordable. Just as delightful are the company's famous Bunnykins cup-and-bowl sets for youngsters. Also intriguing are the china-headed dolls, with costumes by Nisbet, and the small and large Toby mugs—cups that are shaped and painted to represent the visages of famous historical figures. A small selection of attractive Royal Doulton china dinnerware is also available.

Don't fail to inspect the small, serene Britannia Square just outside the shop entrance furthest from World Showcase Promenade. But for its somewhat reduced scale and the distinctively Floridian climate, it almost feels like London itself. The statue in the center of this Georgian enclave is of William Shakespeare, and the crests on the shop's upstairs windows are those of four major U.K. schools—Oxford, Cambridge, Eton, and Edinburgh.

COUNTRY MANOR: This emporium features an array of soaps, bubble baths, potpourris, powders, and other sweet-smelling items with names like elder flower, cucumber, white birch, wild thyme, Scottish heather, honeysuckle, and country garden. Rounding out the offerings here is a wide selection of tasty cookies ("biscuits" to Britons) and delicious shortbread.

THE TEA CADDY: Fitted out with heavy wooden beams and a broad fireplace to resemble the Stratford-upon-Avon cottage of Shakespeare's Anne Hathaway, this shop sponsored by Twinings Tea stocks English teas, both loose and in bags, in a variety of flavors. Wares also include teacups and teapots, an assortment of milk and cream jugs shaped like old women, and tea cozies shaped like rabbits and cats.

FRANCE

The buildings here have mansard roofs and casement windows so Gallic in appearance that you expect to see some sad bohemian poet looking down from above. A canal-like offshoot of the World Showcase Lagoon seems like the Seine itself; the footbridge that spans it recalls the old Pont des Arts. There's a kiosk nearby like those that punctuate the streets of Paris, a sidewalk café at which to sip a glass of wine and watch the crowds go by, an elegant bookstore, and a bakery whose absolutely heavenly rich aromas announce its presence long before it's visible. Shops sell perfumes, fine leather wares, jewelry, crystal, and other luxury items. Their roofs are real copper or slate, and the cabinetry is crafted finely enough to dazzle even the most skilled woodworker. Les Halles—the iron-and-glass-ceilinged market that Paris counted as one of its most beloved institutions (until its demolition a few years ago)—lives again (near the Palais du Cinéma exit). Even the Eiffel Tower is here, perched atop the motion picture theater and looking far taller than its mere 74 feet thanks, again, to the use of forced perspective (described in our paragraphs on Canada). Erected from designs scaled down from the blueprints for Gustave Eiffel's 1889 original—and complete right down to the tiny elevators and the turn-of-the-century beacon lights illuminated after dark, Disney's version makes a great backdrop for photographs.

But perhaps most special of all are the people. Near the Eiffel Tower and on the Promenade in front of the pavilion, mimes in black trousers and striped French T-shirts, and a strolling trio, starring a jolly-looking 300-pound accordionist named Bibi La Crème and a similarly neckerchiefed, beret-hatted guitarist and bassist, are on hand to entertain. The music is evocative, the repertoire familiar—"Frère Jacques" and "Sur le Pont d'Avignon" are standards. Similarly, hostesses who hail from Paris and the French provinces answer questions in lyrically French-accented English.

Some interesting background notes: The dusty rose-colored, lace-trimmed costumes that the hostesses wear were inspired by the dresses in the Impressionist painter Edouard Manet's *Le Bar aux Folies-Bergères*, and the park to the west of the pavilion, with its tall Lombardy poplars, was inspired by Neo-Impressionist Georges Seurat's painting *A Sunday Afternoon on the Island of La Grande Jatte*. The main entrance to the pavilion recalls the architecture of Paris, most of which was built during the Belle Epoque ("beautiful age") years of the last half of the 19th century when, following the designs of city planner Baron Georges Eugène Haussman (he's also responsible for the master plan of Washington, D.C.), thoroughfares were widened and seven stories became the standard height for city buildings. The lane known as La Petite Rue ("the little street") is inspired by small provincial byways. The sinuously curved, Art Nouveau–style facade of the entrance to the arcade between La Signature and Plume et Palette ("pen and palette") recalls the entrances to Paris's great underground transportation system, the Métro. Don't miss the quiet garden on the opposite side of this arcade—one of the most peaceful spots in World Showcase.

Horticulturally, France offers still other delights, beginning on the World Showcase Promenade. Here a row of Western sycamores that normally grow to 60 or 80 feet—planted in lieu of London plane trees—are being pruned French-style to a height of about 18 feet so as to develop knots on the end of each branch. These make a distinctive abstract pattern in winter, and in spring send out spiky leaf-bearing shoots that provide bountiful shade in summer. To the west, on the opposite side of the Promenade, a small square edged with miniature rose bushes has been planted to outline the shape of a *fleur de lis*.

PALAIS DU CINEMA: This intimate, elegant little "palace of cinema," a theater not unlike the one at Fontainebleau, is the setting for showings of *Impressions de France*, a lyrical and enchanting 18-minute-long travel film that takes viewers from one end of France to the other. The film shows off a beautiful tree-dotted estate; fertile fields and vineyards at harvest time; a village flower market and a luscious pastry shop; the ribbed tongue of a glacier and a harbor full of squawking gulls; black-clad Breton ladies with headdresses made of starched lace shaped into unique styles that reveal the wearer's origin; Paris on Bastille Day—in all some four dozen locations (out of 140 originally shot). Several scenes take place in world-famous landmarks like the Eiffel Tower; Versailles and its gilt Hall of Mirrors (just outside Paris); Mont St. Michel, close to the Brittany-Normandy border in the northwest corner of the country; the French Alps near Mont Blanc, in the southeast; and Cannes, the star-studded resort city on the Mediterranean coast. The automobile competition is Cannes' Bugatti Race; the chateau—which Francophiles will immediately recognize as one of those in the Loire River valley—is fabulous Chambord. (This scene, incidentally, was shot from a helicopter which could fly within three feet of any object being photographed.)

All this is even more appealing thanks to a superbly melodic sound track almost entirely made up of the music of French classical composers such as Jacques Offenbach (1819-1880), known for his operettas; Charles Camille Saint-Saëns (1835-1921), a conductor, pianist, organist, and composer celebrated for his lush melodies; Claude Debussy (1862-1918), who did with sound what the Impressionist painters did with light; and Erik Satie (1866-1925), known for his piano works. Selections include Debussy's *Syrinx*, the haunting piece for solo flute, and his *Afternoon of a Faun*, which accompany an aerial shot of fertile fields. Listen for Offenbach's *Gaieté Parisienne* in the biking sequence and Satie's *Trois Gymnopédies* in the Alps scene. The Aquarium section from Saint-Saën's *Carnival of Animals* accompanies the swamp scene, and the same composer's *Organ Symphony* is heard during the Eiffel Tower ascent. The whole is woven together with transitional segments written and arranged by long-time Disney musician Buddy Baker.

The exceptionally wide screen adds yet another dimension. This is not a CircleVision 360 film, made with the nine cameras needed for the motion pictures at China and Canada. Instead, the France film was shot using only five cameras, and it is shown on a screen made up of five projection surfaces, each measuring 21 feet in height and 27½ feet in width—200 degrees around. It's one of Epcot Center's best films.

Note that a queue usually begins to build here at about 10:45 to 11 A.M. and clogs the courtyard through most of the afternoon. Therefore, the best time to see the film is first thing in the morning or in the evening.

PLUME ET PALETTE: One of the loveliest of the World Showcase shops, this one is devoted to art and books. The best of the Art Nouveau style is reflected in the sinuous curves embellishing the wrought-iron balustrade edging the mezzanine and the moldings that decorate the shining cherry-wood cabinets and shelves. The woodworking is superb, and one case seems more beautiful than the next. Stained glass in purple, yellow, and lavender ornaments the top of one of them. Stylized tulips painted in a delicate antique rose color and pale green embellish still others. The curtains are a beautiful dusty pink with white lace.

All this makes a fine backdrop for an array of merchandise that includes collectible French character dolls, miniatures, small china boxes, French notebooks and notepapers, tapestries, and an interesting selection of cookbooks and books on food. On the mezzanine level, a handful of fine oil paintings (by well-known French landscape artists) are for sale from $300 to $3,000 each, along with prints of French countryside scenes.

LA SIGNATURE: Another beautiful spot with wallpaper that resembles watered silk, a fine chandelier, brass-and-crystal sconces, and velvet curtains, this shop sponsored by the French fashion designer Guy Laroche stocks lovely silk scarves and ties, elegant leather belts and handbags, quality costume jewelry, and, as might be guessed from the fragrant aroma, fine perfumes.

LES HALLES: French cookies, candies, and chocolate bars, plus artificial flowers—some handcrafted with crystal beads—are the stock in trade at this area located at the exit from the Palais du Cinéma. The area is modeled on France's now-demolished Les Halles, designed by the architect Victor Baltard (1805-1874).

LA CASSEROLE: The sign above the door boasts *Tout pour le gourmet* ("everything for the epicure"), and this shop presents a selection of very sophisticated cooking equipment. There are black bread pans, which give each loaf an extra thick crust; heavy copper skillets, known for providing an even heat; and some attractive all-cotton damask tablecloths in white with blue or rose designs; not to mention madeleine pans, for making the kind of small, mild-flavored tea cookies that inspired the nineteenth-century French novelist Marcel Proust to one of the lengthiest reveries in the history of fiction. To round out the offerings, there is an array of herbs and conserves even more exotic than those offered in the U.K.'s Tea Caddy.

LA MAISON DU VIN: Selections in this lovely shop range from the inexpensive to the pricey, from a few dollars for a *vin ordinaire* to upwards of $115 for the sweetish, golden Sauternes wine known as Château d'Yquem 1976 or even $185 for a Carruades de Château Lafite-Rothschild 1961. Wine tastings are held here to sample the offerings (a small charge is levied, but you can keep the glass). Those who don't want to carry their purchases all over World Showcase may have them dispatched to Package Pickup for retrieval at the end of the day.

MOROCCO

Nine tons of tile were handmade, handcut, and shipped to Epcot Center to create this newest addition to World Showcase. To capture the unique quality of this North African country's architecture, 19 Moroccan artisans were brought to Epcot Center to practice the mosaic art that has been a part of their homeland for thousands of years. Koutoubia Minaret, a detailed replica of the famous prayer tower in Marrakech, stands guard at the entrance. A courtyard with a fountain in the center—and flowers everywhere—leads to the Medina (Old City). Between the traditional alleyways and the more modern sections are the pointed arches and swirling blue patterns of the Bab Boujouloud gate, a replica of the one that stands in Fez. An ancient working waterwheel irrigates the gardens of the pavilion and the motifs repeated throughout the buildings include carved plaster and wood, ceramic tile, and brass.

ROYAL GALLERY: This museum houses ever-changing exhibits of Moroccan art, artifacts, and costumes.

CENTER OF TOURISM: This informative center offers literature useful in planning a visit to Morocco, and the Royal Air Maroc desk makes it easy to book a trip if the mood strikes. There is a three-screen projection area where a continuous slide show depicts the lifestyles and landscapes of the country.

SHOPPING: The center of the Medina houses an outdoor marketplace that includes an array of shops; merchandise includes carpets, leather goods, ceramics, jewelry, brasswork, and clothing from the region.

JAPAN

Occasionally, when the group known as the "Four Seasons of Edo" are performing in this pavilion, the surrounding area resounds with the most amazing drumming that most visitors will ever hear. The staccato rhythm is as rapid as the fire of a machine gun, and the booms are deeply resonant and loud.

But for the most part, serenity rules in Japan. The principal entertainment, aside from the Four Seasons of Edo, is a young man known as Nasaji Teresawa, who pursues the 2,400-year-old art of snipping and swirling blobs of brown rice toffee into the shapes of swans, unicorns, crabs, and a score of other remarkable creatures.

The landscaping, designed in accordance with traditional symbolic and aesthetic values, also contributes to the peaceful mood. Rocks, which in Japan represent the enduring nature of the earth, were brought from North Carolina and Georgia (since boulders are scarce in the Sunshine State). Water, symbolizing the sea (which the Japanese consider a life source), is abundant; the Japan pavilion garden has a little stream and a couple of pools inhabited (in good weather) by colorful fish. A small bamboo device at the edge of one of these rivulets regularly fills up with water falling from above, and then, weighted by its contents, empties out and makes regular, but somehow soothing, clacking noises in the process. Evergreen trees, which in Japan are symbols of eternal life, are here in force.

Disney horticulturalists created this very Japanese landscape without using very many plants or trees native to that country, where the climate is so different from that in Florida. The evergreens near the brilliant vermilion *torii* gate are native Florida slash pines. The palm near the courtyard entrance to the Yakitori House is a sago palm, which is among the oldest living bits of flora on earth. The curly-leafed trees alongside the stream are corkscrew willows. Among the few trees actually native to Japan are the two Japanese maple trees (identifiable by their small leaves) not far away (near the first stairway from the Promenade on the left side of the courtyard as you face it), and the prickly branched, prickly leafed monkey puzzle trees near the walkway to the Promenade, on The American Adventure side of the pagoda; needle-sharp thorns make this the only species of tree that monkeys cannot climb.

Visitors who have actually been to Japan will be interested to observe that most of the structures inside the pavilion have their Japanese antecedents. The pagoda that occupies such a prominent place along World Showcase Promenade was modeled after an eighth-century structure located in the Horyuji Temple in Nara. The brilliant vermilion *torii* gate on the shores of World Showcase Lagoon derives from the design of the one at the Itsukushima shrine in Hiroshima Bay, one of the most beautiful sites on the inland sea.

MITSUKOSHI DEPARTMENT STORE: There are kimonos in silk, cotton, and polyester; attractive all-cotton T-shirts bearing Japanese characters; expensive, almost sculptural traditional headdresses that seem fabricated of lacquer-stiffened netting; and an excellent selection of bowls and vases meant for flower arranging. But on the whole, no one would ever apply the term "charming" to this spacious store set up by Mitsukoshi—an immense, three-century-old retail firm that was once dubbed "Japan's Sears." Some of the china dinnerware and crystal glasses, the paperweights and desk ornaments, etc., are too often seen elsewhere in the U.S. in department stores or inexpensive chain import stores to arouse more than passing interest. It's unfortunate that this familiarity also makes it easy to dismiss some of the other merchandise that, though it appears to be of the same trinket quality, has considerable meaning in Japanese culture. One example are the dolls, of which there are literally rows and rows, priced from $87 to $92, and clad in elaborate kimonos sashed with wide, stiff *obis*. These are traditionally given to female children on Girls' Day, a popular Japanese national holiday. The blank-eyed, egg-shaped pâpier-maché scarlet masks, which come in a wide range of sizes from small to very large, are part of the traditional New Year celebration; Japanese color in one eye when making a New Year's resolution, keep the one-eyed "face" in plain view throughout the next 365 days as a reminder of the holiday vow, and celebrate success when the year draws to its close by completing the face.

The structure housing the merchandise was inspired by a section of the Gosho Imperial Palace, which was constructed in Kyoto in the year A.D. 794 and is widely recognized as a fine example of early Japanese architecture.

THE AMERICAN ADVENTURE

When it came to creating The American Adventure, the centerpiece of World Showcase, the Disney imagineers were given virtually a free hand. So the 110,000 bricks of the imposing colonial-style struc-

ture that houses the show and a counter-service restaurant are real brick—made *by hand* from soft, pinkish-orange Georgia clay. The show inside stands out because of its wonderfully evocative settings, its innovatively detailed sets, and the 35 superb Audio-Animatronics players, some of the most lifelike ever created by the Disney organization: The American Adventure's Ben Franklin even walks up stairs. The digital sound system is also the most advanced that the Disney organization has ever used, and the show is the most technically complex, involving the world's largest rear-projection screen (72 feet in width) and a number of very sophisticated sets that rise up from below the stage to the delight and awe of the audience.

For the moment, there are no shops here. Entertainment outside the building on the Promenade is provided by a fife and drum corps spiffily outfitted in scarlet and inside the building by a superb vocal group called The Voices of Liberty.

Be sure to note the four luxuriant trees in front of the building. They were planted in 1969 on Hotel Plaza Boulevard, the main thoroughfare of Walt Disney World Village Hotel Plaza, and along with a handful of their contemporaries (which can be seen in their pruned and unpruned states throughout Epcot Center, most notably trimmed diagonally alongside Future World's Universe of Energy) have been moved four times in the intervening years.

Presented by the Coca-Cola Co. and American Express.

THE AMERICAN ADVENTURE SHOW: One of the truly outstanding Epcot Center attractions, this 29-minute presentation celebrates the American spirit from our nation's earliest years right up to the present. Beginning with the arrival of the Pilgrims at Plymouth Rock and their hard first winter on the western shore of the Atlantic, the Audio-Animatronics narrators—Ben Franklin and a cigar-puffing Mark Twain—recall certain key people and events in American history—the Boston Tea Party, George Washington and the grueling winter at Valley Forge, the influential black abolitionist Frederick Douglass, the celebrated 19th-century Nez Percé chief Joseph, and many more. The Philadelphia Centennial Exposition is remembered, along with women's rights campaigner Susan B. Anthony, telephone inventor Alexander Graham Bell, and the steel giant and philanthropist Andrew Carnegie. Naturalist John Muir converses on stage with Teddy Roosevelt. Charles Lindbergh, Rosie the Riveter, Jackie Robinson, Marilyn Monroe, Dwight and Mamie Eisenhower, Elvis Presley (wriggling his pelvis), and Walt Disney are all represented. So are John Wayne, Lucille Ball, Margaret Mead, John F. Kennedy, Martin Luther King, Muhammed Ali, and Billie Jean King. The idea is to recall episodes in American history, both negative and positive, which most contributed to the growth of the spirit of America, either by engendering "a new burst of creativity" (in the designers' words) or "a better understanding of ourselves as partners in the American experience." The presentation is hardly comprehensive; instead, it's "a hundred-yard dash capturing the spirit of the country at specific moments in time."

Throughout the show, the attention to historical detail is meticulous. Every one of the rear-projected illustrations was executed in the painting style of the era being described. Accordingly the Chief Joseph and Susan B. Anthony figures are speaking their originals' very own words. The exact dimensions of the cannonballs in another scene were carefully investigated—then reproduced. In the Philadelphia Centennial Exposition scene, Pittsburgh's name is spelled without the *h* that subsequent years have added.

For information about how each of the various historical figures actually spoke during their lifetimes, researchers contacted about half a dozen historians and cultural institutions—the Philadelphia Historical Commission, Harvard's Carpenter Center of Visual Arts, the State Historical Society of Missouri, the Department of the Navy's Ships Historical Branch, and others. When recordings were not available, educated guesses were made: Bell's voice was created on the basis of contemporary comments about his voice's clarity, expressiveness, and crisp articulation, coupled with the fact that his father taught elocution. To select Will Rogers's speeches for the Depression scene, whole pages of quotes were collected, reviewed, edited, and reedited; the voice is the humorist's own, from an actual broadcast, as is that of FDR's, here heard over the radio in the roadside gasoline stand scene. That particular scene was suggested by a *Life* magazine photograph; details were based upon research in architectural magazines from the 1930s. Even the type of radio and the style of microphone and the price (18 cents) and the color (red) of gasoline in the tanks were the result of researchers' close scrutiny.

One of the most interesting aspects of the show is its inner workings, however. Underneath the entire theater is a movable carriage device that designers have dubbed "the war wagon," measuring 65-by-35-by-14 feet and weighing 175 tons. The basement that supports "the war wagon" is itself supported by pilings driven approximately 300 feet into the ground; it carries ten different sets and during the presentation rolls forward or backward to position the appropriate set underneath the stage at the appropriate time. Also, because the height of the space underneath the theater is relatively limited, the sets themselves were specially designed to allow certain sections to contract telescopically as proved necessary for storage. All of these operations are controlled by computers.

The twelve life-size statues on either side of the stage represent the "Spirits of America." These are, on the left, from front to rear, Individualism, Innovation, Tomorrow, Independence, Compassion, and Discovery; and, on the right, from front to back, Freedom, Heritage, Pioneering, Knowledge, Self-Reliance, and Adventure. The 44 flags flanking the Hall of Flags corridor in the escalator area are those that have flown over the United States. Revolutionary War flags, Colonial flags, and even flags representing the countries that had claims to American soil before Independence can all be seen. A special highlight of the show is the majestic music played throughout by the Philadelphia Symphony Orchestra; the "Golden Dream" finale, one of several memorable Epcot Center theme songs, may soon be available on record or tape—so if you like it, be sure to ask at the Centorium. The pavilion's carillon plays the same music on the hour.

As one of the most compelling of all the World Showcase attractions, The American Adventure is occasionally quite busy. Perhaps the best time to schedule a visit to the show is first thing in the morning or in the evening. Seats in the front of the house give the optimal view of the Audio-Animatronics characters (although all seats provide an acceptable view). While waiting for the show to begin, be sure to read the quotes on the walls—Wendell Wilkie, Jane Addams, Charles Lindbergh, Ayn Rand, Archibald Macleish, Herman Melville, Thomas Wolfe, and George Magar Mardikau are all represented.

AMERICA GARDENS THEATRE BY THE SHORE: A variety of entertainment, including an exceptionally lively show of folk dances and songs, is presented periodically in this lakeside amphitheater in front of The American Adventure pavilion. The folk show is particularly worth a detour; get performance times from the information desks at Earth Station (on your way into the park), or check at any WorldKey Information System kiosk. Showtimes are also posted on the promenade at east and west entrances to the amphitheater.

Be sure to note the pruning of the Western sycamores overhead; the old-fashioned pollarding method used, which involves trimming the treetops flat and allowing the lower branches to fill out and interlock, will eventually produce a thick canopy. The flower beds outside are usually planted in red, white, and blue; the bushes alongside are East Palatka holly.

ITALY

The arches and cut-out motifs that adorn the World Showcase reproduction of Venice's Doge's Palace are just the more obvious examples of the attention to detail lavished on the individual structures in this relatively small pavilion. The angel atop the scaled down Campanile was sculpted on the model of the original right down to the curls on the back of its head—then covered with real gold leaf, despite the fact that it was destined to be set almost a hundred feet in the air. The other statues in the complex, including the sea god Neptune presiding over the fountain in the rear of the piazza, are similarly exact. Even the marble-like facade resembles that of which the real Doge's Palace is constructed. And the pavilion even has an island like Venice's own, its seawall appropriately stained with age, plus moorings that look like barber poles, with several distinctively Venetian gondolas tied to them. St. Mark the Evangelist is also remembered, together with the lion that is the saint's companion and Venice's guardian; these can be seen atop the two massive columns flanking the small arched footbridge that connects the landfall to the mainland. The only deviation from Venetian fact is the inaccurate site of the Doge's Palace in reference to the real St. Mark's Square.

The pavilion is equally interesting from a horticultural point of view. The island boasts a brace of kumquat trees, citrus plants typical of the Mediterranean, and a couple of olive trees that can be seen on both side walls of the Arcata d'Artigiani; originally located in a Sacramento, California, grove, they were moved to Anaheim and then were piled onto a flatbed truck, their branches spreading wide, for the trip to Florida. But they got only as far as the Arizona border. As Disney gardeners tell the story, that state's regulation prohibiting loads beyond a given width is so erratically enforced that no problems had been anticipated. So it came as quite a surprise when the inspector on duty decreed that the trees be trimmed to ten feet. A chain saw soon materialized, and within minutes the ancient olives were shorn. Despite horticulturalists' fears, the trees survived, leaving only their scars to remind visitors of the ordeal; the darker bark is what remains of the original, while the lighter areas are the new growth. The tall trees that stand like dark columns at various points in the pavilion are Italian cypress, which are very common in Italy; Florida slash pines replace that nation's abundant Italian stone pines, which would not grow here.

Entertainment is another highlight of the pavilion. A very lively group known as the Teatro di Bologna puts on 15-minute shows such as "The Great Impasta," in which selected members of the audience have the chance to play heroes, heroines, and the vilest of villains in a style reminiscent of the Renaissance *commedia dell' arte*. The Teatro di Bologna players are very funny (if very broad) and shouldn't be missed. And, inside *Alfredo's*, the waiters and waitresses sometimes burst into song, and when the street players' audience isn't generating too loud hoots and cheers, old favorite opera arias and familiar Italian street songs can be heard through the open window.

ARCATA D'ARTIGIANI: This open-air market on the western edge of the piazza is a good spot for a sweet snack with its selection of tasty Italian chocolates and other goodies for sale. Handsome terra-cotta planters and woven baskets add to the atmosphere.

FINE LEATHER GOODS: The reasons for Italy's fame as a producer of fine leather goods are immediately obvious in this small shop, just inside the Arcata d'Artigiani. The workmanship of the key chains, satchels, briefcases, hand bags, attaché cases, and other items is as appealing as the shop is fragrant with the smell of real leather. The prices are on the high side, but that heavenly scent—one of the best things about this shop—is absolutely free, so don't fail to look in (and breathe).

LA GEMMA ELEGANTE: Located to the rear of the piazza on its eastern edge, this small shop focuses on jewelry. There are gold and silver chains galore, and some are expensive, but it's also possible to find handsome—and affordable—beads, earrings, and pendants made of Venetian glass; intricate glass-mosaic brooches and pillboxes bearing images of tiny bouquets; cameos; and coral necklaces.

IL BEL CRISTALLO: The production of fine glassware has been a tradition in Italy for centuries, and so a shop like this one just off the Promenade on the Germany side of the piazza was a must for the pavilion. Typical Venetian glass paperweights and other items, their bright colors trapped in smooth spheres or teardrops of clear or milky glass, small porcelain figurines and flower bouquets so finely crafted that they look almost real, pastel flowers made of beads, and lead crystal bowls and candlesticks are all on display. Inlaid wood pictures may be purchased, and so can a handful of wonderful music boxes made in the Italian city of Sorrento. The name of the shop means "the beautiful crystal."

GERMANY

There are no villages in Germany quite like this one. Inspired in part by towns in the Rhine region and Bavaria, and in part by communities in the German north, it boasts structures reminiscent of those found in such diverse urban enclaves as Frankfurt, Freiburg, and Rothenburg ob der Tauber. There are stairstepped rooflines and towers, balconies and arcaded walkways, and so much overall charm that the scene seems to come straight out of a fairy tale. The beer hall to the rear is almost as lively as the one at Munich's famed Oktoberfest, especially during the later shows, and the shops, which offer a range of merchandise from wine and sweets to ceramics and cuckoo clocks, toys and books and even art, are so tempting that it's hard to leave empty-handed. The various elements that make up the Germany pavilion are described here as they would be encountered while walking from west to east (counterclockwise) around the cobblestone-paved central plaza, which is known as the St. Georgsplatz, after the statue at its center. St. George, the patron saint of soldiers, is depicted with the dragon that legend says he slew during a pilgrimage to the Middle East.

Try to time your World Showcase peregrinations to bring you to Germany on the hour, when the handsome, specially designed glockenspiel at the plaza's rear can be heard to chime in a melody composed specifically for the pavilion.

DER BUECHERWURM: This two-story structure, whose exterior is patterned after a merchants' hall known as the *Kaufhaus* (located in the southern German town of Freiburg in Breisgau), stocks prints and English books about Germany; handsome prints of German cities full of gabled old houses and gloriously spired cathedrals; and an assortment of souvenir items like ashtrays and vases and spoons bearing images of German cities. Germany has given the world some of its greatest composers, and busts of some of those men—Brahms, Mozart, Wagner—can be found here, the bases equipped with music boxes that play some of their most famous melodies. The building itself is worth noting. In order to correctly reproduce the statues of the German emperors on the facade, designers hired a photographer who, shooting from a "cherry picker," submitted close-ups from a number of angles. Observant travelers may remember that the Freiburg building has one additional statue—that of Emperor Maximilian, omitted here in the interests of maintaining the proper proportions. (Film and sundries are available here.)

VOLKSKUNST: This small, exceptionally appealing establishment is full of a burgher's bounty of German timekeepers, plus a scattering of other items made by hand in the rural corners of the nation. The latter include angels dressed in velvet and brocade, with fine wax faces and glossy hair, perfect for the tops of the very best Christmas trees; sturdy wooden shoes; folk dolls with walnut heads; beer steins in all sizes, from the petite to the enormous and expensive ($2,700); wood carvings made in the southern German town of Oberammergau; bright, fringed Tyrolean scarves; nutcrackers; and a whole collection of "smokers," carved wooden dolls with a receptacle for incense and a hollow pipe for the smoke to escape. As for cuckoo clocks, some are small and unprepossessing, and some are so immense that they'd look appropriate only in some cathedral-ceilinged hunting lodge. The largest measures about five feet in height and is embellished not only with carvings of birds and rabbits and a hunting horn and crossed rifles, but also with a genuine pair of antlers. A must.

DER TEDDYBÄR: Located alongside Volkskunst, this toy shop would be a delight if only for the lively mechanized displays high up on either side of the entrance and against the rear wall; some of the stuffed lambs and the dolls in the full-skirted folk dresses (known as *dirndls*) have been animated so that tails wag and skirts swirl in time to German folk tunes. The shop is also home to one of WDW's very best selections of toys. There are wonderfully detailed LGB-brand miniature trains and the expected assortment of expensive stuffed keepsakes from Steiff, as well as wooden-headed hand puppets and marionettes that represent German grandmothers and grandfathers, children, and clowns. Cradles and baby buggies with colorful tops are tempting as well, along with modeling clay and all kinds of building blocks. Last but not least, the collection of dolls is simply wonderful.

WEINKELLER: The Germany pavilion's wine shop, situated between the cookie shop and the Biergarten toward the rear of St. Georgsplatz, offers approximately 250 varieties of German wines produced and bottled by H. Schmitt Soehne, one of Germany's oldest and largest vintners. Wine tastings are held here on occasion. The selection includes not only those meant for everyday consumption, but also fine estate wines whose prices run into the hundreds of dollars per bottle. These are white with few exceptions, because white wine constitutes the bulk of Germany's vinicultural output. (In fact, only 20 percent of all German vintages are red.) Long, tall beer mugs and glasses, corkscrews, wine glasses in traditional German colors of greens and ambers, fragile crystal goblets, brass ice buckets, decanters, and other accessories are also available. The setting itself is quite attractive—low-ceilinged and cozy and full of fir cabinets that have been embellished with carvings of vines and bunches of grapes. The original designs, which decreed that all those grapes be painted purple, were altered to include plenty of green fruit, the main ingredient in white wine.

SÜSSIGKEITEN: It is a mistake to visit this tiny, tile-floored confectionery shop on an empty stomach: Chocolate cookies, butter cookies, and almond biscuits mix with candy cinnamon stars, caramels, nuts, and pretzels on the crowded shelves; and there are boxes upon boxes of *Lebkuchen*, the spicy crisp cookies traditionally baked in Germany at Christmas, not to mention jujubes (which the packages announce as *Gummibaeren*). Children enjoy the special alphabet cookies and animal crackers, both of which are different from those made in U.S. bakeries. Don't miss the attractive display of old Bahlsen cookie tins by the door. Incidentally, Bahlsen, the shop's sponsor, is among the first companies in the world to pack baked goods in air-tight wrappers to preserve freshness; the firm's logo is an Egyptian hieroglyph that means *long life*.

PORZELLANHAUS: This porcelain shop stocks the products of the German firm of Hutschenreuther. There is some dinnerware—and it is sleek, elegant, and reminiscent of the Danish-made Royal Copenhagen, with its delicate blue ornamentation. And there are some handsome bud vases and cup-and-saucer sets meant for collecting.

But in general, the shop's stock in trade is the array of elaborately sculpted and exquisitely detailed birds, horses, fish, and other figurines (with prices that can run into thousands of dollars). Dog fanciers might succumb to one of the dachshunds, hounds, bulldogs, poodles, Great Danes, Samoyeds, boxers, spaniels, or collies in the cases; nature lovers might prefer the polar bear or the owls, or the deer or the birds. The name of the shop translates roughly as *house of porcelain*.

GLAS UND PORZELLAN: Featuring glass and porcelain items made by the German firm of Goebel, this is an attractive establishment with rope-turned columns, curved moldings, delicate scrollwork, and tiny carved rosettes. But no matter how attractive the backgrounds, the stars of the show are the Hummel figurines, which Goebel manufactures. Cherubic, rosy-cheeked children, shown carrying baskets, trays, umbrellas, and other items, as in the drawings of a young German nun named Berta Hummel, are favorites of collectors around the world. One group features redheads, while others have youngsters perched on the edges of ashtrays. There is always an elaborate showpiece at the center of the shop, and every two or three months, for a couple of weeks at a stretch, artisans from the factory are on hand to demonstrate the process by which Hummel creations are painted and finished. The rest of the time, an excellent display (which includes figurines in all stages of completeness) tells the story.

CHINA

Dominated by a Disney equivalent of Beijing's Temple of Heaven, and announced by a pair of banners whose Chinese characters offer good wishes to passers by ("May good fortune follow you on your path through life" and "May virtue be your neighbor"), this pavilion offers a level of serenity that makes an appealing contrast to the hearty merriment of nearby Germany and the Latin gaiety of adjacent Mexico. Part of this quiet environment is the by-product of the soothing traditional Chinese music that plays over the sound system. The attractive gardens also make a major contribution. They are full of rose bushes (because roses are native to China), and there is a century-old mulberry tree (to the left of the main walkway into the pavilion), with a pomegranate tree and a wiggly looking Florida native known as a water oak nearby. In addition, a new, spacious emporium devoted to Chinese wares has opened, and a Chinese restaurant is in the works. However, all this is secondary to the fabulous motion picture shown inside the Temple of Heaven—a CircleVision 360 film that must be counted among the best of all the World Showcase attractions.

WONDERS OF CHINA: LAND OF BEAUTY, LAND OF TIME: This 19-minute presentation shows the beauties of a land that few Epcot Center visitors will ever see first hand—and does it so vividly that it's possible to see the film over and over and still not fully absorb all the wonderful sights. The Disney crew was the first Western film group to film certain sites, and their remarkable effort includes such marvels as Beijing's Forbidden City; vast, wide-open Mongolia and its stern-faced tribesmen; the 2,400-year-old Great Wall; the Great Buddha of Leshan, eight centu-

ries old and dramatically imposing; the muddy Yangtze River and the 3,000-year-old city of Suzhou, whose location on the Grand Canal, which is generally believed to be the largest man-made waterway in the world, encouraged Marco Polo to call it the Venice of the East. There are shots of Shanghai as well as Hangzhou, where a handful of Chinese are shown doing their morning exercises along the river's edge. Also shown are Huangshan Mountain, wreathed in fog; the Shilin Stone Forest of jagged rock outcroppings in Yunnan Province; Urumqi, whose distance from the sea in Xinjiang Province earned it the title as the most inland city on earth; Lhasa, in Tibet, and its Potala Palace, boasting a thousand rooms and ten times that many altars. Just as fantastic are the Reed Flute Cave and the bizarrely shaped hills of Kweilin above, to say nothing of the very European looking city of Shanghai. To complete the picture there are fields of snow and of wheat, high meadows and beaches dotted with tropical palms, harbors and rice terraces, calligraphers, checkers and Ping Pong players, lightning-fast acrobats, championship horseback riders, camels and a panda bear, glittering ice sculptures, and millions of bicycles.

Almost every step of the way, the film crews were besieged by curious Chinese, even in empty Mongolia. For the Huangshan Mountain sequence, which lasts only seconds, the crew and about three dozen hired laborers had to carry the 300-pound camera uphill for nearly a mile. The Chinese government would not permit Disney cameramen to shoot aerial footage in some areas, so Chinese crews were sent aloft to record the required scenes, first on videotape and later—after approval from the Disney director in charge of the project—on film. You can see for yourself just how well this collaboration worked.

Be sure to spend some time before viewing the film examining the details that embellish the building that houses the theater. The design is based on that of the Hall of Prayer for Good Harvest, the major section of Beijing's Temple of Heaven complex, which was built in the year 1420 (during the Ming Dynasty) and reconstructed after being damaged by lightning in 1896. The name of the World Showcase structure is represented by the characters above the entrance. The number of stones in the floor was chosen for auspicious associations; the center stone is surrounded by nine stones because nine is a lucky number in China. Around the edge of the room rise twelve columns—because twelve is both the number of months in the year and the number of years in a full cycle of the Chinese calendar. Closer to the room's center, there are four columns—one for each of the seasons; the japonicus vines entwining each column symbolize long life, while the square beam that they all support alludes to earth, and the round beam above signifies heaven. The dragons on the beams allude to imperial strength, while the phoenixes are reminders of peace and prosperity. The measurements and proportions are all similarly symbolic. Be sure to stand on the round stone in the absolute center of the anteroom: Every whisper is strikingly amplified.

Also, when exiting, pass by the exhibit of ancient Chinese art and artifacts. Changed about every six months, it invariably includes fine pieces from well-known collections. Note that the best time to see the film is during the first couple of hours that Epcot Center is open in the morning and again just before closing.

BOUNTIFUL HARVEST: This vast Chinese emporium, located off the narrow, charming Street of Good Fortune at the exit to the film, offers a huge assortment of Chinese merchandise—silk robes, prints, paper umbrellas and fans, embroidered items, change purses and glasses cases, and more. Trinkets, medium-priced items, and expensive antiques are all available in an array that may be matched in few other places in the U.S. The calligraphy on the curtains on the store windows wishes passersby *good fortune, long life, prosperity, health, and happiness.*

MEXICO

The tangle of tropical vegetation surrounding the great pyramid that encloses this pavilion and the Cantina, the Mexican restaurant at the lagoon's edge on the Promenade, provide only the barest suggestion of the charming area inside. Dominated by a reconstruction of a quaint plaza at dusk, this area is rimmed by balconied, tile-roofed, colonial-style structures. Crowding a pretty fountain are a quartet of stands selling all sorts of Mexican handicrafts, and off to the left is an attractive shop stocked with still other handsome wares. Marimba and mariachi bands keep things lively. To the rear, the *San Angel Inn*, a corporate cousin of the famous Mexico City restaurant of the same name, serves authentic Mexican fare. Behind it, the pavilion's main show chronicles Mexican culture from earliest times right up to the present.

Queues for the boat ride often extend into the Promenade in the morning—but if you just want to visit the shops and see the pre-Columbian artifacts just inside the pyramid entrance, it's perfectly fine to walk straight in, bypassing the line.

Note that the pyramid itself was inspired by Mesoamerican structures dating from the third century A.D. The serpent heads on either side of the stairway allude to the Aztec god Quetzalcoatl.

EL RIO DEL TIEMPO: SAIL THE RIVER OF TIME: In the course of this six-minute boat trip, sprinkled with vignettes of pre-Columbian, Spanish-Colonial, and modern Mexican life, visitors greet a Mayan high priest, watch stylized dances by performers in vivid costumes, and are assailed by vendors at a lively market. A band costumed to look like skeletons entertains at one juncture (in a reference to the Day of the Dead, a holiday celebrated in Mexico with candies and sweets shaped like skulls or skeletons). In addition, there are a handful of film clips depicting present-day Acapulco (with its cliff divers and flying dancers), Tulum, Manzanillo (and its speed boats), and Isla Mujeres (with its gorgeous sea life). The assemblage of film, Audio-Animatronics figures, and props is reminiscent of the Magic Kingdom's If You Had Wings and It's A Small World. Long lines, which prevail from mid-morning on, usually thin out in the afternoon as the crowds drift into the more distant parts of World Showcase. If you are in the area, skip the boat ride the first time around and return in the evening or late in the afternoon when the crowds are likely to be far smaller.

PLAZA DE LOS AMIGOS: Brightly colored paper flowers, sombreros, wooden trays and bowls, peasant blouses, baskets, copperware, and black pottery make this shopping area (*mercado* in Spanish) at the plaza's center as bright and almost as lively as one in Mexico itself. The colorful pâpier-maché piñatas that figure so strongly in the scenery here are so popular that Epcot Center has to buy them from suppliers by the railroadcar-full. Irresistible.

ARTESANIAS MEXICANAS: This shop stocks more expensive versions of some of the merchandise sold in the mercado—more elaborately made dresses, plus some fine pieces of silver and turquoise jewelry, onyx ashtrays and bookends, plaques and bookends plated with silver, bird cages from Jalisco, elaborate candelabra both glazed and unglazed, belt buckles and barrettes, and more.

HOT TIPS

• Get precise, up-to-date information about the procedure for getting reservations in Epcot Center restaurants as soon as you arrive in Central Florida. Call 824-4321 for *information*, not reservations.

• Preferred reservation times at Epcot Center's full-service restaurants are usually fully booked within an hour of the official park opening time. So be sure to arrive at Epcot Center at least one half hour ahead to get a jump on the day and help assure that you get the restaurant and seating time of your choice. Study the special box on Epcot Center restaurant reservations in the *Good Meals, Great Times* chapter. Remember, too, that non-prime dining hours are often available to late reservation makers, so adjustment of your eating schedule may well help you to try the restaurant of your choice.

• Have dinner at one of the WDW resort hotels or in WDW Village if you don't have a reservation and want something more elaborate than what Epcot Center's fast food eateries are offering. (But if your time is limited, consider eating at one of these establishments, because Epcot Center fast food is well above the national norm.)

• Save the shops, and CommuniCore East and West and the World of Motion's TransCenter, for the congested midafternoon hours. Go to as many attractions as possible in the peaceful early morning and late afternoon hours.

• Visit World Showcase in the morning—it's uncongested until about 11 A.M. See Future World in the evening, avoiding the busy morning hours. Remember that throughout Epcot Center, the queues are longest during midday and shortest (sometimes nonexistent) during the evening hours.

• Don't queue for the World Showcase Promenade buses. You'll get there faster by walking, and you'll spend a comparable amount of time on your feet.

EVERYTHING ELSE IN THE WORLD

131 Walt Disney World Village
137 Fort Wilderness Campground
138 River Country
142 Discovery Island
144 Wonders of the World

The Magic Kingdom and Epcot Center take up only about 350 acres of Walt Disney World—the *overall* World comprises 43 square miles, much of it crammed with all sorts of diverse and irresistible activities. These attractions are of a quantity and quality seldom found anywhere else on the globe.

There is superb golf and tennis; there are beaches for sunbathing; lakes for speedboating and sailing; canoes for rent and winding streams on which to paddle along; bicycles for hire; campfire sites; nature trails; and picnic grounds. And that list still doesn't include River Country, a Disney creation of the kind of old-fashioned swimming hole of which most people only dream; Walt Disney World Shopping Village, an assortment of shops seldom found outside the most cosmopolitan cities; and the nonpareil botanical garden and bird sanctuary that's called Discovery Island.

Among the other activities worth mentioning at WDW is the program known as the Wonders of Walt Disney World, in which youngsters attending grades five through ten are offered the opportunity to go behind the scenes—to meet the Disney entertainers and receive instruction from Disney cartoonists; to visit the World's extraordinary 7,500-acre conservation area; or to tour the WDW solar-powered office building (among other unique ecological operations). Developed in cooperation with educators from all over the country, this learning program has earned such widespread acclaim that many schools grant excused absences to those who participate.

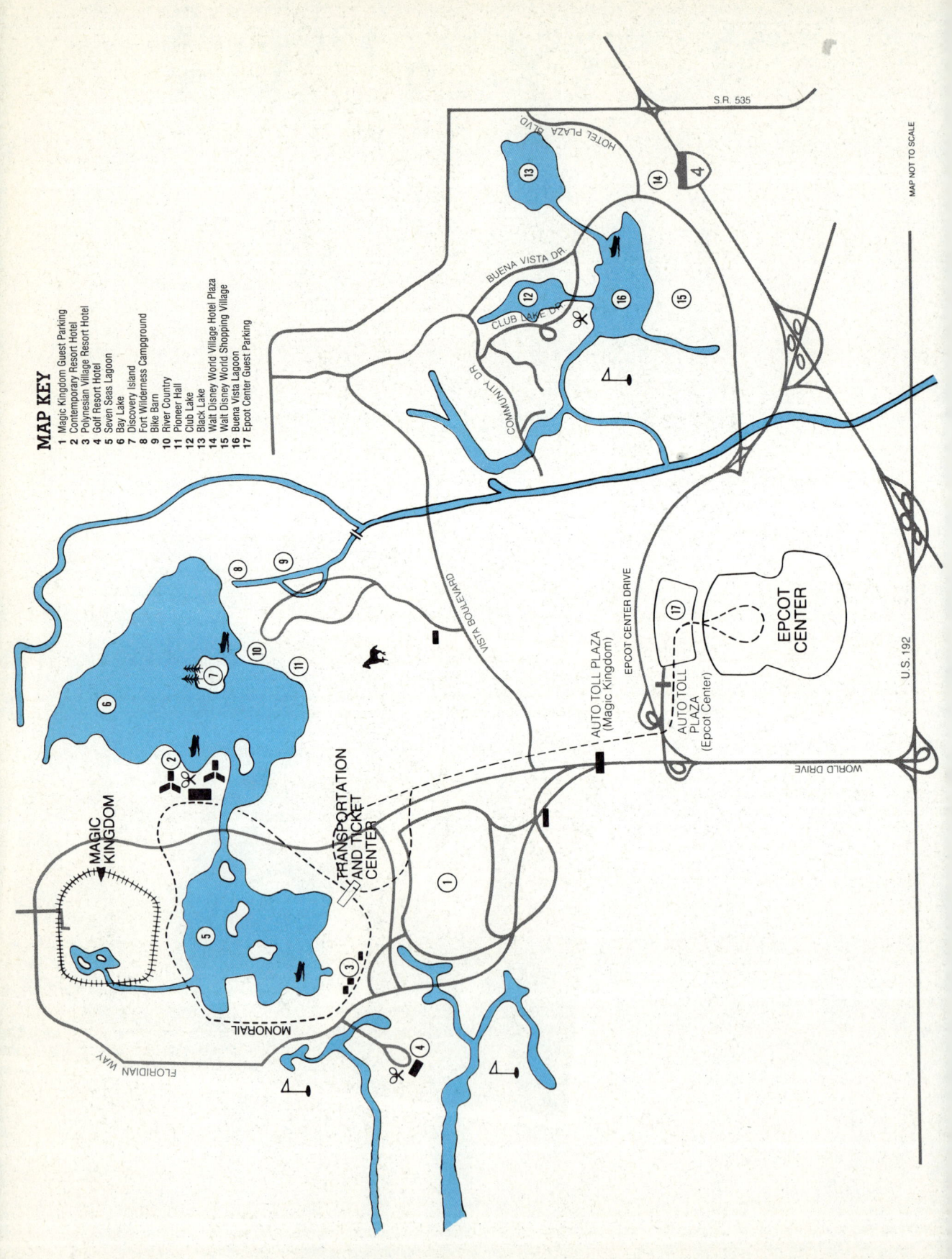

WALT DISNEY WORLD VILLAGE

SHOPS

A visit to Walt Disney World Shopping Village can involve eating in a restaurant, meeting a film star, listening to first-rate jazz over some frothy cream-and-liqueur concoction, or just sitting on a bench by the water looking at the boats zipping back and forth across Buena Vista Lagoon. But for most people, those are the extra added attractions of a complex whose real raison d'être is shopping.

Arranged in eight low-lying, shingle-sided buildings flanking the hexagonal Captain's Tower on the shores of Buena Vista Lagoon, the Walt Disney World Shopping Village boutiques stock everything from baby bonnets to silk dresses, thousand-dollar bottles of wine to toy soldiers and stuffed animals—and then some. There is one store devoted exclusively to Disney merchandise, but that was added only because of popular demand; the merchandise in the other stores differs little from what might be found in any other fine shopping area in America.

The best way to take it all in is simply to wander at will. Stop for lunch or a snack after a couple of hours, then go out and stroll some more. The descriptions below suggest the types of merchandise that each store offers. Particular items may not be there when you are, but comparable goods should be available. Note that weekends are fairly busy, but even then the pace tends to be leisurely. Kids who get bored by their elders' browsing can be turned loose at the marina, or at an innovative playground near the Village Stage (where the annual Christmas pageants are presented).

CHRISTMAS CHALET: If anything can set a mind to dreaming of white Christmases when the mercury is hitting 95° outside (and the humidity is just about the same), this lovely little shop is it. Arranged at the edges of the rooms there are small treasures in traditional reds and greens—ornaments covered with feathers, others made of wood, metal, glass, felt, and calico. The selection is one of the best of its type anywhere.

Located about 5 miles from the Magic Kingdom and only 2½ miles from Epcot Center, Walt Disney World Village comprises a number of hotel and villa-type accommodations (with and without kitchen facilities), the Lake Buena Vista Club, the Walt Disney World Conference Center, the Walt Disney World Shopping Village, several lakes, and a number of sports facilities—among other things. It is relatively quiet, and the pace is far more leisurely than that which exists around the Polynesian Village and Contemporary Resort hotels. In the Buena Vista Lagoon, along whose shores the shopping area was constructed, there are even a few alligators.

But the Village is still convenient to the main activities of the World and is easily accessible from either of the two exits from I-4. The best route is the exit off the Epcot Center interchange. But it's also possible to take the exit from S.R.-535 (although this route usually is more congested and far less scenic). Red-flagged buses also make the trip to and from Epcot Center, the TTC, and the Shopping Village on a regular basis; holders of ID cards issued by WDW resorts and WDW Village Hotel Plaza establishments, as well as bearers of certain Passports, can ride them at no extra charge.

In addition, there are Christmas wreaths made of velvet and calico, and other more ingenious and occasionally truly startling combinations. You even may find a Santa squirt gun, or a special Christmas jump rope.

POTTERY CHALET: This large store adjoining the Christmas Chalet offers the kinds of kitchen utensils and tableware that otherwise might be found only in a good housewares-oriented department store. There are things with which to cook and things to put on the table, light fixtures and canisters, cut crystal and pressed glass, music boxes and wind chimes, aprons and place mats. The selection of cookie cutters is particularly excellent; they come in both metal and plastic, in geometric, animal, and human shapes. There are several just for cutting different styles of gingerbread men. In addition, there's a huge display of animal figurines—tigers and dogs, owls and cats (domesticated and otherwise), hippos, and even parrots. It's a shop for rambling, and lots of fun for lovers of knickknacks.

CHALET CANDLE SHOP: The big deal in this small, sweetly scented shop (which actually is a part of the adjoining Pottery Chalet) is the lacy, ornamental, and carved candles festooned with multicolored ribbonlike curls of wax. Not everyone may care for this product, but there are plenty of other items in wax and paraffin here, in all sizes and shapes.

CHINA, CRYSTAL & SILVER: The gleaming $30,000 Lalique crystal table at the center of this shop (also part of the Pottery Chalet) may not be here forever, and some figures from the realistic set of *Wizard of Oz*-character figurines may have been sold by the time you arrive. But there always is plenty of fine, delicate merchandise on display, by such top makers as Hummel, Waterford, and Belleek, to say nothing of Disney characters crafted of pewter.

2R'S READ'N & RITE'N: Party supplies, stationery, cards for all occasions, desk accessories, and assorted gift items are all for sale at this emporium near the Chalet Candle Shop and the Lite Bite Snack Spot. Bookworms, however, will be most grateful for its excellent selection of hardbound and paperback books, the best in all of WDW. There's something for the very serious-minded, something to tickle the funny bone, and tomes at all levels of literature in between. Stamps are available here.

CRISTAL ARTS: This shop sells roughly the same sort of cut-glass merchandise available at Main Street's Crystal Arts and Adventureland's La Princesa de Cristal in the Magic Kingdom. Large green, blue, or red cut-glass bowls and vases are available, along with clear-glass mugs and other items engraved to customers' specifications with initials, messages, or pictures. Note: If you bring a favorite photograph with you to this shop, the engraver can have it reproduced on a plate or other item.

TOLEDO ARTS: Adjoining Cristal Arts on the east, Toledo Arts offers leather items, porcelain figurines, swords and ships, carved olive-wood boxes, napkin rings, salt-and-pepper shakers, and statues; plus other items, many imported from Spain. Damascene work, which involves etching a metal surface with acid, then encrusting it with silver or gold, is also sold, and craftsmen are usually on hand to demonstrate the process.

GREAT SOUTHERN CRAFT COMPANY: Fine handmade silver and leather goods are the featured offerings here. Don't miss the selection of finished handcrafts in the Country Craft Boutique. Located between Toledo Arts on the west and Port of Entry on the east.

LILLIE LANGTRY'S OLD-FASHIONED PHOTO STUDIO: Main Street in the Magic Kingdom has a photo studio in the Camera Center, and Adventureland has Laffite's Portrait Deck. Lillie Langtry's is the last-but-not-least of the trio of locations where guests can pose for sepia-toned prints in Edwardian suits or flounced-and-furbelowed gowns of a degree of frilliness rarely found outside a film studio's wardrobe department.

PORT OF ENTRY: If you were to shop your way around this planet, picking up local products in all the markets and souvenir shops as you went, you could open a store like this one when you returned home. Europe is represented by Delft knickknacks, small windmills, and piggy banks. From Mexico come pottery figurines, piñatas, copper kettles, and pots. The artisans of India are represented by carved bangles and boxes, clothing, and candleholders. From Guatemala come pots and a wealth of baskets. Straw and rattan items have been collected from all corners of the globe. And there are leather goods, carved marble items, necklaces, bracelets, and more from Africa and the Orient. Not far from the Captain's Tower and the Village marina.

BATH PARLOR: This is the place for elegant bath towels, fancy toilet seats, bathroom rugs, laundry bags, bath brushes, and all sorts of other appurtenances for the perfect toilette. A few gag items (striped, polka-dotted, or initialed toilet paper, for instance) are also available, along with a selection of sleepwear.

SACHET IN: Located alongside the Bath Parlor, this boutique is devoted to things fragrant—not just sweet-smelling sachets for drawers and closets, but also fancy soaps, of which the shop has Orlando's widest selection.

SIR EDWARD'S HABERDASHER: Named after Edward Moriarty, a Disney executive, this shop, full of good-quality clothing for men and boys, is an oasis of traditional masculinity in a bustling village otherwise filled with trifles and treasures that seem to appeal most to the feminine heart. Located near Sachet In, close to the parking lot.

GOURMET PANTRY: Not long ago, one vacationer searching for coffee and orange juice for the next day's breakfast passed up this store on the assumption that he'd find only escargots and smoked oysters. Wrong! These things can be found here, but there also are breads and pastries, meats and cheeses, cereals, yogurt, beer and soft drinks, and many more items—both mundane and exotic. Unusual teas and specially blended, freshly ground coffees are also available, and, occasionally, free tastes are offered to passersby. Villa and Treehouse guests take note: purchases will be delivered to your room at no extra charge; if you aren't going to be home, the delivery person will even stash perishables in your refrigerator. To order by phone, touch "1" on your room telephone, or, when calling from outside, dial 828-3886.

CHARACTER SHOP: When the Walt Disney World Shopping Village was first planned, no provision was made for a store selling Disney souvenirs. Popular demand changed that, and this was the result. Dumbo, Jiminy Cricket, Minnie and Mickey, Chip and Dale, Tigger and Eeyore, Tramp and his Lady are all here—stuffed, in porcelain, and emblazoned on everything from T-shirts and back scratchers to pencils and carry-all bags. There even are windup toys, hats, visors, blue-and-white Alice-in-Wonderland dresses with pinafores, and white-polka-dotted red Minnie dresses (also sold at Tinkerbell Toy Shop in Fantasyland in the Magic Kingdom). Be sure to look for the larger-than-life stuffed Mickey.

TOYS FANTASTIQUE: The rocking-horse sign outside is one of the Disney sign shop's most handsome efforts, and there are even greater delights inside, among the toys that are the products, some handmade, of both Europe and America. This is a toy shop to end all toy shops. The stuffed animals and dolls come in enough variety to make a collector of even the most staid grown-up. There are model kits, imported die-cast toys, windup bath toys, and electric trains with all the necessary fittings and accessories. And the doll boutique often features a selection of Madame Alexander dolls.

CANDY SHOPPE: Adjoining the Gourmet Pantry, this small, fragrant enclave sells Godiva chocolate, fudge, chocolate barks and creams, red licorice, peppermint sticks, hard candies, and just about everything else that ever made a sweet tooth ache. And that includes chocolate chess sets, dart boards, cars, and the like.

IT'S A SMALL WORLD AFTER ALL: Doting aunts and uncles, not to mention fond grandparents, will find the children's clothing that crowds the racks and shelves here well-nigh irresistible. The prices are generally on the high side (relative to what Mom herself might spend at home), but business booms nonetheless. Adjoining Toys Fantastique.

COUNTRY ADDRESS: This very good woman's clothing store offers a range of merchandise from the middle-priced and polyester to the oh-so-chic and expensive fashions by designers such as Anne Klein. Active and spectator sportswear and separates, as well as swimsuits, are offered in addition to dresses and evening wear. Next to It's a Small World.

24KT PRECIOUS ADORNMENTS: Elegant gold and silver jewelry is the main lure here. Located in the same building as the Village Restaurant and Lounge, at the north end of the Shopping Village, near Country Address.

VILLAGE GIFTS AND SUNDRIES: When you run out of shampoo or film, or want to stock up on cosmetics or buy a magazine, or if you run out of any number of other necessities, this is the place to look. If you need something that nobody else seems to carry, Village Gifts and Sundries might have it. There are even Kodak rental cameras available here. Occupies the west end of the building next to the Village Restaurant and Lounge, near 24KT.

VILLAGE SPIRITS: Spirits, liqueurs, ales, and other alcoholic products from all around the world are stocked at this shop next door to Village Gifts and Sundries. Inexpensive wines from California and New York keep company with vintages priced at $100 and more a bottle, plus a few very rare (and expensive) foreign wines bought at auction. Some very good values. Decanters, glasses, serving trays, and other bar items in abundance are also on sale, as well as the strawberry tequila served in Cap'n Jack's popular margaritas.

SHOE TIME: In these days of ever-climbing prices, the store buyer here has managed to put together a selection of stylish, high-quality, casual-to-dressy footwear that won't break the bank. Handbags and other accessories are also available, as well as Etienne Aigner designs. Behind Heidelberger's Deli and opposite Village Spirits.

PLUS YOU: An excellent selection of luggage and totes for men and women as well as accessories in all price ranges for teeny-boppers and female executives alike can be found here; worth a look. Adjoins Shoe Time.

MISS MERRILY'S FASHIONS: Kicky dresses, shorts and trousers, flowing skirts and blouses to match, with a supporting cast of French-cut jeans and other junior-sized clothing in trendy styles, jam this lively shop (once aptly named Miss Merrily's Madness). Opposite Village Gifts and Sundries.

SASSY'S: This boutique, next door to Miss Merrily's, stocks preteen clothing from shoes to lingerie, accessories, school clothes, and designer jeans, and various gift items.

WINDJAMMER DOCK SHOP: You go through this shop on the way to Cap'n Jack's Oyster Bar. The first section is devoted to women's fashions—Javanese batik shorts; skirts and tops; cool, crinkly cotton sundresses; a fine selection of costume jewelry; and shorts in a paint store's worth of colors, and just about any style imaginable.

RESTAURANTS

For a complete listing of all Walt Disney World Village restaurants, bars, and snack shops, see *Good Meals, Great Times*.

LAKESIDE ACTIVITIES

The 35-acre Buena Vista Lagoon that borders this village of cedar-shingled shops also gives it much of its atmosphere: When the sidewalks radiate heat, the water looks cool and inviting; in the slanting rays of the late afternoon sun, it glistens like a sheet of silver.

And there's always something going on. Little Water Sprites zip to and fro, speeding to the dock from feeder canals to the west, while more laid-back folk float gently along in pedal boats or V-hulled tent-topped metal canopy boats.

It's pleasant to sit and watch all this acitivity—from the benches at the Buena Vista Lagoon marina, centrally located in Walt Disney World Shopping Village; over mammoth salads and gooey ice cream sundaes at the Ice Cream Parlor on the lake's west shore; or over frozen fresh strawberry margaritas at Cap'n Jack's Oyster Bar. Those who opt to participate need walk only a few steps to the marina, where boats can be rented from morning until dusk. Opening and closing hours change from season to season; call 824-4321 for details. No swimming is allowed. (Prices subject to state tax.)

WATER SPRITES: These tiny craft are very popular. Though they don't really move very fast, they feel as if they do; and, in any event, they get up enough speed to cover quite a lot of territory on Buena Vista Lagoon. Half-hour rentals cost $8. There are usually lines of people waiting for boats between 11 A.M. and 4 P.M.; plan accordingly. The minimum age to rent or drive one of these boats (even with an accompanying adult) is 12.

CANOPY BOATS: These metal, V-hulled, 16-foot craft can accommodate up to ten adults; some people stock up on picnic supplies at the Shopping Village's Gourmet Pantry and turn an afternoon sail into a party. Cost is $12 per half hour.

PEDAL BOATS: These craft as well as Aqua cycles can be rented for $3 per half hour or $6 per hour.

CELEBRATIONS & SPECIAL EVENTS

There's nearly always something going on under the Captain's Tower in Walt Disney World Shopping Village. Some weeks the place might be stacked high with shiny new hardcover books; on another day, it might be cool and green, with an array of plants for sale. Crafts demonstrations and art shows are staged now and again, along with occasional manufacturers' promotions. In the past, these have included a barnyard festival with animals from the petting farm at Fort Wilderness and birds from Discovery Island; a citrus promotion; a Trivial Pursuit promotion; and the dollmaker Madame Alexander, who was introducing a new line that had collectors lining up in the wee hours of the morning.

In addition, there are a number of annual events—some in celebration of holidays. All of these are free.

WDW VILLAGE WINE FESTIVAL (JANUARY): Sixty wineries from California, other parts of the U.S., and Europe participate in this annual festival.

BOAT SHOW (OCTOBER): Because this Central Florida region has no ocean beaches, most events of this type are staged in shopping malls and exhibition halls. Here, however, boats are displayed not only throughout the Shopping Village, but also in the water; and with over 200 boats from all manufacturers, this is the area's biggest in-the-water boat show.

HALLOWEEN: The Captain's Tower, made to look as spooky as a contemporary structure can be, with festoons of cobwebs and displays of Halloween merchandise, is the centerpiece of a number of activities around the Shopping Village. There's a Halloween Procession that allows local children (and vacationing youngsters with the foresight to bring an outfit) to join assorted costumed witches, ghosts, goblins, and Disney villains—*Sleeping Beauty's* Maleficent and *Snow White's* Wicked Witch— in a grand march around the Shopping Village.

FESTIVAL OF THE MASTERS: This art show, which takes place in November each year, is generally considered one of the state's best because only artists who have won an award in the past three years are invited to enter.

CHRISTMASTIME: Thanksgiving marks the beginning of the Christmas season here when a Christmas tree is set up in the village. Then the *Glory and Pageantry of Christmas,* a reenactment of a nativity play fashioned after a thirteenth-century pageant whose origins are in southern France, makes its annual debut. In all, there are appearances by some three dozen characters garbed in period costumes made from brocades, satins, silks, velvets, wool, rough homespun, and monk's cloth—a baker, butcher, candlemaker, flower seller, fruit and vegetable peddler, weaver, and others. A concert of carols precedes each evening's tableau.

USEFUL STOPS

A Guest Services facility is located in the Pottery Chalet with an outdoor walk-up window facing Lite Bite and the Read'n & Rite'n shop. Services include reservation assistance, ticket sales, lost and found, film and stamp sales, wheelchair and stroller rental, gift certificates, gift wrap, and general information.

LOANER CAMERAS: Kodak cameras and film are available at Village Gifts and Sundries. A refundable $50 deposit is required.

BUS TRANSPORTATION: The WDW Shopping Village bus stop and shelter is located next to Sir Edward's Haberdasher. From there, you can get green-and-gold-flagged buses (those labeled with a "V") to the Lake Buena Vista Club and the Villas and Treehouses; blue-and-white-flagged buses to Walt Disney World Village Hotel Plaza; and red-flagged buses to Epcot Center and the Transportation and Ticket Center. (From there, monorails and ferries go to the Magic Kingdom, gold-flagged buses to the Contemporary Resort, green-flagged buses to the Golf Resort and the Polynesian Village, and blue-flagged buses to Fort Wilderness.) For more information on transportation within the rest of the World, see *Transportation and Accommodations.*

FOREIGN CURRENCY EXCHANGE: This can be done at the Sun Bank during regular banking hours. See *Getting Ready to Go.*

TRAVELER'S CHECKS: These can be purchased at the Sun Bank (see above); outside the bank, there is an American Express Cardmembers Cheque Dispenser, which cardholders (who have previously obtained a special number) may use to purchase traveler's checks.

FORT WILDERNESS

In a part of the state where campgrounds tend to look like a pasture—barren and very hot—the Fort Wilderness Campground, located almost due east of the Contemporary Resort Hotel, is an anomaly—a forested 650-acre wonder of tall slash pines, white-flowering bay trees, and ancient cypress hung with streamers of gray-green Spanish moss. Seminole Indians once hunted and fished here.

In all, there are some 828 woodsy campsites arranged in several campground loops; along some of them, Fleetwood trailers are available for rent, completely furnished and fitted out with all the comforts of home. For information about these campsites, see *Transportation and Accommodations*.

Scattered throughout the campground loops, there are a number of sporting facilities—tetherball, horseshoe and volleyball courts, and, among other conveniences, large playing fields. Fort Wilderness has riding stables, a marina full of boats, a canoe livery, a beach, a jogging-and-exercise trail, electric carts and bikes for rent, and a nature trail. Some of these facilities are available for the use of campground guests only; some are limited to guests at WDW-owned resort hotels and villas as well; and some can also be enjoyed by guests lodging at the establishments at the Walt Disney World Village Hotel Plaza and off the property.

There's also a petting farm where goats and ducks and other farm animals run free inside a white rail fence, and it's fun to walk through the barn that houses the large, sleek horses that pull the Magic Kingdom's Main Street trolleys.

Two stores, the Settlement and Meadow trading posts, stock campers' necessities and some Disney souvenirs. And then there's Pioneer Hall, widely known as the home of the Hoop-Dee-Doo Musical Revue (described in *Good Meals, Great Times*). This rustic structure (made of western white pine shipped all the way from Montana) also encompasses a cafeteria and game room.

Last but not least in the Fort Wilderness catalogue, there's River Country. This eight-acre expanse of water-oriented recreational facilities embodies everyone's idea of what the perfect old-fashioned swimming hole should be like. It's a separate attraction, with its own hours and admission fees.

HOW TO GET TO FORT WILDERNESS

BY CAR: From outside the World, take the WDW exit off I-4 onto U.S. 192, go through the Magic Kingdom Toll Plaza, and, bearing to your right, follow the Fort Wilderness or River Country signs. This is probably the most expeditious way to go, even for WDW resort guests coming from other parts of the World.

BY BUS: Take the gold-flagged bus from the Contemporary Resort, the green-flagged bus from the Polynesian Village, the red-flagged bus from WDW Shopping Village and Epcot Center, or the red-and-white-flagged bus from Walt Disney World Village Hotel Plaza establishments to the Transportation and Ticket Center. Change there to the blue-flagged bus to Fort Wilderness. Count on 30 to 45 minutes in transit. To ride the red- and red-and-white-flagged buses, you must show an ID card from one of the WDW-owned properties or a Hotel Plaza establishment; certain Passports will also do.

In addition, special black-flagged buses make the trip to Pioneer Hall from the Polynesian Village and the Golf Resort in time for the Hoop-Dee-Doo Musical Revue.

BY BOAT: Guests at WDW-owned properties, and those with admission tickets to River Country or Discovery Island, also can go by boat from marinas in the Magic Kingdom (green-flagged, about 30 minutes' ride); from the Polynesian Village (gold-flagged, about 15 minutes' ride); and from the Contemporary Resort (blue-flagged, about 25 minutes' ride).

SOUVENIRS AND SUPPLIES

Staple food items and all sorts of other necessities of the camping life are available, along with souvenirs, at Fort Wilderness's two stores—the Settlement Trading Post, located not far from the beach at the north end of the campground; and the Meadow Trading Post, located near the playing fields and the campfire area near the center of Fort Wilderness.

The trading posts' deli counters will also make up sandwiches to go, for picnics on the beach or at River Country.

For a complete list of places to eat in Fort Wilderness, see *Good Meals, Great Times*.

HOOP-DEE-DOO MUSICAL REVUE

Sturdy, porch-rimmed Pioneer Hall is best-known Worldwide as the home of the Pioneer Hall Players, an energetic troupe of singing-and-dancing-and-wisecracking entertainers who keep audiences chuckling and grinning and whooping it up for two hours, during a procession of barbecued ribs, fried chicken, corn on the cob, strawberry shortcake, and other stomach-stretching viands. If you have time for only one of the Disney dinner shows, make it this one (for more details, see *Good Meals, Great Times*).

RIVER COUNTRY

THE PERFECT SWIMMING HOLE

It's next to impossible to go through childhood reading such classics as *Huck Finn* and *Tom Sawyer* (and other such great tales of growing up) without developing a few fantasies about what it would be like to swim in a perfect swimming hole. A group of Disney imagineers (who actually knew a commercial re-creation of such a place as kids) have concocted a Disney version on a somewhat larger scale at River Country, a water-oriented playground that occupies a corner of Bay Lake near Cypress Point at Fort Wilderness Campground.

Fred Joerger—the same Disney rock-builder who created Big Thunder Mountain, Schweitzer Falls at the Jungle Cruise, and the caves of Tom Sawyer Island (among other things) in the Magic Kingdom—has helped design scores of rocks used to landscape one of the largest swimming pools in the state; more have been piled into a small mountain for guests to climb up—and then slide down. The rocks, scattered with pebbles acquired from stream beds in Georgia and the Carolinas, look so real that it's hard to believe they aren't.

More to the point, the place is great fun. Slipping and sliding down the curvy water chutes at top speed; getting tangled up, all arms and legs, in the whirlpools of Raft Rider Ridge; and whamming into the water from the swimming pool's high slides makes even careworn grown-ups smile, grin, giggle, chortle, and roar with delight. People who climb to the top with trepidation embark on the lightning-fast journey to the bottom only because it seems too late to back out; at the bottom they rush back for more. Line-haters queue up—over and over again. Those who associate lakes with muck and weeds go into ecstasies over the way the soft sand on the River Country bottom squiggles between their toes.

WHAT TO DO: There are several basic sections of River Country—the 330,000-gallon swimming pool, one of the largest in Florida's Orange County; Bay Cove (aka the "Ol' Swimmin' Hole"), the big walled-off section of Bay Lake that most people consider the main (and best) part of River Country; an adjoining junior version of the above for small children, with its own beach; and the grassy grounds, with picnic tables and a squirting fountain in which to play. On the edge of the lake, there's also a boardwalk-nature trail through a lovely cypress swamp, and a wide (if not terribly long) white-sand beach.

Heated in winter, the oversized swimming pool has two sets of diving rocks (in graduated sizes) at one end. On the other side of the pool is the pair of water slides that begin high enough above the water to make an acrophobe climb right down again. They plunge at such an angle that it's impossible to see the bottom of the slide from the top. Daredevils who don't chicken out are shot into the water from a height of about seven feet—hard enough, as one commentator observed, to "slap your stomach up against the roof of your mouth." Gutsy kids adore the experience; those who like their thrills a bit tamer might prefer to watch.

The heart of River Country, Bay Cove—actually a part of Bay Lake—is fitted out with rope swings, a ship's boom for swooping and plunging, and assorted other constructions designed to put hearts into throats as swimmers plunge from air to water. The big deals, however, are the two flume rides—one 260 feet long (accessible by a boardwalk and stairway to the far right of the swimming hole as you face it) and a smaller one, 100 feet shorter (accessible by a stairway to the left of that) and the white-water raft ride.

The flumes, which are like overgrown, steep-sided waterslides, corkscrew through the greenery at the top of the ridge known as Whoop-'N-Holler Hollow, sending even the most stalwart shooting into the water, usually like greased lightning. Timid folk will find it easy to control speed, however. The rule of thumb is to sit up to slow down, and lie back to speed up. Be warned that once you lie down to accelerate, getting up is virtually impossible. Reclining with arms at sides guarantees a slower ride than lying back with hands above the head. Arching your back so that only shoulders and heels are on the flume's surface increases the pace still further. Combining positions allows for braking and accelerating at will.

White Water Rapids, as the white-water raft ride mentioned above is known, involves a more leisurely trip through a series of chutes and pools in an inner tube, from the crest of Raft Rider Ridge (adjoining Whoop-'N-Holler Hollow) into Bay Cove. It's not a high-speed affair like the flumes, but some people like it better. The pools are contoured so that the water swirls through them in whirlpool fashion. You tend to get caught in the slow circling water, and when other tubers come sliding down the chutes at you, bare arms and legs get all tangled up.

ADMISSION: River Country is an attraction in its own right, with a separate admission charge that includes transportation to the site and use of all the facilities. A River Country and Discovery Island combination ticket, which includes transportation and admission to both, is also available.

	Guests at WDW resorts/children 3 through 12	All other guests/children 3 through 12
River Country admission (During summer months after 5 P.M.—$2 off for all ages, or $20 family rate)	$8/$5.75	$8.75/$6.50
River Country/Discovery Island combination ticket	$10.75/$6.75	$11.50/$7.50

A 2-day River Country ticket is available to resort guests only at resort ticket locations or at the River Country ticket window. This ticket is good for any two days during a seven day period; prices are $11.25 for adults and $7.50 for children (3 through 12).

Prices are subject to change.

NOTE: Children under ten must be accompanied by an adult. Some of the River Country adventures require swimming ability.

WHEN TO GO: Daytime temperatures in Orlando are such that it's possible to enjoy River Country almost all year round, though it is perhaps most pleasant in spring—when the weather is getting hot but the water is still cool. In summer, the place can be very busy indeed.

Ticket windows close as the crowd approaches capacity. During WDW's busiest times of year, that may happen as early as 11:30 A.M. It's worth noting, however, that those who already have tickets will be admitted anyway. Consequently, if you plan to visit River Country in the afternoon of a summer day, it's smart to buy your combination River Country/Discovery Island ticket at the ticket booth at the entrance to the Magic Kingdom on your way into the park.

One of the World's best-kept secrets is the joy of River Country after 5 P.M. in the summer. Crowds begin to thin out dramatically then, but usually not so much that the place is empty; and a special reduced admission ticket is offered after 5 P.M. After dark, the surroundings are lighted and it's possible to watch the Electrical Water Pageant from the beach as it passes by around 9:35 P.M.

HOW TO GET THERE: From the Transportation and Ticket Center, blue-flagged buses drop passengers off within walking distance of River Country. It's also possible to go by boat. Launches leave regularly from the dock near the gates of the Magic Kingdom. For guests arriving at River Country by car, a tram picks up at the River Country parking lot and takes guests to the entrance. River Country tickets or IDs from WDW resorts are required.

TOWELS, DRESSING ROOMS, SUPPLIES: Men's and women's dressing rooms, and coin-operated lockers are available. Quarters for these can be obtained at the concession window, but to avoid waiting in line for change, it's best to bring your own.

Towels are available for rent at 25¢ each at the concession window, but they're small, so you'll probably want to bring at least one beach towel.

FOOD: Pop's Place, the main snack stand, sells quarter-pound burgers, hot dogs, beer and soda, and the like. The Waterin' Hole, a smaller stand nearby, offers a more limited selection during peak season.

Picnicking is permitted. You can eat on the beach or seek out a table on the shady lawns. (Sorry folks, no alcoholic beverages are allowed to be taken into River Country.)

MORE

Fort Wilderness Campground is one of the liveliest spots in the World.

BEACHES: The campground does not have its own swimming pool (and to use the one at River Country it's necessary to pay the River Country admission), but the clear waters of Bay Lake, which lap the 315-foot-long, 175-foot-wide, white-sand beach at the north end of the campground, are delightful, and swimming is allowed inside the roped-off areas. Open to guests at WDW-owned properties only.

BIKE RENTALS: Tandems, dirt bikes, surreys, and assorted other two-wheelers can be hired at the Bike Barn for trips along Fort Wilderness's bike paths and circuitous roadways—or just for getting around. Cost is $2 to $3 per hour, or $5 to $7 per day.

BLACKSMITH SHOP: The pleasant fellow who shoes the draft horses that pull the trolleys down Main Street in the Magic Kingdom is on hand at some time every day to answer questions and talk about what he does; occasionally guests can watch him at work, fitting the big animals with the special polyurethane-covered, steel-cored horseshoes that are used here to protect the horses' hooves.

BOAT RENTALS ON BAY LAKE: Zippy little Water Sprites, sailboats, pontoon boats, and pedal boats (described in *Sports*) are available for rent at the Fort Wilderness marina, at the north end of the campground.

CAMPFIRE PROGRAM: Held nightly near the Meadow Trading Post near the center of the campground, it features Disney movies, a sing-along, and cartoons. It's free for Walt Disney World resort guests only. Chip and Dale usually put in an appearance.

CANOE RENTALS: Fort Wilderness is ribboned with tranquil canals, sometimes in full sun and sometimes canopied by tall trees, which make for delightful canoe trips of one to three hours—or longer if you take fishing gear and elect to wet your line. Rentals are available at the Bike Barn ($2 per hour, $7 per day).

CHECKERS: Boards are set up in the Settlement Trading Post.

ELECTRIC CART RENTALS: Available at the Bike Barn for sight-seeing or transportation around the campground.

ELECTRICAL WATER PAGEANT: This twinkling cavalcade-of-lights (described in more detail in *Good Meals, Great Times*) can be seen from the beach here nightly at 9:45 P.M., and, during the hours that the Magic Kingdom is open late, at 9:35 P.M., from River Country.

FISHING EXCURSIONS ON BAY LAKE: WDW's restrictive fishing policy means plenty of angling action—largemouth bass weighing two or three pounds, mainly—for those who sign up for the special 8 A.M. and 3 P.M. fishing excursions offered to guests at WDW-owned properties. The fee is $75 (each additional hour, $25), and includes gear, driver/guide, and refreshments; no license is required. Guests whose accommodations have kitchens may keep their catch; for everyone else, it's catch-and-release.

FISHING IN THE CANALS: Largemouth bass can be caught here as well. Those without their own gear will find cane poles and lures for sale at the trading posts; equipment is also available for rent at the Bike Barn. No license is required.

THE HORSE BARN: The world champion Percheron eight-horse hitch that pulls the trolleys down Main Street in the Magic Kingdom calls this corner of Fort Wilderness home. You can watch them chomping placidly on their food, and occasionally see young colts and fillies as well. The Tri Circle D insignia above the barn door is also the WDW brand: two small circles, Mouse ears–style, atop one large one with the letter *D* inside.

FORT WILDERNESS FUN

JOGGING AND EXERCISE TRAILS: This 2.3-mile course, punctuated by exercise stations every quarter mile or so, is one of the Fort Wilderness attractions that draws WDW resort guests from all over the property. The weather is often steamy, but things are pleasant in the early morning—especially because most of the running trail is in the shade. You may just jog the whole length; or you can stop periodically to do the chin-ups, sit-ups, and other exercises outlined on nearby signs.

LAWN MOWER TREE: The tree that somehow, mysteriously, grew around a lawn mower is a Fort Wilderness point of interest, worth hunting down. It's just off the sidewalk leading to the marina.

MARSHMALLOW MARSH EXCURSION: A nightly (during the summer months) marshmallow roast and sing-along follows a canoe trip and a short hike to the northern end of the campground, where a handful of big split logs is arranged around a fire ring. The Electrical Water Pageant, which can be seen just offshore, is part of the entertainment. Bring mosquito repellent. For Walt Disney World resort guests only; cost is $5 for adults, $4 for children.

PETTING FARM: This fenced-in enclave just behind Pioneer Hall is now home to some extra-friendly goats, a fully grown brahma bull, some sheep, a few rabbits, exotic chickens and pigeons, and a goose—the sole remaining member of an original trio, two thirds of which were promptly dispatched elsewhere when they developed the decidedly unamiable habit of chasing youngsters; the nasty twosome once trapped a woman in her trailer for four hours. (The colony of prairie dogs didn't work out either, because members persisted in burrowing out of their compound; no sooner would their Disney caretakers try to thwart them—by digging a bigger hole and installing a below-ground-level wire fence—than the little creatures would gnaw right through it.) Though mainly designed for youngsters, the Petting Farm is also a lot of fun for the adult crowd, and it's a good place to pass the time while waiting for seating at the Hoop-Dee-Doo Musical Revue in nearby Pioneer Hall.

SOFTBALL AND BASEBALL DIAMONDS: Located in the meadow near the Bike Barn, these can be used by guests at WDW-owned properties. No balls and bats are available; bring your own. Free.

TRAIL RIDES: Offered from the corral at the kennel and livery area near the River Country parking lot, these trips depart five times daily, and take riders past an Indian village, some Western wagons, and assorted other frontier-type props. These add a bit of atmosphere—but not nearly so much as the occasional sight of a real cougar or bobcat (extremely rare, but not totally nonexistent either) and deer (which are abundant here). Galloping is not part of the game, so you don't need riding know-how to sign up. Cost is about $5 per person for both day visitors and for guests at WDW-owned properties. No children under 9 are allowed. Reservations are necessary; phone 824-2734.

VOLLEYBALL, TETHERBALL, BASKETBALL, AND HORSESHOE COURTS: Open only to guests at WDW-owned properties, these are scattered throughout the camping loops. No charge.

WATER-SKI TRIPS: Ski boats with driver and equipment can be hired at $35 an hour at the marina. Includes instruction. Reservations should be made two to three days in advance. Call the Contemporary Resort (824-1000; ask for the marina).

WILDERNESS SWAMP TRAIL: A mile and a half long, this smooth footpath into the woods skirts the marshes along the shore of Bay Lake, then plunges into a forest full of tall, straight-standing cypress trees. Near Marshmallow Marsh, at the northern end of the campground.

DISCOVERY ISLAND

This 11½-acre landfall (a member of the American Association of Parks and Aquariums) on the southeast shore of Bay Lake, a natural marvel full of exotic birds and a whole United Nations of plants, is a delightful place to go for a change of pace from the Magic Kingdom. Here you're in the domain of the animals and man is just a visitor. The mood is different from anywhere else in the World, and the scenery is remarkably lush.

Before the World began, this island was flat and scrubby, just a tangle of vines. But Disney planners, thinking of Robert Louis Stevenson's classic *Treasure Island*, decided to turn it into a horticultural and zoological paradise. They cleared the vegetation, brought in 15,000 cubic yards of sandy soil, and added 500 tons each of boulders and trees. They built hills, carved out lagoons, sowed grass seed, and planted 20 types of palm trees, 10 species of bamboo, and dozens upon dozens of other plants from Argentina, Bolivia, the Canary Islands, China, Costa Rica, Formosa, the Himalayas, India, Japan, Peru, South Africa, Trinidad, and other nations around the world. Then they added winding paths, built aviaries and filled them with birds, and added a few props to carry through the Treasure Island theme. A wrecked ship salvaged from off the coast of Florida was installed on the beach, and a Jolly Roger waved from the lookout post. The creation was dubbed Treasure Island.

Since then, that theme has been abandoned and the island's name changed. But the ship is still there, as is the vegetation (lusher than ever). And the avian population is flourishing so well that the droning of the motors of the Water Sprites on Bay Lake is almost drowned out by chirps and tweets, crows and hoarse caws, cries and squeaks, and the lonely-sounding squawks of peacocks.

Now nobody makes any bones about the fact that the birds and the extraordinary vegetation constitute the island's chief attraction. Far from taking a backseat to the man-made, nature is the big deal on Discovery Island. The sweet-smelling flowers in pinks and reds and yellows that polka-dot the billowing greenery, the ferns that hang in the forests, the trees that canopy the footpaths, the butterflies, the dense thickets of bamboo, and the graceful palms—not to mention the birds themselves—are all very real; during Discovery Island hours—that is, from 9 A.M. to 5 P.M. (to 6 P.M. during the summer) every day—visitors provide (as curator Charlie Cook tells it) a good show for the birds and animals.

WHAT TO SEE: It's possible to walk the length of the paths and boardwalks that wind through the island in 45 minutes or so. But spending the better part of a day—or at least several hours—is a far better idea, since there is so much to see that it warrants more than just a rushed look. This is especially true in spring, when the birds are in breeding condition—looking their best, putting on courting displays, and sometimes collecting materials for nests. Even during other seasons, however, each stop yields rewards. An ibis might be spotted building its nest. A sleeping tortoise—dinosaur-like, with the papery, wrinkled skin of an old woman's neck—suddenly rouses himself and creeps forward to join a clump of rocks that turns out to be other tortoises.

Many animals run free. Peacocks trail their spotted trains of iridescent green, blue, and gold around the grounds. They lose their tail feathers every September, and spend the winter growing new plumage in preparation for their springtime mating dance—a slow turning to and fro, sometimes punctuated by a quiver and a shudder of their graceful fans. A type of chicken developed in Poland, where chicken breeding is a popular hobby, occasionally chases the peacocks. The large rabbit-like animals are Patagonian cavies, members of the guinea pig family, who in the wild live in burrows to escape predators. Keeping quite calm, you can approach them slowly to examine them at close range.

In addition, there are a number of special points of interest, which are marked on maps available on the island:

COOCOO CABANA: The macaws, cockatoos, and other trained birds that comprise the José Carioca Flyers make their home here and at a small enclosure dotted with perches nearby. One six-year-old bird can stand on his head. Little green ones named Moe, Larry (the greenest; actually a female), and Curly (the shyest) know how to roll over. Andrew waves good-bye. Each one has his own trick, and you can stand and watch the caretakers putting them through their paces for hours.

TRUMPETER SPRINGS: The trumpeter swans who live here, the largest members of the waterfowl family, belong to a species that once was nearly extinct—as a result of hunting in the early part of the century.

BAMBOO HOLLOW: The sturdy bamboo here was planted on the island's windward side as protection against occasional harsh weather and wind.

CRANE'S ROOST: The large, red-banded Sarus cranes, the small Demoiselle cranes, and the striking gold-crested African crowned cranes engage in wonderfully elaborate courting dances every spring.

AVIAN WAY: One of the largest walk-through aviaries in the world, this large enclosure, occupying close to an acre, is the home of the United States' most extensive breeding colony of Scarlet ibis. Their incredible color, even richer than that of ibis in the wild, derives from a diet that is especially rich in carotenes. Even those in the forest are striking. The early South American explorers who first saw them thought that the trees were covered with blood.

Also in the aviary are white peacocks, albino animals with tails that look like the train of a lacy wedding gown, and elegant African Crowned cranes, almost as common in Africa as cats and dogs are in the United States; they have a voracious appetite for insects that aids in controlling insect pests, and farmers keep them for that purpose.

PELICAN BAY: Brown pelicans became almost extinct because the chemical DDT, washed into rivers and absorbed by fish that the birds subsequently ate, caused their eggs to have such thin shells that even the weight of the mother pelican nesting on them broke them before hatching. It only has been since Florida's 1965 ban on the chemical that the population has grown again. The Discovery Island birds, though now healthy, have suffered injuries that have left them crippled in ways that would make it impossible for them to survive in the wild.

FLAMINGO LAGOON: Native flamingos—which nested in colonies some 20,000 strong when John James Audubon visited Florida in the early part of the 19th century—have not lived in the wild here since around 1920. The Discovery Island birds are Caribbean flamingos. They have grown accustomed to man's presence, as the early Florida flamingos could not, and are breeding.

TURTLE BEACH: Early explorers used to lead Galapagos tortoises, now rare and endangered, onto their ships; because the animals can live for some time without food or water, they provided the crews with fresh meat for the duration of a trip. There are 11 here; the largest weighs some 500 pounds.

EAGLE'S WATCH: The pair of southern bald eagles here belong to a species that nests in the wild only in Florida. Sharp-eyed and white-headed, the birds seen here are on loan from the U.S. Department of the Interior.

HOW TO GET THERE: Watercraft from the Magic Kingdom, the Polynesian Village, and the Contemporary Resort, Fort Wilderness, and River Country all call regularly at Discovery Island; to ride these, you must show a Discovery Island admission ticket or a WDW resort ID.

ADMISSION: Cost is $4 ($2 for children 3 through 12); combination tickets that include River Country admission as well are also available (described in this chapter's River Country section). Some Eastern Airlines packages (described in the *Getting Ready to Go* chapter) include admission to both Discovery Island and River Country.

PHOTOS: The birds on Discovery Island offer wonderful photographic possibilities. Don't forget your camera. Film is available on the island.

BEACH: Swimming isn't allowed, but the peaceful strand flanking the shipwreck is great for sunbathing and sandcastle building—or just for sitting and watching the brightly colored sails of the Hobie Cats (from the Fort Wilderness marina) go by.

FOOD: It's fun to pack a picnic, with supplies from the Gourmet Pantry at Walt Disney World Shopping Village or one of the Fort Wilderness Campground's trading posts, for lunch on the beach near the handsome old wreck (which is still aging gracefully along the Bay Lake shore). Ice cream sandwiches and bars, frozen juice bars, frozen chocolate-covered bananas, and beer and soft drinks are also available at the island snack bar, the Thirsty Perch.

WONDERS OF THE WORLD

BEHIND THE SCENES

There isn't a Magic Kingdom visitor around who wouldn't like to see Disney character costumes being made, or to go backstage at the Diamond Horseshoe and ask the dancers how they make it look so easy, or to talk to a Disney character artist in person and watch him draw Donald Duck. Outdoor lovers who hear of wildlife-rich WDW's 7,500-acre nature preserve, not normally open to the public, would give their eyeteeth to explore its glass-smooth waterways.

Wonders of Walt Disney World, a program offered to students in the fifth through tenth grades, shows off these aspects of WDW (and more) in four special courses devoted to the creative arts, ecology, energy, and entertainment. The inside look at parts of this 43-square-mile complex is one that any adult would envy. The Wonders of Walt Disney World program is even more enriching because the on-property experience is augmented by excellently produced books designed to prepare kids for what they'll be learning before they arrive, and to help them follow through on the knowledge they've acquired once they're back home again. Developed in cooperation with educators from the Orlando area and from out of state, the program has won accolades from teachers and state school superintendents all over the country; many educational institutions give students credit for their participation and grant excused absences to those who complete the course. (Therein lies the other positive aspect of the program: it allows families to vacation at Walt Disney World during spring, winter, and fall—when crowds are smaller and things are generally more manageable.)

ALL ABOUT THE PROGRAMS: The WDW section of the program, distinct from the pre- and post-trip work that each participant completes, lasts about six hours. Each student is given a Kodak instant camera to use during the session to record his or her impressions; the cost of the film, as well as the cost of lunch and the pre- and post-trip materials, is included in the $45 fee. Only one program per visit is recommended for each participant.

CREATIVE ARTS: A visit by a Disney artist, who shows students how to draw a character or two and then critiques them as they execute their own versions, is the highlight of the *Disney Creative Arts* course. There's also a walk through the Magic Kingdom and Epcot Center, during which the Wonders program instructor points out some of the parks' design elements—the careful painting of signs and buildings to make them look antique (though they're really not), the scaling of the buildings on Main Street so that they look bigger than they are, and instances of the use of colors, shapes, and texture to produce effects. Features of Epcot Center are examined in the same detail.

ECOLOGY: *The Wonder and Beauty of Our World* course begins with a film describing Floridian ecosystems in general; then proceeds with tours of 11½-acre Discovery Island and the 7,500-acre conservation area, where students look for air plants and orchids, ospreys and egrets, alligators, and bald cypress. Each youngster is given not only a camera and binoculars to use during the session, but also a nature log in which to record his or her observations. There's talk of the interrelationships of soil and water and plant and animal life, and of the ways in which the destruction of one of these elements can mean the ruin of the whole community; there's no development-is-bad message here, just a caution, and adult bird watchers and other nature lovers (as well as photographers who normally wouldn't be interested in yielding to their kids' pleas for a trip to WDW) usually look more favorably on the idea when this course comes to their attention.

ENERGY: During *The Energy That Runs Our World* course, students visit the Universe of Energy at Epcot Center for an overview of the subject; learn how energy is produced, distributed, used, and conserved; and talk about transportation systems from the steam-powered motors of the past to the linear induction motors that power the WEDway People-Mover, a Disney-developed prototype for mass transit. On a trip through the Magic Kingdom, youngsters discuss the ways in which energy is used there; and at the Walt Disney World Central Energy Plant—a facility that few outsiders ever see—they learn about the World's computerized energy distribution system and see how its prototype solar-powered office building actually works.

ENTERTAINMENT: *The Walt Disney World of Entertainment* course has students looking not just at the onstage performers, but also at the people backstage and the audience. Lighting, music, pacing, sets, and timing are all discussed as well. Students meet a Disney character (and practice walking and communicating like that character) and talk to the performers at the Diamond Horseshoe and other Disney showfolk.

MORE INFORMATION: To find out more and make reservations, write two months in advance of your trip to Wonders of Walt Disney World; Box 40; Lake Buena Vista, FL 32830. Or call 828-2405 to check if there's an opening in the program at the last minute. The Wonders program is also available to purchasers of Walt Disney World packages and Eastern Airlines packages.

SPORTS

147 Tennis Everyone
148 A Matter of Courses
150 Waters of the World
152 More Fun Stuff

Many first-time visitors don't realize that Walt Disney World is much more than just the Magic Kingdom and Epcot Center. Within WDW's 27,000-odd acres there are more tennis courts than at many tennis resorts, more holes of championship-caliber golf than at most golf centers, and so many acres of other diversions—from fishing and bicycling to boating and swimming—that the quantity and variety are matched by very few other vacation destinations.

So while the golfers in the family are earnestly pursuing a perfect swing on one of the trio of first-class layouts, tennis buffs can be wearing themselves out on the courts, sailors can be sailing, water skiers can be skimming back and forth across powerboat wakes, and anglers can be dangling a cane pole in a canal—in the hopes of bringing in a big bream for dinner.

Instruction (formal or impromptu), as well as guides, drivers, and assorted leaders and supervisors (as required), make each sports offering as much fun for rank beginners as for hard-core aficionados. Moreover, the ready accessibility of all these WDW sporting activities—via an excellent system of public transportation (see *Transportation and Accommodations*)—means that no member of a visiting family or group need give up play time to chauffeur others around. By the same token, excellent supervision in all sports areas keeps to a minimum any parental fears that youngsters might get into trouble the moment they stray off to play without accompaniment.

Finally, staying in one of the WDW-owned hotels, in the villa complex, or in the WDW Fort Wilderness Campground is quite different from lodging off the property and visiting the World by the day, for certain sporting activities that are available to WDW resort guests are off limits to day visitors. However, most sports facilities are available to all, and except for the potential logistical problem of coordinating a day's-end rendezvous back at the car, the functional design and convenient placement of WDW sports and recreational facilities make them as compelling for off-property lodgers as for guests at WDW's own resorts. (Prices noted herein are subject to change and do not include applicable state tax.)

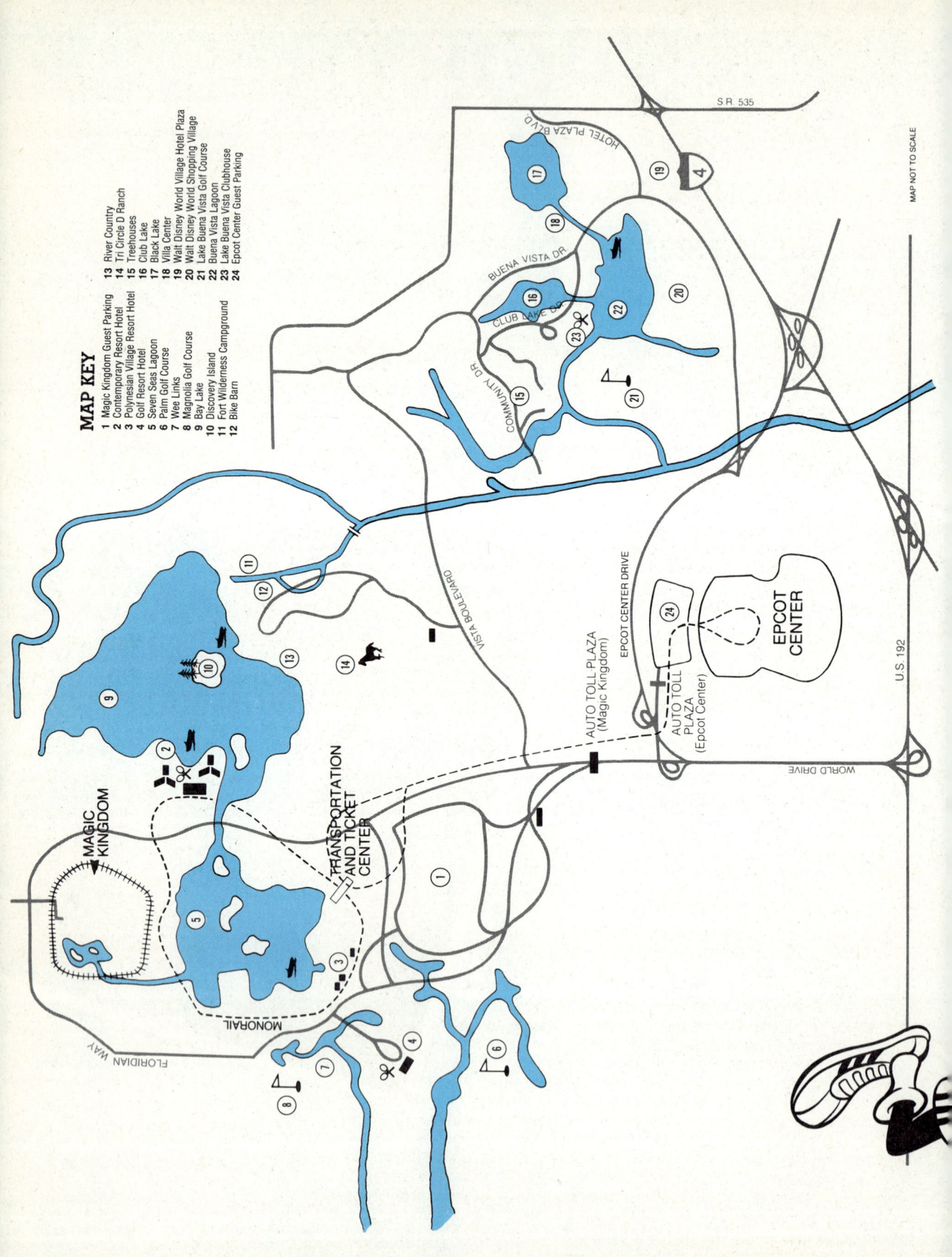

TENNIS EVERYONE

No one comes to Walt Disney World just for a tennis vacation; there just isn't the country-club ambience of a tennis resort where everyone is totally immersed in the game. But the facilities and instruction program at WDW are extensive enough that such holidays are certainly within the realm of possibility. And at the very least, a game of tennis on one of the World's 11 courts is a good way to rest up from a mad morning in the Magic Kingdom, for there's seldom a problem arranging court time.

Only in February, March, and April do the courts at the three separate tennis locations enjoy fairly heavy usage, but even then there is usually a lull between noon and 3 P.M., and again from dinnertime until 10 P.M. Even in these busy months, however, it's usually possible to get a reservation. Of the three sets of courts, those at the Lake Buena Vista Club are usually the least crowded, with those at the Golf Resort also available for play most of the time.

WHERE TO FIND THE COURTS: There are six tennis courts at the Contemporary Resort Hotel, just beyond the garden wings to the north of the Tower. This is WDW's major tennis facility. It boasts a backboard, plus a practice "lane" (about half as long and wide as a normal court) with an automatic ball machine which shoots out about 400 balls per half hour to backhands or forehands, or both. There are two additional courts tucked away behind the Golf Resort, and three, cradled by adjacent woods and a section of the golf course, at the Lake Buena Vista Club. All WDW tennis facilties are hard courts and are open from 8 A.M. to 10 P.M. daily (hours may vary during winter months). All are lighted for play after dark.

COURT FEES: To WDW resort guests, the cost is $4 an hour for singles, $6 for doubles. Use of the backboard is free, except during busy periods, when the regular court fees are charged. Guests pay $6 per half hour to use practice lanes and $7.50 for the on-court ball machine.

RESERVATIONS: Courts can be reserved 24 hours in advance. Call 824-3578 to play at the Contemporary Resort; 824-1469 for the Golf Resort; 828-3741 for the Lake Buena Vista Club. The limit on the number of hours a day any single group of players can occupy a court—a restriction in effect only during very busy periods—is two hours for any single morning, afternoon, or evening. But that still means that you can spend up to six hours a day on any given court even at the busiest times, and the fact is that these restrictions on court time have never yet been imposed.

For players without partners, the "Tennis Anyone?" program will help find an opponent. Just call the Pro Shop at the Contemporary Resort to get your name posted.

INSTRUCTION: The tennis program at the Contemporary Resort offers adult clinics ($20) and junior development lessons for players aged 4 through 16 ($10) upon request. Video cameras are used to record players' on-court efforts for subsequent review at both clinics; children as young as 3 and adults as old as 80 have participated. Nobody will try to radically change your game; the idea is to help you play better with what you have.

Private lessons are also available, by appointment at the Contemporary Resort only. The cost is $25 per hour and $12.50 per half hour with a staff professional; $30 per hour and $15 per half hour with head pro Steve Babb, who supervises the entire WDW tennis program and is one of the rare players in the world who plays equally well with either hand. Videotape reviews are included as part of hour-long lessons at the Contemporary Resort for an additional $10.

For more information about private lessons and group development sessions, call 824-3578.

TOURNAMENTS: Individual tournaments may be arranged by calling the Pro Shop at the Contemporary Resort. The fee for running such a tournament is $50.

RACQUET RENTAL: Good-quality racquets are available for rent for $1 an hour for adults. Balls may be purchased (for $4.25 per can of three) or rented by the basket for $2. Some boast a Mickey Mouse logo.

LOCKERS: Locker facilities are available at all tennis court areas. There is no charge for the use of a locker.

A MATTER OF

Most people probably don't think of Walt Disney World immediately when they contemplate a golf vacation. Yet there are three superb courses right in the Vacation Kingdom: the Magnolia and the Palm flank the hotel named for the sport, the Golf Resort, and extend practically to the borders of the Magic Kingdom. In addition, just a short drive away, there's the Lake Buena Vista Golf Course, whose borders are punctuated by the units of yet another lodging facility christened in honor of the game, the Fairway Villas.

None of these three Joe Lee-designed courses will set anyone's knees to knocking in terror, though all three courses are demanding enough to provide the site for an annual stop on the PGA Tour tournament trail. Depending on the tee from which a golfer chooses to play, the Disney courses are challenging and/or fun, and they are constructed to be especially forgiving for the mid-handicap player. What's more, they're remarkably interesting topographically, considering that the land on which Lee started was about as hilly as a formica tabletop.

At all three, the green fees (including the required cart) are about $28 for WDW resort guests and $33 for day visitors; twilight rates, in effect beginning at 3 P.M., are $17 for all.

For tee-off times on any of the three courses, just phone 824-2270. Especially from February through April, it's a good idea to reserve starting times well in advance for play in the morning and early afternoon (though starting times after 3 P.M. are almost always available at the last minute). Those with confirmed reservations at a WDW resort (which include guests at any of the six hotels at Walt Disney World Village Hotel Plaza) can reserve as far in advance as desired the year round. Day visitors can reserve only seven days ahead for play between January 1 and April 30.

THE GOLF COURSES

AT THE GOLF RESORT: The wide-open, tree-dotted Magnolia, which flanks the hotel to the north, plays from 5,903 (ladies) to 7,253 (championship) yards at par 72; it was ranked by *Golf Digest* magazine among the nation's top hundred courses. The par-72 Palm to the south—shorter and tighter, with more wooded fairways and nine water hazards—plays from 5,785 to 6,951 yards. Together, this pair (and the Lake Buena Vista Club course) hosts the big Walt Disney World Classic every year, a good indication of the quality of the play to be found. Driving ranges are located near the Magnolia and Palm courses. (There's also one at the Lake Buena Vista course.)

The Wee Links: This six-hole, 1,525-yard experimental beginners layout—a championship-course-in-miniature nestled on a 25-acre corner of the Magnolia—was designed especially with the young beginner in mind. The design incorporates sand and water traps, tees and greens, just like an adult layout. But the traps are small and flat, and the water hazards are shallow enough to allow easy ball retrieval. The yardage is measured in "junior yards"—that is, only two feet to the yard; and the greens are made of a special low-maintenance artificial turf called Mod Sod (which can be top-dressed to allow greater control of roll speed) instead of more-difficult-to-care-for grass. The PGA Tour, which funded the course, hopes that its ease of maintenance and low cost will encourage other communities around the country to establish similar layouts—and eventually lead to "little leagues" for young duffers.

The $3 fee for juniors (under 18) includes Spalding junior clubs and a Wee Links Lesson covering the fundamentals of the swing, golf etiquette, and the rules of the game (offered daily at 8:30 and 11 A.M. and 2 and 4 P.M., mainly for rank beginners). The $3 fee covers 12 holes of play (2 rounds). Adults pay $6

COURSES

to play on the Wee Links, and it should be noted that this is a walking course only.

AT THE LAKE BUENA VISTA CLUB: Located to the south of the clubhouse and the Buena Vista Lagoon, this par-72 layout plays from 6,002 to 6,540 yards. The shortest of the trio, with the narrowest fairways, it bears less resemblance to the Magnolia than to the Palm, and lacks the water hazards that characterize the latter.

INSTRUCTION: The Walt Disney World Golf Studio is the most compelling aspect of the golf instruction available at WDW. Each Golf Studio instructor works to help golfers develop their own styles by building on what skills they already possess. Instruction is provided via small classes with a high teacher-student ratio. Part of each lesson is recorded on videotape and then, back in the Pro Shop, given a thorough viewing and critique. Then, to hammer in what has just been learned, the instructor repeats his suggestions and admonitions on an audio cassette tape that students can take home.

The studios, which last about two hours each, are offered at 9 and 11:30 A.M. and 2:30 P.M. Monday through Friday, and at 9 and 11:30 A.M. on Saturday at the Magnolia driving range. Call 824-2250 for reservations; the studio fee is $35, $40 including nine holes of golf.

Private Lessons: These are available at both the Golf Resort and at the Lake Buena Vista Club at $20 per half hour with an assistant ($25 with Golf Resort head pro Eric Frederickson or LBV head pro Rina Ritson, the first woman golf pro ever to hold the top position at a major golf club).

Call 824-2250 to book private lessons at the Golf Resort, 828-3741 to arrange instruction at Lake Buena Vista.

EQUIPMENT RENTAL: Spalding Executive and Top-flight rental clubs ($10), buckets of range balls ($2.50 each), and shoes ($3) are all available at the Pro Shop—what you rent here may be better than your own gear.

TOURNAMENTS

The Walt Disney World Golf Classic, a popular spectator event that ranks as the most important on WDW's sports calendar, takes place in the fall, usually in October, and features most of the pro tour's top players. So guests who plan to play golf during their WDW vacation are advised *not* to schedule a visit for tournament week.

You can play alongside the pros if you pay for it: $3,200 is the price of a one-year membership in the Classic Club. As a tourney sponsor, each member plays with one of the competing pros daily, for three of the four days of the tourney. While the pros are competing for cash prizes, the amateurs vie for trophies and plaques in a separate but simultaneous competition. The $3,200 fee also includes six nights' lodging during the tournament, and the waiver of green fees for a year and admission to the Magic Kingdom for a week. For details, phone 824-2255.

At other times of year, smaller private competitions are held for civic, corporate, and social groups; to arrange for one (at no charge beyond the green fees), contact the Tournament Coordinator at 824-2275.

WATERS OF THE

BOATING

Walt Disney World is the home of the country's largest fleet of pleasure boats. Most of the action is centered on two lakes—the 200-acre Seven Seas Lagoon, the body of water that the ferries cross and the monorails circle as they carry guests between the Transportation and Ticket Center and the Magic Kingdom; and 450-acre Bay Lake, which is connected to the Seven Seas Lagoon by the Water Bridge.

Cruising on Bay Lake and the Seven Seas Lagoon can be excellent sport, and a variety of boats are available for rent at the marinas at the Contemporary Resort, on the eastern shore of Bay Lake; at Fort Wilderness, to the southwest beyond Discovery Island; and at the Polynesian Village, which occupies the southern edge of the Seven Seas Lagoon.

In addition, boaters can explore the waters of Walt Disney World Village—including 35-acre Buena Vista Lagoon.

To rent, day visitors and resort guests alike must show a resort ID, a driver's license, or a passport. Rental of certain craft may carry other special requirements (described below).

Note that no privately owned boats are permitted on any of the WDW waters.

SPEEDBOATS: Particularly when the weather is warm, there are always dozens of small boats zipping back and forth across the surface of Bay Lake, the Seven Seas Lagoon, and the lakes at Walt Disney World Village. These are called *Water Sprites*, and they are just as much fun as they look. Though they don't go too fast, they're so small that a rider feels every bit of speed, and they get you around quickly enough so that a lot of watery terrain can be covered in a half-hour rental period ($8).

You can rent them at the Contemporary Resort, Polynesian Village, Fort Wilderness, and WDW Village marinas. During warm weather, lines of people waiting to rent these zippy little craft usually form at about 11 A.M. and remain fairly constant until about 4 P.M. The minimum rental age is 12. Even with an accompanying parent or adult, children under 12 are not allowed to drive.

SAILBOATS: The size of Bay Lake and the Seven Seas Lagoon—and their usually reliable winds—make for good sailing, and the Contemporary Resort, Polynesian Village, and Fort Wilderness marinas rent a variety of sail craft. *Sunfish*, which can hold two, go for $5 an hour. *Capris*, accommodating from one to six—more stable because of their leaded keel, wider beam, and greater weight, and consequently better for beginners—cost $10 an hour. *Hobie Cat 14s* and *16s* cost $10 and $12 an hour respectively; catamaran experience is required. The Hobie 16, which has a main and a jib, requires two to sail, but cannot accommodate more than three. Sailing conditions are usually best in March and April and before afternoon thundershowers in the summer—and that's when demand is greatest. So don't tarry. Get to the marina when the urge to sail strikes.

PONTOON BOATS: *Flote Botes*—motor-powered, canopied platforms-on-pontoons, really—are perfect for families, for water lovers who aren't experienced sailors, and for older visitors more interested in serenity than thrills. They're available at the resort marinas ($30 an hour).

CANOPY BOATS: These 16-foot, V-hulled, motorized boats-with-canopies are also good for slow cruises, and can accommodate up to ten adults. They can be rented for $12 per half hour at the WDW Village Marina.

PEDAL BOATS: These craft are for rent for $3 per half hour or $6 per hour at all WDW lakeside marinas, for excursions on the WDW lakes. They're also available for resort guests only at Fort Wilderness's Bike Barn.

CANOEING: A long paddle down the glass-smooth, wooded Fort Wilderness canals is such a tranquil way to pass a misty morning that it's hard to remember that the bustle of the Magic Kingdom is just a launch ride away. Canoes are for rent at Fort Wilderness's Bike Barn ($3 per hour, $7 per day). Most trips last from one to three hours; those who take fishing gear can easily stay out longer. Canoes are restricted to the canals of WDW.

OUTRIGGER CANOES: It takes eight to paddle one of these long, skinny Polynesian-style canoes. They're available at the Polynesian Village Marina ($1 per guest per hour), and are permitted on the Seven Seas Lagoon.

WATER SKIING: Ski boats with driver and full equipment ($35 an hour) are available at the Fort Wilderness and Contemporary Resort marinas. Anyone is allowed to water ski, but there is no discount on the posted price even if you bring along your own skis and other gear.

WORLD

SWIMMING

Between Bay Lake and the Seven Seas Lagoon, Walt Disney World resort guests have five miles of powdery white sand beach at their disposal. And that doesn't include the nine swimming pools that come in all shapes and sizes. River Country (see *Everything Else in the World*) may be the ultimate "swimming hole," but each pool has charms of its own.

BEACHES: When Walt Disney World was under construction in the mid-1960s, Bay Lake, with an eight-foot layer of muck on its bottom, was found to be unpolluted, though murky. It was drained and cleaned, and below the muck, engineers unearthed the pure white sand that now edges parts of the shore, most notably behind the Contemporary Resort and across from it on the lake's Fort Wilderness shore. These two sections of beach, plus the one at the Polynesian Village, make up WDW's principal sandy areas. They aren't the walk-forever strands found on Florida's east and west coasts, but they are long enough that most people never bother to go all the way to the end.

POOLS: There are two each at the Contemporary Resort Hotel, the Polynesian Village, and the Walt Disney World Village area Vacation Villas; plus one each at the Lake Buena Vista Club, the Golf Resort Hotel, and at River Country. The resort pools are for registered guests only. There's no charge for admission, towels, or chairs anywhere, except for the admission and towel charge at River Country. One of the pair of pools at the Polynesian Village has a water slide built into great Disney-made boulders that are part of the landscaping; to get to the carved-out stairway that leads to the top, duck under a waterfall. River Country's pool has two similar (but scarier) slides that end abruptly seven feet above the water. For lap-swimming, the best is the big 20-by-25-meter pool at the Contemporary Resort. When it isn't crowded (early in the morning and around dinnertime), the lifeguard is usually happy to haul in the rope that separates the deep and shallow ends. There are no diving boards at any of the pools; to practice cannonballs, head for River Country, where there are large boulders made especially for leaping.

Lifeguards are on duty during most daylight hours. There is no formal swimming instruction at WDW.

In addition, all six of the establishments at Walt Disney World Village Hotel Plaza have pools.

DAY VISITORS: Pools and beaches at the resort hotels are not open to day guests (or to guests staying at the hotels at Walt Disney World Village Hotel Plaza). If you're just at WDW for the day and want to take a break from the afternoon heat, head for River Country. See *Everything Else in the World*.

FISHING

The 70,000 bass with which Bay Lake was stocked in the mid-1960s have grown and multiplied as a result of WDW's restrictive fishing policy. No angling is permitted on Bay Lake or the Seven Seas Lagoon except on the two-hour Fort Wilderness fishing expeditions (for WDW resort guests only). There's one leaving the campground marina each morning at around 8 A.M. and one each afternoon at around 3 P.M.; a maximum of five fishing persons can be accommodated on each. The fee is $75 for two hours ($25 for each additional hour), and includes gear, driver/guide, and coffee and pastries (in the morning) or soft drinks (in the afternoon). No license is required. Largemouth bass weighing two to three pounds each are the most common catch, though occasionally someone will reel in a bream or a bigger largemouth. Bass up to nine pounds have been recorded.

Guests at WDW accommodations with kitchens may keep the contents of their creel; for everyone else, it's catch-and-release. By the way, there are no official WDW facilities for cleaning fish you catch. Fishing on your own is permitted in the canals in the Walt Disney World Village area and at Fort Wilderness. Fort Wilderness campers can toss in their lines from any shore; villa guests can cast from the banks of the nearest canal or rent a canopy boat and chug back into remoter waters for their sport. (The waters around the Treehouses are particularly productive.) Licenses are not required. No gear is available for rent, but cane poles and lures are for sale at the Fort Wilderness trading posts.

MORE FUN STUFF

JOGGING: Except in winter, late fall, and very early spring, the weather is just too steamy in Central Florida to make for the exhilarating jogging found in cooler climes. If you run early in the morning in warm seasons, the heat is somewhat less daunting. (The scenery is also usually good enough to take your mind off the perspiration.) Guests staying at Walt Disney World Village accommodations can just head out the door and run as they please along the winding drives where everything is green and blessedly quiet. Fort Wilderness offers a 2.3-mile course (partially paved) punctuated by exercise stations.

Jogging maps that outline the Fort Wilderness route, as well as the best courses from the Contemporary Resort, the Polynesian Village, the Golf Resort, and around Walt Disney World Village, are available at Guest Services desks in hotels and villa check-in areas; mileages range from 3.4 to 4.2 miles round-trip.

FORT WILDERNESS'S EXERCISE TRAIL: This 2.3-mile course gives joggers the chance to do chin-ups, sit-ups, and other exercises on special apparatus. Signs explain all the maneuvers—and it's almost all in the shade. There is no charge.

HORSEBACK RIDING: Trail rides into the pine woods and scrubby palmetto country—past an Indian village, some Western wagons, and assorted other western-style props—leave from the corral at Fort Wilderness (near the River Country parking lot) at 9 A.M., 10:30 A.M., noon, 1 P.M., and 2 P.M. daily. This is not for big-time gallopers—you can't ride off on your own—and the horses have been culled for gentleness so that the trips are suitable even for nonriders. Cost is $5.25 a person for both day visitors and resort guests (no children under nine are accepted). For advance reservations, which are necessary, phone 824-2734.

WALKS: There are lovely nature trails through the moss-hung remains of a cypress swamp near River Country (about ¼ mile), and near Marshmallow Marsh at Fort Wilderness. The latter, about a mile long, leads along the reedy, sunny shores of Bay Lake, then heads into the cool woods before looping back to the starting point.

BIKING: Pedaling along the eight miles of bike paths at Walt Disney World Village and the lightly trafficked roads there and at Fort Wilderness can be a pleasant way to spend a couple of hours—especially in the winter or in the mornings and late afternoons during the rest of the year, when it's not too hot. Both areas are sufficiently spread out that two-wheelers are a practical means of getting around in general as well. If you don't bring your own bike, you can rent one at Fort Wilderness's Bike Barn or at the Villa Center near the Vacation Villas at Walt Disney World Village for $2 an hour or $5 a day. Tandems are available at the Bike Barn and at the Villa Center ($3 an hour or $7 a day). Anyone is allowed to ride bikes on the property.

THE SPA: The Contemporary Resort's Olympiad Health Club (located on the hotel's third floor) has Nautilus gym equipment—perfect for a good workout. Afterward, it's almost not necessary—though it's decidedly pleasant—to relax in the sauna or in individual whirlpools; or to indulge yourself in a massage—45 minutes to an hour of sheer heaven at the hands of the Spa's U.S. Air Force–trained masseur (also a licensed RN and respiratory therapist). For use of the facilities, the cost is $4; whirlpools are an additional $5, and massages an extra $25. Appointments for massages must be made in advance. The hours at the health club are 9 A.M. to 6 P.M. daily, closed Sunday. Facilities are open to men and women at alternate times. Call 824-3410 for appointments and further information on hours. Note that the Spa is open to both day and resort guests.

VOLLEYBALL, TETHERBALL, AND HORSESHOES: Courts are scattered throughout the Fort Wilderness camping loops. But they're open to WDW resort guests only.

SOFTBALL AND BASEBALL: Diamonds, complete with backstop, are located in the meadow near Fort Wilderness's Bike Barn, and are available for the use of WDW resort guests. But bring your own balls and bats.

GOOD MEALS, GREAT TIMES

154 Restaurant Directory
156 In the Magic Kingdom
160 In Epcot Center
166 In the Hotels
168 WDW Village
173 Nightlife

In the Magic Kingdom, fast food is king: even machines that broil 2,800 hamburgers an hour have a tough time keeping up with the demand, and in the course of just a single year, enough burgers are served to allow an individual to eat one for every inch of the 400 miles from Orlando to Atlanta. And that's in addition to enough French fries to fill ten boxcars, and a quantity of ice cream sufficient to build a minor mountain in an Olympic-size swimming pool.

But by no means is that all of the Walt Disney World food story. Epcot Center has added international flavors to the WDW palate—it's now possible to sample everything from maple syrup pie and bratwurst to bangers and mash, fettucine all' Alfredo, and mole poblano. Elsewhere in the World, sample some of the country's most unusually delectable French toast for breakfast; for lunch, it's de rigueur to eat quiche and salad or seafood-stuffed crepes, or a fruit-and-cottage cheese platter. For dinner, there's fried chicken or roast beef, or more ambitious meals that end with a flambéed hot fudge sundae or an elegant amaretto-flavored soufflé. Restaurants at WDW run the gamut from a simple snack shop to an elegant salon.

In the following pages, we'll describe many meals worth a detour at any time of day. Specialties do change from time to time, though the basic types of food available remain the same. Hours at most establishments also vary from one season to the next. Prices are comparable to those for similar meals elsewhere in the United States (and they move upward as relentlessly); children's menus, or special rates for youngsters at buffets, are widely available. Occasionally, a restaurant will close for a few weeks for refurbishing. So consult bulletin boards in the individual resort hotels, or call Guest Services at your hotel for up-to-the-minute details.

HOW TO USE THIS CHAPTER

Because the number of restaurants, snack shops, cafeterias, and other miscellaneous eateries around the World is so large and so varied, this chapter offers meal information in three different ways. To find a specific restaurant, we've provided an alphabetized directory to all restaurants on the property—with their exact locations. So if you know the name of a desired dining place, this directory will tell you where to find it.

If you are getting hungry in a particular area of the World, and want to know what's available in the immediate vicinity, the second section of this chapter offers an area-by-area rundown of nearly all operative eateries. Detailed data on each restaurant's atmosphere, decor, and menu specialties are also included.

Finally, to help in the planning of systematic programs for eating a broad swath across the World, this chapter also contains a meal-by-meal selection of eating places. These restaurants are organized by breakfast, lunch, and dinner specialties, and we've indicated certain entries for which we think it's worth going a bit out of your way. Note that menus and prices may vary during the year.

This chapter contains eating places within the boundaries of Walt Disney World only. For recommendations of restaurants *outside* the World, please refer to the "Where To Eat" section of the *Orlando* chapter.

The letters that conclude each restaurant entry are a key to the meals served there: breakfast (B), lunch (L), dinner (D), or snacks (S).

RESTAURANTS OF WDW

The list below includes all the restaurants and snack spots currently operating in Walt Disney World—at the hotels, at Fort Wilderness Campground, at Walt Disney World Village, and in the Magic Kingdom and Epcot Center.

Adventureland Veranda: Magic Kingdom; at the east edge of Adventureland, between the bridge to the Hub and the Swiss Family Island Treehouse

Aloha Isle: Magic Kingdom; in Adventureland, adjoining the Adventureland Veranda on the west

Aunt Polly's: Magic Kingdom; in Frontierland, on Tom Sawyer Island

Au Petit Café: Epcot Center; on the World Showcase Promenade in the France pavilion, in World Showcase

Barefoot Snack Bar: Polynesian Village; on the lobby level of the Great Ceremonial House

Baton Rouge Lounge: WDW Shopping Village; on the main deck of the *Empress Lilly*

Beach Shack: Fort Wilderness Campground; near the beach

Biergarten: Epcot Center; to the rear of the St. Georgsplatz in the Germany pavilion, in World Showcase

Bistro de Paris: Epcot Center; upstairs at the France pavilion, in World Showcase

Boulangerie Pâtisserie: Epcot Center; France pavilion, around the corner from Les Chefs de France, in World Showcase

Campfire Snack Bar: Fort Wilderness Campground; inside Pioneer Hall

Cantina de San Angel: Epcot Center; on the World Showcase Promenade opposite the Mexico pavilion's pyramid, in World Showcase

Cap'n Jack's Oyster Bar: WDW Shopping Village; on the edge of Buena Vista Lagoon

Captain Cook's Hideaway: Polynesian Village; on the first floor, adjoining the Polynesian Princess boutique

Coconino Cove: Contemporary Resort; at the south end of the Grand Canyon Concourse (fourth floor)

Columbia Harbour House: Magic Kingdom; in Liberty Square near the entrance to Fantasyland

Coral Isle Cafe: Polynesian Village; on the second floor of the Great Ceremonial House, around the corner from Papeete Bay

Crystal Palace: Magic Kingdom; near the Adventureland Bridge, at the north end of Main Street

Diamond Horseshoe: Magic Kingdom; in Frontierland at the edge of Liberty Square

Dock Inn: Contemporary Resort; in the Marina Pavilion near the beach

El Pirata y El Perico: Magic Kingdom; in Adventureland, opposite Pirates of the Caribbean

Empress Lounge: WDW Shopping Village; aboard the *Empress Lilly*

Empress Room: WDW Shopping Village; aboard the *Empress Lilly*

Enchanted Grove: Magic Kingdom; east side of Fantasyland, opposite Tomorrowland Terrace

Farmers Market: Epcot Center; on the first floor of Future World's The Land

Fiesta Fun Center Snack Bar: Contemporary Resort; first floor

Fife and Drum: Magic Kingdom; in Liberty Square, behind the Silversmith Shop

Fisherman's Deck: WDW Shopping Village; aboard the *Empress Lilly*

Fort Sam Clemens Snack Bar: Magic Kingdom; in Fort Sam Clemens on Tom Sawyer Island, in Frontierland

The Good Turn: Epcot Center; on the second floor of Future World's The Land

Gulf Coast Room: Contemporary Resort; on the second floor near the escalators

Heidelberger's Deli: WDW Shopping Village; near the edge of the parking lot

King Stefan's: Magic Kingdom; in Cinderella Castle

Lake Buena Vista Club: WDW Village

Lake Buena Vista Club Snack Bar: WDW Village; at the Lake Buena Vista Club

Lancer's Inn: Magic Kingdom; in Fantasyland, near Cinderella's Golden Carrousel

Le Cellier: Epcot Center; near Victoria Gardens and the *O Canada!* film's exit in the Canada pavilion, in World Showcase

Les Chefs de France: Epcot Center; France pavilion, in World Showcase

Liberty Inn: Epcot Center; alongside The American Adventure

Liberty Tree Tavern: Magic Kingdom; in Liberty Square

Lite Bite: WDW Shopping Village; near Crystal Arts and Toledo Arts

L'Originale Alfredo di Roma Ristorante: Epcot Center; on the east side of the piazza in the Italy pavilion, in World Showcase

Lunching Pad: Magic Kingdom; near Mickey's Mart, in Tomorrowland

Main Street Bakery: Magic Kingdom; on the east side of Main Street, halfway between the Hub and Town Square

El Marrakech: Epcot Center; Morocco pavilion, in World Showcase

Meadow Trading Post: Fort Wilderness Campground; near the playing fields

The Mile Long Bar: Magic Kingdom; in Frontierland, between Pecos Bill and the Country Bear Jamboree

Mitsukoshi Restaurant: Epcot Center; on the second floor of the large building on the west side of the plaza in the Japan pavilion, in World Showcase

Monorail Club Car: Contemporary Resort; on the east side of the Grand Canyon Concourse (fourth floor), near the escalators

Odyssey Restaurant: Epcot Center; astraddle the Future World/World Showcase boundary, near the Mexico pavilion

Outer Rim: Contemporary Resort; on the east side of the Grand Canyon Concourse (fourth floor)

Papeete Bay Verandah: Polynesian Village; second floor of the Great Ceremonial House

Pecos Bill Cafe: Magic Kingdom; near the Walt Disney World Railroad's Frontierland depot

Pinocchio Village Haus: Magic Kingdom; in Fantasyland, adjoining It's A Small World on the east

Player's Gallery: Golf Resort; adjacent to the Trophy Room on the main floor

Plaza Pavilion: Magic Kingdom; east of the Plaza Restaurant, on the edge of Tomorrowland

Plaza Restaurant: Magic Kingdom; on Main Street around the corner from Sealtest Ice Cream Parlor

Pop's Place: Fort Wilderness Campground; inside River Country

Promenade Lounge: WDW Shopping Village; on the Promenade Deck of the *Empress Lilly*

Pueblo Room: Contemporary Resort; south end of the Grand Canyon Concourse (fourth floor)

Refreshment Corner: Magic Kingdom; on the west side of Main Street, opposite Sealtest Ice Cream Parlor

Refreshment Outpost: Epcot Center; next to the Canada pavilion, in World Showcase

Refreshment Port: Epcot Center; between the China and Germany pavilions, in World Showcase

Rose & Crown Pub & Dining Room: Epcot Center; on the World Showcase Promenade, in the United Kingdom pavilion

Round Table: Magic Kingdom; in Fantasyland near Cinderella's Golden Carrousel

San Angel Inn: Epcot Center; inside the Mexico pavilion's pyramid, in World Showcase

Sand Bar: Contemporary Resort; in the Marina Pavilion near the beach

Sand Trap: Golf Resort; downstairs next to the Pro Shop

Sealtest Ice Cream Parlor: Magic Kingdom; on the east side of Main Street, opposite Refreshment Corner

Settlement Trading Post: Fort Wilderness Campground; near the Fort Wilderness marina and Pioneer Hall

Sleepy Hollow: Magic Kingdom; in Liberty Square, opposite Olde World Antiques

South Seas Dining Room: Polynesian Village; on the west side of the second floor of the Great Ceremonial House

Space Bar: Magic Kingdom; at the base of the StarJets in the center of Tomorrowland

Starboard Lounge: WDW Shopping Village; on the main deck of the *Empress Lilly*

Stargate Restaurant: Epcot Center; in Future World's CommuniCore East

Station Break: Magic Kingdom; underneath the Walt Disney World Railroad's Main Street depot

Steerman's Quarters: WDW Shopping Village; aboard the *Empress Lilly*

Sunrise Terrace Restaurant: Epcot Center; in Future World's CommuniCore West

Sunshine Tree Terrace: Magic Kingdom; in Adventureland, adjoining the Enchanted Tiki Room

Tambu Lounge: Polynesian Village; adjoining Papeete Bay, on the second floor of the Great Ceremonial House

Tangaroa Snack Isle: Polynesian Village; in a separate building near the east swimming pool

Tangaroa Terrace: Polynesian Village; in a separate building on the eastern edge of the property

Terrace Buffeteria: Contemporary Resort; on the Grand Canyon Concourse (fourth floor) immediately to the right of the elevators

Terrace Cafe: Contemporary Resort; adjoining the Terrace Buffeteria

Thirsty Perch: Discovery Island

Tomorrowland Terrace: Magic Kingdom; at the Fantasyland edge of Tomorrowland, opposite the Grand Prix Raceway

Top of the World: Contemporary Resort; on the 15th floor

Tournament Tent: Magic Kingdom; in Fantasyland, near the Fantasy Faire Theater

Town Square Cafe: Magic Kingdom; east side of Town Square at the south end of Main Street

Trail's End Cafe: Fort Wilderness Campground; in Pioneer Hall

Trophy Room: Golf Resort; off the lobby

Troubadour Tavern: Magic Kingdom; in Fantasyland, next to Peter Pan's Flight

Verandah Restaurant: WDW Shopping Village

Villa Center: Vacation Villa pool area

Village Ice Cream Parlour and Bake Shop: WDW Shopping Village; next to Verandah Restaurant

Village Lounge: WDW Shopping Village; next to the Village Restaurant

Village Restaurant: WDW Shopping Village; on the shores of Buena Vista Lagoon

Yakitori House: Epcot Center; on the east side of the Japan pavilion's plaza, in World Showcase

IN THE MAGIC KINGDOM

MAIN STREET

FULL SERVICE

Town Square Cafe: This is one of the best bets for Magic Kingdom meals. The lunch and dinner menus offer simple baked chicken, beef stew, and chopped sirloin, plus a chef's salad and a variety of straightforward sandwiches, such as chicken or tuna salad, ham and cheese, and a delicious concoction known as a Monte Cristo—a batter-dipped, deep-fried turkey, ham, and Swiss cheese sandwich. For dessert: apple pie or crepes angelica—pancakes filled with coconut cream and topped with vanilla ice cream, strawberry melba sauce, and shredded coconut. Patterned after a well-known New Orleans restaurant, the setting here is genteelly Victorian, with plenty of polished brass and curlicued, beautifully painted woodwork. The terrazzo-floored patio gives diners a fine view over the action in Town Square. A special children's menu is available.

Full breakfasts are also served: eggs, pancakes, waffles, cold cereals (with skim milk on request), biscuits, Danish pastry, and bacon, sausages, and smoked ham. B, L, D.

Plaza Restaurant: This airy, many-windowed establishment, around the corner from the Sealtest Ice Cream Parlor, is done in mirrors with sinuously curved Art Nouveau frames. The menu offers hot dishes, along with quiche, chef's salad, and thick sandwiches—plus milk shakes, floats, and the biggest, gooeyest sundaes in the Magic Kingdom. Café mocha, which combines chocolate and coffee, is another specialty. L, D, S.

CAFETERIA SERVICE

Crystal Palace: One of the Magic Kingdom's landmarks, and its only cafeteria. Modeled after a similar structure that once stood in New York State and after another that still graces San Francisco's Golden Gate Park, it serves standard cafeteria fare. There are Swiss steak, baked fresh fish, barbecued chicken dishes, assorted casseroles, and healthy-looking salads. Jell-O and ambrosia and an assortment of tempting pies and cakes are also available.

This is civilized fare, and the fact that it's here at all is just more proof—as if any were needed—that the Magic Kingdom is not just for kids. The place is huge but not overwhelming, because the tables are well-spaced throughout a variety of nooks and crannies. Tables in the front look out onto flower beds and the passing throng beyond, while those at the east end have views into a secluded courtyard.

Not long ago, songbirds used to fly into the structure as guests came through the doors—and then became so lost they couldn't get out. Keen observers, looking carefully into the topmost reaches of the tallest dome, will see the remedy—an owl, still and brooding to all appearances, but actually a stuffed incarnation of the songbird's natural enemy. Its presence has far reduced the avian traffic through the dining area.

The Crystal Palace is also one of the few spots in the Magic Kingdom to serve full breakfasts—scrambled eggs and hashed brown potatoes, biscuits, sausage, bacon, ham, hotcakes, Danish pastry, and cold cereal. B, L, D, S.

FAST FOOD AND SNACK SPOTS

Refreshment Corner: The small, round tables at this spacious, old-fashioned, red-and-white stop on the west side of Main Street (located near the Crystal Palace) spill out onto the sidewalk. Except when the weather is terrifically hot, it's a delightful spot for fast food—hot dogs (regular and jumbo sizes), brownies, and soft drinks. Old time Coca-Cola ads cover the walls, and during busy periods a pianist is on hand to plink away on the restaurant's white upright. L, D, S.

Main Street Bakery: This genteel little tearoom, with its small, round tables and cane chairs, is a good place for a light breakfast, a midmorning coffee break, or a midafternoon rest stop. Assorted cakes, Danish, and a variety of other Sara Lee-made sweets are the temptations. B, S.

Sealtest Ice Cream Parlor: Ice cream freaks from all over the country converge on this corner of the Kingdom, which boasts the World's best variety of ice cream flavors—six in all: vanilla, heavenly hash, chocolate, strawberry, butter pecan, and lemonberry swirl the last time we looked. S.

Station Break: Located underneath the Main Street train station, this refreshment stand is especially good for grabbing coffee and a piece of Danish pastry in the morning on the way into the park—or for picking up a ham and cheese sandwich, potato chips, and a soft drink to munch on at nearby tables. The atmosphere is hardly noteworthy, but waiting time is nearly nil. B, L, D.

VENDORS

Throughout the Magic Kingdom, there are ice cream wagons that sell ice cream sandwiches, Mouse Bars, and three especially wonderful frozen treats—orange-juice bars, strawberry bars, and frozen chocolate-covered bananas, invented by a Disney employee.

Popcorn wagons all over the park contribute their lovely aromas all day long.

At Epcot Center, vendors purvey soft drinks, strawberry bars, pineapple-orange-juice bars, and ice cream galore.

ADVENTURELAND

FAST FOOD AND SNACK SPOTS

Adventureland Veranda: Bougainvillea cascades over the edges of a red tile roof that looks as if it came straight out of the tropics. Tables are clustered outside on a small patio and inside under slowly rotating fans hung from mahogany ceilings. Off to the east end of this pretty, sprawling restaurant are a couple of open-air patios with views of Cinderella Castle. Screened from the gazes of passersby, these are among the most delightful meal sites in all the Magic Kingdom. Special Adventureland Veranda teriyaki-sauced beef and chicken are among the offerings. Other Americanized versions of Oriental specialties also have their fans. Cornstarch is heavily used, and the chefs occasionally stir-fry the vegetables into sogginess. For dessert: Key lime and pecan pies, apple turnovers, and banana nut rolls.

Note that waiting lines here usually take about five minutes longer than those of similar lengths in other fast-food establishments because of the greater number of choices. L, D, S.

> ### WHERE TO STAY ON A DIET
>
> Dieters need not abandon all restraint for want of suitable foodstuffs at WDW. A number of restaurants offer foods that are suitable for a variety of diets. All are open for lunch and dinner.
>
> #### MAGIC KINGDOM
>
> Main Street: Crystal Palace, Town Square Cafe, Plaza Restaurant
> Adventureland: Adventureland Veranda
> Liberty Square: Liberty Tree Tavern
> Fantasyland: King Stefan's
> Tomorrowland: Lunching Pad, Tomorrowland Terrace
>
> #### EPCOT CENTER
>
> The Land: Farmers Market

Aloha Isle: Adjoining the Adventureland Veranda (on the west), this refreshment stand often sells pineapple spears and juice along with other tropical offerings. S.

El Pirata y El Perico: In English, the Spanish name of this snack stand, directly across from Pirates of the Caribbean (outside La Princesa de Cristal), means The Pirate and The Parrot. The offerings: hot dogs, burritos, nachos, brownies, and ice cream bars. L, S.

The Oasis: Tucked away near the Jungle Cruise. The perfect spot for a soft drink. S.

Sunshine Tree Terrace: So close to the Tropical Serenade (Enchanted Tiki Birds) that you can hear the Audio-Animatronics parrot José squawking his spiel. Offerings here are some of the tastiest in the Kingdom: orange and grapefruit juices, orange slush, orange-Danish pastry, and, in winter, hot citrus-flavored tea, not to mention the excellent citrus swirl—soft-serve ice cream swirled through with a not-too-sweet frozen-orange-juice concentrate. B, S.

FRONTIERLAND

FULL SERVICE

Diamond Horseshoe: Several times daily, from about noon until early evening, a troupe of singers and dancers presents a sometimes corny, occasionally sidesplitting, always entertaining show in this Wild West dance-hall saloon. Waitresses serve potato and corn chips, freshly baked pie, fruit punch, and cold sandwiches before the show begins. Reservations are required, and they're hard to come by. They must be made in person, and you can't count on getting them if you arrive much more than an hour after the Magic Kingdom opens. Those who miss the deadline can line up for possible cancellations, but with little hope of success except on days when the weather is so bad that some visitors depart early. L, S.

FAST FOOD AND SNACK SPOTS

Pecos Bill Cafe: This is not one of those Magic Kingdom eateries that is tucked away so that only those who look will find it. Sooner or later, almost every guest passing from Adventureland into Frontierland—ambling by the Frontierland depot of the Walt Disney World Railroad on the way to Big Thunder or the Country Bear Jamboree—walks by Pecos Bill. And, as a sidewalk café, this establishment—fitted out with leather-seated chairs, ceilings made of twigs, and red tile floors—has few peers. There are tables indoors (in air-conditioned rooms) and outdoors, under umbrellas in an open-air courtyard. Hamburgers, cheeseburgers, steak sandwiches, and hot dogs are the staples. L, D, S.

Mile Long Bar: The bar, a gleaming and intricately detailed beauty with a brass rail on which to lean and a set of antlers above, just goes on and on, or so it seems at first glance. Actually, it's the mirrors at either end that produce the effect that gives this relatively small refreshment stand its name. Three shaggy animal heads hang on the walls, in keeping with the Wild West theme. Guests who stand around long enough will see one animal turn to another and wink, for these are Audio-Animatronics figures just like the ones on the walls at the Country Bear Jamboree. The fare is as basic as the decor is intriguing. Definitely worth a peek. L, D, S.

Aunt Polly's: The much-trumpeted sense of getting-away-from-it-all that islands always convey comes home once again out on Frontierland's Tom Sawyer Island. Though only a couple of minutes' ride across the Rivers of America via the Tom Sawyer

Island Rafts, this landfall manages to seem remote even when there are dozens of youngsters clamoring through its caves, over its hills, and across its rickety barrel bridges. Therein lies the charm of Aunt Polly's. While the adults in a party get some well-needed R&R sipping lemonade in the shade of the old-fashioned porch and watching the gleaming white riverboats docking or chugging by, the kids can go out exploring and, at nearby Fort Sam Clemens, ping the toy rifles perched on the gunholes as if there were no tomorrow—an activity as delightful for youngsters as it is dispensable for grown-ups. It doesn't even matter that Aunt Polly's offers a selection barely wider than the fare that that lady might have served her youthful nephew—peanut butter-and-jelly and submarine sandwiches, apple pies, cookies, iced tea, lemonade, and soda. An excellent choice for lunch. L, S.

Fort Sam Clemens: Also on Tom Sawyer Island. Brownies, soft-serve ice cream, fruit juices, and orange and strawberry slushes are available. S.

LIBERTY SQUARE

FULL SERVICE

Liberty Tree Tavern: At this pillared and portico'd eatery opposite the riverboat landing, the floors are made of wide oak planks, the wallpaper looks as if it might have come from Williamsburg, the curtains hang from cloth loops, and the venetian blinds are made of wood. Pieces of pewter and Windsor and ladder-backed chairs are scattered throughout the premises, there's a spinning wheel and a hope chest in the waiting room, and an old-fashioned writing desk and a cradle, copper bowls, and tea kettles arranged near the wide fireplace. The window glass was made using eighteenth-century casting methods, and most of the tables and chairs were mass-produced (for sturdiness's sake). So the Liberty Tree Tavern's charm is not of a mismatched and random type.

At lunch, the staples are oversized salads and entrées such as pot roast; for dessert, there's apple cobbler, brown Betty, and pecan pie. The menu is similar, if a bit fancier, at dinnertime. Walnut bread, Philadelphia pepper-pot soup, and New England clam chowder are served at both meals. L, D.

FAST FOOD AND SNACK SPOTS

Columbia Harbour House: This is a fast-food chicken and fish house with some class. Though the fish has been frozen and is only served fried, good cornbread muffins and corn chowder are also available, and there are enough antiques and other knickknacks decking the halls to raise this place, located near the Liberty Square entrance to Fantasyland, above the ordinary. Model ships, copper measures, harpoons, and nautical instruments, and little tie-back curtains, small-print wallpaper, and low-beamed ceilings give the place a cozy air—despite its size. L, D, S.

The Fife and Drum: Located in the peaceful nook behind the Silversmith Shop, this refreshment stand

---

MAGIC KINGDOM MEALTIME TIPS

• The hours from 11 A.M. to 2 P.M., and again from about 5 to 7 P.M., are the mealtime rush hours in Magic Kingdom restaurants. Eat earlier or later whenever possible.

• When a restaurant has more than one food-service window, don't just amble into the nearest queue. Instead, inspect them all, because the one farthest from a doorway occasionally will be almost wait-free.

• Lines at the Adventureland Veranda don't move as quickly as those at most other fast-food eateries.

• Sit-down restaurants offering full-scale meals are usually less crowded at lunch than they are at dinner.

• To avoid queues, eat at a restaurant that offers reservations—King Stefan's at both lunch and dinner and the Diamond Horseshoe, a western-style saloon in Frontierland that serves cold sandwiches and presents an amusing show, at lunchtime. Reservations are available in person on the day of the meal; book them as soon as you arrive in the Magic Kingdom.

offers soft drinks, potato chips, soft-serve ice cream, and Coke floats. S.

Sleepy Hollow: Iced tea, soft drinks, brownies, Toll House chocolate chip cookies, and a special Legendary Punch (fruity and not half bad) are for sale at this snack stand located opposite Olde World Antiques, near the Liberty Square bridge. In peak season, ham and cheese sandwiches are also served here. You can eat on a secluded brick patio outside. B, L, D, S.

FANTASYLAND

FULL SERVICE

King Stefan's Banquet Hall: The hostesses at this establishment (named for Sleeping Beauty's father) wear thirteenth-century-style French headdresses and long medieval gowns with over-skirts. The hall itself is high-ceilinged and as majestic as the old mead hall it is supposed to represent. The delightful cold-vegetable salad and quiche on the noontime menu make lunch here pleasant indeed. At dinner, there are prime ribs, seafood, and chicken all served with rice and vegetables. There's also a children's menu.

Reservations are required for both lunch and dinner. To make them, present yourself at the Castle door as soon after arriving in the Magic Kingdom as possible. L, D.

FAST FOOD AND SNACK SPOTS

Pinocchio Village Haus: This is another of those Magic Kingdom restaurants that seems a lot smaller from the outside than it really is, thanks to a labyrinthine arrangement of a half dozen rooms decorated with antique cuckoo clocks, European tile-fronted ovens, oak peasant chairs, and murals depicting characters from Pinocchio's story—Figaro the Cat, Cleo the Goldfish, Monstro the Whale, and Geppetto, the puppet's creator. The menu offers fried chicken with French fries and plain hamburgers, cheeseburgers, and hot dogs. L, D, S.

Enchanted Grove: A small stand that's the perfect spot for orange and grapefruit juice and orange slush. S.

Troubadour Tavern: Soft drinks and chips are available at this small refreshment stand west of Cinderella's Golden Carrousel. S.

The Round Table: Ice cream gets top billing here—soft-serve cones in chocolate, vanilla, and chocolate-vanilla swirl; sundaes topped with chocolate, strawberry, or blueberry sauce; floats in root beer or piled high atop rich, frosted brownies. S.

Tournament Tent: Hungry folk can buy ham and cheese subs, soft drinks, and fruit punch. L, D, S.

PIZZA

Lancer's Inn: This is the only place in the Magic Kingdom that serves pizza; it can be ordered with pepperoni or plain cheese. For dessert, Key lime and apple pies are available, though the ice cream specialties at the Tournament Tent and The Round Table can be pretty irresistible. L, D, S.

TOMORROWLAND

FAST FOOD AND SNACK SPOTS

Tomorrowland Terrace: The largest fast-food spot in the Magic Kingdom, where the menu is (for the most part) refreshingly familiar—hamburgers, cheeseburgers, and hot dogs are the staples. The names of the specialties remind you that this sprawling establishment is in Tomorrowland—the Orbit Burger and the Moon Burger are two examples. L, D, S.

The Lunching Pad: This small spot between the Space Port and Mickey's Mart, near the Tomorrowland Information and Ticket Booth, serves natural foods and fresh fruit. L, S.

Plaza Pavilion: Just east of the Plaza Restaurant, this sleek pink-and-purple-and-orange spot on the edge of Tomorrowland serves hamburgers, hot dogs, fried chicken, and soft drinks. Everything comes with a side order of French fries. Some particularly pleasant tables look past the graceful willow trees nearby, toward the Hub Waterways and an impressive topiary sea serpent. L, D, S.

The WEDway Space Bar: Located at the base of the StarJets in the center of Tomorrowland's vast concrete plaza, this small spot offers ham and cheese submarine sandwiches, plus assorted desserts and a variety of soft drinks. No menu item stands out, and the place never seems too busy. L, S.

A WORD TO THE WISE

Ride Space Mountain *before* eating, not afterward. The trip can uncomfortably jostle even the strongest stomach.

IN EPCOT CENTER

Restaurants within each area of Epcot Center are described as they would be encountered in Future World while moving counterclockwise from Spaceship Earth and in World Showcase while walking counterclockwise around World Showcase Lagoon. Note: Reservations are an absolute must at certain restaurants, and they aren't easy to come by without following the instructions in the box on page 163.

FUTURE WORLD

FAST FOOD AND SNACK SPOTS

Sunrise Terrace Restaurant: Fried cod, fried shrimp, and fried chicken are the specialties at this fast-food emporium located in CommuniCore West, opposite the Stargate Restaurant. This is not, however, a typically utilitarian fast-food establishment but is instead a comfortable place, decorated in violets and grays (with touches of scarlet) and some unusually beautiful neon lights. And the food is not conventional, frozen, prebreaded fare. It's freshly batter-dipped instead. Chef's salads, cornbread muffins, clam and corn chowder, and fruit tarts and peanut butter cookies round out the offerings. Like the Stargate Restaurant, the Sunrise Terrace stays open until Epcot Center closes, so it's a good spot to stop for a snack on your way home. During busy seasons, continental breakfasts and French toast are served in the mornings. B, L, D, S.

Farmers Market: One of the most interesting of the Epcot Center eateries, and a new wrinkle on the Walt Disney World fast-food scene, the Farmers Market consists of a handful of very special counter service stands located on the lower level of The Land pavilion. Each of these boasts a unique menu. The soup-and-salad stand offers New England fish chowder, chicken gumbo, impressive fruit salads served in half a pineapple, tuna- and chicken-salad-stuffed tomatoes, and generous vegetable salads with Swiss cheese. **The Bakery**'s morning offerings include bagels and cream cheese, sticky buns, Danish pastries, and bran, corn, and blueberry muffins. After 11 A.M., apple, pecan, Boston cream, orange chiffon, and lemon meringue pies appear, along with cheesecake and chocolate cake, rich-looking brownies, hermit cookies with cinnamon, and loaves of date-nut bread and cheese bread (the same cheese bread served upstairs in The Good Turn)—plus chocolate chip cookies baked on the premises. (These are so delicious that some Disney employees make special trips to The Land just to get them.)

The **barbecue store** sells barbecue beef sandwiches, barbecue chicken breast sandwiches, half chickens, beans, and cornbread muffins. **The Cheese Shoppe** offers cheese and fruit platters and quiches—not only the standard variety that come with cheese, or with bacon, onions, and mushrooms, but also a widely celebrated, newly developed pizza quiche. A **sandwich stand** regales the hungry with several types of hefty combinations, while an **ice cream stand** tempts guests with cooling cones and cups. **The Potato Store** serves steaming baked potatoes stuffed with beef-in-wine sauce, cheddar cheese with bacon, and other fillings. Even the **Beverage House** here offers something special—not only chocolate, strawberry, or vanilla milk shakes, chocolate milk, buttermilk, hot chocolate, and an array of soft drinks, but also vegetable juice, peach nectar, papaya juice, and orange juice.

Each stand has a farm-style facade done in bright colors, not unlike those that might be found in agricultural exhibit buildings at a midwestern state fair. With bright, umbrella-topped tables nearby, the effect is as cheery as possible. Because of the wide variety of foods available here, this is one of the best bets in Epcot Center for a family that can't agree on what to eat. It's also a good spot for weight watchers. B, L, D, S.

Odyssey Restaurant: Located practically astride the Future World/World Showcase dividing line, near the Mexico pavilion, the Odyssey is accessible via three walkways—one near the Mexico pavilion, the World of Motion, and the World Showcase Plaza's World Key Information System kiosk. This handsome, hexagonally shaped establishment looks less like a fast-food eatery than a moderately fancy sit-down restaurant. That's partly because of the decor, a subtle amalgam of rusts and ochres with a carpeted floor and walls and a profusion of green plants. It's also partly because the food service lines are tucked away from view, out of the way of the main dining area. The fact that tables are spread over several levels enhances the already pleasant ambience by making the whole place feel smaller than it really is. There's never the feeling of having arrived in a cavernous mess hall.

As for the menu, it's absolutely all-American: hamburgers, hot dogs, plus platters of chicken, tuna, and ambrosia salads. Best of all, the restaurant—located just a bit off the main pedestrian path—is less heavily patronized than some other more immediately visible spots. L, D, S.

Stargate Restaurant: This large fast-food establishment, located in CommuniCore East, is handsomely decorated in shades of blue, mauve, and magenta. It's a particularly good bet when the weather is temperate enough to allow dining on the tables on the terrace outside—or when bound for World Showcase with finicky eaters in tow. It's also one of the few Epcot Center restaurants open for breakfast. Cold cereals, Danish pastries, fruit cups, blueberry muffins, and cheese omelets served with creditable home-fried potatoes are available then. But the real specialty is the extremely satisfying, if extravagantly named, "Stellar Scramble." Made of cheese, ham, onions, green pepper, and scrambled eggs, this "breakfast pizza" might not win any prizes among connoisseurs of haute cuisine, but it's unquestionably tasty. At lunch and dinner, offerings include pepperoni or cheese pizzas, hamburgers, fruit salads, and chef's salads. The peanut butter cookies are good, too. The Stargate Restaurant stays open until the park closes. B, L, D, S.

does so it provides a fine view over the thunderstorm, sandstorm, prairie, and rain forest scenes of the "Listen to the Land" boat ride down below. The scenes were designed with diners in mind and provide them with a peek into a farmhouse window out of viewing range of the waterborne passengers below. This also is the only full-service, sit-down restaurant in Epcot Center that offers a complete breakfast. Reservations are necessary for both lunch and dinner; those holding reservation confirmation tickets for either meal may bypass any queue that exists at the pavilion's front entrance within half an hour of their scheduled meal seating time. B, L, D.

WORLD SHOWCASE

FAST FOOD AND SNACK SPOTS

Refreshment Port: A perfect stop for a quick thirst quencher. Located right next to the Canada pavilion. S.

Yakitori House: The nature of the food offered at this small but comfortable establishment in the Japan pavilion is representative of the pace of life in that country. The average Japanese spends only about seven minutes consuming his guydon, a beef-stew-like concoction flavored with soy sauce, spices, and the Japanese rice wine known as sake, and served over rice. That, together with bits of skewered chicken known as yakitori, which are basted with soy sauce and sesame oil as they broil, plus yakitori and teriyaki sandwiches and Japanese sweets and beverages, makes up the offerings here. Located in the Japanese gardens to the left of the plaza, the restaurant occupies a scaled-down version of the 16th-century Katsura Imperial Summer Palace in Kyoto; sliding screens, traditional umbrellas, lanterns, and kimono-clad hostesses add to the atmosphere. L, D, S.

Liberty Inn: To many foreigners, American food is synonymous with hamburgers, hot dogs, and French fries, and these are the staples at the Liberty Inn, located alongside The American Adventure on the far end of the World Showcase Lagoon. Chili, chocolate pudding, apple turnovers, chocolate chip cookies, and Danish pastries (only in the morning) round out the selections. As a result, the place is a delight

FULL SERVICE

The Good Turn Restaurant: Sleek wood-trimmed booths, upholstered in garnet-red velvet and illuminated with handsome brass lamps, make this an exceptionally attractive restaurant. The regional American foods, which are the house specialty, only add to the establishment's appeal. Dinners feature such appetizers as melon and ham, stuffed baked mushrooms, and fried cheddar cheese with mushrooms and walnuts in pastry. Prime ribs, broiled steaks, barbecued beef, duckling with black currant sauce, baked red snapper with lemon butter, stir-fried shrimp and vegetables over linguine, and broiled lime-marinated chicken are offered as entrées. French fried sweet potatoes make a very tasty side dish. At lunch, the menu includes several of the same items, along with a trio of hearty soups and a selection of salads and sandwiches. A basket of very nibbleable cheese bread goes on every table. An added bonus is that the restaurant revolves, and as it

for small children, and also quite a pleasant spot for their parents. There's veranda seating, a pretty fountain, and a full complement of antique-looking decoys, chests, candlesticks, samplers, and other bric-a-brac. The restaurant is large, so there's ample seating for everybody. B, L, D, S.

Refreshment Outpost: Another good spot for a refreshing cold drink. Between the Germany and China pavilions. S.

Cantina de San Angel: Located along the World Showcase Promenade, just outside the entrance to Mexico's pyramid, this fast-food stand serves quick snacks like tacos de carne, beef-filled soft tortillas; tostadas con pollo, tortillas topped with chicken and refried beans; and—perhaps best of all—churros, a sort of fried dough rolled in cinnamon and sugar. This last tasty treat makes the Cantina perfect for a continental breakfast, but it's also first rate for a rest on a hot afternoon. Dos Equis and Superior brand beers are available, and the establishment's plant-edged terrace makes a fine grandstand for viewing the passing parade. B, L, D.

CAFETERIA SERVICE

Le Cellier: This low-ceilinged, stone-walled establishment tucked away on the lowest level of the Canada pavilion just off Victoria Gardens (not far from the exit from the *O Canada!* film), looks a little like the ancient wine cellars for which it is named. It offers a full menu of Canadian foods—which are a lot more interesting than one might initially have thought. The savory, Quebec-born pork-and-potato-filled pie known as tourtière is dished out in enormous slices, each one fully three inches high and covered with a tempting golden crust. After 5 P.M., roast prime ribs are available. Tangy Canadian cheddar cheese adds zip to some appetizing fruit platters, and Canadian bacon and baked salmon (shipped frozen, alas, from Canada's West Coast) complete the selection of entrées. For dessert there's maple syrup pie, a sweet cousin to pecan pie, and trifle, a British culinary inspiration made of layers of yellow cake, custard, strawberries, and real whipped cream—all soaked with sherry. And Labatt's beer is on tap. The combination of all this should make Le Cellier a prime destination for those who haven't been able to get a dinner reservation at one of the more publicized World Showcase restaurants but still want something more substantial than the fast-food eateries are offering. Queue haters should be sure to avoid mealtime rush hours, which run from about 11:30 A.M. to 2 P.M. and again from about 5:30 to 8 P.M. (Line is also longer right after *O Canada!* film is over, but don't be deceived as it moves quickly.) L, D, S.

Boulangerie Patisserie: This bakery-and-pastry shop in the France pavilion is not hard to find: Just follow your nose and then watch the crowds line up to consume the establishment's elegant croissants and brioches, napoleons, éclairs, fruit tarts, and chocolate mousse. These are served by ladies wearing black pinafores with ruffled white blouses, under the management of the stellar trio of chefs who run the popular Les Chefs de France restaurant not far away—Paul Bocuse, Gaston LeNôtre, and Roger Vergé. Hint for those who hate to wait: Arrive before 10 A.M. (this has become a favorite "breakfast" stop among Epcot Center experts) or stop here about half an hour before park closing. B, S.

FULL SERVICE

Rose & Crown Pub & Dining Room: The fare here is "pub grub"—that is, fish and chips, steak-and-kidney pie, chicken-and-leek pie, and cottage pie (made of spiced ground beef, mashed potatoes, and melted cheddar cheese). For lunch, however, it's also possible to order "bangers and mash" (grilled sausages with fried onions and mashed potatoes), hot roast beef with gravy and still more mashed potatoes, traditional cold veal-and-ham pie, and a really delicious fresh vegetable platter served with a Stilton cheese and walnut dressing. At dinner the standard offerings are supplemented with roast prime ribs and horseradish sauce and, as appetizers, a dish known as Scotch eggs—hard-boiled, covered with sausage meat and fried, then chilled and served with mustard sauce on the side. (It's usually inedible back in Great Britain, but it's really quite tasty here in

Florida.) For dessert there's traditional sherry trifle, a confection of layered whipped cream, custard, strawberries, and sherry; and raspberry fool, strictly whipped cream and raspberry puree. Bass India Pale ale from England, Tennent's lager beer from Scotland, and Harp lager beer and Guinness stout, both from Ireland, are on tap. They're served cold, in the American fashion, or at room temperature, as Britons prefer.

Meanwhile, a lute player in jerkin, tights, and full-sleeved shirt—a cape slung over his shoulder—is often on hand to entertain with Elizabethan madrigals or other appropriate melodies. And the decor is really beautiful, mainly polished woods, etched glass, and brass accents. In fine weather it's pleasant to lunch under the sunny yellow umbrellas on the terrace outside and watch the sleek *FriendShip I* and *II* ferries chugging across the Lagoon. On the little island just to the east, the wind ruffles the leaves of the Lombardy poplars, a species of tree that is found along roadsides all over Europe.

Horticulturally speaking, it's also interesting to note the vines on the pub's northwest wall. These Virginia creepers grow amazingly fast and, when Epcot Center opened, showed only a few tentative tendrils close to the ground. The spreading tree nearby is a laurel oak, distinguished from the southern live oaks more widely seen at Epcot Center by its upright growth and its leaves, which are shiny on both sides instead of just one.

As for the pub's architecture, it incorporates three separate styles. The wall facing the World Showcase Promenade reminds one of urban establishments popular in Britain since the 1890s, while that on the south is reminiscent of London's *Cheshire Cheese* pub, with its brick-walled flagstone terrace, slate roof, and half-timbered exterior. The canal facade, with its stone wall, decorative doorways, and clay tile roof, evokes the charming pubs so common in the British countryside.

The pub section of the Rose & Crown serves such snacks as Stilton cheese and fresh fruit platters—

EVERYTHING YOU NEED TO KNOW ABOUT EPCOT CENTER RESTAURANT RESERVATIONS

It's important to confirm that the procedures described below are still in effect at the time you arrive at WDW. To check, call 824-4321. Also, try to arrive five minutes before your reserved seating time. As we went to press, the following system was in effect:

For dinner reservations: Must be made *on the day of the meal* at the World Key Information System screens in Earth Station—the building immediately past the waiting area for Spaceship Earth, as one walks through Future World from the Entrance Plaza. Shortly after the opening of Epcot Center, a line of would-be reservation makers has usually developed, and those at the end have less of a chance of booking a table at a popular establishment (such as Alfredo's or Les Chefs de France) at a popular time like 7:30 P.M.

For this reason, and because nobody really wants to wait on an unproductive line, it's helpful to arrive at the Epcot Center turnstiles about half an hour before the published park opening. Most recently, reservations have been available within the first hour of Epcot's opening for all restaurants, although the precise desired dining time may not be open. Decide in advance where you want to eat and when (and choose a couple of possible alternate dining locales) and then send the speediest member of your party on ahead to Earth Station to make the reservations. (It will help if you've familiarized yourself the night before with the location of Earth Station and the World Key Information System stations.) Each of the restaurants has something special about it, and there's always a good menu selection even for unadventurous eaters—even in the more exotic restaurants of World Showcase. By the same token, don't arbitrarily dismiss the idea of an early seating if you can get it: If you lunch at 11 A.M., a 5 P.M. dinner date will not only be welcome, but more important, it will provide the opportunity to spend the most pleasant and uncrowded evening hours enjoying the Epcot Center attractions. And whatever you do, don't abandon the idea of an Epcot Center restaurant experience altogether.

For lunch reservations: This meal provides guests with another chance to enjoy the most popular Epcot Center restaurants. It also has another important appeal: With a reservation for 1 P.M., it's possible to spend some of the most crowded hours in the park consuming a pleasant meal while less fortunate visitors are waiting on some of the longest lines of the day. Reservations for lunch must be made in person *at the restaurant itself on the day of the requested seating* or *until* 11:30 A.M. on the World Key Information System (see top of left hand column of type in this box). So complete this chore as early in the day as possible. Also note that you may be able to walk right in—say, if the time you have in mind is something not too popular (like 10:45 A.M.). Restaurants open for lunch between 10:30 and 11 A.M.

If all else fails: It sometimes happens that someone holding a reservation does not show up at the appointed seating time (reservations are held for only 15 minutes), so it certainly doesn't hurt to stop and inquire about a table when passing a restaurant for which you have a sudden appetite.

and the above-mentioned Scotch eggs—along with all the brews noted above and traditional British mixed drinks like shandies (Bass ale and ginger beer), lager beer with lime juice, black velvets (Guinness stout and champagne), and black and tans (Bass ale and Guinness stout). This drinking-and-snacking spot is quite popular, so it's often necessary to queue up at the door. But the wait is seldom very long since few guests linger over their drinks. Reservations are not accepted in the pub area but are required for the adjacent dining room. L, D, S.

Les Chefs de France: Three-star restaurants are rare even in France (for 1983 the august Michelin guide listed only 18 of them), so it's a notable coup that WDW has somehow managed to lure three of France's finest cuisineurs to run this rather remarkable restaurant. Paul Bocuse and Roger Vergé each operate his own three-star restaurant in France (Bocuse's is outside Lyon, Vergé's just north of the French Riviera), and together with Gaston LeNôtre (widely recognized as France's premier preparer of pastries and other delicious dessert delicacies) they form a most unusual, absolutely formidable gastronomic trio. Bocuse, Vergé, and LeNôtre operate this unique World Showcase restaurant, and they have designed a menu that features fresh ingredients readily available from Florida purveyors. One or more of the French chefs makes regular visits to WDW to supervise preparation and adjust certain items on the menu, though there has been very little need to tinker up to now.

As you might expect, the fare here is fiercely French, but the foundation of the menu is nouvelle cuisine, which involves lighter sauces, using much less cream and butter than the classic style of French cooking. At dinner, appetizers include chilled potato, leek, and watercress soup, salmon soufflé seasoned with tarragon and served with a white butter sauce, oysters baked with spinach and champagne sauce, and ramekins of snails in garlicky herbed butter and hazelnuts. Diners choose entrées from among fresh grouper doused with a rich lobster sauce, roast duck with wine sauce and prunes, fresh red snapper topped with salmon mousse and wrapped in puff pastry, roast veal with a mushroom sauce, and chicken fricassee in a mild vinegar brown sauce. At lunch the menu offers quiches, platters of French cheeses, country-style pâtés, a veal pâté wrapped in pastry, and sandwiches of ham and cheese on crusty French bread or sausage on a croissant. Hot dishes are offered, such as Lyon-style sausage baked in pastry (and doused with a beef-and-wine-flavored Bordelaise sauce), and a shrimp, crab, and fish casserole in a rich lobster sauce. A beef stew redolent of wine and a rich onion soup are available at lunch and dinner, as are an array of absolutely fabulous pastries and desserts and the thick, strong coffee known as café filtre (it's the French equivalent of Italian espresso). The atmosphere is as much a delight as the food. Tablecloths are sparkling white linen, and decorative touches of brass and etched glass abound. A modest wine list accompanies both lunch and dinner menus. Note that this can be one of the most expensive of all World Showcase restaurants. Reservations necessary. L, D.

Le Bistro de Paris: Located above Les Chefs de France, this new restaurant evokes early 20th-century Paris. Peach and green curlicues decorate the ceiling above brass light fixtures and sconces, large mirrors, colored leaded glass, and simple wood chairs. A traditional bistro menu (created by the same trio of French chefs responsible for the fare at Les Chefs de France) features cassoulet, steamed filet of fresh grouper, chicken breast in puff pastry, and braised beef. (There's a separate menu "for the little gourmet"—kids under 12—at reduced prices.) Reservations accepted. L, D.

Au Petit Café: Located prominently in front of the France pavilion, along the World Showcase Promenade, this sidewalk café is a delightful place to stop for a snack or light meal. Under a large canopy with small round tables and black-jacketed waiters, it's as pleasant as it can be, and it can't be beat as a people-watching headquarters. But no reservations are accepted, and long lines often mean a 45 minute wait. Don't stop here if you're very tired or absolutely ravenous. L, D, S.

El Marrakech: The tastiest part of the new Kingdom of Morocco Showcase features a variety of examples of traditional and modern Moroccan cuisine. Waiters are dressed in *djellaba* (long robes) and *babouche* (pointed slippers). Moroccan menu specialties include *tagine belghenmi* (lamb stew with vegetables), *couscous* (coarse steamed wheat served with lamb or chicken), and *bastila* (flaky pigeon pie). Reservations accepted. L, D.

Mitsukoshi Restaurant: This complex of dining and drinking spots, all operated by the Japanese firm for which it is named, occupies the second level of the large structure on the west side of the Japan pavilion plaza. Reservations necessary.

• Tempura Kiku: This small corner of the restaurant is devoted to the batter-dipped, deep-fried chicken, beef, seafood, and fresh vegetables that are collectively known as tempura. The individual tidbits are crisp, tasty, and altogether delicious. L, D.

• Teppanyaki Dining Rooms: The style in these five rooms is not unlike that popularized by the Benihana chain all around America: Guests sit counter-style around large flat grills, while white-hatted chefs chop vegetables, meat, and fish at lightning speed and then stir-fry it all just as quickly. Whether or not all the chopping and cooking is accompanied by a mildly comic routine depends on the sense of humor of the chef, but in any case the

establishment is quite convivial. The seating arrangements make it quite natural to strike up a conversation with fellow diners; in fact, it's almost impossible to keep to yourself. The exchange can

> ## WHERE TO EAT IN EPCOT CENTER IF YOU DON'T HAVE RESERVATIONS
>
> In Future World try the Farmers Market for quiche, barbecue, soups, salads, sandwiches, ice cream, and pastries. The Odyssey Restaurant, near World Showcase Plaza, is another good bet. So are Sunrise Terrace (in CommuniCore West) and the Stargate Restaurant (in CommuniCore East).
>
> In World Showcase, there's Le Cellier, a cafeteria in the Canada pavilion; France offers the informal full-service eatery known as Au Petit Café (though there are usually queues), and Japan has its Yakitori House, good for skewered bits of barbecued beef and chicken. The American Adventure has the Liberty Inn. Outside Mexico (on the World Showcase Promenade), there's the Cantina de San Angel.

often yield valuable hints and tips on what to see during the next day or two, besides being lots of fun. L, D.

L'Originale Alfredo di Roma Ristorante: This restaurant's *trompe l'oeil* ("trick the eye") perspective paintings make diners believe they're seeing real scenes rather than mere murals, and lend real character to the decor of this popular establishment. But the real stars here are the waiters and waitresses, who habitually burst into glorious song and keep guests laughing and singing with such gusto that passersby on the piazza outside sometimes wonder what all the merriment is about. The food is just as noteworthy. As in the famous Roman restaurant of the same name, the specialty is fettucine all'Alfredo—wide, flat noodles tossed in a sauce made of butter and imported Italian Parmesan cheese. But many other sizes and shapes of pasta, all of it made right on the premises, are also available; they are significantly enhanced by tomato, meat, pesto (basil, garlic, and Parmesan), or carbonara (egg, bacon, cream, and Pecorino cheese) sauces. There are also a number of less familiar Italian preparations involving chicken, eggplant, seafood, sausage, and veal, which are all really excellent here. For dessert, choose from a number of specialties such as ricotta cheesecake, spumoni, tortoni, or custard with a caramel syrup. Even if you don't eat here, it's fun to stop and just peer through the glass kitchen windows to watch the cooks cranking out the rigatoni, ziti, linguine, lasagna, fettucine, and spaghetti (which, the eminently readable menu reminds guests, was brought to America by Thomas Jefferson when he returned to the United States from Europe in 1786). Reservations necessary. L, D.

Biergarten: Located at the rear of the St. Georgsplatz in the Germany pavilion, this huge, tiered restaurant is set in a courtyard rimmed with geranium-studded balconies and punctuated by an old mill. It's every bit as jolly as Italy's Alfredo's, especially in the evenings, partly because of the long tables that encourage a certain togetherness among guests, partly because Beck's beer is served in 33-ounce steins. But equal credit for the *gemütliche* atmosphere must go to the restaurant's lively half-hour-long dinner shows, in which yodelers, dancers, and other traditional southern German musicians—each appropriately clad in lederhosen or dirndls—play accordions, cowbells, a musical saw, and a harplike stringed instrument known as the "wooden laughter." The performances are exceptional, and the Biergarten offers an extremely entertaining evening. The food is hearty and very German: smoked pork loin, roast chicken, the spicy marinated beef known as sauerbraten, grilled bratwurst, bauernwurst, and bierwurst, and jaegerwurst, potato salad, "wine"-kraut, and potato dumplings make up the offerings. Although there's no big show at lunchtime, a few "street" entertainers are usually on hand—and the setting is pleasant nonetheless, with the big mill waterwheel slowly turning and the sounds of water splashing into the millstream blending with the rousing oompah music. L, D.

San Angel Inn Restaurante: A corporate cousin of the famous Mexico City restaurant of the same name, the food at this establishment, located to the rear of the plaza inside the Mexico pyramid, may come as a surprise to most visitors. Although the tacos and tortillas and other specialties that usually fall under the broad umbrella of Mexican food are available, the menu also offers a wide variety of more subtly flavored fish, poultry, and meat dishes. To start, there's ceviche—made of marinated mackerel here—as well as guacamole (avocado dip). Suprema de jicama, a compote made of sweet Mexican turnip and oranges, is also available—and delicious. As entrées, the menu offers pollo en pipian, chicken strips simmered in pumpkin seed sauce; mole poblano, chicken simmered with spices and a bit of chocolate; huachinango à la Veracruzana, fresh red snapper poached in wine with onions, tomatoes, and peppers; and much more that is good and tasty. Mexican desserts are largely unfamiliar to Americans, with the possible exceptions of the custard known as flan, and arroz con leche, best known in the United States as rice pudding. Still, such desserts as crepas de cajeta, thin pancakes filled with milk caramel; helada con cajeta, vanilla ice cream with a milk caramel topping; and chongos zamoranos, milk curds in syrup, are well worth trying. Dos Equis and Superior brand beer, tart lemon- or tamarind-flavored waters, the traditional hot Mexican milk known as atole, and gigantic, delicious margaritas make good accompaniments. Just as intriguing as the food is the restaurant's location overlooking yet another pyramid, a smoldering volcano, and every now and again a show of thunder and lightning realistic enough to have diners reaching for umbrellas—all part of the pavilion's main attraction, El Rio del Tiempo. Reservations necessary. L, D.

IN THE HOTELS

CONTEMPORARY RESORT

Most of the hotel's restaurants are located on the Grand Canyon Concourse on the fourth floor, but there are also restaurants on the second and fifteenth floors, and snack spots by the marina and in the first-floor Fiesta Fun Center.

Terrace Buffeteria: On the Grand Canyon Concourse, this establishment opens at 7 A.M. and closes at 10:30 P.M. daily. Omelets and other egg dishes, grits and biscuits, cereal and French toast are served at breakfast, and chicken, baked fish, meat loaf, and assorted soups and salads at dinner. B, D, S.

Terrace Cafe: On the Grand Canyon Concourse. Serves a bountiful, all-you-can-eat Italian buffet—one of the World's best buys—every evening. And each morning there's a buffet-style character breakfast. For lunch, the menu features sandwiches and a taco bar. No reservations. B, L, D.

Pueblo Room: On the Grand Concourse, tucked away behind Coconino Cove, and quieter than other Grand Concourse eating spots. At breakfast, the roster of fairly standard offerings includes a two-egg omelet, pancakes, and steak and eggs. At lunch, choose from salads, hearty sandwiches, hamburgers with a choice of six toppings, and a fruit and cottage cheese platter. Dinners feature tossed greens and an assortment of fairly straightforward meat, chicken, and seafood dishes, among them prime ribs, veal, jumbo shrimp in garlic-lemon butter, and roast duckling. Children's portions are available at lunch, and there's a special children's menu at dinner. Reservations accepted for dinner only, but not required. B, L, D.

Outer Rim: On the Grand Canyon Concourse, opposite the Terrace Cafe, with a good view over Bay Lake. Dinner includes chicken cordon bleu, prime ribs, and shrimp in garlic-lemon butter and white wine. Children's portions are available for youngsters under twelve. No reservations. D.

Gulf Coast Room: One of the most elegant of Walt Disney World's continental restaurants, with a subdued, relaxed atmosphere that seems worlds away from the bustling Grand Canyon Concourse and the congestion of the elevator lobbies. Grilled lamb chops, New York strip steaks with herb butter, seafood en brochette, sautéed red snapper, and veal marsala are specialties of the house. There are delicious flambéed coffees for *après*. Carlos, the strolling guitarist, plays just about any song a guest may request. Children who don't delight in the leisurely pace of the service can be dispatched to the Fiesta Fun Center Snack Bar. Jackets are required for men. Reservations are suggested; phone 824-3684. D.

Top of the World: This view-filled room on the hotel's fifteenth floor offers bountiful, all-you-can-eat buffets for breakfast, lunch, and brunch on Sunday. The dinner show features Broadway at the Top, a lively revue of Broadway musicals, at 6 and 9:15 P.M. nightly. The menu includes duckling, prime ribs, veal, and red snapper. The setting, with excellent views of the Magic Kingdom, is one of the best in the World. After dark, the golden spires of Cinderella Castle glitter under floodlights, and the white lights edging the rooflines of Main Street wink and twinkle like distant fireflies. Reservations are required for the dinner shows; phone the WDW Central Reservations Office at 824-8000. For Sunday brunch reservations, call 824-3611. B, L, D.

Fiesta Fun Center Snack Bar: On the first floor, serves light fare until midnight. B, L, D, S.

Dock Inn: Submarines, ham and cheese sandwiches, hot dogs, frozen-juice bars, frozen bananas, and ice cream bars are the stock-in-trade at this stand at the marina behind the hotel. B, L, D, S.

THE POLYNESIAN VILLAGE

Some of WDW's more interesting eating spots are located here.

South Seas Dining Room: A character breakfast, Minnie's Menehune, is featured here. Dinner is served buffet style in this smallish room; roast beef and roast pork, Oriental-Polynesian dishes, vegetables, and salad fixings are standard offerings. B, D.

Papeete Bay Verandah: Serves sit-down dinners daily, breakfast and lunch buffets Monday through Saturday, and a copious brunch buffet on Sunday. The breakfast buffet features all sorts of fresh fruit, French toast, eggs, grits, and smoked fish. The hot-and-cold lunch buffet is a favorite; one highlight is the coconut-spiked rice pudding for dessert. The kabobs, prime ribs, and red snapper are the best choices for dinner, but more adventurous diners may be tempted by some of the Polynesian-style offerings. Among the appetizers are scallops marinated in coconut milk with a touch of horseradish and sour cream; shrimp, kingfish, spinach, and cabbage steamed in ti leaves; and thin salted salmon fillets seasoned with lemon, scallions, and tomatoes. Main courses include Pua'a (pork loin seasoned and rolled in crushed peanuts and served with a fried banana), chicken pago-pago (a marinated chicken breast glazed with a honeyed sesame sauce and served in a pineapple half), almond duck tempura (a crispy boneless duck), or Laulua pig and prawns (pork fillet and prawns stuffed with cheddar cheese and crab meat, served with shrimp fried rice). The Papeete Lovo includes a selection of several of the more popular entrées. For dessert, the menu offers poached pear marinated in apricot brandy and served with a strawberry cream sauce; macadamia-nut pie with passion-fruit ice cream; rum-flavored banana-rice pudding served in a fresh coconut; and melon balls and lime sherbet doused with coconut milk. The room itself is large and open and offers fine views across the Seven Seas Lagoon all the way to Cinderella Castle. After dark, Polynesian dancers and a small combo entertain quietly. Reservations are requested for dinner; phone 824-1391. B, L, D.

Coral Isle Cafe: On the second floor of the Great Ceremonial House, around the corner from Papeete Bay. This standard coffee shop with faintly South Seas decor serves the usual assortment of eggs every morning (including an interesting shrimp-and-cheese-stuffed omelet), plus granola and other cereals, and wonderful banana-stuffed French toast, one of the best of all Walt Disney World dishes. At lunch and dinner, the house does a booming business in big fruit salads, shrimp and crab-meat salads, chef's salads, and a variety of sandwiches. The assortment of hot entrées is expanded during the evening hours. Drinks, including the special Polynesian concoctions served at the Tambu Lounge, are available. A good choice when you want a no-fuss meal. B, L, D, S.

Tangaroa Terrace: This sprawling establishment, on the eastern edge of the property near the Oahu longhouse, has never been as heavily patronized as some of the other Polynesian Village restaurants because of its somewhat remote location. Increasingly, however, the word is spreading about its star breakfast offering, banana-stuffed French toast made with sourdough bread (eggs and other more usual breakfast selections also are available), and its dinners of prime ribs, steak, snapper, and a variety of more exotic entrées in an Oriental mode—sautéed pork fillets topped with mushrooms and pea pods, teriyaki steak, stir-fried shrimp and vegetables, macadamia-nut duckling, as well as fresh seafood daily. Reservations are a good idea; phone 824-1361. B, D.

Barefoot Snack Bar: A good spot for continental breakfasts, hamburgers, hot dogs, ham and cheese sandwiches, fruit salads, and snacks; beer in cans is also available. The most unusual specialty: coconut hot dogs. L, D, S.

Tangaroa Snack Isle: Most guests discover this snack bar on their way to Tangaroa Terrace, the game room, or the east pool, to which it is extremely convenient. Hamburgers and hot dogs, a variety of submarine sandwiches, chef's and fruit salads, and light snacks like yogurt and ice cream cones are all available. Canned beer is sold here, as well. L, D, S.

THE GOLF RESORT

Trophy Room: This is the hotel's only full-service restaurant, and it ranks among the most pleasant spots in the World for a meal. Many Disney executives come here for lunch because even when there are lines at the Polynesian Village and the Contemporary Resort, the Trophy Room is fairly quiet. Also, the food is quite good. At breakfast and lunch, there are immense all-you-can-eat buffets. At dinner, crab claws and shrimp cocktail are among the appetizers, as well as a platter piled with French-fried zucchini, mushrooms, and cheddar cheese. Entrées include steaks, prime ribs, duck in a peach-brandy sauce, chicken breast, pork tenderloin, seafood platters, and red snapper. French-fried ice cream, served on a peach half with a vanilla sauce, is offered both at lunch (on the à la carte menu) and at dinner; it's truly scrumptious. At the Sunday brunch buffets you can choose unlimited Bloody Marys, screwdrivers, champagne, or wine. B, L, D.

Sand Trap: The perfect spot for snacks—right at poolside. L, D, S.

DINNER WITH THE DISNEY CHARACTERS

A family-style dinner consisting of thinly-sliced prime ribs, chicken, or fish is served in the Trophy Room at the Golf Resort and features a visit by a handful of the Walt Disney characters—larger than life and always appealing. And each youngster takes home a special Disney trinket. Begins early, about 5 P.M. Cost is about $12.50 for adults, $10.50 for juniors, and $7.50 for children; reservations are required. Call 824-8000.

WDW VILLAGE

Some of the World's best restaurants are located in this enclave on the southeastern edge of the property—in the Lake Buena Vista Club, which has its own restaurant and a snack bar, and many more in the Shopping Village scattered among the boutiques, and nearby aboard the gleaming *Empress Lilly* riverboat restaurant. It's worth noting that while the restaurants hereabouts really hop at dinnertime, none is terribly crowded at lunch, except on Saturday and Sunday, when Orlando and Kissimmee residents make the trip to WDW Village for a day of shopping. And these restaurants have the added advantage of being just a couple of hundred yards' dash from the marina, so that kids can go off and hire a pedal boat or a Water Sprite (at least during lunchtime and in late afternoon) while parents linger over coffee or drinks.

Verandah Restaurant: This airy, gardenlike establishment—with linen napkins and all—serves three meals a day. There's the usual range of egg dishes at breakfast, and oversized sandwiches and salads, patty melts, burgers, chicken, ham, and similar fare at lunch. Prime ribs, beef Wellington, seafood platters, and veal Parmesan are staples at dinnertime. Wine, beer, and cocktails are available. B, L, D, S.

Village Ice Cream Parlour and Bake Shop: Right next door to the Verandah Restaurant, this is a perfect spot for ice cream. Banana splits and strawberry royales are only two of many creations. Baked goods and regular and soft-serve ice cream round out the offerings. S.

Cap'n Jack's Oyster Bar: The menu at this waterside spot is so full of good things—seafood marinara, stuffed clams, ceviche, crab claws, clams and oysters on the half shell, and Maryland crabcakes—that it's as terrific for a light lunch or dinner as it is for a snack, even though the place is nominally a lounge. Cap'n Jack's is a terrific place to be, especially in late afternoon, as the sun streams through the narrow-slatted blinds and glints on the polished tables and the copper above the bar. And the house's special frozen strawberry margaritas—made with fresh fruit, strawberry tequila, and a couple of other potent ingredients—are as tasty as they are beautiful. They're served in big balloon-shaped goblets, with a slice of lime astraddle the rim: tart, slightly fruity, and altogether delightful. L, D, S.

Heidelberger's Deli: This is the best sandwich spot in the World, though it's not likely to fully satisfy delicatessen devotees from Los Angeles or New York. Four different kinds of breads and five types of rolls are offered, not to mention a whole case of meats, cheeses, and other fillings. Every sandwich comes with a choice of potato salad, cole slaw, baked beans, or sauerkraut. Beer, wine, and soft drinks are available. L, D, S.

Lite Bite: This is the shopping area's fast-food spot, serving hamburgers, hot dogs, fried chicken, salads, and assorted soft drinks and beer to eat inside or out. L, D, S.

Village Restaurant: This unassuming dining room is one of the most pleasant restaurants in Walt Disney World—and there's no waiting since reservations are now accepted (828-3723). There are fine views over Buena Vista Lagoon, and the sunshine that streams through the windows keeps a whole garden's worth of house plants robust and green all year. Fresh fish is usually available here, even when you can't get it elsewhere in the World. At lunch, the menu offers shellfish salads, eggs Benedict, quiche, and an interesting omelet stuffed with crab and artichoke hearts, as well as a selection of terrific sandwiches and homemade soups. Adjoining the Village Restaurant is the living room–like Village Lounge. Fitted out with comfortable low sofas and club chairs, it presents the kind of top-name jazz performers who don't usually venture far away from big cities; there is a minimum charge of $5 during busy periods. (This charge does not apply to guests waiting for dinner at the Village Restaurant.) A great spot for after-dinner drinks. Valet parking is available. L, D.

Lake Buena Vista Club: The menu at this coolly elegant, country club–like establishment is ambitious, even at breakfast, when it offers blueberry crepes with vanilla sauce, omelets, and eggs Florentine (drenched in Hollandaise sauce and served on a bed of spinach atop an English muffin). Interesting fruit and vegetable salads and sandwiches, and entrées featuring fresh fish (flown in from Boston), crepes, omelets, and several low-cal plates are available at noon, along with the house's special Gold Brick sundae—vanilla ice cream doused in a scrumptious, crunchy, milk-chocolatey sauce. Both at lunch and dinner, the menu offers onion soup des Halles, a thick, rich Parmesan- and Swiss-cheese-topped broth for which the chef is locally famous. Things are even fancier at dinner, and Sunday brunch is one of the World's most popular. Reservations are requested for dinner and brunch; phone 828-3735. B, L, D.

Lake Buena Vista Club Snack Bar: The only breakfast fare is coffee and pastries; otherwise hot dogs, subs, and other snacks are available. B, L, D, S.

Villa Center: Located in the Vacation Village pool area. Sandwiches, soft drinks, and beer are served. L, D, S.

ABOARD THE EMPRESS LILLY

Named after Walt Disney's wife, this 220-foot-long Disney version of the stern-wheelers that plied the rivers of America during the nineteenth century rises gleaming and white at the west edge of the Buena Vista Lagoon, ornate as a Victorian ball gown, looking perpetually ready to sail off into the sunset. She really isn't, of course. Permanently moored, she's stacked from bottom to top with restaurants and lounges, and always bursting at the seams with diners and merrymakers having a very good time indeed.

In some very interesting ways, the *Empress Lilly* is authentic, however. Like early riverboats, she has tall stacks like those that once allowed the sparks vented from the boiler's fire to cool off before hitting the all-wood deck or the often-flammable cargo. She also has "hog chains" strung between the two slanted poles that extend from the hull through the third deck. (Steamboats were flat-bottomed, with a superstructure light enough to allow them to draw only a few feet of water; the hog chains kept the boat from sagging in the middle from the weight of its cargo, and from "warping" or sinking at the stern from the weight of the heavy engine, boiler, and paddle wheel.) Since the *Empress* represents a cross between an excursion boat and a showboat, she has her share of jigsaw-cut gingerbread trimming, not only on the second story, or Promenade Deck, but also on the first level, the main deck. The railings on both decks are elaborate; the posts are turned and then bracketed to create an archway effect.

The hallways and public rooms are full of polished Honduras mahogany, Victorian-style flowered carpets, old-fashioned prints and brass fixtures, and tufted Victorian love seats with damask and velvet upholstery; the curtains are swagged or sheer. Each of the restaurants and lounges is a little different. Note that shorts are not permitted on board after 5 P.M. Valet parking is available near the boat.

Fisherman's Deck: This seafood spot on the forward Promenade Deck has a huge curved expanse of window—180 degrees' worth—and in the afternoon, the sunlight that washes the pale cream-colored tongue-in-groove paneled walls and the blue tufted Victorian side chairs is as remarkable as the food. At lunch, the chefs offer first-class poached salmon; smoked whitefish and salmon; crab meat, shrimp, and avocado salads; sandwiches made with grilled crab meat, cheddar, tomato, and bacon; and fresh red snapper. The fried-oyster-and-bacon-stuffed omelet is one of several dishes on the menu that might have been served in nineteenth-century riverboating days. At dinner, shrimp cocktail, oysters en brochette, crab claws with avocado-mustard sauce, snapper, prawns en brochette, and Maine lobster (seasonal) are the specialties; the Empress Delight includes a bit of everything—pompano, oyster and bacon en brochette, and crab-meat-stuffed lobster. At both lunch and dinner, there are also limited offerings for meat eaters. No reservations are accepted; give your name to the hostess and then wait over drinks in the Promenade Lounge on the starboard Promenade Deck, or the always-lively Baton Rouge Lounge, on the forward main deck. Note that Central Florida is big on "fresh frozen" fish; if you prefer yours fresh-fresh, be sure to check the precise chill on that day's offerings before ordering. L, D.

Steerman's Quarters: This ornate main deck salon, full of heavy red upholstery and turned mahogany spindles and paneling, is named for the steering gear that would have occupied this area in one of the original stern-wheelers. Meat is the big deal—cold prime ribs with minced horseradish, ground steak in puff pastry, strip steak, beef tenderloin—though oysters on the half shell and shrimp cocktail are available, along with specialty crepes stuffed with seafood in white-wine sauce, or diced chicken in Mornay sauce. At dinner, prime ribs and a half-dozen grilled meats are orderable. While you're waiting for your food, you can sit by a big glass window that seems only inches away from the paddle wheel's gleaming white arms and watch the turning wheel. No reservations are accepted; give your name to the hostess and wait in the Starboard Lounge or in the Baton Rouge Lounge. L, D.

The Empress Room: The most amazing thing about this restaurant (located amidships on the Promenade Deck) is not its food (though the menu is one of WDW's most ambitious), but the service, the atmosphere, and the Louis XV surroundings—light-painted paneling, damask wallpaper, a shallow-domed ceiling with an Italian brass chandelier glittering with crystal droplets, and, between the tables-for-four along the wall, dividers fitted out with paneling and etched glass. Parts of the elaborate moldings are covered with enough real gold leaf (worth $8,000 when the *Empress* was constructed in 1977) to form a cube measuring 1¾ inches on a side.

The culinary offerings include hot and curried spinach and oyster soup or chilled avocado soup, Bibb lettuce and fresh mushroom salads, country pâté, smoked duck with creamed horseradish, crab meat sautéed in butter with brandy, Dover sole stuffed with salmon mousse and mushrooms and doused with a Vermouth sauce, whole young chicken in a cream-and-cider sauce, and more. The quality of the food preparation is often erratic, and a bit less garlic (and seasonings in general) would keep the cuisine more haute. But this is among the most elegant eating places in the World; the restaurant seats guests from 6 to 9:30 P.M., and a 20 percent surcharge is added to each check for service. Not all the fish here is fresh; if this matters to you, be sure to get a status report before ordering. Jackets are required for men, and reservations are a must; they are available to all up to 60 days in advance (828-3900). D.

FORT WILDERNESS CAMPGROUND

Most people cook their own meals; supplies are available at the Meadow and Settlement Trading Posts (open from 8 A.M. to 10 P.M. in winter, to 11 P.M. in summer). Deli-style sandwiches can be concocted there for carry out.

Trail's End Cafe: This informal, log-walled, beam-ceilinged cafeteria offers standard breakfasts (plus a seven-inch breakfast pizza, grits, biscuits and gravy, and bread pudding) every morning; and during the rest of the day, hearty lunches and dinners featuring barbecued chicken, fish, chicken pot pie, turkey à la king, franks and beans, spare ribs, and more. Specially priced children's portions are available. Pizza is served every night from 9 P.M. until 12:30 A.M. Beer and sangría are available by the glass or by the pitcher. B, L, D, S.

Campfire Snack Bar: Hot dogs, chili dogs, hamburgers and cheeseburgers, French fries, chili and beans, soft drinks, lemonade, beer, and sangría are among the offerings. L, D, S.

Beach Shack: Located near the Bay Lake beach. Ham and cheese subs, potato chips and Fritos, ice cream bars and sandwiches, grape- and orange-juice bars, and frozen bananas are available. Among the potables are sarsaparilla to sip and beer to tipple. L, D, S.

LATE-NIGHT PIZZA
The thin-crusted variety is available from 9 P.M. to 12:30 A.M. in Pioneer Hall, while silent movies and sing-alongs entertain.

WDW VILLAGE HOTEL PLAZA

At the Americana Dutch Resort: This gleaming white high-rise has two eating spots: the Only Steak and the Flying Dutchman, a somewhat fancier and more expensive eating spot that offers an all-you-can-eat buffet at breakfast time, sandwiches and hot entrées at lunch, and Florida and Maine lobsters, steak, veal specialties, and some of the rare fresh fish served in WDW at dinner. B, L, D, S.

At the Howard Johnson's: The restaurant and the adjacent coffee shop here offer the standard HoJo menu in standard HoJo style—food that is reassuringly predictable, if not overwhelmingly tasty, at a speed that brings to mind the old phrase about molasses in winter. The ice cream is worth the wait, however, and it's served 24 hours a day. B, L, D, S.

At the Hotel Royal Plaza: This sprawling resort boasts a pleasant (but unremarkable) coffee shop, The Knight's Table, which is open from 7 A.M. until midnight daily. B, L, D, S. Pizza is available at the Giraffe Lounge from 10 P.M. to 2 A.M. The ambitious El Cid offers specialty veal dishes as well as steak Diane, chateaubriand, rack of lamb, and fresh Maine lobster. D.

At the Viscount Hotel: This hotel's restaurant, the Palm Grill, offers a buffet at breakfast with lunch and dinner served à la carte from an American and international menu. B, L, D. Next to the restaurant is the new Ice Cream Parlor, which serves sodas, shakes, scoops, and sundaes. Pizza and hot dogs are also available here. L, D, S.

At the Buena Vista Palace: Among this hotel's interesting eating spots you'll find the garden-like Watercress Café, where meals or snacks are available either inside or outside on a patio with a lake view, around the clock. B, L, D, S. The Outback Restaurant, decorated in earth tones with an Australian theme, serves a buffet breakfast, and steaks and lobster are the fare at the dinner hour. B, D. Arthur's 27, as elegant in its way as the Empress Room on the *Empress Lilly*, serves continental cuisine—and offers a wonderful view. D.

At the Hilton: There are three restaurants here. The American Vineyards offers regional American specialties like hickory-smoked Vermont turkey, Florida stone crab claws, and quail. D. The County Fair gives guests the option of serving themselves from the buffet or ordering from the menu; the Boarding House section features family-style dining and an all-you-can-eat policy. B, L, D. For hot dogs and hamburgers al fresco, there's the Pool Terrace Broiler. L, D.

MEAL BY MEAL

When you're looking for something special in the way of a meal, and you're willing to go a bit out of your way to find it, the descriptions below should provide sufficient suggestions to sate your appetite. What follows are the highlights of WDW breakfasts, lunches, and dinners, as well as some suggestions for avoiding mealtime crowds at the eatery of your choice. This is a selective, not a comprehensive, list; for complete information see the preceding listings under "Restaurants of WDW."

BREAKFAST

Most people opt for eggs and bacon or something similar at their own hotel. But those who decide to go farther afield will be amazed at the choices available. For instance, the French toast served at the Polynesian Village Resort's Coral Isle Cafe and Tangaroa Terrace—made with thick slices of real sourdough bread, stuffed with bananas, deep fried, and then rolled in cinnamon and sugar—is one of the best breakfast concoctions ever.

Except during the busiest periods, restaurants in the Magic Kingdom are good choices for quick morning meals. Most fast-food spots serve coffee and Danish pastry from park opening until about 11 A.M.

BREAKFAST WITH DISNEY CHARACTERS

Food takes second place to Donald Duck, Minnie Mouse, Goofy, and the rest of the Disney gang, who take turns making special appearances at these especially delightful breakfast-time affairs. Breakfast à la Disney on the *Empress Lilly* riverboat restaurant at Walt Disney World Village takes place at 9 A.M. and 10:30 A.M. daily; the scrambled eggs-and-bacon meal is served banquet style. (To reserve, phone the *Empress Lilly* at 828-3900.) Another character breakfast which takes place daily from 8 to 11 A.M. at the Terrace Cafe in the Contemporary Resort features an enormous buffet. No reservations are necessary. The third spot for dining with the characters at breakfast is Minnie's Menehune at the South Seas at the Polynesian Village. There is continuous seating between 8 and 10 A.M. (To reserve, phone Central Reservations at 824-8000.)

At most breakfast spots in the hotels, there are likely to be lines between 8 and 10 A.M., the morning rush hour. So allow yourself plenty of time at these hours—or eat earlier or later, or stop at a snack shop for something light to stave off hunger until time for a lineless breakfast (or an early lunch). It's also possible to use the long card you'll find hanging from the doorknob of any WDW guest room to order breakfast from Room Service the night before. Be forewarned: ordering from Room Service on the same morning can mean waiting up to two hours for your food.

In Epcot Center, the Stargate Restaurant in Future World's CommuniCore East offers cheese omelets, cold cereals, Danish pastries, and the Stellar Scramble (informally known as breakfast pizza). The only full-service restaurant serving a full breakfast is The Good Turn restaurant in The Land; the Farmers Market downstairs offers bagels and cream cheese as well as eggs and delicious pastries. Mexico's Cantina de San Angel serves deep-fried, cinnamon-and-sugar-dusted dough called churros, which are delicious, and France's Boulangerie Patisserie, where queues run to 45 minutes during most of the rest of the day, is relatively uncrowded before 10:30 A.M.—despite the fact that it offers delicious brioches and croissants and excellent coffee.

LUNCH

Breaking up a day in the Magic Kingdom with lunch at one of the resorts can provide the energy to keep going until closing time. A few of the eating spots do get crowded around midday, but the Pueblo Room at the Contemporary Resort, the Coral Isle Cafe at the Polynesian Village, and the Trophy Room at the Golf Resort are usually particularly peaceful. The Golf Resort's special dessert—French-fried ice cream, served on a peach half and drizzled with vanilla sauce—is well worth ordering, even though it costs extra. The buffets at Papeete Bay in the Polynesian Village and at the Top of the World in the Contemporary Resort are also worth a detour. Lunch highlights in Walt Disney World Shopping Village are Heidelberger's Deli and Cap'n Jack's Oyster Bar. If you can't tear yourself away from the Magic Kingdom for even an hour to go elsewhere for lunch, there's still no lack of selection. Hamburgers and French fries are for sale at practically every turn, and then there are the Monte Cristos (batter-dipped, deep-fried turkey, ham, and Swiss cheese sandwiches) served at the Town Square Cafe, or the vegetable and fruit salads available at the Crystal Palace, both on Main Street; the Philadelphia pepper pot soup, clam chowder, and black walnut bread served at the Liberty Tree Tavern in Liberty Square; the teriyaki-sauced beef and chicken at the Adventureland Veranda; peanut butter and jelly sandwiches at Aunt Polly's on Tom Sawyer Island in Frontierland; pizza at Lancer's Inn in Fantasyland; and chocolate crepes at King

Stefan's in Cinderella Castle; and health food at the Lunching Pad in Tomorrowland.

As at breakfast, crowds can be a problem; the three hours between eleven and two are the busiest. To avoid the rush, eat a light breakfast and a big early lunch—or have a late breakfast and a late lunch. If necessary, snatch a midmorning snack to tide you over until things get less hectic.

Another option (especially during the summer and holiday periods) is to leave the Magic Kingdom altogether for lunch at Walt Disney World Shopping Village or at one of the resort hotels, which are less crowded than the Magic Kingdom at noon.

Except on Saturdays and Sundays, when local residents usually come out to shop, none of the Walt Disney World Shopping Village restaurants are ever horribly crowded at lunchtime.

The hours between 11 A.M. and 2 P.M. in the Magic Kingdom are very busy, however, even though the lines usually move fairly quickly. It's usually far swifter to eat earlier or later. When there are several food service windows operating, evaluate them all before wandering into the nearest queue: Occasionally, the one farthest from the doorway will be almost (if not entirely) wait free. Note that the lines at the Adventureland Veranda generally move more slowly than those at other fast-food establishments because of the greater variety of offerings. Also, while the sit-down restaurants offering full dinners—such as Cinderella Castle's King Stefan's and Liberty Square's Liberty Tree Tavern—are crowded at lunch, they're busier still at dinnertime.

SUNDAY BRUNCHES

These grand spreads take over the Lake Buena Vista Club (9:30 A.M. to 2 P.M.), the Golf Resort's Trophy Room (10 A.M. to 3 P.M.), and the Top of the World at the Contemporary Resort and the Papeete Bay at the Polynesian Village (both 9 A.M. to 2:30 P.M.) every Sunday. All feature hot dishes along with traditional breakfast fare, fruit, and pastries. While no alcoholic beverages are included in the brunch price at the Papeete Bay Verandah or at the Top of the World, champagne is included at the Lake Buena Vista Club; the Trophy Room offers unlimited Bloody Marys, screwdrivers, wine, or champagne. The especially varied Trophy Room buffet often includes oysters on the half shell, seafood Newburg, and quiche Lorraine. Prices range from about $8 to $11 (less for children under 12 and juniors aged 12 to 18). Make reservations in advance: Papeete Bay (824-1391); Trophy Room (824-1484); Lake Buena Vista Club (828-3735); and Top of the World (824-3611).

In Epcot Center, midday is a good time to sample some of the full-service restaurants offering ethnic specialties. Linger over their culinary delights, out of the heat of the midday sun, while crowds of other guests are lining up for attractions. For hamburgers and other standard fast-food fare, try the Stargate Restaurant in CommuniCore East, Liberty Inn in The American Adventure, and the sleek, attractive Odyssey Restaurant near Mexico and the World of Motion. The Farmers Market, in The Land, offers a huge variety, from baked potatoes and soups and salads to barbecued sandwiches and more, and is a good choice for a family that can't arrive at a consensus. The pizza quiche offered at The Cheese Shoppe there is a favorite, and the chocolate chip cookies from the nearby Bakery make a good dessert. Ethnic fast foods are available at Japan's Yakitori House and Mexico's Cantina de San Angel. Among full-service eateries, The Land's Good Turn restaurant is special for its imaginatively conceived regional American offerings, not to mention that delightful cheese bread. In World Showcase, meat pies and Epcot Center's best salad (the fresh vegetable platter) may be found at the Rose & Crown Pub & Dining Room; stir-fried meats and vegetables are the prime fare in the Mitsukoshi restaurants; hearty German food is offered in Germany's Biergarten; and fairly elaborate Mexican fare comprises the menu in Mexico's San Angel Inn Restaurante. The delightful Au Petit Café on the World Showcase Promenade in France is the only sit-down restaurant that doesn't require reservations, but the waiting line is almost always about 45 minutes long. The most elaborate cooking is done at Italy's Alfredo's and at France's Les Chefs de France.

DINNER

There's an awesome choice, from the humblest snack center to the *Empress Lilly*'s ambitious Empress Room. Walt Disney World is not exactly a bastion of haute cuisine, but that doesn't mean that dinner experiences are anything less than pleasant. Service is almost unfailingly good (slipping just slightly during the busiest seasons), and the best of Walt Disney World's dinners are just fine. For a night on the World, some good choices are the Steerman's Quarters, Fisherman's Deck, and the Empress Room, all on the *Empress Lilly*; the Village Restaurant on the shores of Lake Buena Vista in Walt Disney World Shopping Village; the Lake Buena Vista Club; the Gulf Coast Room in the Contemporary Resort; and the Papeete Bay Verandah in the Polynesian Village.

For family fare: Children are welcome at every WDW restaurant, but the leisurely pace of service at some places makes some kids fidget. But there are plenty of choices that are particularly well suited to dining en famille. Restaurants at the Contemporary Resort especially good for families are the Terrace Buffeteria and the Terrace Cafe; the South Seas at the Polynesian Village is another good choice.

The decision about where to dine may ultimately depend on the plan for the rest of the day. Especially in slack periods, the familiar long lines at the most popular attractions in the Magic Kingdom are practically nonexistent from about 6 P.M. onward, and even in the busiest times, the queues ease up a bit as the afternoon wanes. So it's a wise visitor who takes advantage of this phenomenon by having a late lunch or a 4 P.M. snack—then dines after 9 P.M. (This plan also allows time to catch the second, less-

DINNER SHOWS

The fact that the Disney organization is the king of family entertainment is nowhere more strongly apparent than amid the whooping and hollering troupe of singers and dancers who race toward the velvet-curtained stage at Fort Wilderness Campground's Pioneer Hall. As you plough through barbecued ribs, fried chicken, corn on the cob, and strawberry shortcake, those enthusiastic performers sing, dance, and joke up a storm until your mouth is as sore from laughing as your stomach is from ingesting all the food. This is the Hoop-Dee-Doo Musical Revue, presented daily at 5, 7:30, and 10 P.M. Cost is about $18 per adult, $15 for juniors (13 through 18), and $10 for children (3 through 12); reservations can be made through the CRO (824-8000) and are required well in advance.

The Polynesian Revue at the Polynesian Village (aka the Luau), presented nightly at 5 and 8 P.M. (and, from the end of March through late August, at 10:30 P.M. as well), also has its moments. The performers' dancing is some of the most authentic this side of Hawaii's well-respected Polynesian Cultural Center—where many of the WDW dancers have studied. The full Polynesian-style meal served at the first two shows is not one of the Disney chefs' better efforts; unless you have young children along, you may prefer to catch the last show (in season), where platters of fruit and cheese provide showtime sustenance. Cost is about $18 for adults, $15 for juniors, and $10 for children. (Late show prices are $10 for adults and juniors, $7 for children.)

The Top of the World at the Contemporary Resort hosts a revue of Broadway hits, Broadway at the Top—plus a view over the Magic Kingdom that will dazzle you even if the music doesn't always. As for the food, prime ribs are an especially good choice (entrées about $10 to $15). Seating is at 6 and 9:15 P.M. for the 7:45 and 11 P.M. shows; the entertainment charge is about $7.50 for adults and $3.75 for children.

The Biergarten at Epcot Center's Germany pavilion features a continuous show to entertain diners throughout the evening; it's complete with traditional German musicians, yodelers, and dancers. The fare here is hearty—everything from sauerbraten to potato dumplings. Entrées range from $7.25 to $13.50.

Plan to arrive 15 minutes or so before starting time, and allow enough time for transportation and parking. (Prices are subject to change and are taxable.)

---

crowded run-through of the Main Street Electrical Parade.)

WDW restaurants outside the Magic Kingdom are busiest in the evening between 7 and 9 P.M. Those in the Magic Kingdom are busiest between 5 and 7 P.M.

ABOUT DINNER RESERVATIONS

In most WDW restaurants, it's first come, first served. The lines that result can be avoided by eating early or late—or by choosing one of the handful of restaurants that accept dinner reservations. (Note that reservations are held for only 15 minutes.)

CONTEMPORARY RESORT: Gulf Coast Room (824-3684).

POLYNESIAN VILLAGE: Papeete Bay Verandah (824-1391) and Tangaroa Terrace (824-1361).

GOLF RESORT: Trophy Room (824-1484).

MAGIC KINGDOM: King Stefan's in Cinderella Castle. Reservations must be made in person at the restaurant on the day of the meal; go first thing after arrival in the Magic Kingdom.

WALT DISNEY WORLD VILLAGE: Empress Room aboard the *Empress Lilly* (828-3900); the Village Restaurant (828-3723); and Lake Buena Vista Club in the villa area (828-3735).

Or plan to take in the dinner show at the Top of the World in the Contemporary Resort, the Luau at the Polynesian, or the Hoop-Dee-Doo Musical Revue at Pioneer Hall—but note that *reservations for these activities must be made well in advance; some seatings sell out a year ahead!* No deposits are required, so there's no reason not to reserve early enough to avoid disappointment. (Call the CRO at 824-8000 for all dinner-show reservations.)

For dinner shows and supper seatings alike, you can book a table as soon as you get your confirmed reservation number if you're staying at WDW resorts; 45 days ahead if you're lodging at one of the Walt Disney World Village Hotel Plaza establishments and *only* if you have made your reservation through the CRO; and 30 days if you're putting up outside Walt Disney World. Empress Room reservations may be made 30 days in advance, no matter where you're staying, and Top of the World dinner reservations aren't available to anyone until 30 days before the dining date. In the case of dinner shows, if you can't get a place for an early performance, try for a later one (usually less heavily booked).

At Epcot Center, it's important to remember every establishment offers unique delights. If you didn't get dinner reservations in advance, don't despair. Try a dinner of tourtière (a Canadian pork pie) and maple syrup pie (for dessert) at Canada's atmospheric Le Cellier. Or sample Mexican specialties at Mexico's Cantina de San Angel (whose lagoon-side tables provide a fine view of the sun setting behind Epcot Center); or the skewered, grilled meats at Japan's Yakitori House. Cravings for more conventional fast foods will be satisfied at the Stargate Restaurant in CommuniCore East, at the Odyssey Restaurant near World of Motion and Mexico, and at the Liberty Inn in The American Adventure. The Odyssey Restaurant also serves more substantial, all-American dinner fare, as does the Sunrise Terrace in CommuniCore West. The Farmers Market, in The Land, offers a little bit of everything.

Other restaurants require reservations (procedures are outlined on page 163). Try not to miss The Good Turn restaurant's cheese bread, the Scotch eggs in the Rose & Crown, the salmon soufflé and the pastries at Les Chefs de France, and the Mexican turnip-and-orange compote at Mexico's San Angel Inn Restaurante. The Biergarten has lively dinner shows and Alfredo's features singing waiters.

SCOOPS, SUNDAES, AND SOFT SERVE

Happily one can now find sugar cones at WDW—albeit only at the Cone Shop on Main Street in the Magic Kingdom, the Farmers Market at Epcot Center, and the Ice Cream Parlour in the Village. And there's something about a hot, humid summer afternoon that makes all of these cooling treats seem especially appealing.

BY THE SCOOP

IN THE HOTELS: Pueblo Room at the Contemporary Resort. Peach brandy ice cream is also served at the Outer Rim in the Contemporary Resort.

South Seas Buffet and Coral Isle Cafe at the Polynesian Village Resort, passion-fruit ice cream at Papeete Bay Verandah at the Polynesian Village.

IN THE MAGIC KINGDOM: Liberty Tree Tavern, Liberty Square; and Town Square Cafe, Main Street.

AT EPCOT CENTER: The ice cream stand at Farmers Market in The Land.

WALT DISNEY WORLD VILLAGE: Lake Buena Vista Club restaurant and snack bar, and Village Restaurant.

CONES

Cone Shop, Main Street, Magic Kingdom; and the Village Ice Cream Parlour and Bake Shop, Walt Disney World Shopping Village. Six flavors each. Tangaroa Snack Isle, Polynesian Village. Farmers Market, Epcot Center.

ASSORTED SUPER SUNDAES

IN THE HOTELS: Gulf Coast Room (doused with Grand Marnier or with flambéed hot fudge) and Pueblo Room and Top of the World, at the Contemporary Resort.

Papeete Bay Verandah (with flambéed pineapple bits, served in a pineapple half), Tangaroa Snack Isle, Tangaroa Terrace, and Coral Isle Cafe, at the Polynesian Village.

Trophy Room, at the Golf Resort.

IN THE MAGIC KINGDOM: Sealtest Ice Cream Parlor and the Plaza Restaurant on Main Street.

WALT DISNEY WORLD VILLAGE: Fisherman's Deck and Steerman's Quarters, *Empress Lilly;* the Verandah Restaurant; and Village Ice Cream Parlour and Bake Shop.

Lake Buena Vista Club (with a special chunky Gold Brick chocolate sauce at lunchtime, and atop bananas Foster and cherries Jubilee at dinner).

SOFT SERVE

IN THE MAGIC KINGDOM: Round Table (with strawberry or blueberry melba sauce, chocolate sauce, or over brownies), Fantasyland; Fort Sam Clemens, Frontierland; Sunshine Tree Tavern (with a tangy frozen orange juice ripple), Adventureland; Fife and Drum, Liberty Square.

WALT DISNEY WORLD VILLAGE: Ice Cream Parlour and Bake Shop.

IN THE HOTELS: Fiesta Fun Center at the Contemporary Resort Hotel.

AT FORT WILDERNESS: Meadow and Settlement Trading Posts.

FRENCH-FRIED ICE CREAM

Trophy Room, Golf Resort.

LEMON SHERBET PUNCH

IN THE MAGIC KINGDOM: Liberty Tree Tavern, Liberty Square.

INTERNATIONAL TREATS

AT EPCOT CENTER: Specialties at L'Originale Alfredo di Roma Ristorante include Italian concoctions like spumoni and tortoni. For a Mexican treat, visit San Angel Inn Restaurante for helada con cajeta (vanilla ice cream with caramel topping).

A TIP FOR THE FINICKY: Soft serve tastes better than the scooped stuff. Frozen yogurt, served at Tomorrowland's Lunching Pad, in the Magic Kingdom, has the most flavor of all.

MOONLIGHT SERENADE

During summer months, guests can arrive at the Lake Buena Vista Club for dinner by boat. When calling for dinner reservations (828-3735), ask to be picked up at the WDW Village dock where you'll be greeted with a glass of champagne to enjoy during your complimentary boat ride.

LOUNGES

No one ever said that the Magic Kingdom's no-liquor policy means that all of the World is a teetotaller. Actually, some of WDW's tastiest offerings are liquid (and decidedly alcoholic), and some of its most entertaining places are its bars and lounges.

CONTEMPORARY RESORT: The watering holes here are sleek, with atmosphere aplenty.

Monorail Club Car: Near the elevators on the Grand Canyon Concourse, this long, skinny bar overlooking Bay Lake is a cozy, companionable sort of place for serious drinking. No entertainment but the company you bring.

Coconino Cove: On the Grand Canyon Concourse, just outside the Pueblo Room. Guests waiting to be seated can have drinks and Mexican snacks here, and watch the monorail glide in and out of the hotel. There's entertainment nightly.

Top of the World Lounge: Adjoining the Top of the World restaurant, this spacious room offers superb views over the Magic Kingdom. This is a good spot to watch the sunset and, when the park is open until midnight, the fireworks. Dash out onto the more easterly of the two observation decks nearby at 10:05 to see the Electrical Water Pageant blipping, bleeping, and glittering on Bay Lake below.

POLYNESIAN VILLAGE: The resort's Polynesian theme has inspired a whole raft of deceptively potent potables like the Blue Lagoon (creme de banana and blue curaçao), Seven Seas (fruit juice, grenadine, orange curaçao, and rum), Chi Chis (a standard piña colada made with vodka instead of rum), and WDW piña coladas (which include orange juice in addition to rum, pineapple, and coconut cream). There's even a special Polynesian Village nonalcoholic treat—the pink Lei-Lani, a delicious orange juice and strawberry mixture.

Barefoot Bar: Adjoining the swimming pool lagoon, serving soda, draft beer, piña coladas, frozen daiquiris, mai tais, and various other mixed drinks. Open from 11 A.M. until 10:30 P.M. in summer (to 5 P.M. in winter).

Tambu Lounge: Cozy and clublike, this lounge adjoining the Papeete Bay Verandah is open daily beginning at 11 A.M., and offers a menu of Polynesian-style appetizers and low-key entertainment nightly. A good spot for a quiet conversation. Open from 11 A.M. until midnight.

Captain Cook's Hideaway: Off the lobby of the Great Ceremonial House, this small, dark nook also has entertainment nightly. Open from 6:30 P.M. to 1:30 A.M.

GOLF RESORT: The **Players' Gallery,** adjoining the Trophy Room, with a view over the Magnolia golf course, serves an assortment of specialty drinks and cocktails—Double Eagles (Kahlua, Amaretto, and brandy with cream on the rocks), Birdies (creme de cacao, orange juice, and grenadine), Lateral Hazards (sangria, triple sec, and rum), and Strawberry Colada Bogeys (light rum, strawberries, pineapple juice, and cream of coconut).

FORT WILDERNESS CAMPGROUND: Beer and sangria are served in Pioneer Hall. For something stronger, take a blue-flagged watercraft to the Contemporary Resort or a gold-flagged watercraft to the Polynesian Village. Be sure to check the operating hours before boarding so that you don't miss the last trip back. Or, if you have a car, make the short drive to Walt Disney World Village.

WALT DISNEY WORLD VILLAGE: Some of WDW's best lounges are here.

Cap'n Jack's Oyster Bar: Agleam with copper, right on the water, this bar serves delicious strawberry margaritas, made with strawberry tequila and real strawberries. The nibbles of steamed clams, oysters, and seafood marinara are good enough for an entire meal.

Village Lounge: This boîte, comfortable as a living room, hosts top jazz musicians and is one of the World's best-kept secrets. There's a $5 minimum during busy periods (which does not apply to guests waiting for dinner at the Village Restaurant).

Baton Rouge Lounge: This spacious lounge on the main deck of the *Empress Lilly* is one of the liveliest spots in WDW, thanks to the quick, barbed tongue of comedian-banjoist Denny Zavett, who appears with the Riverboat Rascals, who play Dixieland and bluegrass between Zavett's sets. Specialty drinks are sold by the pitcher—things like Mississippi River Water, concocted of white creme de cacao, fruit juices, and blue curaçao; Huckleberry's Cooler, made with blackberry brandy, blue curaçao, and grape and citrus juices; and Scarlett O'Haras—Southern Comfort, cranberry juice, and a splash of lemon-lime flavoring. The Bayou chips—crunchy homemade potato chips sold by the basket—are delicious enough to make it easy to abandon dinner plans altogether. Open from 11 A.M.

The Empress Lounge: Almost as elegant as the Empress Room, whose guests this mahogany-paneled bar is meant to pamper before and after a meal. The Empress Lounge features a harpist who happens to look like Snow White. Aboard the *Empress Lilly*.

Starboard Lounge: On the starboard main deck of the *Empress Lilly*, this room offers an assortment of appetizers—sautéed crab meat, oysters and cherrystone clams on the half shell, to name a few—along with assorted sweet after-dinner drinks (Buena Vista Coffee, for instance, is laced with Amaretto and brandy and topped with whipped cream; Starboard Coffee includes Drambuie, brandy, Tia Maria, Grand Marnier, and a dollop of whipped cream).

Promenade Lounge: On the starboard Promenade Deck on the *Empress Lilly*, above the Starboard Lounge, this sitting area—with its old-fashioned wallpaper and paneled wainscoting—seems more like a Victorian parlor than a bar.

IN EPCOT CENTER: All restaurants, including some of the counter-service establishments, offer alcoholic beverages with meals. Restaurants such as The Good Turn in The Land and the San Angel Inn Restaurante have small bars at which patrons may wait for tables.

Then there are a few places that specialize in spiritous liquid refreshments:

Rose & Crown Pub & Dining Room: The pub section of this watering hole that's part of the United Kingdom pavilion is a veritable symphony of polished woods, brass, and etched glass. Beer is available along with a score of specialty drinks imported from the other side of the Atlantic.

Matsunoma Lounge: In addition to the exotic sake-based specialty drinks available here, this establishment offers a fine panoramic view over the whole of Epcot Center—including the World Showcase Lagoon with Spaceship Earth as a backdrop—one of the best vistas of the property that is available.

Biergarten: Just outside this restaurant in Germany there's a small shaded terrace where steins of beer and sausages are available.

MORE SPECIAL NIGHTTIME FUN

The Magic Kingdom, open late during several busy periods of the year, takes on additional dazzle after dark. In peak seasons, there's the Main Street Electrical Parade, a procession so spectacular that it alone is worth the trip to WDW—even though it's necessary to visit during a busy period in order to see it.

And Epcot Center is particularly lovely at night, when the lights sparkle on the Lagoon and Spaceship Earth is all aglow. But there are always a dozen or so other special happenings and events going on after dark throughout WDW.

FIREWORKS: During summers and holidays when the Magic Kingdom is open late, there are fireworks at 10 P.M. nightly. The show lasts just five minutes, but packs as much dazzle as those many times its length.

LASERPHONIC FANTASY: This show (during summer months and holidays when Epcot Center is open late) features laser lights, fireworks, and dancing water fountains which can be seen from any point on the promenade at 10 P.M.

ELECTRICAL WATER PAGEANT: Best seen from the nearest beach, this sparkling show is composed of a 1,000-foot-long string of illuminated floating creatures. Guest Services or City Hall can tell you when and where the Electrical Water Pageant can be seen—usually at 9:05 P.M. from the Polynesian, 9:45 P.M. from Fort Wilderness, 10 P.M. from the Contemporary Resort, and, during the hours that the Magic Kingdom is open late, at 9:35 P.M. from River Country and 10:20 P.M. from the park itself.

MARSHMALLOW MARSH EXCURSION: This entertainment—offered only during the summer—consists of a trip by canoe through the winding Fort Wilderness waterways, a hike along a footpath (for a few hundred feet) to a well-hidden campfire spot on the lakeshore, a merry sing-along, a story-telling fest, and a marshmallow roast. Cost is about $4, and reservations are required; to make them, appear in person on the day of the trip at the Pioneer Hall ticket booth, or call 824-2788. Depending on demand, the excursion may be open to resort guests only.

RIVER COUNTRY: This archetypical, all-American swimming hole is open until 10 P.M.—under the lights—during the summer, and crowds are minimal. River Country admission is $2 less for adults and $1 less for children, after 5 P.M.

CAMPFIRE PROGRAM: This event at Fort Wilderness, held nightly near the Meadow Trading Post at the center of the campground, features a sing-along, Disney movies, and cartoons.

DISNEY MOVIES: A good choice when feet refuse to take even one more step. Full-length Walt Disney feature films are shown nightly at the Contemporary Resort for WDW guests, in the theater near the Fiesta Fun Center—usually at 4:30, 7, and 9 P.M. Movies are also shown at the Fort Wilderness Campground every evening at the campfire.

TENNIS: The courts at the Contemporary Resort, the Golf Resort, and the Lake Buena Vista Club are open until 10 P.M. year round. (See *Sports*.)

MEETINGS AND CONVENTIONS

178 Accommodations
179 Facilities
180 After Hours

Among Walt Disney World's 20,000 employees, there are photographers and videotape experts, printers and computer wizards, carpenters and sign painters, specialty merchandise and floral designers and pyrotechnics specialists, even singers and dancers—and all of their talents and expertise are at the disposal of meeting planners. Just a single WDW account manager works with each individual meeting client to map out an overall conference plan; then the full corps of support forces is mobilized to make these ideas become reality. Only a single phone call is required when questions arise, no matter how many diverse areas may be involved.

The fact that the readers of *Meetings and Conventions* magazine have rated Walt Disney World among the nation's top meeting centers for many years suggests the quality of the meetings that this system can produce. While other meeting centers may outstrip Walt Disney World in some single area, the total meetings package—accommodations, food, service, amusements, and meeting facilities—has few equals. Between the *Contemporary Resort Hotel* and the Walt Disney World Cenference Center at Walt Disney World Village—where the bulk of meetings are held at WDW—there are facilities to handle television broadcasts, major press conferences, and virtually any other complex technical undertaking, including the sorts of multimedia shows that usually have to be contracted to outside firms at other meeting sites.

Sophisticated audio systems can be installed: When one meeting of chief executive officers required an individually controlled mike for each of its 65 attendees, the Disney sound men designed and executed an elaborate control grid just for that event. When another group requested a single-slab conference table to seat 30, Disney carpenters built one—right on the property—with only three days' notice. For delegates' leisure time, WDW offers special attractions that some 150 million people over the past dozen years have traveled from around the world to see—among them the Magic Kingdom and Epcot Center. Banquet entertainment is developed by the same creative staff that puts together the SRO shows at the Pioneer Hall and Diamond Horseshoe theaters. All of this puts WDW at the forefront of site choices for meetings requiring extensive support facilities and first-class frills.

WDW meetings are not for everyone, however. Groups who want to convene all day every day might do just as well to take their conventions to a site where participants won't be so sorely tempted by the beaches, the golf courses, and the Magic Kingdom. And while both entertainment and banquet prices at WDW are at least comparable to (and occasionally less than) those elsewhere, the overall package may be too costly for some economy-minded groups, since no discounts are given on room rates.

ACCOMMODATIONS

World Conference Center floor plan.

1 SYCAMORE 2 MAGNOLIA 3 JACARANDA 4 CYPRESS
7 SANDPIPER 6 SEA GULL 5 BLUE HERON

MEETING, BANQUET, & AUDIOVISUAL FACILITIES

Rooms for meetings and banquets are scattered all over the property, with the bulk concentrated at the Contemporary Resort Hotel (used mainly for large groups) and the Walt Disney World Conference Center (designed with small- and middle-sized meetings in mind). There are extensive audiovisual facilities at both sites.

CONTEMPORARY RESORT HOTEL: Most meeting facilities are located on the second floor of the Tower. The 11,968–sq. ft. Ballroom of the Americas, at the north end of the hotel, is the largest single facility, accommodating up to about 1,400 seated theater-style, or about 1,000 for a banquet. It can be divided into two smaller rooms, each with a capacity of about half the above numbers. The 8,777–sq. ft. Grand Republic Ballroom holds slightly fewer people; it can be split into three rooms ranging in size from 2,080 to 4,290 sq. ft. In addition, there are five other rooms nearby of 800 to 1,160 sq. ft. each; and on the 15th floor there are two others measuring 697 sq. ft. and 1,247 sq. ft. Both have wonderful panoramic views over the rest of the World.

CONFERENCE CENTER: This sleek cedar creation is located on the banks of Club Lake at Walt Disney World Village. It was designed expressly with small- and medium-size meetings and seminars in mind, and may be one of the most innovative structures of its type in existence. Four large rooms, each with its own light, sound, and projection systems, can be combined in a wide assortment of configurations, the largest comprised of 6,500 sq. ft., to seat 505 theater-style. In addition, there are three smaller meeting rooms, the 400–sq. ft. Sea Gull, the adjacent 460–sq. ft. Sandpiper (with which the Sea Gull can be combined), and the 805–sq. ft. Blue Heron—each with big lakeview windows, sophisticated lighting (which, among other things, automatically turns up the room's lights when the sun goes behind a cloud), and rearview projection screens that can be supplemented by AV equipment rented from Disney's own equipment pool. All seven rooms are extremely attractive; the chairs are comfortable enough for all-day sitting; and, despite the fact that you're just a 15-minute drive from the Magic Kingdom, the whole facility has a relaxed, away-from-it-all atmosphere.

OTHER BANQUET AND MEETING SPACE:
A smallish meeting could be arranged at the quiet but centrally located *Golf Resort Hotel,* using the 1,024–sq. ft. Tournament Room for meetings and individual hotel suites for cocktail receptions. Another option is the third deck of the *Empress Lilly* riverboat restaurant at Walt Disney World Village; dinner for as many as six dozen can be set

AND FACILITIES

up in the airy room known as the Skipper's Table, cocktails can be served at the polished bar of the adjacent Texas Lounge, and receptions for as many as 250 can be staged in both rooms and on the promenade decks outside. Larger quarters are available at the *Lake Buena Vista Club* across the lagoon. Conceivably, drinks could be served aboard the *Empress Lilly*, and then meeting attendees might cruise across the lagoon in canopied Flote Botes for dinner in the Lake Buena Vista Club's 2,275-sq. ft. Vista Room. The *Kingdom Queen* ferryboat also can be used to provide entertainment and dining space, while the smaller *Seminole* ferryboat can accommodate 225 people for a reception.

Still larger conventions are possible in Orlando—albeit outside Walt Disney World—at the Orange County Convention/Civic Center which opened in March 1983. It offers 150,00 sq. ft. of exhibit and meeting space. Details: Orlando/Orange County Convention Bureau; 9800 International Dr.; Orlando, FL 32819; 305-345-9800.

AUDIOVISUAL EQUIPMENT: Lecterns, microphones, projectors, viewers, screens, special lenses, tape recorders, videotape equipment, record players, lights, and sound equipment of virtually any type can be rented on a daily or per-use basis. In addition, technicians are available to record meetings, set up sound and lighting systems, and edit and splice film and tape.

LODGINGS

Large meetings use the rooms and suites at the *Contemporary Resort Hotel*, with overflow lodged at the *Polynesian Village Resort* and the *Golf Resort Hotel*. Smaller groups use the *Club Lake Villas*, the *Fairway Villas*, the *Vacation Villas*, or the *Treehouses*, just a couple of minutes' electric cart ride away from the Conference Center. The L-shaped rooms at the Club Lake Villas each have a patio and a wet bar, and a sitting area separate from the sleeping area.

All meeting-related and personal charges can be handled by individual invoices or on a single master bill, or billed to individual American Express and MasterCard credit cards. Note that the Disney organization requires all reservations to be confirmed 45 days in advance. And attendees who want to remain after the conclusion of a convention should book stayovers as soon as meeting plans are finalized, or risk finding no room at the inn. Some of these arrangements must be concluded as much as a year in advance. For more basic information about the WDW lodgings, consult *Transportation and Accommodations*.

AND MORE

Meeting planners who can't secure the dates of their choice at Disney-owned properties should be sure to look into the facilities at the Buena Vista Palace and at the Hilton at Walt Disney World Village. See our chapter *Transportation and Accommodations* for more detailed descriptions, then contact the hotels for specifics.

AFTER HOURS

One of the main attractions of Walt Disney World as a meeting site is the availability of ample banquet and entertainment space, plus post-meeting pastimes of a sort that just are not found in many other spots on earth. And where else in the world can your banquet table's floral centerpiece be surrounded by a ring of Mouseketeer hats that can be worn when a meeting gets a bit too serious?

ENTERTAINMENT: Normally, meeting planners choose one of several popular WDW theme parties, each performed by an all-Disney cast: The Fabulous Fifties, which revives the songs and dances of the decade using a spectacular a/v show presenting the fads of the era; America Is, a good-humored patriotic salute to "Mom, the Flag, and Apple Pie"; Vaudeville on Bourbon Street, featuring slapstick comedy along with a barbershop quartet, pearly band, honky-tonk piano, banjo duo, and Dixieland quartet; Taste of Americana, showcasing the best of American music and food; Celebrate It's A Musical World, an extravaganza of melodies from many lands—it's an international show with an enormous cast; and the folksy, down-home Country-and-Western Show. For large groups, it's also possible to stage a sort of moveable feast—a different party in each of several rooms, each festivity featuring the appropriate food (served buffet style) and entertainment. For these occasions, the Taste of Americana show is the best bet.

Anyone with a penchant for playing impresario (and the funds to pay the piper) can concoct a special affair-of-a-lifetime just by marshalling the resources of the Walt Disney World talent pool. One company, for instance, ended a clambake on the beach with a pyrotechnical display set off from a barge out on the lake—the company logo emblazoned in fireworks. Similarly, WDW chefs can be called upon to produce far more sophisticated menus than those normally offered. WDW is, above all, a special paradise for the creative meeting planner.

Children attending a meeting with their parents can be entertained by Disney movies; magicians, mimes, and caricature artists; rock bands; and hot-dogs-and-corn-on-the-cob banquets of their own. Or you can just use the Magic Kingdom as a nonpareil babysitter.

Disney liaison people can fill you in on all your choices and provide specific guidance.

AFTER-MEETING DIVERSIONS: Arrangements can be made for meeting guests to take advantage of just about everything in the WDW vacation inventory—River Country, the Magic Kingdom, Epcot Center, Discovery Island, horseback rides at Fort Wilderness, the three golf courses (and the Walt Disney World Golf Studio instructors), the tennis courts, and more—often at group rates. Account representatives can even set up golf and tennis tournaments.

FOR MORE INFORMATION: Contact Walt Disney World Sales; Box 40; Lake Buena Vista, FL 32830; 305-828-3200.

ORLANDO

183 Getting Around
184 What to Do
188 Where to Eat
191 Nightlife

The city of Orlando has become so closely identified with Walt Disney World that it's easy to forget that it's an important city in its own right, with its share of assets and problems just like any other sizable community in the country. Now boasting a population of about 135,000, it began as a campground for soldiers during the mid-nineteenth-century Seminole War; it is said to have been named for a sentry who sent out an alarm of an Indian attack, then died of wounds he sustained in the ensuing battle.

Later, a Philadelphian brought sugar cane to the area, but the agricultural venture failed, and cattlemen took over—the area is still one of the country's largest beef producers. Citrus is also big business in these parts; the acres around Clermont have more citrus groves than almost any other region of comparable size in the world.

Florida has long been known for its citrus production, but it has been the recent influx of major corporations establishing headquarters in Orlando that has provided the greatest impetus to the city's current commercial boom. Harcourt Brace Jovanovich was among the leaders in 1982, and Westinghouse, General Electric, and AT&T (among others) have quickly followed suit.

The city of Orlando is surrounded by small towns—among them Ocoee, Maitland, Windermere, Kissimmee, Fern Park, and Winter Park. The boom that all of these towns have enjoyed since the coming of Walt Disney World has left many of them crisscrossed by wide, treeless highways, and bordered by fast-food restaurants, used car lots, and other unbeautiful legacies of the modern commercial age. But Winter Park, Windermere, and Maitland are exceptions. There are neighborhoods where the lawns are large and green and dotted with palms or huge old live oaks, thickly veiled by Spanish moss. There the houses of gleaming white stucco are sprawling, with roofs of red-orange ceramic tile in the Spanish style. Just to go for a drive through this area can be a visual treat.

Orlando, Kissimmee, and the other communities are also home to many attractions other than those contained inside Walt Disney World, and many restaurants in these surrounding towns are well worth investigating. This chapter will steer you to many of them. (Unless otherwise noted, all phone numbers are in the area code 305.)

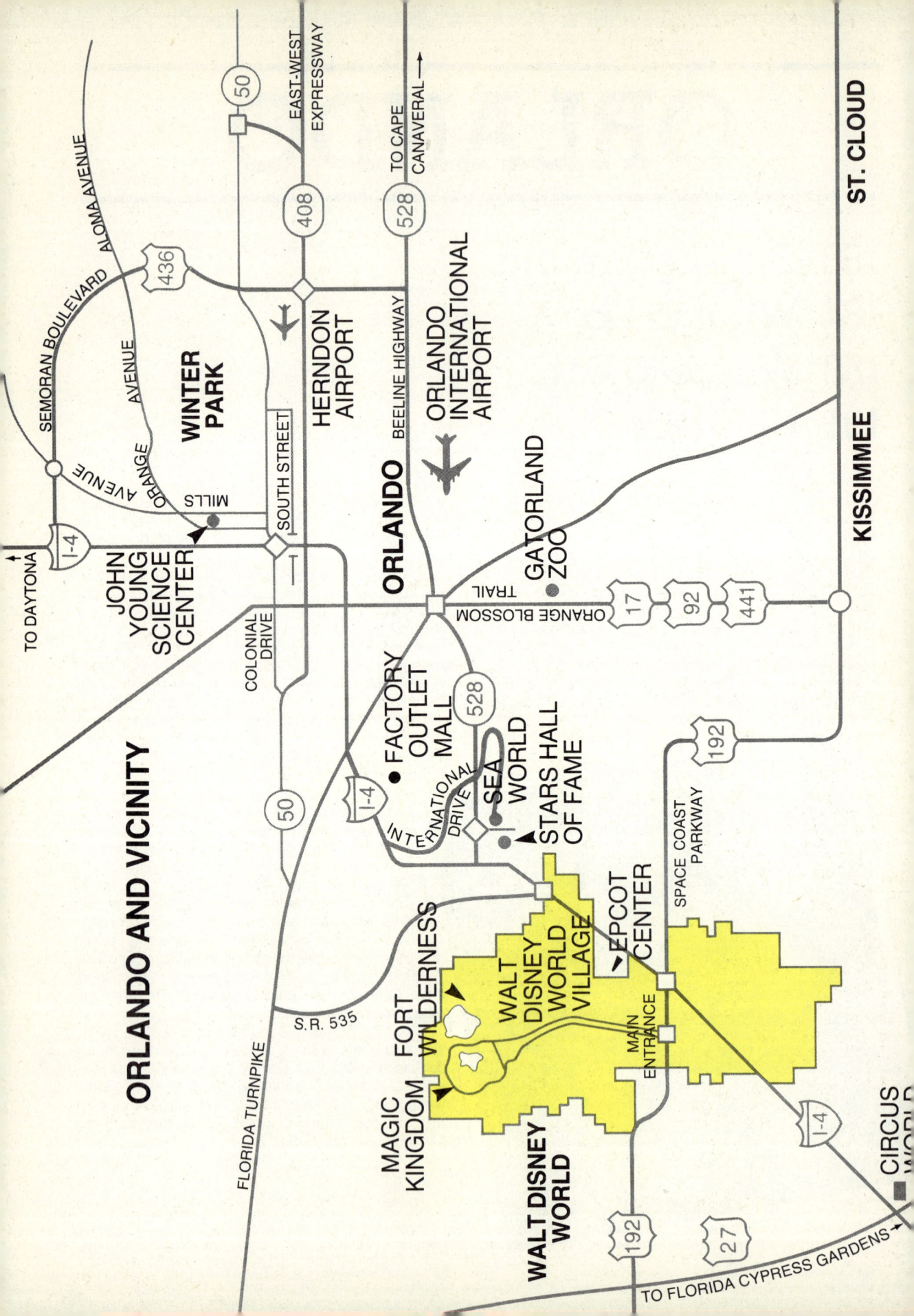

GETTING AROUND

Unless you spend all your time inside Walt Disney World, it's most convenient to have a car. (For a description of Orlando geography and the interlocking surrounding roads, see "Orlando-area Highways" in *Transportation and Accommodations*.)

CAR RENTALS: Those who don't bring the family car can rent one at any one of some 60 car rental agencies—Orlando has one of the largest number of fleet vehicles of any city in the nation—and the rates (most on an unlimited mileage basis) are relatively modest. When shopping around for the best car rental deal, keep in mind that rates right at the airport are usually higher than at car rental agencies elsewhere in town. Also be sure to include the cost of collision damage insurance in your calculations, for it can vary enough from agency to agency to make a substantial difference in the cost of a rental lasting a week or more. (Note that most vacation packages that include a rental car do not include collision damage insurance; if you opt not to take it, the agency will require a large deposit—either in cash or by credit card.) Many firms allow you to drop a rental car elsewhere in Florida at no extra charge; if that matters to you, be sure to ask. Eastern Airlines "Super 7" packages include a rental car, and National Car Rental Co.—the "official" car rental firm of WDW and the only car rental facility on the property—offers special deals.

The larger Orlando-area car rental firms include Alamo (toll-free 800-327-9633; or, from Florida, 800-462-5266); Avis (toll-free 800-331-1212; from Oklahoma, 800-482-4554); Budget (toll-free 800-527-0700; from Texas, 800-442-0700; or, in Dallas, 214-980-0400); Hertz (toll-free 800-654-3131; from Oklahoma, 800-522-3711; or, from Oklahoma City, 405-755-4424); General Rent-A-Car (toll-free 800-327-7607; from Florida, 800-432-0659); and National (toll-free 800-328-4567; or, from Minnesota, 800-862-6064).

BUS TRANSPORTATION: City buses are not nearly adequate for vacationers' purposes, but a number of firms provide transportation from hotels all over the city to the major attractions—not only WDW, but also Circus World, Cypress Gardens, Church Street Station, Stars Hall of Fame, Sea World, the Altamonte Mall, and the like. You don't have to worry about parking, and frequent service is provided. Fares are high enough that those who plan to do much traveling around will find it less expensive to rent a car. Gray Line and Rabbit are among the big tour operators; American Sightseeing Tours has service from the airport to many area hotels. Hotel desks can provide up-to-the-minute details.

TAXIS: Several firms provide service, among them the City Cab Company (422-4561), Yellow Cab Company (423-5566), and Ace Taxi (859-7514). The normal price of a cab ride from the Orlando International Airport to Walt Disney World is about $30.

LIMOUSINE SERVICE: The Airport Limousine Service (859-4667) is conveniently located at the Orlando airport. Service to the WDW-area hotels is $7 to $9 per person.

WHAT TO DO

Though it has no beaches, the Orlando area is so full of natural attractions it would be easy to spend a whole vacation here, even if there were not a single man-made attraction in sight. Meandering streams, like Reedy and Shingle creeks, in the few remaining still-wild areas make for fine flat-water canoeing; big lakes like Tohopekaliga, the state's third-largest, are known Florida-wide for their bass fishing action, and many largemouth fishing tournaments have been staged here. And the sugary-sand beaches and the placid surf of the Gulf Coast are only about 80 miles away, while the hard, wide beaches and the pounding waves of the Atlantic, only about 60 miles distant, can be reached by car in just an hour.

Add to that an assortment of golf courses, tennis courts, and all manner of other man-made attractions—not to mention Walt Disney World itself—and it can become fairly difficult not to hit upon a plan of action that satisfies every visitor's vacation desires.

BALLOON TRIPS: A great way to experience the Central Florida scene is to float above its pinewoods and farmlands and enjoy the beautiful skyscape. The ride is the smoothest imaginable; it's absolutely delightful—and it's like nothing you've ever tried before. Two companies that offer such lighter-than-air ascensions are Phineas Phogg's—an establishment at Church Street Station (described below in the "Nightlife" section of this chapter) and Orange Blossom Balloons, Inc. Weather permitting, balloons go up early in the morning, before the ground breezes begin to stir. For the Phineas Phogg ride, passengers meet at Church Street Station and return about four hours later. The fee (about $95 per person) includes a champagne brunch comprised of cheese, bread, and fruit—plus gifts of assorted trinkets. Reservations, which are required, can be made at the Church Street Station antique store, or by phone at 422-2434. Orange Blossom Balloons, Inc. offers an equally spectacular experience (complete with a fancy breakfast after the flight) for the same all-inclusive price—which includes hotel pick-up. Reservations, as well as a deposit, are necessary. Contact them at 10511 Gardenwood Rd., Orlando, FL 32821; 855-5632. Advice: wear trousers and comfortable shoes.

CATTLE AUCTIONS: Before Kissimmee took to calling itself the Gateway Community to Walt Disney World, its main claim to fame was as the "Cow Capital of the South" because of the extensive cattle industry in the surrounding area. That business is still flourishing, as any Sunday drive along the narrow streets and county highways around Kissimmee will demonstrate. The live cattle auctions that take place at 1 P.M. every Wednesday at the Kissimmee Livestock Market (on S.R.-527 north) are as full of Stetsons and cowboy boots, blue jeans and cigar-chomping cattle dealers as ever. It's worth a visit. Details: Kissimmee—St. Cloud Convention & Visitors Bureau; Box 2007; Kissimmee, FL 32742; 847-5000.

CIRCUS WORLD: A 1982 issue of *Tampa* magazine rated Circus World as Florida's third-best tourist attraction (behind WDW and Busch Gardens), and it does boast features that even Walt Disney World doesn't. The multimillion-dollar theme park is on 850 acres southwest of Orlando at I-4 and U.S.-27. There's the Cinema Circus, which uses a you-are-there system called IMAX and a six-story-high movie screen to show how it feels to perform on a high wire, somersault through the air on a flying trapeze, work with the big cats, or put elephants through their paces. There's a wonderful display of miniature circus models and circus memorabilia, worthy of a museum (Chicago's celebrated Museum of Science and Industry mounted a special exhibition for just such a collection only a few years ago). Kids can have their faces made up as clowns, complete with whiteface and red noses. You can ride elephants, and feed and play with baby animals. There's an open-air Great Western Stampede and Aqua Circus, a high-wire acrobatic diving show. A circus spectacular features performing elephants and several first-rate acts, and the Be-A-Star Circus (perhaps most fun of all) gives audience volunteers (strapped into safety harnesses) the chance to fly on a trapeze and walk the high wire.

Not to mention the midway where you can compete in games of chance, and, where you can get jostled and jolted until your knees turn to jelly on an array of thrill rides. The Flying Daredevil—a new-style roller coaster that lurches into a 50-foot drop, zooms through a 360-degree loop, climbs to a 50-foot-high platform, pauses, and then zooms backward through the loop and back to the starting point—leaves even dedicated thrill-ride lovers a bit jangled. A recent addition here is Jumbo the Giant Wheel, a sixteen-story-high Ferris wheel.

At press time, admission was $12.95 for adults ($10.95 for children under 12; under 3, free), and hours were 9 A.M. to 6 P.M. Details: Circus World; Box 800; Orlando, FL 32802; 422-0643 or 813-424-2421.

FISHING: Bass anglers make a big deal about Florida's third-largest lake, Tohopekaliga—which is full of the kind of shoreline weed beds, reeds, grass, cattails, and other vegetation that make fine feeding grounds for lunkers; the record catch stands at 16 pounds, 8 ounces. There are several fishing camps where boats can be rented and bait purchased; the Kissimmee–St. Cloud Convention and Visitors Bureau (Box 2007; Kissimmee, FL 32742; 847-5000) can send a list.

FLORIDA FESTIVAL: This multipeaked tent full of shops and eateries is a good place to visit in combination with Sea World (its parent operation just across the narrow road), either for lunch or for dinner after a day of watching sea creatures and water-skiers. The boutiques stock merchandise that tends toward the trinkety, but the food stands offer a variety of dishes like fried chicken; tacos and burritos; conch

11:30 P.M. daily. No admission charge. Details: Florida Festival; 7007 Sea World Dr.; Orlando, FL 32821; 351-3600.

FLORIDA CYPRESS GARDENS: It's said that a traveler would have to visit 70 countries at different times of year to see all the plants and flowers that can be viewed in a single day at this 223-acre attraction, developed in the mid-1930s. The Original Gardens, with their elaborate plantings of some 8,000 species (including 27 varieties of palm)—best seen on foot along meandering pathways or on electric-motored boat rides for which there's a slight additional charge—are as lush and lovely as ever. The Gardens' water-ski shows are also thrilling, with athletes skiing barefoot and backward, performing graceful water ballets and assorted stunts, and swooping high above the crowd in hang gliders. In 1980, after 44 years of operation, two new areas were added: the Living Forest (where there are displays of various exotic animal species, live shows featuring birds and alligators, a walk through a large aviary, and areas where youngsters can cuddle the llama, pat the bunny, and hitch a ride on a 300-pound tortoise) and Southern Crossroads, an assortment of shops, restaurants, and theaters (for magic shows and a you-are-there sort of movie). The most recent addition here is Kodak's revolving Island in the Sky—with spectacular views from 150 feet up. You may be shopped out by the time you get here from WDW, but Cypress Gardens, lovely as it is, is well worth a day's visit. Be sure to call ahead to find out about any special events that may be coming up here at the time of your visit; hang-gliding competitions, car meets, water-ski championships, and various other events frequently scheduled here are often worth a detour. At press time, operating hours were 8 A.M. to dusk daily, and admission fee was $10.50 ($7 for children under 12; under 6, free). Details: Florida Cypress Gardens (Orlando office); 5750 Major Blvd.; Orlando, FL 32805; 351-6606.

GATORLAND ZOO: Good for a couple of hours and an eyeful of literally thousands of alligators ranging in length from about eight inches (the newborns) to fifteen feet (the three-quarters-of-a-ton elders of the clan). An assortment of snakes is also on view. Some of the alligators can be fed, and some of the snakes can be handled. Located between Kissimmee and Orlando on U.S. 17-92-441, about 20 minutes from the WDW main gates. At press time, operating hours were 8 A.M. to 7:30 P.M. daily in summer (to 6 P.M. in winter), and admission was $4 ($3 for children under 12; under 3, free). Details: Gatorland Zoo; 14501 S. Orange Blossom Trail; Orlando, FL 32821; 855-5496.

chowder; gyros; fresh, steamed, and fried seafood; spareribs; oysters on the half shell; alligator; hearts of palm (aka swamp cabbage); and more. Al E. Gator's, the only full-service restaurant on the property, serves gator, conch, flounder, and such. Stay around afterward for drinks and live entertainment (the same group of banjo players, guitarists, and singers that keeps things moving at the Sea World water-ski show), and you have one of Orlando's more amusing evenings. Open from 11:30 A.M. to

LOCH HAVEN ART CENTER: Orlando's art museum has permanent displays of paintings and sculpture, as well as frequent special exhibits. The Orlando Science Center (described below) is nearby. At press time, hours were 10 A.M. to 5 P.M. from Tuesday through Friday, from noon on Saturday, and from 2 P.M. on Sunday. Free. Details: Loch Haven Art Center; 2416 N. Mills Ave.; Orlando, FL 32803; 896-4231.

MYSTERY FUN HOUSE: Wavy mirrors, a mirror-maze, crazy ladders, and more—all fine for a couple of hours on a rainy day when youngsters are really stir crazy. Located near the Court of Flags and the Sheraton Towers in the Florida Center area, eight miles from the WDW main gate. At press time, admission was $4.95 ($3.95 for children 4 through 12; under 4, free); hours were 10 A.M. to 11 P.M. daily. Details: Mystery Fun House; 5767 Major Blvd.; Orlando, FL 32819; 351-3359.

SEA WORLD: Imagine a fine big-city aquarium. Then add plenty of greenery and some water-skiers, whales, dolphins, sea lions, and sea otters (all performing to hopelessly corny scripts)—and you have a fair idea of what Sea World is all about. The Shamu Experience show reveals the 4,000-lb. black-and-white killer whale in balletic leaps and rolls, in the company of a pair of sprightly dolphins. The Shark Encounter exhibit features an amazing film that includes a sequence depicting a savage sharks' feeding frenzy; there's also a waterskiing show, a seal-and-otter show, the Cap'n Kids' World playground, and Undersea Fantasy that teaches all about coral reefs. Best of all, perhaps, are the feeding pools, where you can toss fish to sea lions and sea otters. Large and small aquariums displaying undersea life from around the world, and exhibits that tell you about tide-pool life, North American river otters, and walruses, are also on view. There's also the Hawaiian Village restaurant, which offers a Polynesian-style menu. There are several refreshment spots on the property, but it's more fun to amble (or bus) across the road to the Florida Festival, a multipeaked tent full of small boutiques and kiosks where you can buy foods indirectly indigenous to Florida—Cuban, Spanish, Italian, and Florida "cracker" specialties (such as alligator, which tastes a bit like a cross between chicken and fish). At press time, park admission was $12.95 ($10.95 for children under 12; no charge for those under 3), and operating hours were 9 A.M. to 7 P.M. daily in fall, winter, and spring (with extended hours during peak holiday seasons), 8:30 A.M. to 9 P.M. in summer. Gates close daily one hour before the park itself. Guided tours are available at a slight additional charge. The park is located at the intersection of I-4 and the Bee Line Expressway, 12 miles southwest of Orlando and a few minutes north of Walt Disney World. Details: Sea World of Florida; 7007 Sea World Dr.; Orlando, FL 32821; 351-3600.

STARS HALL OF FAME: The world's largest wax museum brings a bit of Hollywood to Central Florida. Located one block from Sea World in a 61,000-sq. ft. building east of I-4, it maintains billboards all along the highway; and visitors come to see the more than

100 "sets" that show off stars at memorable moments in their careers—Shirley Temple in a scene from the 1934 film *Bright Eyes*; Lionel, Ethel, and John Barrymore in the 1932 *Rasputin and the Empress*; Mary Pickford and Douglas Fairbanks in the 1929 *Taming of the Shrew*; and Greta Garbo and John Gilbert in *Queen Christina* (1933), to name a few. Mae West, Rudolph Valentino, W. C. Fields, Fred Astaire and Ginger Rogers, Clark Gable and Vivien Leigh, Edward G. Robinson, Elizabeth Taylor, and many more are all immortalized in wax here, looking fairly true to life (some more so than others, though great art it's not). A multi-media show, the Rock 'n Roll Time Machine, highlights the fads and fashions of the past 25 years. A cafeteria, a games area, gift shops, and snack bars provide other diversions—usually enough to fill up a couple of hours. Wheelchairs are available; parking is free; and bilingual information is available. At press time, operating hours were 10 A.M. to 10 P.M. daily (box office closes at 8:30 P.M.), and admission was $7.95 ($5.95 for children under 12; those under 4, free). Details: Six Flags' Stars Hall of Fame; 6825 Starway Dr.; Orlando, FL 32821; 351-1120.

WET 'N WILD: Walt Disney World's River Country may be the archetypal all-American swimming hole, all trees and clean-and-clear lake water. But this latter-day version of the chlorinated, concrete-paved, and shadeless municipal swimming pool may seem more familiar to many visitors, and among connoisseurs of water slides, Wet 'n Wild gets top marks. This is the place to explore the water slide in all its manifestations. There's the Kamikaze, an undulating, 300-foot-long slide that sends you into the water at cruising speed; the three-story Waterflumes slideways; the twisting and turning 60-foot-high Corkscrew, which ends by shooting you into a mystery tunnel; the Banzai Boggan, a gut-wrenching water roller coaster. Raging Rapids is a 450-foot rafting adventure, with whirlpools and wind and rain tunnels. A ski tow ride, a superspeed slide, a huge surf lagoon where you can ride the big waves on air mattresses, a simple swimming pool, a shallow area where you can splash around in a fountain and sit underneath a waterfall, a bubble machine that makes the water feel like whipped cream, and a beach round out the aquatic offerings. The place is jammed most afternoons in summer, and there are lines for all the slides. So unless you're going to sunbathe, you may enjoy yourself more in the evening. Special low rates are available. Towels and rafts are available for rent on the spot, but it's best to bring your own. Hours vary from season to season; admission fee at press time was $9.50 ($7.50 for children under 13; under 3, free). Located on International Drive. Details: Wet 'n Wild; 6200 International Dr.; Orlando, FL 32819; 351-3200.

ORLANDO SCIENCE CENTER: Located near the Arts Center in Loch Haven Park, this "hands-on" museum has special science exhibits, a Discovery Room for youngsters, and the John Young Planetarium that stages not only star shows (in the afternoons), but also elaborate light shows that are big favorites of the teenage set. At press time, hours were 9 A.M. to 5 P.M. from Monday through Thursday, 9 A.M. to 9 P.M. on Friday, noon to 9 P.M. on Saturday, and noon to 5 P.M. on Sunday; admission was $2 ($1.50 for children under 18 and senior citizens over 55; those under 5, free). Details: Orlando Science Center; 810 E. Rollins St.; Orlando, FL 32803; 896-7151.

WINTER PARK: This upper-crust community about a half-hour's drive north of Walt Disney World is full of one-of-a-kind restaurants (described in "Where to Eat," below) where expensive meals are the stock in trade. The Langford Resort Hotel offers a handsome and informative little walking-tour guide, available at the hotel for the asking. It includes stops at a number of the small museums here that you might want to visit on your own, among them the following:

Morse Gallery of Art: Houses a remarkable collection of the work of the stained glass artist Louis Comfort Tiffany—windows, lampshades and vases, drinking glasses, desk sets, and dishes, many of them from Laurelton Hall (Tiffany's Oyster Bay, Long Island, summer home, which burned to the ground in 1957). The works of John LaFarge, Frank Lloyd Wright, Rene Lalique, Emile Galle, and Victor Durand, a few of Tiffany's contemporaries, are also on display. At press time, hours were Tuesday through Saturday, from 9:30 A.M. to 4 P.M., Sunday from 1 P.M. to 4 P.M. (closed Mondays, Christmas, New Year's, Thanksgiving, and July 4); and admission was $2.50 ($1 for children and students). Details: Morse Gallery of Art; 133 E. Welbourne Ave.; Winter Park, FL 32789; 645-5311.

Beal-Maltbie Shell Museum: Some 100,000 species of shells—nearly 2,000,000 shells in all—assembled between 1888 and 1945, and added to since then by Cocoa Beach resident Dr. James H. Beal—are displayed in this red-tile-roofed building on the pretty Rollins College campus. At press time, hours were 10 A.M. to 4 P.M. from Monday to Friday, and admission fee was $1 (50¢ for children under 13; under 6, free). Details: Beal-Maltbie Shell Museum; Rollins College; Winter Park, FL 32789; 646-2364.

SHOPPING: If Walt Disney World Shopping Village doesn't wear out your wallet, the Orlando area has three major shopping malls that will be happy to finish the job. The Altamonte Mall (½ mile east of I-4 on S.R.-436 in Altamonte Springs) is a vast shopping complex featuring four major department stores—Jordan Marsh, Burdine's, Sears, and Robinson's. Fashion Square (3201 East Colonial Drive in Orlando) has Sears, Robinson's, and Burdine's, among many other shops. Colonial Plaza Mall (East Colonial Drive at Bumby Street) houses about a hundred stores, including a Woolworth's, Ivey's, and a branch of Jordan Marsh.

Factory outlets: Among the several in the Orlando area are the Danskin Factory Outlet at the Interstate Mall in Altamonte Springs, which stocks leotards, tights, skirts, tops, and more in women's and children's sizes (339-3840); just north of there on S.R.-436, at Casselberry Square, in Casselberry, there's the Polly Flinders Outlet, which features savings of up to 60% on the kind of high-quality hand-smocked dresses that make little girls look like little girls (830-1310); and there's the Dansk Factory Outlet at 7000 International Drive in Orlando (351-2425). There is also a new mall entirely devoted to factory outlet shops. It includes everything from clothing and sporting goods to books and records to jewelry and cosmetics—and all merchandise is discounted approximately 25 to 75 percent off normal retail prices. There are more than 70 shops under one roof, and food and refreshments are also available. The Factory Outlet Mall is located at 5401 West Oakridge Road, just north of International Drive (352-9600).

WHERE TO EAT

Orlando is not one of those cities like New Orleans or New York that gets especially high marks for food. As recently as ten years ago, Central Florida was almost entirely rural; away from downtown Orlando, much of the area still is. That means that steak houses are still among the fanciest places to celebrate a birthday or an anniversary; that most French and continental restaurants offer the kind of buttery, creamy, complicated concoctions that the lighter, more contemporary French cooking known as *nouvelle cuisine* made passé in more cosmopolitan centers; and that the differences between fish fresh out of the sea and fish that has been frozen is not as widely appreciated as might be expected in a town so close to both the Gulf of Mexico and the Atlantic Ocean.

Nonetheless, the growth of the city has brought chefs here from all over the world, and the variety and the quality of Orlando restaurant meals has improved considerably during the last decade, so that now—while there's little of the kind of subtly sophisticated cooking available in the world's gastronomic centers—just plain good food is abundant, and first-class mealtime experiences, ones that derive their enjoyment as much from atmosphere as from food, are more than easy to find. A selection of the best spots follows.

As an indication of what you should expect to spend for a meal, we've classified restaurants as **expensive** (lunches over $10, dinners over $30), **moderate** (lunches from about $8 to $10, dinners from $15 to $30), and **inexpensive** (lunches under $8, dinners under $15). These prices are for an average meal for two, not including drinks, taxes, or tips. Operating hours were correct at press time; but it's advisable to call in advance just to make sure that the restaurant will be open when you arrive. Acceptance of credit cards is signaled after each listing with AX = American Express; CB = Carte Blanche; DC = Diners Club; MC = MasterCard; and V = Visa.

JORDAN'S GROVE: The building is an immaculately restored old house and the food is American, done imaginatively. The menu varies from day to day, usually including two ambitious dishes each of red meat, fish, fowl, veal, and pasta, as well as appetizers, soups, salads, and desserts. Specialties include roast lamb with a garlic-lemon sauce, spinach fettuccine with walnuts and gouda cheese, and a lasagna made of pasta, seafood, and mousseline of shrimp. Open from 11:30 A.M. to 2:30 P.M. Tuesday through Friday, and from 6:30 to 11 P.M. Tuesday through Sunday. Brunch 11:30 to 2:30 Sunday. Reservations required. AX, CB, DC, MC, V. 1300 S. Orlando Ave., Maitland; 628-0020. Expensive.

LE CORDON BLEU: Almost every Orlando food fancier has his favorite Winter Park dining spot, and this one gets a good share of votes for its renditions of locally popular specialties like artichoke bottoms filled with crab meat and glazed with Mornay sauce; snails in garlic butter; rack of lamb; chicken in wine sauce; and duck à l'orange. A platter of fresh vegetables is listed among the house specialties for vegetarians. Open from 11:30 A.M. to 2:30 P.M. Monday through Friday and 5:30 to 11 P.M. Monday through Saturday. Reservations accepted. AX, CB, DC, MC, V. 537 W. Fairbanks, Winter Park; 647-7575. Expensive.

LIMEY JIM'S: A favorite of many Orlando residents for a special night on the town. Rack of lamb, veal vignerone, prime ribs, fresh Florida pompano, and chicken with lobster are the specialties. Open from 6 to 11 P.M. daily for dinner. Reservations accepted. AX, CB, DC, MC, V. At the Hyatt Orlando, at 6375 W. Space Coast Pkwy., Kissimmee; 396-1234 from Kissimmee, or 239-4100 from Orlando. Expensive.

MAISON & JARDIN: Locally nicknamed the "Mason Jar," this is an elegant place with high ceilings and white arches, widely spaced tables, and vast windows that take in the formal gardens that surround the mansion building in which meals are served. Appetizers include mushrooms thermidor, escargots in garlic butter, and blinis à la Russe (with caviar). The many meat, fish, and fowl entrees are equally ambitious. Steaks are available with or without sauces (though this is definitely not a steak house). Open for dinner Tuesday through Saturday from 6:30 to 10:30 P.M. and on Sunday from 6 to 9:30 P.M., and for brunch on Sunday from 11 A.M. to 2 P.M. Reservations accepted. AX, CB, DC, MC, V. 430 S. Wymore Rd., Altamonte Springs; 862-4410. Expensive.

PARK PLAZA GARDENS: With gardenlike awnings, skylights, and lush greenery, this is one of the two prettiest eating spots in Winter Park (the other is La Belle Verriere, which has a collection of stained glass as spectacular as its food is disappointing). Park Plaza Gardens offers consistently rich concoctions of seafood, fowl, and meat, liberally sauced with cream, butter, and herbs. Open for lunch from 11:30 A.M. to 3 P.M. daily, and for dinner from 6 to 10 P.M. Sunday through Thursday and to 11 P.M. on Friday and Saturday. Reservations accepted for dinner only. AX, CB, DC, MC, V. 319 Park Ave. S., Winter Park; 645-2475. Expensive.

SPINELLI'S: The place to go for delicious Italian food. Northern Italian as well as continental cuisine, served in two dining rooms—one formal, one more casual (but no shorts). Veal, beef, and chicken specialties include saltimbocca and a chicken breast and crabmeat dish called pollo Spinelli. Lobster is also served. Open Monday through Friday for lunch from 11:30 A.M. to 2 P.M. For dinner, open Monday through Saturday 6 P.M. to 10 P.M., and on Sunday from 5 to 9 P.M. Reservations suggested. AX, CB, DC, MC, V. 1200 Pennsylvania Ave., St. Cloud; 892-2435. Expensive.

CHARLIE'S BLUE CRAB: This dining spot is spiffily outfitted in brass and polished wood. The waiters here wear black tie. But don't worry, diners needn't dress formal. The specialty is mesquite-grilled fresh fish, and there are also crab cakes, fried shrimp, steamed lobster, clam chowder, and oysters, both iced and sautéed—practically everything you can imagine in the way of seafood, and all of it skillfully prepared. Open 11:30 A.M. to 10:30 P.M. daily. No reservations. AX, MC, V. 2415 Aloma Ave., Winter Park; 677-7352. Moderate.

AL E. GATOR'S: This full-service restaurant in the Florida Festival, opposite Sea World, features foods popular throughout Florida, and the menu lists such dishes as cracked conch chowder, stuffed flounder, crab quiche, and mango muffins. Reuben sandwiches are fixed with swamp cabbage (aka hearts of palm), and alligator meat—which tastes a bit like chicken and a bit like fish—is on the menu. The deep-fried potato skins alone are worth a trip. Open from 11:30 A.M. to 10:30 P.M. Sunday through Thursday, to 11 P.M. on Friday and Saturday. Reservations accepted. AX, CB, DC, MC, V. 7007 Sea World Blvd., Orlando; 351-3326. Moderate.

BARNEY'S STEAKHOUSE: The salad bar has 30 entrees, but the big sellers are steaks, prime ribs, and seafood. Voted Orlando citizens' favorite steak house in the 1983 Orlando *Sentinel* reader survey. Open for dinner from 5 to 11 P.M. daily. Reservations accepted only for eight or more. AX, CB, DC, MC, V. 1615 E. Colonial Dr., Orlando; 896-6864. Moderate.

CASA D'ANTONIO'S: An unprepossessing, dimly lit restaurant done in varying shades of red. The food is hearty southern Italian (lasagna, spaghetti, stuffed shells, baked ziti, and such), with good red sauce. This is the stereotypical Italian restaurant according to most of America. Open from 5 to 10 P.M. daily except Sunday. Reservations accepted. AX, MC, V. 1336 Orange Ave., Winter Park; 629-1139. Moderate.

FREDDIE'S STEAK AND SEAFOOD HOUSE: This clubby, very masculine eating spot north of Winter Park (in Fern Park) attracts more than its share of male conventioneers and other big meat eaters for its selection of steaks and prime ribs. But the seafood, particularly the fresh pompano and grouper, has its local fans as well, and Orlando residents often drive here to celebrate something special. Open for dinner only, daily except Sundays from 4:30 P.M. until 1:30 A.M. Reservations accepted. AX, CB, DC, MC, V. 603 U.S.-17-92, Fern Park; 339-3265. Moderate.

LA CANTINA: The decor is fairly nondescript, but the steaks are huge and usually good, and there are Italian specialties as well—veal parmigiana, lasagna, and spaghetti. Many of the Disney executives from California make a beeline for the place when they get to town. Locals also keep it jammed, and the wait for a table sometimes stretches to as long as an hour—except in the early evening. Open Tuesday through Thursday from 5 to 10:30 P.M., to 11:30 P.M. on Friday and Saturday (closed on Sunday and Monday). No reservations accepted. AX, MC, V. 4721 E. Colonial Dr., Orlando; 894-4491. Moderate.

LILI MARLENE'S AVIATORS PUB AND RESTAURANT: One of two eating spots in the Church Street Station complex, Lili Marlene's is less notable for its food (though the nutty, earthy flavor of the crisply French fried baked potato skins, now offered only at lunch, will haunt you for weeks afterward) than for the decor—high paneled and beamed ceilings, stained-and-leaded glass windows, ceiling fans, stunning chandeliers, oak pews and round and square tables, wide-planked wooden floors, and a scattering of model airplanes throughout. The long, polished, and mirrored bar is more splendid still. Fish, steaks, and chicken are available. Open for lunch from 11 A.M. to 4 P.M. daily, and from 5:30 P.M. to midnight daily for dinner. No reservations accepted. AX, MC, V. 129 W. Church St., in Church Street Station, Orlando; 422-2434. Moderate.

TWO FLIGHTS UP: Hefty and unusual sandwiches, unusual entrees (chicken, fish, beef, vegetables), terrific meal-sized salads. And the specialty here is veal. Liza Minelli loved the place when she was in town; the high noise level, the fanciful food, and the high-tech decor make it about as New York–trendy as the Orlando area gets. Open Monday through Saturday from 11:30 A.M. to 2 A.M. Reservations accepted for large parties. AX, DC, MC, V. 329 Park Ave. S., Winter Park; 644-9868. Moderate.

GARY'S DUCK INN: The theme at this big restaurant—which has nothing at all to do with duck—is nautical; the menu offers plenty of seafood—shrimp, lobster, scallops, and various seafood platters. And the portions are large, so this is a fine spot for families. Open from 11:30 A.M. to 10 P.M. Sunday through Friday, and from 5 to 11 P.M. on Saturday. No reservations accepted. AX, MC, V. 3974 S. Orange Blossom Trail, Orlando; 843-0270. Moderate to inexpensive.

BEE LINE RESTAURANT: Doctors and lawyers, construction workers and tourists, all manage to find their way to this casual, hard-to-find Tex-Mex cafe. The tacos are the best in town, and the guacamole is great. The place seats about 100, and there's hardly ever a wait. Open for lunch from 11:30 A.M. to 2 P.M. Tuesday through Friday, and for dinner from 5 to 10 P.M. Tuesday through Saturday. No reservations, no credit cards. 4542 Hoffner Ave., Orlando; 857-0566. Inexpensive.

BENNIGAN'S: One of the more interesting of the several chain restaurants on International Drive. Quiches and appetizer platters made up of fried mushrooms, fried zucchini, and fried mozzarella cheese are the specialties, and sirloin and strip steaks are popular. The French fried baked potato skins and the nachos are terrific. Open from about 11 A.M. until 2 A.M. weekdays, with brunches served from 10 A.M. to 3 P.M. on weekends. The happy hours, from 11 A.M. to 7 P.M. and from midnight to 2 A.M. daily, give you two drinks for the price of one. Reservations accepted for large groups only. AX, MC, V. 6324 International Dr., Orlando; 351-4436. Inexpensive.

CHESAPEAKE CRAB HOUSE: This single, red-painted, cinderblock building, not much bigger than a Dairy Queen built in the early 1960s, is usually

jammed at mealtimes with enthusiastic, hammer-wielding eaters whanging away at blue claw crabs, picking over the shells, and piling up the empties in the center of white butcher paper covered tables—hardly big enough to contain all the mounds, let alone pitchers (and mugs) of beer and soft drinks (the only libations served here). Informal, to say the least, and fairly inexpensive. Open from 5:30 to 10 P.M. Monday through Saturday (closed Sunday). No reservations or credit cards accepted. 1700 N. Orlando Ave., Maitland; 831-0442. Inexpensive.

EAST INDIA ICE CREAM COMPANY: With small round tables that crowd together inside under one of those impossibly ornate pressed-tin ceilings, and reappear outside on a covered terrace among a platoon of lush, oversize tropical plants, this is certainly one of the prettiest places for light meals in Orlando. Waffles, bagels, cereal, Danish pastry, and eggs in more imaginative combinations than usual are offered at breakfast, while big deli-style sandwiches appear for lunch and dinner. But the star of the show is the ice cream produced daily on the premises in out-of-the-ordinary flavors, then sauced (if you choose) with chocolate mint, hot fudge, butterscotch, marshmallow, or other toppings. Open from 8 A.M. to midnight Monday through Thursday, to 1 A.M. on Friday and Saturday, and from 10 A.M. to midnight on Sunday. No reservations or credit cards accepted. 327 Park Ave. S., Winter Park; 628-2305. Inexpensive.

LEE AND RICK'S OYSTER BAR: Though the decor is basic—linoleum floors, formica-topped tables, and plywood-paneled walls—you can't beat the food: oysters on the half shell raw or steamed (by the bucket if you ask), rock shrimp by the dozen, scallops, snapper, flounder, snow crab, smoked mullet, and combination platters thereof. Beer is available by pitcher or glass; sangria and chablis by the glass or carafe. Open for lunch from 11:30 A.M. to 4 P.M. Monday through Saturday, and for dinner daily from 4 to 11 P.M., til 10 P.M. on Sundays. Reservations accepted. AX, MC, V. 5621 Old Winter Garden Rd., Orlando; 293-3587. Inexpensive.

ORIENT IV: Orlando's best for Szechuan and Hunan-style Chinese cooking. Tung-Ting shrimp, Tai-Chin chicken, and dry sautéed beef are the best-sellers. Open for lunch from 11:30 A.M. to 3 P.M. Monday through Saturday, and for dinner from 3 to 10:30 P.M. Monday through Thursday, until 11 P.M. on Friday and Saturday, and from 1 to 9:30 P.M. on Sunday. Reservations accepted. AX, CB, DC, MC, V. 104 Altamonte Ave., Altamonte Springs; 830-4444. Inexpensive.

ROSSI'S: A funky, family-owned pizza house—a welcome change from the chains. The double-crusted pizzas stand out. Assorted other Italian specialties also are available. Open for lunch from 11 A.M. to 3 P.M. Monday through Friday, for dinner from 3 to midnight Monday through Thursday, to 1 A.M. on Friday and Saturday, and from 4:30 to 11 P.M. on Sunday. Reservations accepted for large groups only. AX, MC, V. 5919 S. Orange Blossom Trail, Orlando; 855-5755. Inexpensive.

NUMERO UNO RESTAURANT: Unpretentious, small, family-run, and the best Cuban restaurant in town. Boliche, paella, and ropa vieja are some of the specialties, all accompanied by fried plantains, corn fritters, black beans, and rice. Open from 11 A.M. to 10 P.M. daily except Wednesday. No reservations. DC, MC, V. 2499 S. Orange Ave., Orlando; 841-3840. Inexpensive.

THE BAVARIAN SCHNITZEL HOUSE: Could pass for a student hangout in Munich. A simple, ebullient place serving huge steins of real, unpasteurized German beer and plenty of good, hearty German food. All food, including the sausages, is made on the premises. Open from 11 A.M. to midnight Monday through Friday, and from 5 to 1 A.M. Saturday. Reservations accepted. AX, DC, MC, V. 65 E. Church St., Orlando; 425-4444. Inexpensive.

NIGHTLIFE

Walt Disney World boasts some of the area's best after-dark entertainment, but not all of it.

DINNER THEATERS: There are a couple to visit: **Once Upon a Stage** features a buffet meal followed by a Broadway-style musical with a professional cast. Expect to pay about $33 to $37 for two, not including drinks (3376 Edgewater Drive, Orlando; 422-3191). At **Shakespeare's of Church Street**, serving wenches bring forth wine, ale, and a six-course repast to be consumed without the aid of forks, while assorted Shakespearean characters engage in such Elizabethan hijinks as singing, dancing, juggling, and jousting. The price is about $25 per person (15 W. Church St., Orlando; 841-4144).

THEATER: In summer, the **Annie Russell Summer Theatre** at Winter Park's Rollins College, which presents student productions during the school year, puts on comedies, musicals, and drama with professional casts (ticket prices vary from production to production; phone 646-2145 for details). The drama department here is excellent; Anthony Perkins is one of the better-known alumni.

NIGHT SPOTS: All the larger hotels have lounges of varying degrees of attractiveness, and many feature live entertainment. **The Crocodile Club**, in Bailey's Restaurant, is the place for the younger set interested in dancing to New Wave music (118 W. Fairbanks Ave., Winter Park; 647-8501). **Harper's**, the bar at Le Cordon Bleu restaurant (537 W. Fairbanks, Winter Park; 647-7858) attracts a young crowd, mainly students from nearby Rollins College. There's live entertainment Tuesday through Saturday. **Cheek to Cheek**, in the Villa Nova Restaurant, draws a more sophisticated, older crowd who enjoy top-name and local music groups (839 N. Orlando Ave., Winter Park; 644-2060) and **Bennigan's** (6324 International Dr., Orlando; 351-4436) is jammed at happy hours. **Park Avenue** (4315 N. Orange Blossom Trail, Orlando; 295-3750) has a lovely decor, a great sound system, and a big dance floor; when the hubbub gets to you, you can sit outside on the lakeview terrace. Attached to Park Avenue is **The Copa Banana**, which on Friday and Saturday nights offers skits and stand-up comedy by a troupe of local comedians. The $4 admission fee to The Copa Banana also gets you into Park Avenue. **Sullivan's Trailway Lounge** (1108 S. Orange Blossom Trail, Orlando; 843-2934) draws Orlando citizens of all ages; it's the kind of place where you're apt to see a couple in their fifties in his-and-hers outfits out for a night on the town with a daughter and son-in-law, and some of the clogging that can be viewed on the dance floor is as lightning-fast as you'll see anywhere.

Florida Festival, opposite Sea World, is also a terrific place to while away an evening; in addition to the many food stands, there are drinks and excellent live entertainment at **Al E. Gator's Bar** (7007 Sea World Blvd., Orlando; 351-3326).

You could put a Woolco inside **J.J. Whispers**, Orlando's state-of-the-art mega-singles bar. In fact, it used to be a Woolco. The cavernous building has been converted into four different entertainment rooms with enough bars and dance floors to satisfy the thousands of singles who line up to get in every Thursday night, the hottest night of the week (5100 Adanson Rd., Orlando; 629-4779).

Special events: Programs of dance, music, and theater are often presented at the **Mayor Bob Carr Performing Arts Centre** (401 W. Livingston St., Orlando; 843-8111). Check the local papers or call for details.

AFTER DARK AT CHURCH STREET STATION

Once a pair of decaying hotels in a depressed section of none-too-lively downtown Orlando, the complex known as Church Street Station attracts Orlando residents out for a lively night on the town. Tourists come by the busloads, and nobody grumbles too much—especially on the way home—about the cover charge (about $5.50), which admits you to the entire complex. Be aware that the merchandise here is expensive and that you may be asked more than once to have your picture taken—for a fee. For information, call 422-2434.

Rosie O'Grady's Good Time Emporium, a vast wood-floored room with ceiling fans and chandeliers overhead and with railroad-station-waiting-room pews providing the downstairs seating, is the best-known of the lounges; the members of the band provide the Dixieland music that keeps the place so lively and cancan dancers (aka waitresses) enter by sliding down a shiny brass firepole onto the small stage. The adjacent **Apple Annie's Courtyard**, decorated with brick floors and plenty of wicker, plants, and fountains, has bluegrass music. **Phineas Phogg's Balloon Works** is the local disco; the rock 'n' roll exhibitions are worth a look even if you don't dance yourself.

Lili Marlene's, described in the "Where to Eat" section of this chapter, is the fourth of the Church Street Station quintet. Note that the cost of many of the specialty drinks here and at Apple Annie's includes a charge for the glass itself, which you may keep; if you don't want it, you may turn it in at the gift shop for a $1 refund.

The **Cheyenne Saloon & Opera House** is located directly across the street from the main complex. Tailored to resemble the original Grand Ole Opry House in Nashville, it boasts an ornate decor and a half dozen bars. A barbecue dinner of pork, ribs, or beef includes all the fixings—baked beans, cole slaw, corn on the cob, buttermilk biscuits, and fruit cobbler for dessert. Nightly shows run the gamut from top-name entertainment to clogging exhibitions, even roping events.

The newest additions to the complex are the **Antique Shop and Depot**, located in the old train station and housing over 15 individual shops and dealers, and **Buffalo Bill's**, an emporium specializing in saddles, guns, western wear, and other memorabilia from the frontier.

Children are welcome—and a common sight—at all the operations in the complex.

FOR MORE INFORMATION

Orlando Magazine, the top city magazine, has a what-to-do pullout section, "The Guide," which covers real estate, food, and local goings-on. And the *Orlando Sentinel* publishes what's-doing sections on Fridays.

The Kissimmee–St. Cloud Convention and Visitors Bureau (Box 2007; Kissimmee, FL 32742; 305-847-5000; toll-free 800-327-9159, or, from Florida, 800-432-9199) can send you information about where to play golf and tennis outside WDW, where to find boating and fishing facilities, as well as listings of special events in the area. The Orlando Area Chamber of Commerce, Tourism Development Dept. (Box 1234; Orlando, FL 32802; 425-1234) can tell you about man-made attractions, local eating spots, and the like.